Clean Your House From A to Z

From Countertops and Carpets to Whirlpools and Walls,
America's Cleaning Experts Show You Fast, Simple,
and Safe Ways to Make Everything Sparkle and Shine

BARNES
&NOBLE
BOOKS
NEW YORK

Notice

The information in this book has been carefully researched, and all efforts have been made to ensure accuracy. Rodale Inc. assumes no responsibility for any injuries suffered or damages or losses incurred during or as a result of following this information. All information should be carefully studied and clearly understood before taking any action based on the information or advice in this book.

Material in this book appeared previously in *Clean It Fast, Clean It Right* (Rodale Inc., 1998)

This edition published by Barnes & Noble, Inc., by arrangement with Rodale Inc.

© 2002 by Rodale Inc.
Illustrations © by Lorraine Dey
Cover photographs © by Rodale Inc. and C Squared Studio/PhotoDisc

Printed in the United States of America
Rodale Inc. makes every effort to use acid-free ∞, recycled paper ♻.

Cover Designer: Christopher Rhoads
Interior Designer: Charles Beasley
Cover Photography: Mitch Mandel/Rodale Images, C Squared Studio/PhotoDisc

ISBN 0–7607–3076–8

2   4   6   8   10   9   7   5   3   1   hardcover

Contents

Introduction

Let's face it: Dirt hurts.

The grit, the grime, the stains and spills that are part of everyday life can damage your clothes, your furnishings, your house, even your health. And despite your best efforts to keep things clean, there always seems to be another spill, more mold, another ground-in stain.

What can you do? Fight back with the advice in this book.

Clean Your House from A to Z offers cures for more than 200 of the most common cleaning problems. You'll find instructions on cleaning bathtubs, boots, countertops, and upholstery. You'll learn how to handle blood stains, juice stains, burn marks, and soot. You'll see how to take the stain out of stainless steel and how to control the dust mites in your mattress. You'll even discover the best way to clean delicate fabrics like silk and linen.

Whether you need help removing stains, beating grease, or eliminating odors, the answers are here.

But this book is more than just a list of how-to tips to make your home and possessions sparkle and shine. It's a handbook that's filled with ingenious shortcuts to save you time, money, and effort.

Unsure which specialty cleaning solutions really work? We'll tell you. Want to cut the cost of cleaning? We'll show you how to make your own cleansers for pennies. Need help right away with a nasty stain? Our "Emergency Action" notes explain exactly how to treat splatters and spills when they first occur so they don't become permanent.

Yes, we know we're making big claims, but we can back them up. You see, the advice in *Clean Your House from A to Z* comes from America's top cleaning experts. When we set out to create this book, we brainstormed all the tough stains, spills, and grime and dirt problems most people encounter. Then we set some of the best consumer writers in the country on a search for the solutions. They interviewed more than 150 industry pros, scientists, and everyday-cleaning experts from coast to coast—people who make a living studying and solving the crime of grime.

The result is a comprehensive guide to cleaning your home and everything you own. Follow the advice in this book, and you'll never have to settle for that "slightly soiled" look again. Follow this advice, and you can enjoy the clean, fresh, and healthy home you deserve.

Acoustical Tile

You never walk on it. And the laws of gravity haven't been revoked—things still spill reliably downward. So what could possibly be tinting your acoustical tile? The main enemies here are cigar and cigarette smoke, cooking vapors, and other airborne contaminants that rise on warm currents and, over time, soil the light-colored tiles. Dark ugly patches form around heating and air-conditioning ducts, where dust and grime collect. Cleaning must be done gently, especially if your tiles are the type that rest on grids, so as not to dislodge the tiles.

Technique: Most acoustical tiles found in homes are made of highly porous, absorbent fiber, so washing with a lot of water is not an option. Rub grime-darkened areas with a putty wallpaper cleaner called Absorene or a foam-rubber wall-cleaning sponge. Be sure that it is the type that is chemically treated and used by fire restorers to repair soot damage. Wall-cleaning sponges are available at hardware stores, janitorial supply stores, and paint stores. "You use it sort of as an eraser to lift the material off," says Martin L. King, a restoration consultant in Arlington, Virginia, and technical advisor to the National Institute of Disaster Restoration in Millersville, Maryland. Common kitchen sponges shouldn't be used because they will smear dirt instead of rubbing it away.

To remove remaining grime, use an acoustical-tile cleaner that incorporates bleaches, available at janitorial supply stores. Follow the manufacturer's directions on the container.

Note: Painting acoustical ceiling tile could cause two problems, says Keith Mullen, technical consultant for Armstrong World Industries of Lancaster, Pennsylvania, the maker of Armstrong Ceilings. First, your ceiling could lose its sound-absorbing quality. Second, painting could change the ceiling's fire rating. So check first with your local building inspector before painting ceiling tile in your home, Mullen says. Mineral fiber ceilings can be painted by spraying, brushing, or rolling, Mullen says; but vinyl- or Mylar-laminated ceilings should not be painted. If you do paint your ceiling tile, use a high-quality paint and be careful not to fill in the little perforations in the material.

A resurfacing product called Coustic-Coat will maintain the tile's fire rating, says Gary Becker, owner of a Coustic Glo franchise in Northampton, Pennsylvania. For the location of a Coustic Glo dealer in your area, consult the toll-free telephone directory.

Speed tips: As part of your routine vacuuming chores, vacuum the tiles using a brush attachment, especially around air-conditioning or heating ducts. "The best thing is to have a well-maintained heating system with clean air ducts and to change the furnace filter regularly," King says.

In a pinch: If you can't get to the store for a foam-rubber sponge or putty wallpaper cleaner, you may rub dirty tiles with a hunk of fresh bread rolled into a ball, which will scrub without doing damage, King adds. Or pat the area with sticky tape.

Caution: Always use a drop cloth, preferably canvas because it's easy to slip on a plastic one. Always wear eye protection. Rubber gloves and a filter mask are also a good idea.

Acrylic Fabric

Acrylic fabric is easy to clean, which is one reason that it is used in everything from sweaters to sweat socks to outdoor furniture.

Technique: For garments, machine-wash in warm water, using a fabric softener during the final rinse cycle. Tumble dry on a low temperature setting. Remove quickly from the dryer. Hand-wash delicates in warm water and dry them flat, says the Acrylic Council in New York City.

When cleaning stains from upholstery, remove as much of the stain as you can with a spoon or spatula if it's solid, or, if liquid, blot up as much as you can. Mix powdered laundry detergent without brighteners in warm water. Using a sponge dipped in the suds, work around the stain from the outside in. For greasy or sugary soft-drink stains, do the above steps and then rinse the area with a mixture of half water, half white vinegar. Place towels on the area and cover with a heavy flat object for several hours, according to Solutia, a fiber producer in New York City.

Speed tips: For a quick general cleaning of acrylic upholstery, sponge lightly with water, or use a spot remover such as K2r or Carbona Stain Devils, available at supermarkets, hardware stores, or discount department stores. Use as little cleaning fluid as will get the job done and liberal supplies of absorbent towels. Always read product label for proper usage and any applicable safety precautions.

Caution: If this fabric has an Achilles' heel (an acrylic heel?), it's heat. When ironing acrylic fabric, "you don't want to get it too hot," says Leon Moser, extension specialist and fabric expert at North Carolina State University's College of Textiles in Raleigh. "All things considered, it has a relatively low melting point." Also, be sure to read the product labels for proper usage and safety precautions before ironing.

Air

Scientists first began studying indoor air pollution during the 1960s and are only now beginning to understand its health effects. Indoor air pollution can come from an almost-unlimited variety of sources, so you shouldn't count on one method or product (no matter how fantastic its claims) to clean the air in your home. Improved building methods in recent years have made "tighter" homes that conserve energy but may actually worsen indoor air pollution by allowing less exchange between inside and out. Mechanical air cleaners can help, but simply opening your windows can do wonders. A balanced approach is best, says Leyla McCurdy, director of indoor air programs for the American Lung Association in Washington, D.C.

Technique: Of the three main strategies for improving indoor air quality, the Environmental Protection Agency ranks controlling the source of the pollution as the most effective method. Ventilating your home ranks second, and mechanical cleaners such as HEPA (high-efficiency particulate air) filters and ionizers are third.

Source Control

Ways of controlling pollution sources are as varied as the sources themselves. They may include covering exposed asbestos, dusting and vacuuming rooms frequently to cut down on airborne particles, restricting smoking, and carefully following instructions when using chemical products. Since asbestos is highly carcinogenic, it's best to hire a professional to work with it.

Ventilation

For ventilation, the best way is also the easiest—open windows and doors regularly (weather and security permitting, of course).

The potential drawback with open windows is that if you live in an area with high levels of outdoor air pollution, you may be letting bad stuff in even as you drive bad stuff out. "In certain climates, it may be better to have a tighter house, then control air quality through mechanical ventilation," says McCurdy. For instance, in the

How Healthy Is Your Home?

Linking health problems to specific pollution sources can be difficult, especially since symptoms caused by bad air in your home may be nearly identical to those for colds, flus, or other common illnesses. But if your symptoms tend to disappear when you leave the house, it may be a clue that your house is making you sick.

Here are some major sources of air pollution in the home, according to the American Lung Association, as well as some suggestions for keeping them in check.

Asbestos
Sources: Asbestos is commonly used in homes, from roofing and flooring materials to insulation. It's rarely a problem unless it's disturbed, as during home renovations, or if it begins to deteriorate with age.

Effects: Asbestos fibers may be inhaled and can cause lung scarring, lung cancer, or other forms of cancer.

Solutions: Exposed asbestos-containing materials should be covered with plastic and duct tape. Any asbestos that is flaking or damaged should be handled by a professional to minimize your exposure and risk.

Asbestos can be difficult to identify unless it's labeled. There's usually no health risk unless the asbestos material is actively flaking or decomposing—that's when particles become airborne, according to the American Lung Association. If you have doubts about a material, go to the phone book and call in an asbestos specialist.

Biological Pollutants
Sources: Biological pollutants include viruses, bacteria, molds, fungi, and mites. They can come from dirty air conditioners, humidifiers, dehumidifiers, and air-cleaning filters. They can also come from plants, pets, and unwashed bedding.

Effects: Biological pollutants can cause fevers, colds, and allergic reactions.

Solutions: Clean your air-filtering appliances regularly, following manufacturers' instructions. Use distilled water in humidifiers. Wash sheets frequently in hot water (at least 130°F) to kill mites. Keep your home ventilated.

Formaldehyde
Sources: Sources of formaldehyde include cigarette smoke; resins in particleboard, fiberboard, and plywood paneling; some adhesives;

tropics, McCurdy says, hot humid air blowing in through open windows and doors can promote mold growth inside.

For additional ventilation, use your bathroom or kitchen exhaust fans as needed. Run your unit air conditioner with the vent control carpet backing; upholstery; and drapery fabrics. It is also found in older foam insulation.

Effects: Formaldehyde can cause headaches, dizziness, lethargy, rashes, nausea, and irritation of the eyes and respiratory tract. High levels may trigger asthma attacks in people with asthma.

Solutions: Restrict smoking. Increase ventilation in your home. Consider replacing or coating particleboard, fiberboard, or foam insulation if it was made prior to the mid-1980s. Since then, many manufacturers have begun making products that emit lower levels of formaldehyde. If you're building a home, specify that you want pressed wood products that emit low levels of formaldehyde.

Nitrogen Dioxide

Sources: Nitrogen dioxide is often a result of poorly vented gas ranges or other appliances, or wood or coal stoves.

Effects: Nitrogen dioxide can cause eye and respiratory tract irritation and, in serious cases, bronchitis.

Solutions: Gas ranges should be fitted with a range hood that vents pollutants outside. Or keep a window open and use an exhaust fan while cooking. Have the gas company regularly inspect your gas furnace, water heater, and clothes dryer to make sure that they are burning efficiently and not emitting gas.

Secondhand Smoke

Sources: Secondhand smoke is a result of cigarettes, pipes, and cigars.

Effects: A proven cancer-causer, secondhand smoke is responsible for about 3,000 lung cancer deaths per year.

Solutions: Don't smoke, and don't allow others to smoke in your home. Or confine smoking to one room and use an exhaust fan there.

Toxic Chemicals in Household Products

Sources: Toxic chemicals include pesticides, heavy cleaning solutions, hobby products, and solvents.

Effects: Effects range from dizziness and nausea to allergic reactions and eye, skin, and respiratory tract irritation.

Solutions: Read and follow all instruction and warning labels carefully. Use toxic chemical products only in well-ventilated areas. Use pump sprays instead of aerosols and, when possible, substitute toxic products with nontoxic products.

open to increase the rate at which air is exchanged from indoor to out. Ventilation is especially important when you're doing anything indoors that may generate pollutants—cooking, painting, using chemicals, using kerosene heaters, or installing new carpet.

Air Cleaners

Mechanical air cleaners include tabletop and floor models as well as larger filters that operate in conjunction with central heating and air-conditioning systems. They come in two general types: filters and ionizers. Mechanical filters, also known as HEPA filters, are generally more effective than ionizers, says McCurdy. HEPA filters are the most efficient mechanical filters for removing small particles that can be breathed deep into the lungs. They operate by drawing air from a room through a series of filters, then expelling cleaned air back into the room. The filters, which must be replaced every few months, depending on how dirty the air is to begin with, are made of tightly woven glass. They trap pollen, mold spores, animal hair, dander, dust mites, dust, and other particles. Many commercial HEPA filters also include a carbon filter to reduce room odors. But HEPA filters are far less effective at removing gases than particles from the air.

Tabletop or room models, sold under brand names such as Holmes, Enviracaire, and Duracraft, range in price from around $99 to nearly $350. In general, the larger the cleaner, the more "air changes per hour" the machine will perform, and the more particles will be removed.

Ionizers are portable devices that charge particles floating in the air so that they stick to walls, floors, tables, drapes, and the like, thus removing them from the air you breathe. The problem with ionizers is that bumping a chair or brushing a curtain can send the particles right back into the air. Also, ionizers do little to remove gases from the air. For gases, ventilation and source control are superior. In addition, some ionizers emit ozone, which may actually add to the air-quality problems in your home.

Plants

Plants look great and add a touch of the outdoors to your home. But the jury's still out on their air-cleaning prowess. Excessive moisture in the your plants' soil may actually provide a breeding ground for microorganisms that could wind up in your air, says McCurdy.

Caution: Don't confuse commercial air fresheners with clean air. Spraying air fresheners in a room just masks odors and introduces more foreign particles into the air. For a simple and inexpensive alternative to artificial air fresheners, pour some warmed vinegar into a dish and set it in it in the room until it evaporates and then keep replacing it until the odor is gone, advises the American Lung Association.

Air Conditioners

Air conditioners exchange air from outside to inside your house. Cutting down on dust and other airborne stuff is essential.

Technique: For room air conditioners (window units), filters should be washed before the unit is used for the first time in the season and once a month when the air conditioner is in use. Wash them more frequently if you have pets or a lot of activity in the house. Slide the filters out of the air conditioner and wash them by hand in warm water, with no soap. Be sure to let them dry thoroughly before reinstalling. If the fans in your unit are easily accessible, wipe them periodically with a soft cloth, says Vincent Brackin, spokesman for the Carrier Corporation in Syracuse, New York. With some units, the air conditioner chassis (the mechanical unit) slides into a metal casing or frame that holds the window open. If you have this type, slide the chassis out every few months and brush away twigs, leaves, or other debris from the casing. Lightly dust the exterior surfaces and grille of the air conditioner as part of your routine housecleaning. This will help prevent dust from building up on the filters.

If you have central air-conditioning, "it's wise to clean or change the filter monthly during periods of high use," says Edward W. Dooley, spokesman for the Air-Conditioning and Refrigeration Institute near Washington, D.C. Some central air-conditioning filters are disposable (they're flimsy and are usually marked "disposable" by the manufacturer). Others may be washed. Methods vary with the make of the filter, and it's best to follow the manufacturer's washing instructions. Dust or vacuum duct outlets and registers as part of your regular home-cleaning routine. The ducts themselves shouldn't require cleaning if the outlets and filters are kept clean. Check the outdoor unit regularly for leaves and other debris.

Speed tips: Unit air conditioner filters may be vacuumed instead of washed. Handheld vacuums are best because a too-powerful suction could suck up and misshape the filter, says Brackin.

Caution: Never apply soap or detergents to the coils inside the air-conditioning unit. If you vacuum the coils, do it carefully. "They're fragile; they're made out of aluminum," says Brackin. "If you bend the coils over, you're preventing the heat exchange from occurring." Always unplug the unit before cleaning inside.

Alabaster

Alabaster is a soft stone that can be damaged easily by water, so proceed with caution.

Technique: For most cleaning jobs, dusting with a dry soft cloth should do the trick. For heavier dirt, rub with a slightly damp cloth dabbed with a small amount of mild dishwashing detergent. Or spit on a cotton swab. No kidding—this method is favored by George Wheeler, Ph.D., stone specialist at the Sherman-Fairchilds Center for Objects Conservation with the Metropolitan Museum of Art in New York City, who says that the enzymes in saliva make a safe and effective cleaning substance. For serious spots or stains, rub gently with a cotton swab dabbed with an acetone cleaner such as nail polish remover or mineral spirits, but use it sparingly.

Caution: Never bathe or splash water on alabaster.

Antiques

The most important steps you take in cleaning antiques involve keeping objects out of harm's way—and dirt's way—in the first place. The actual cleaning of objects should be kept to a minimum. "Do-it-yourselfism is very American," says Joyce Hill Stoner, Ph.D., professor of art conservation at the Winterthur/University of Delaware Program in Art Conservation in Newark. "With antiques, we want to quell that as much as possible."

Aggressive cleaning is likely to wipe away history along with the grime. Scour an antique coin or a bronze statue to a shine and you're likely to significantly lessen its value. Go after an old painting with a cloth and a can of cleaning spray and you could destroy the work altogether.

When anything other than the lightest cleaning is required, it's best to let a professional conservator handle it unless you have special knowledge or experience. When in doubt, says Timothy Lennon, conservator of paintings at the Art Institute of Chicago, "leave the thing alone. If it does need attention, get an expert." After all, he adds, "you wouldn't advise people to fill their own teeth."

Technique: The environment in which your antiques sit plays such an important role in their well-being. So establishing an antique-friendly home is key. Fastidious housecleaning will help keep dust and grime from collecting on antiques. Vacuum carpets and rugs and dust other room surfaces frequently to reduce the level of airborne pollutants that might find their way onto your antiques. Air filters can help as well.

Whenever possible, keep valued items away from the kitchen and entrance areas to the kitchen. Cooking near antiques increases their exposure to airborne grime. "I treated a painting at an Italian restaurant that just reeked of oregano and tomato sauce," Dr. Stoner says. "And you can't clean it the way you'd clean a wall." For the same reason, it's best to keep smoking to a minimum.

Other than outright dropping or otherwise damaging a piece, the biggest dangers to antiques come from light and moisture. "You want a clean dry environment with balanced humidity," Lennon says.

Moisture and light can be especially harmful to objects made from organic materials. These include wooden furniture, textiles, paintings, and books. Objects made from stone, metal, or glass are less susceptible, but it's still a good idea to protect those objects from strong light or changes in humidity.

Natural sunlight, with its concentration of ultraviolet rays, is the most damaging. Whenever possible, keep prized objects away from areas that are regularly exposed to direct sunlight. Sunlight can fade colors in paints or dyes, yellow the varnish on a painting, bleach paper, and even weaken textile fabric. Even indirect sunlight over time can do damage, and light damage, like lead poisoning, is cumulative—meaning that it only intensifies over time. Use curtains and blinds liberally.

"In general, try to cluster things of great value and sensitivity in rooms that are less likely to be used, and draw the curtains," says Steven Weintraub, conservation consultant with Art Preservation Services in New York City.

Maintaining an even level of humidity is crucial to protecting antiques. Too much moisture in the air promotes mildew growth and encourages insects. But the opposite extreme is damaging as well. Super dryness can promote cracks in wood, ivory, paint, and other materials. Constant fluctuations are as damaging to objects as a moisture-laden or overarid environment. Paper, for example, expands and contracts with the humidity or aridity of the air around it. Too many changes and the paper simply breaks apart.

Use humidifiers and dehumidifiers as needed throughout the year to help maintain a reasonably steady relative humidity level of 30 to 70 percent. Beyond that range, "you can be assured that there's going to be significant risk of damage," Weintraub says. A

Not Just Any Old Conservator Will Do

The United States has no formal licensing program for art and antiques conservators. Just about anyone can hang out a shingle.

So if you're looking for a professional to clean an antique item for you, it's not a good idea to simply pick the first name you come across in the phone book.

A good place to start is your local art museum. Many museums set aside a day or two periodically to allow residents to take in their antiques for evaluation by the conservation staff. At any rate, the staff may be able to direct you to good professionals in your area.

If there is more than one museum in your area, call them all. "If the same conservator's name comes up at two different museums, that's good," says Joyce Hill Stoner, Ph.D., professor of art conservation at the Winterthur/University of Delaware Program in Art Conservation in Newark.

If there aren't good museums nearby, or if you simply want more information about finding conservators, you can write to the American Institute for Conservation of Historic and Artistic Works (AIC) at 1717 K Street NW, Suite 301, Washington, DC 20006. The AIC has brochures to help your search and also runs a referral service.

Here are some AIC tips on selecting a conservator.

- Ask potential conservators about their training, length of experience, and whether conservation is their primary activity.
- Ask whether they have experience dealing with the type of objects you own that need attention and whether they belong to conservation organizations.
- Ask for references, including lists of previous clients. Contact some of those clients.
- Expect to receive a written preliminary examination report detailing the condition of the object as well as proposed treatment, the limitations of that treatment, and the cost and duration. A good conservator will notify you of major or unexpected changes in the treatment and will provide written and, in some cases, photographic documentation of the treatment.
- Conservators, like physicians, don't always agree. Don't be shy about getting a second opinion.

"thermohygrometer" will measure relative humidity in a given room. These devices can often be purchased for about $100. Contact your local art museum or a local conservator for advice on finding a good thermohygrometer in your area.

Here are general tips for cleaning various types of antiques.

Furniture

Dust most antique furniture surfaces with dry, clean lint-free cloths that are frequently washed. Especially delicate areas may be cleaned with a sable brush with an air bulb attached to the stem for gently blowing dust away. These are available from camera equipment stores.

If extra cleaning is required on wood furniture, the National Committee to Save America's Cultural Collections suggests a solution of 50 parts distilled water to 1 part Murphy Oil Soap. Dip a clean soft cloth in the solution and wring it out so that it is damp rather than wet. Gently wipe the surface of the furniture. Use a cloth dampened with plain water to rinse, then dry with a clean soft cloth.

Caution: Always test the solution on an inconspicuous corner of the furniture before applying widely. Do not use any other cleaning solutions. Never let moist cleaning cloths sit on furniture. Read the product label for proper use and safety instructions.

Metal Objects

You can remove dust and other surface dirt from metal objects using a clean soft brush. To remove fingerprints or oily or greasy deposits from gold, bronze, copper, or brass, dip the brush in a little ethyl alcohol and brush gently.

Caution: Always test the ethyl alcohol using a cotton swab on an inconspicuous corner of the piece to make certain that you aren't damaging the object. Don't attempt to polish antique metal objects. Not only can this erase historically significant marks but also you're rubbing away part of the metal itself. "Every time you polish it, you have less substance there. Every time you polish metal, it's thinner," Dr. Stoner says.

Paintings

About the only cleaning you should consider attempting yourself on an old painting is light dusting with a sable brush. Even this must be done with extreme care. Before you dust with the brush, check the painting carefully for loose pieces of frame or lifting paint that may be dislodged by the brush. Any other cleaning or restoration work should be done by a professional art conservator.

Caution: Do not use cleaning solutions or sponges on antique paintings. Don't even use a feather duster, cloth, vacuum brush, or handheld vacuum cleaner. "The danger would be lifting loose paint off the surface," Lennon says. Before using any product, read the label for proper use and safety precautions.

Avoid touching the front or back of the painting. Oils from your fingers can damage the paint or varnish on the painting itself, while finger pressure on the back may promote cracks in the painting. Never lift a painting or other antique unless you've thought out exactly where you're going to put it down.

Avoid old-time, word-of-mouth cleaning prescriptions like the plague. One such prescription calls for rubbing a painting with a raw potato. "This makes a delicious scum for cockroaches," Dr. Stoner says.

Textiles

Textiles, whether they're on display or in storage, should be inspected and vacuumed regularly. This will remove dust and help protect against insect damage. Always work on a padded surface. For example, you can place a mattress pad over your dining-room table and cover it with a clean white sheet. Use a low-power, handheld vacuum cleaner. For added protection of the fabric, place a clean fiberglass window screen over the fabric and vacuum through it.

Caution: Don't eat, drink, or smoke when cleaning textiles. You only increase the chances of a damaging stain, crumbs that will attract insects, or smoke residue.

Aquariums

An aquarium is an inherently unnatural environment for fish. To reduce their stress level, you should compensate by making sure that the stuff you put inside the tank, including cleaning supplies, is as natural as possible.

Technique: You can clean out an aquarium that hasn't been used in a while with a solution of 1 teaspoon aquarium salt (non-iodized salt) to ½ gallon water. Wipe the aquarium down with the solution and a clean soft cloth. Then rinse thoroughly with plain water. Use the same method to clean out a new aquarium before using it for the first time.

An older aquarium may have a whitish film on the sides. "This is caused by hard water or calcium deposits," says Lance Reyniers, president of Python Products, a Milwaukee-based manufacturer of aquarium maintenance equipment. If the film is heavy or the grime stubborn, you should use a solution specially made for cleaning aquariums. These solutions, available at aquarium stores, are stronger than the homemade saltwater solution but still safe for fish.

When your aquarium is actually in use, you keep the water clean using a variety of filters and regular water changes. There are three basic types of filters, all of which may be used at the same time to filter out different pollutants. A biological filter, which sits at the bottom of the tank underneath a layer of gravel, screens out ammonia released by fish and other aquatic animals. Mechanical filters remove such debris as uneaten food and solid waste. A chemical filter uses carbon or other substances to screen out chemical pollutants.

There are many filters on the market. The ones you use and the frequency with which you clean and change them will depend on the type and number of fish you have, the size of your tank, and other factors. Get specific advice from your aquarium store.

Every two weeks or so (more often if you have a crowded tank) change 5 to 10 percent of the water in your tank. "Smaller, more frequent water changes are healthier and less stressful for fish," says Reyniers. "In the natural environment they're constantly in new water."

The bottom of the tank is where the dirty water is, so water should always be removed from the bottom of the tank using a siphon. There are a variety of siphoning products and methods available, from sophisticated water change systems made by Python Products and other companies to a simple hose. At the very least, it's a good idea to use a siphon that is equipped with a mesh to prevent gravel from being sucked up.

Use an aquarium thermometer to measure the water temperature before you change the water and while you are replacing it. You can use a hose attached to your faucet or a clean bucket that has not contained cleaning supplies. Adjust the hot and cold knobs on your faucet as needed to make sure that the temperature in your aquarium does not change during the process.

Aquatic plants help clean the water in the tank by removing carbon dioxide and producing oxygen, and they help create a natural environment for the fish.

Caution: Here's one rule that you should remember when cleaning an aquarium: Fish hate soap, be it mild hand soap or harsh detergent. Even traces left behind after you think you've rinsed it all away may be enough to stress or even sicken fish. The bottom line is this: Don't use soap to clean an aquarium. Don't even use buckets or cloths that have had soap on them. Keep soap-free supplies and tools on hand that you use only for your aquarium. Never change the water in your aquarium within 48 hours of a major rainfall or snow melt in your area. These events prompt municipal water systems to increase chlorine levels in the water supply, which can be harmful to fish, says Reyniers.

Asphalt

Asphalt is tough and durable, but removing stains isn't always easy. For a bad stain, you may have to decide between living with it or resurfacing the asphalt.

Technique: To rid an outdoor basketball court or driveway of routine dirt and grime, "a hose with a good nozzle should get most of the stuff up," says Ross Bentsen, education director of the Asphalt Institute in Lexington, Kentucky.

For more serious cleaning jobs, pour some general household cleaner such as Spic and Span into a bucket of warm water. Using the mixture, scrub the surface with a stiff brush. For mixture amounts, follow the manufacturer's instructions on the cleaner container.

Speed tips: If you've spilled paint on asphalt, you better get it up quickly or be prepared to live with it. If you catch latex paint before it seeps in, it may be removed with plenty of water and the previous cleaning method. Oil-based paint is nearly impossible to remove.

Caution: Use cleaning solutions sparingly on asphalt. Anything you use will inevitably wash its way into your yard, or your neighbor's. When cleaning asphalt, don't use a petroleum-based product such as WD-40 cleaner and lubricant, Bentsen says. Asphalt is an oil-based product, and the cleaner will cut through the asphalt just as it cuts through the stain.

Asphalt Stains

Asphalt is a petroleum-based product, so a petroleum-based product such as WD-40 cleaner and lubricant, which dissolves oil and petroleum stains, will cut it down to size.

Technique: To remove a fresh asphalt stain, such as one picked up on the bottom of your sneakers from a road construction site, rub with a cloth sprayed with WD-40.

Caution: To avoid making a stain worse, always test-clean a small obscure portion of whatever you're cleaning. Always read any product label for proper use and safety precautions.

Awnings

Most residential awnings are made of woven fabric, either canvas or synthetic fibers. Periodic cleaning will keep them looking good. Awnings should be cleaned every five to seven months to remove dust, grime, and other atmospheric residue. "If you wait a year, the sun bakes it in," says Bob Van Gelder, owner of Awning Care Plus, which has been cleaning awnings in the San Francisco area for more than 20 years.

Technique: For routine cleaning of awnings that are relatively easy to reach, homeowners may do the job themselves. For heavier jobs or on hard-to-reach awnings, the best step is to call a professional, who will attack the problem with a pressurized water cleaner that flushes dirt and grime away.

For routine jobs, Van Gelder swears by a "truck brush." As the name implies, truck brushes (available at janitorial supply stores) are long-handle brushes with soft flexible bristles designed for cleaning the sides of large trucks. Mix 2 ounces mild liquid dishwashing detergent, such as Joy or Ivory, into a gallon of water. Dip the brush in the mixture and gently scrub the awning. For bird droppings use the same cleaning solution, but try a stiffer-bristle brush if the spot doesn't come right off. When you're finished scrubbing, spray the awning thoroughly with a garden hose.

Minor tree sap stains can be removed with acetone. Put a small amount on a sponge mop and rub the sap stain.

Note: For colored awnings, test-clean by applying a small amount of acetone to an inconspicuous corner with a cotton swab. Allow it to dry and check that the color hasn't faded. Extensive sap stains require professional help.

Speed tips: Some awnings may be removed easily from their frames. If you have this type, it may pay to take the awning down and give it a good cleaning on the ground, using the same cleaning methods as above. Some awning services will remove the awnings for you and replace them when they're clean if you want to do the cleaning yourself.

In a pinch: If you can't find a truck brush, any long-handle brush with soft bristles should work.

Caution: How you reach your awnings will of course depend on how they're positioned around your house. Always use caution when working on ladders, and avoid leaning a ladder against an awning frame. Avoid harsh household detergents, which may cause colors to fade. Before starting to clean your awnings, read any product labels for their proper use and safety precautions.

Barbecue Grills

Grease, gunk, and crawly things can threaten your outdoor feast.

Technique: On gas grills, the flame coming from the burners should be blue when shaded and invisible in sunlight. If the flame is yellow or orange, it's a good indication that the tubes or burner are dirty. Once a year, brush the burner with a wire brush, and poke each burner hole with a nail or drill bit to clear away gunk. Of course, do this when your grill is cool. Venturi tubes, which transfer gas from the valve to the burner, should be checked at least once a year for spiders. There are either one or two venturi tubes connecting the gas supply to the bottom of the burner. "Spiders love to build nests inside the venturi tubes, and they can block the flow of gas," says John Bassemier, president of Bassemier's Fireplace and Patio in Evansville, Indiana, and past president of the National Barbecue Association. Dealers sell special venturi-tube brushes, but you can insert a pipe cleaner or plastic straw into the tubes and twist it to collect and clear spiderwebs and nests, Bassemier says.

The basket (the inside of the grill) and the grill grid (the cooking surface) can be cleaned by leaving your grill on high for several minutes after you're through cooking. If it's not a gas grill, let the grid sit over the hot coals after you're finished cooking. Another way to clean the grid is to place it, after it has cooled, on several sheets of newspaper. Coat the grid with an oven cleaner or commercial grill cleaner. Then place more newspaper over the top. Dampen the newspaper with enough water so that the paper clings to the grid, and place weights on top. Let it sit for several hours or overnight; then brush the grids clean with a grill brush and rinse with water. The inside of the grill can be scraped with a grill scraper or a putty knife.

HOW I DO IT

Hog Wild

Mention ribs and places like Texas and Arkansas spring to mind. But Steve Ross, proprietor of Roscoe's Rootbeer and Ribs in Rochester, Minnesota, cooks up a mean enough rack to have won national competitions in 1993, 1994, and 1996. Cooking up to 5,000 pounds of loin back ribs per month, Ross has cleaned an awful lot of secret sauce from his grills and smokers.

"I don't like to use a strong detergent on any cooking surface. Each night, we remove the grill racks and soak them in hot water and mild liquid dishwashing detergent, then in the morning rinse thoroughly and wipe them down. On the sides of the grills and the insides of the smokers, we use wallpaper scrapers to get rid of carbonized meat and sauce. Then we wipe the surfaces with a cloth. Once a week we give all the surfaces an extra-thorough cleaning, getting into all the crevices. You'll never get the cookers completely cleaned, though, and you don't really want to. I'm a firm believer that smokers and grills get seasoned over time.

"When we cook on the road, at competitions, we use a giant portable contraption called a Maxi Barbecue Chicken and Rib Cooker. (It holds 600 chickens or 180 slabs of pork ribs.) To clean this, we spray it inside and out with an organic degreaser called Jungle Jake, then let it sit overnight. In the morning, we take it to a do-it-yourself car wash and hose it down."

Speed tips: When cleaning a gas grill by flame, place a double thickness of aluminum foil over the grill grids, enough to fully cover them and hang out over the edges. Light the grill and then close the lid. When the cover comes down, the foil sticking out will bend over, creating a seal. Leave on high for a maximum of 30 minutes or until smoking stops, whichever comes first, says Bassemier. The foil will intensify the heat, cleaning better and faster. Never leave the gas on for more than 30 minutes when cleaning with this method. Prolonged heating can warp the grill basket.

In a pinch: If your gas grill has lava rocks, these will become greasy on the top over time. Turn them periodically to allow the grease to burn off.

Caution: Never use a scraper on the inside of your grill if it's made of porcelain. This can cause scratches that can weaken the grill.

Baseboards

Baseboards are usually coated with durable, shiny oil-based paint, which means that they can stand up to fairly aggressive cleaning methods.

Technique: You can use a nylon scrub pad or fine (#00) steel wool with liquid dishwashing detergent or a household cleaner such as Spic and Span, says Martin L. King, a restoration consultant in Arlington, Virginia, and technical advisor to the National Institute of Disaster Restoration in Millersville, Maryland. For mixture amounts, follow instructions on the cleaner container.

Caution: Occasionally, you will come across baseboards painted with flat paint. These demand a gentler touch. Use a terry towel or sponge with a dilute solution of liquid dishwashing detergent and water.

Baskets

Most baskets are made from reeds. A good dousing every now and then won't just keep them clean—it will also extend their lives. "It keeps the reed flexible and pliable, and the basket will last for years," says Nancy Varner, manager of Basketville in Toano, Virginia, which is near Colonial Williamsburg and is one of the nation's largest stores specializing in baskets. Other baskets are made from wood, usually white oak or white ash, and should be cleaned with much less water.

Technique: You can wash a reed basket in the kitchen sink using the spray attachment, or take it out back and spray it down with your garden hose. Use a little mild dishwashing detergent and a soft-bristle brush to scrub away dirt or stains, and then rinse thoroughly. Let the basket air-dry outdoors in the sun or in a sunny window. Although water is good for the reed, if the basket is allowed to remain wet, it will begin to rot. The basket should dry in a few hours.

For painted baskets, use the same method as above but don't scrub with a brush, which may scratch the paint. Use a soft cloth instead.

Heavy amounts of water may damage wooden baskets. Instead of spraying or immersing them, wipe them down with a soft cloth dampened with plain water.

In a pinch: A white basket that has become stained or scuffed up will look like new with a coat of white spray paint.

Caution: Avoid using harsh detergents, which could mar the surface of the basket. For the same reason, avoid using a brush with metal bristles. Don't put the basket away while still wet.

Bathtubs

A little routine cleaning on a regular basis will lessen the need for the longer more difficult process of scrubbing away caked-on soap scum.

Technique: After each use, wipe your bathtub with a sponge and rinse it with water. This will prevent soap from building up. About once a week give your tub a more thorough cleaning.

Before you run out and purchase expensive cleansers made specifically for bathrooms, try cleaning your tub with other types of detergents or cleaners already lying around the house. Bon Ami or a mild liquid dishwashing detergent on a sponge makes a good general bathtub cleaner. Bon Ami acts as a polisher, too. A liquid laundry detergent such as Tide, applied with a sponge, does an excellent job of cleaning away grime as well as discoloration caused by hard water, says Neil Pirthipal, a customer service representative at American Standard in Piscataway, New Jersey. If your bathtub has adhesive strips on the bottom to prevent slipping, try scrubbing these with some Bon Ami and a soft nylon-bristle brush. If a grittier cleanser is required, put some baking soda on a damp sponge. It's natural, safe, and won't scrape bathtub surfaces.

In a pinch: Need something a little tougher than a sponge? Try scrubbing the tub with a nylon net ball or pad (available in your grocery store cleaning section). You can even roll up an old nylon stocking into a ball.

Caution: Avoid using abrasive cleansers, pads, or brushes that might scratch or dull the surface of the tub, Pirthipal says. Never use cleansers containing acetone or ethyl alcohol to clean a fiberglass tub. They will damage the fiberglass finish. Never use steel wool instead of a nylon brush to scrub no-slip surfaces. "If pieces get imbedded in the skid-resistant surface, it will cause rust stains," says Pirthipal.

Bicycles

Cleaning your bicycle is similar to cleaning your car. A thorough going-over periodically, including a good waxing, won't just make your ride sparkle. It will help your bicycle perform better and last longer.

Bikes these days fall into two major categories: mountain bikes and road bikes. Cleaning methods for both are similar, but mountain bikes, with their wide tires made for negotiating muddy trails, are likely to get a lot dirtier and need extra attention.

Technique: For most items, waxing comes at the end of a cleaning process. But your bicycle should be waxed before you take it out and get it dirty in the first place. "The key to protecting the frame is to prepare it for the duty it's going to perform," says Jim Langley, senior technical editor for *Bicycling* magazine, in Soquel, California. "This will go a long way toward making it easy to clean after a muddy or dirty ride." If your bike isn't that dirty, often a wipe down with a clean cloth, followed by waxing, will suffice.

You can find waxes made especially for bicycles at just about any good bicycle store, but car wax will do as well. The key is to find something easy to apply since bike frames have lots of tubes and joints. Liquids are generally easier to work with than pastes. Apply the wax with a clean soft cloth, following the instructions on the container.

Cleaning a bike involves two major areas: the frame and the drivetrain. A bicycle should be supported right side up, off the ground when cleaning. Hang it on an open garage door by hooking the saddle tip on a metal brace, a sturdy tree branch at the right height, a bike stand, or any other place where you can safely secure it. Simple bike stands can be found for under $20 in some bike shops. Or you can invest in a repair stand, which costs $125 to $150.

Drivetrain

The drivetrain includes the chain, pedals, derailleurs, rear hub, and other mechanical parts of the bike. This is a messier job than cleaning the frame and should be done first. These parts should be cleaned about once a month if you ride regularly, or whenever you notice a buildup of grime. Clean the chain a few links at a time by spraying with a degreaser such as WD-40 and wiping with a cloth. When those links are clean, advance the pedals slightly and work on a new section of the chain. Once the chain is clean, use your finger to lift it off the chainring. These are the large metal wheels with teeth that hold the chain. Use a screwdriver to remove gunk from between the teeth. Slide a cloth between the rings, slipping it back and forth like dental floss.

Spray a degreaser such as WD-40 on the derailleurs, crankset, cogs, and pedals, wiping with the cloth as you go. Always spray mechanical parts from the top to avoid getting degreaser inside components and eliminating necessary lubricants. The main goal here is to get rid of any built-up gunk. "You don't want it spotless," Langley says. "You still want it lubed." When you're done, apply drops of bicycle lubricant (available at bike stores) to the chain, pedals, and other parts.

Frame

First use a garden hose without a spray attachment to dribble water over the entire frame. Mix ¼ cup mild liquid dishwashing detergent (enough to create suds) in a bucket of water. Use a sponge to soap down the entire frame, including the handlebars, grips, and seat. While washing, inspect the frame for signs of rust. Minor rust spots can be removed by rubbing with medium fine (#0) steel wool. Significant rust should be checked out by a bike mechanic because it could lead to structural failure of the frame.

Use a nylon-bristle brush to get rid of stubborn, dried-on mud. Use a smaller nylon brush to go after dirt in crevices the sponge can't reach. Then dribble water over the frame until the soap is gone. When you're finished washing, dry the frame with clean soft cloths, then wax.

Wash the wheels and tires with the same solution. Wash the tires slowly and methodically, taking the opportunity to inspect them for signs of damage. Look for nicks or cuts and debris embedded in the tread. The sidewalls of the tires are usually made of fabric. Check them for signs of fraying. If the tires are damaged, they should be replaced.

Speed tips: Instead of applying bike or car wax to your frame, you can use a furniture spray such as Pledge instead. Just spray it on and wipe to a shine. It goes on a lot faster than the waxes. The drawback is that this treatment won't hold up as long—you'll have to do it every few days.

Caution: Never clean a bike while it's standing on the ground without solid support. It might fall over. That's the number one cause of bicycle damage, Langley says.

Don't use a spray attachment to hose your bike down, and don't take it to one of those do-it-yourself car washes with high-pressure hoses. Water will get into crevices and wash away necessary lubricants, which will cause expensive components to wear rapidly. For the same reason, don't wash a bike upside down or spray degreaser directly into drivetrain parts. Don't use a tire protectant, such as Armor All, on your tires. They'll get slippery and you could lose control when riding.

Bird Feeders

You want to keep bird feeders clean, but you must be careful not to leave soapy residue that can harm your feathered dinner guests.

Technique: Bird feeders should be given a thorough cleaning at least every three months. Wash plastic feeders with water and rinse thoroughly. Wooden feeders should be taken apart (if possible), brushed out, and cleaned with a wire brush. You may even want to sand the surfaces from time to time with a piece of sandpaper. Rinse wooden feeders thoroughly, but do not use soap because it will be impossible to get all the soap out of the wood, says John Bianchi, communications director and spokesman for the National Audubon Society in New York City. Hummingbird feeders should be flushed every few days with very hot water because they can develop molds that hummingbirds are particularly sensitive to. Take down the feeder, pour out any sugar water, and rinse the feeder under very hot water at a sink.

Blankets

Most blankets, even woolen ones, may be machine-washed. Whenever possible, no matter what the blanket is made of, closely follow the cleaning instructions on the care label. And watch how you dry the blanket, or it'll lose its shape.

Technique: With woolen blankets, dry cleaning is most often recommended. But if you have the time and the desire, you can wash them at home, with care. If you choose the home method, machine-wash one blanket at a time in cool water on the gentle cycle. "Friction and heat cause wool to shrink," says Charlotte Hughes, manager of blanket operations for Cascade Woolen Mill in Oakland, Maine. You can wash the blanket by hand by gently swishing it in a tub of cool water with a mild laundry detergent such as Ivory Snow or a teaspoon of mild liquid dishwashing detergent. There are several methods for drying a wool blanket. You can dry it in a machine dryer on the "No Heat" setting. Or you can spread the blanket flat on a picnic table to dry or hang it on a taut line that doesn't bow under the weight of the blanket. If drying outdoors, keep the blanket in the shade. After the blanket has dried, you can fluff it in a machine dryer on the "No Heat" setting.

Vellux blankets are velvetlike synthetic blankets made from two thin layers of polyurethane foam with a surface of flocked nylon that gives it the velvety feel. These can be machine-washed in warm water using your usual laundry detergent. Machine dry them on medium heat and remove immediately. Washing Vellux blankets twice a year will keep them fluffy and help maintain their thermal properties. Do not spot-clean or dry-clean.

Cotton holds up well to laundry detergent. Cotton blankets may be washed right along with your regular laundry. Loose-knit cotton blankets should be washed on a delicate cycle to avoid pilling. Dry them on a taut line that doesn't bow under the weight of the blanket.

Caution: Hanging your blanket (especially a woolen one) on a droopy line will cause it to dry in the shape of the droop. Make certain that the line is taut, or lay the blanket flat. For wool, find a shady spot for drying because direct sunlight may cause the wool to shrink.

Blinds

More heat and cold is transferred through your windows than through your walls. Because dust and other airborne pollutants are drawn to areas where energy transfer is the greatest, window blinds become virtual dust magnets.

Technique: No matter what your blinds are made of, dusting is the first cleaning step. For routine maintenance, dust venetian or vertical blinds regularly using a lamb's wool duster or a soft house painting brush. Or go over the blinds using a vacuum cleaner with a brush attachment. Close the blinds fully and clean one side, then turn them so the slats are facing the opposite way and clean the other side.

Blinds in or near kitchens can become grimy, and nicotine from smoking may leave a yellowish film on blinds in other rooms. If your blinds are made from a synthetic material such as vinyl or from metal with a baked-on coating, you can wash them with a cleaner like Windex or Formula 409 and a soft cloth. Or you can make your own effective cleaner by mixing a couple of ounces of trisodium phosphate (available at hardware stores) in a bucket of water. Be sure to protect your eyes, wear rubber gloves and a long-sleeve shirt, and follow all safety precautions on the product label. Wipe the blinds with a soft cloth dipped in the mixture, then go over them again with a cloth dipped in plain water. If you have trouble getting between the slats, use a soft clean paintbrush or wrap a tongue depressor–size piece of wood in a terry towel or paper towel.

If wooden blinds need more than just dusting, you can use a cloth dampened with the trisodium phosphate mixture. But be careful not to slop on the water. You don't want to oversaturate wood.

For heavier cleaning of blinds covered with fabric, mix 3 to 4 ounces mild liquid dishwashing detergent in a bucket of water. Beat the mixture into a sudsy froth. Take a damp sponge and skim some foam off the top without dipping into the water. Scrub the fabric with the foam. Then rub with a clean terry cloth. "That extracts the soil, plus it dries the surface," says Cliff Zlotnik, owner of Unsmoke/Restorx, a property restoration and cleaning company in Braddock, Pennsylvania, and a member of the Association of Specialists in Cleaning and Restoration in Millersville, Maryland.

Vinyl or coated metal mini-blinds can be washed in the bathtub. The Window Covering Safety Council, in New York City, recommends this method. Extend the blind to its full length and remove it from its support brackets. Place it gently in your bathtub with warm water mixed with 1 to 2 cups of powdered automatic dishwasher detergent. There should be enough water to completely submerge the blind. Hold the blind by its headrail and dip the blind up and down in the water several times to loosen dirt and dust. Use a sponge to wash each slat. Wear rubber gloves to avoid irritating your hands in the dishwasher detergent.

When the blind is clean, empty the tub of the soapy water and refill the tub halfway with plain cold water. Dip the blind up and down until soap is off, then drain the tub. If it's necessary to rinse more, refill the tub again halfway. Gather the blind and place it upright in a corner of the tub and allow it to dry for several hours. If the slats are still damp, rehang the blind anyway and wipe slats dry with a soft cloth.

In a pinch: If you don't have time to clean or if your blinds are really dirty, there are professional blind-cleaning services. They use an "ultrasonic bath" method, which uses sound waves vibrating through water to clean the blinds. Often you can get a lower rate if you deliver your blinds to the cleaner and pick them up yourself.

Caution: It's a good idea to test any cleaning solution on an inconspicuous part of your blind before cleaning the whole blind. Just dab some of the solution on with a cotton swab. This is especially advised for fabric or painted wood blinds. Often these are imported, and it's difficult to know what dyes or paints have been used.

Blood Stains

As with most stains, the quicker you get to a blood stain, the better chance you have of getting it out. But work patiently and follow the steps. "There are no quick ways to clean a blood stain," says Jane Rising, instructor in the education department at the International Fabricare Institute in Silver Spring, Maryland.

Technique: First, blot the stain with cool water. Then blot with a mild liquid dishwashing detergent mixed with water. Flush thoroughly with water. If the stain persists, try mixing the detergent and water with a couple of drops of ammonia. Flush thoroughly with water. If the stain still won't go away, and the fabric is colorfast, soak it in an enzyme-containing product such as Shout. Test for colorfastness first in an inconspicuous spot. Flush thoroughly with water.

If all else fails, blot the stain using a bleach containing hydrogen peroxide, as long as the bleach is safe for the color and fabric of your garment. Or soak the cloth in a nonchlorine colorfast bleach, such as Biz, for several hours or overnight. Use ½ scoop Biz in 2 gallons warm water.

If that doesn't work, you can try a rust remover, such as Whink or Rit, and follow the label directions. It's important to flush thoroughly with water between each step so that individual cleaning solutions don't mix on the fabric. Follow the cleaning instructions on the garment. If you have treated the fabric with an aerosol stain protector, such as Scotchgard, reapply it after you've cleaned the fabric.

To remove a blood stain from fabric that has been Scotchgard-treated at the factory, follow the manufacturer's instructions very carefully to protect any warranty. For furniture, read the label under the cushion and check the cleanability code. A "W" means use a water-based cleaner to clean; an "S" means use a cleaning solvent, not water; a "W-S" means use either water or a solvent; and an "X" means use neither, just vacuum. In general, for carpets that have been stain-treated at the factory, the following method can be used to remove a water-based stain such as blood. Blot up as much as you can with paper towel. Mix ¼ teaspoon clear dishwashing detergent and 1 cup lukewarm water.

Don't use laundry detergent because it may contain brighteners and other additives. Blot from the outside to the center of the stain. Blot with plain white paper towels or terry towels until the towel no longer picks up the stain. Rinse with clear water. If the stain is gone, place white paper towels over the area and weight down, changing towels periodically until the area is dry. The paper toweling will wick up stains from deep in the carpet. If the stain is stubborn, try a solution of 2 tablespoons nonsudsing ammonia with 1 cup lukewarm water. Rinse and blot as mentioned previously. Immediately follow with a mixture of 1 cup white vinegar and 2 cups water to neutralize the ammonia. Blot and rinse as mentioned previously, and weight down paper towels over the stain until dry.

In a pinch: If a minor blood stain happens at work or someplace you can't get to cleaning supplies easily, "blot it with water immediately," Rising says. "Often, that will take care of it."

Caution: Never rub or brush a stain because this may spread the stain or damage the fabric. Make certain that you have flushed completely between each cleaning step with clean water. Make sure, if you've used bleach, to flush it completely away. Bleach left on fabric can weaken it. Be sure to test any cleaning method on a small obscure corner of the fabric before attacking the stain, even if you've used the method before, to make sure that the colors and the fabric can withstand the cleaning. Read the labels on clothing for cleaning instructions. Follow the product label carefully for proper use and safety precautions.

Boats

Always start with the gentlest approach when cleaning a boat. Use stronger methods sparingly, and then be sure that they're suitable for your boat's materials.

Technique: Regardless of what your boat is made of, cleaning starts with a bucket of freshwater and mild soap or liquid dishwashing detergent. Soap the boat down thoroughly with a good sponge, then rinse with generous amounts of freshwater.

Wooden Boats

Since wooden boats are painted, "you are essentially cleaning paint, which means that solvents are out. Soap and water is the best routine," says Randy Cobb, plant engineer for Old Town Canoe Company, the venerable maker of canoes and other small boats located in Old Town, Maine. For crusted-on dirt that the sponge won't clean, try one of the least abrasive Scotch-Brite pads, which are white, tan, or beige. Using anything more abrasive may damage the surface.

Fiberglass Boats

Start with soap and water. If that doesn't do the trick, go after tough dirt or oily stains with a little mineral spirits (paint thinner), applied sparingly on a soft cloth. Then rinse the boat thoroughly. Don't use lacquer thinner or acetone, which are stronger solvents and can damage fiberglass.

Of Rats and Men

Ah, to take to the high seas in an old English sailing ship. The excitement! The adventure! The vermin! Well, you had to figure it wasn't *all* excitement and adventure. Among the less glamorous tasks was cleaning the ship of rats and cockroaches after a long sea voyage.

James Horsburgh, a ship captain from the early nineteenth century, describes the following method, which doubled as a way to check for leaks. The description appears in *The Naval Chronicle*, a multivolume British naval journal of that era. First, a large pot filled with red-hot charcoal was lowered onto the ballast in the hold and covered with shakings (pieces of old rope, canvas, and other sweepings) that had been moistened and dipped in tar.

"But in order to make certain of destroying the vermin," Horsburgh writes, "I also placed upon the ballast a small kettle, with sulphur on fire, and immediately closed the hatch, securing it with clay. In a few minutes, the smoke began to issue out at many parts of the ship, which enabled the carpenter to mark them with chalk, by which means a leak was discovered in the stem (the bow), of 10 years standing, or from the time the ship first floated; and many efforts had been made at various times to discover it, without success.

"After 40 hours, the hatches were opened, and the rats were found in a petrified state, but the cockroaches were as lively as ever."

Vinyl-Covered Boats

Many small boats today are made from a vinyl composite material called Royalex. These hulls have a vinyl exterior with a hard plastic layer underneath and a foam plastic core. After soap and water, go after tougher grime with some denatured alcohol, available at hardware stores, on a cloth. These boats have a tendency to mildew, especially if stored in a shed for a long time. Denatured alcohol will clear mildew away without damaging the material. For truly stubborn stains, apply a little acetone—very sparingly. Heavy use of acetone or other solvents may weaken the foam core and will remove some of the vinyl skin.

Polyethylene Boats

Some canoes, kayaks, and small boats are made of this rugged but flexible plastic, somewhat similar to the plastic used for liquid laundry detergent containers. If the boat needs more cleaning after soap and water, apply a limited amount of paint thinner or acetone with a cloth, Cobb says. Small amounts of lacquer thinner may be used as a last resort.

Aluminum Boats

If the aluminum is painted, use the same cleaning method as for wooden boats. Unpainted aluminum boats are rugged; they can withstand any of the aforementioned cleaning methods.

Speed tips: If you use your boat in salt water, hose it down with freshwater thoroughly and as soon as possible after each use. This will prevent a saltwater film from building up and limits corrosion.

Caution: Don't use thinners or other solvents on a painted boat. Use them sparingly on other boats. "You never want to get any more aggressive than necessary," Cobb says. Always rinse cleaning agents thoroughly with water.

Bone

Objects made of bone are porous and frequently brittle. Over-clean and you may wind up being bad to the bone.

Technique: Smooth bone, such as handles for knives or letter openers, may be wiped with a slightly dampened cloth or cotton swab. Bone carvings should be dusted with an artist's sable paint-brush, available at art stores. Don't use cloth or swabs on carvings, as you may break off brittle pieces or lodge bits of cloth or cotton in crevices, warns Stephen Koob, a conservation specialist at the Freer Gallery of the Smithsonian Institution in Washington, D.C.

Speed tips: You can vacuum bone pieces instead of dusting. Use a small battery-operated vacuum cleaner, available at electronics stores.

Caution: Never submerge bone in water. Even getting it wet is a bad idea—mold grows easily. Never use soap or wax, both of which can leave a residue that will turn the piece yellow. Bone that you don't want to clean yourself or that is stained or damaged by fire should be taken to a professional conservator. To find one in your area, contact the American Institute for Conservation of Historic and Artistic Works, 1717 K Street NW, Suite 301, Washington, DC 20006.

Books

In cleaning books, as in making the perfect omelet, the best rule is keep to it light and simple.

Technique: "Unless there is a need to clean, just dusting books with a soft cloth is the thing to do," says Karen Muller, executive director of the Association for Library Collections and Technical Services, a division of the American Library Association in Chicago. Food or fingerprint smudges on the cover of a hardcover book or a paperback with a hard finish may be cleaned with a damp, but not wet, sponge or cloth. For smudges on conventional paperbacks, use a very soft eraser and rub gently. Go super gently on colored paper, to make sure that you don't rub off color. For leather-bound books, wipe with a clean dry cloth, or carefully vacuum off the obvious dust.

There is no surefire method for removing the musty smell from old books, but the Northeast Document Conservation Center in Andover, Massachusetts, suggests this nifty (if somewhat involved) method. It requires two clean garbage can–type containers, one small enough to fit into the larger with room to spare. Place the book in the smaller can, and put that in the larger can. Then place some odor-absorbing material such as baking soda, plain charcoal briquettes, or cat litter in the bottom of the larger can, around the base of the smaller. Cover the big can and let it sit for several days,

HOW I DO IT

Guarding the Bard

In 1623, seven years after the death of William Shakespeare, two of his actor friends collected and published 36 plays in an edition called the First Folio. Without the remarkable efforts of John Heminges and Henry Condell, at a time when plays were rarely considered literature worth saving, many Shakespearean dramas would have been lost forever. Of the fewer than 300 remaining copies from the original edition, the Folger Shakespeare Library in Washington, D.C., owns 80, the world's largest collection.

"First Folios are worth three-quarters of a million dollars apiece, so we don't just 'clean them,' " says conservation director Frank Mowery.

"Like all of our rare books, they're kept in a walk-in vault with a constant 68°F temperature and 50 percent humidity. Consistency is essential. Paper expands and contracts as it gains and loses moisture. After too many fluctuations it breaks apart, just like a piece of metal that has been bent back and forth. Fifty percent humidity is moist enough to keep the paper from getting brittle but too dry for silverfish and other destructive insects that get their water from what they eat.

"We have sophisticated atmospheric control systems that keep the vault nearly dust-free, but once a year a staff member dusts the books with a lint-free cloth sprayed with a spray-on cleaner and polish, like Endust, or with a static-free Dust Bunny, a cloth that creates a magnetic attraction to dust.

"Scholars are permitted to handle the books, but they must wash and dry their hands thoroughly before doing so. You might think that gloves would be required, but we don't permit them. Even with ultra-thin gloves you lose some of your feel, increasing the chance of tearing a page or dropping a book.

"You may not have access to all this sophisticated climate control machinery, but you can preserve your own books by using humidifiers and dehumidifiers as the climate demands, to stabilize the humidity in your home library."

checking periodically. Don't leave your treasure where the trash collector might mistakenly haul it off.

Speed tips: To keep an entire shelf of books looking good, use a vacuum cleaner with a long, soft brush attachment to clean the spines. Then lightly dust the tops and edges of the books. Do not press down because you may damage the tops.

Caution: For leather books, conservationists no longer recommend leather dressings such as neat's-foot oil or lanolin, as they once did. The current consensus is that dressings may discolor or stain leather books, make them sticky, or absorb into other books or papers. Dressings may also increase the chance of mold.

Boots—Leather, Rubber

Good-quality boots will stand up to years of trekking through the mud and over rough terrain, provided that you treat them nicely once they're safely back home.

Technique: Rubber boots require relatively simple care. Just take them out back and put the hose to them when they get muddy. Even hard caked-on mud should soften after a few moments under the hose. "I'm always in mud with my rubber boots, and it does not take much to get hardened mud off them," says Rocky Rodrigues, footwear representative for L.L. Bean, the venerable outdoors store in Freeport, Maine, that started making and selling boots in 1912. Remove any remaining mud with a soft towel or cloth.

There's not much you can do to prevent cheap or imitation rubber boots from fading and cracking. But you can prolong the life of any rubber boot by storing it out of direct sunlight. If shiny boots are your thing, apply a coat of automotive tire and vinyl protectant such as Armor All for tires once or twice a year, Rodrigues says.

The biggest concern with leather boots is not getting them wet but getting them dry in the right way. Not that you want to soak your boots just for the fun of it, but most full-grain leather work boots or hiking boots can stand up to a hosing if they've gotten really muddy. The important thing is to let them dry at room temperature, away from direct sources of heat. Radiators, ovens, and blow-dryers will certainly dry boots faster, but you run the risk of cracking or warping the leather.

Saddle soap, available in tins at many shoe stores, will do a good job of cleaning routine dirt and stains from leather boots. Just follow the instructions on the can. But saddle soap may wipe away some needed moisture. Remember that leather is a hide and, just like your skin, should be kept soft. If the boots feel dry after using saddle soap, apply a commercial leather conditioner.

Suede and nubuck boots should be brushed as needed to keep them looking good. Suede is made from leather that has been split, with the soft inside turned out. Nubuck is full-grain leather that has been lightly sanded to produce a soft, suedelike exterior. For suede, you can use a brass suede brush. Nubuck has a shorter nap that may be damaged by a metal brush, so use a horsehair or soft nylon brush or similar soft brush instead. Brush against the nap to lift dirt particles. Then brush back into place by stroking in the direction of the nap, says Rodrigues. You can use a block eraser, available at shoe stores, to erase light stains on nubuck. If you want to use a protectant spray on your suede or nubuck shoes, use one that contains fluoropolymers, not silicon.

Note: Commercial waterproofing products, widely available at shoe stores, will help protect your boots against rain and stains. Carefully follow the instructions on the container. Boots should be clean before you apply waterproofing. Also, you may want to wear new boots a few times before waterproofing them. Some manufacturers apply a polish to make boots look great on the shoe-store shelves. This should be allowed to wear away before applying waterproofing.

In a pinch: It's unlikely that dress boots will ever get as dirty or need the type of heavy-duty cleaning as work boots, but you can spot-clean them using clear tap water applied to a clean towel.

Caution: For boots made of exotic hides or materials, carefully follow the instructions of the manufacturer or the store where you purchased them.

Bowling Balls

Dirt and mineral oils (used to coat lanes) gunk up the surface of the ball and can hurt its performance.

Technique: "Cleaning oil off a ball is like cleaning grease off dishes," says Larry Vezina, team leader of the specifications and certification department for Bowling, serving the American Bowling Congress and Women's International Bowling Congress, both in Greendale, Wisconsin. Place the ball in your kitchen sink carefully and wash it with hot water and liquid dishwashing detergent. Some bowlers actually place their ball on the lower rack of the dishwasher and run it through a regular cycle (remove dishes first).

In a pinch: Use a spray glass cleaner and rub with a soft cloth.

Caution: Avoid acetone cleaners (such as nail polish remover), which may soften the ball.

Brass

A shiny alloy of copper and zinc, brass is used in everything from lamps to candlesticks to buttons. General cleaning is simple and easy. Keeping brass shiny is a different story. How hard you work at it depends on whether the metal is lacquered.

Technique: Dust brass objects regularly using a soft cloth. Old T-shirts are great to use. Occasionally, grease or grime from particles in the air will collect on a brass object. Rub the object with a soft damp cloth. Dry the object right away to prevent water spots. Or rinse in a solution of a rinse agent such as Jet-Dry and water to prevent water spots, and then dry thoroughly.

Most brass objects and fixtures are lacquered to protect them from oxidation, a natural tarnishing process that occurs when oxygen interacts with the metal. Lacquered brass does not need to be polished until the lacquer begins to wear away. "If it's not handled a lot, the lacquer could last 10 years," says James W. McGann, vice president for quality at Virginia Metalcrafters in Waynesboro, which creates all the brass and bronze pieces used at Colonial Williamsburg.

When lacquered brass does finally begin to tarnish, it must be completely removed before you polish or relacquer it. You can use any commercial lacquer thinner, available at hardware stores. Be sure to follow the directions carefully. Stubborn lacquer that has been baked on may have to be removed by a professional metalworker. Relacquering should also be done by a professional. Check your phone book for metal finishers, antique dealers, or lighting repair shops to locate a professional.

Unlacquered brass or brass that has had its lacquer removed will have to be polished regularly to maintain its shine. Doorknobs and other objects that are touched frequently should be polished once a month to stay shiny. Other pieces should be polished every two to three months. You can use any of several dozen commercial brass polishes on the market. One popular brand is Brasso, which is widely used by the U.S. military. Getting a brass piece back to its original shine may be difficult or impossible using the standard home methods. If you're really finicky, a professional metalworker may come closest using a buffing wheel and jeweler's rouge.

Speed tips: To remove wax from a brass candlestick, dampen a soft cloth with warm water, which will melt the wax as you rub.

In a pinch: You can make your own brass polish, says McGann, by mixing 1 tablespoon salt with 1 tablespoon flour. Stir in 1 tablespoon white vinegar. Apply the paste with a soft damp cloth, rub gently, rinse, and wipe dry with a dry soft cloth.

Caution: Never use harsh cleansers or abrasive pads to clean brass. These can scratch the metal. Handle brass pieces as infrequently as possible. Oils from your fingers can leave permanent marks on unlacquered pieces and hasten the deterioration of lacquer. "If you handle a piece of brass with sweaty hands, it'll show fingerprints by tomorrow," McGann says. If you have a piece of brass that you think may be a valuable antique, don't polish it until you've had it examined by a professional conservator. The patina, a fine film that forms naturally on antique brass and other objects, is considered historically significant.

Brick

Because of brick's rough rugged surface, you may be tempted to really apply the pressure when cleaning. But take care—it's more delicate than you think. The trick is to apply the right amount of pressure without damaging the brick or mortar.

Technique: "If it's just general dirt, it could be relatively effective to get out there with a garden hose with a spray attachment," says Brian Trimble, senior engineer for the Brick Institute of America in Reston, Virginia.

For tougher cleaning jobs, mix ½ cup trisodium phosphate (available at hardware stores) with ½ cup dry laundry detergent in 1 gallon water. When using trisodium phosphate, wear eye protection, rubber gloves, and a long-sleeve shirt, and follow safety precautions on the product label. Hose down the bricks thoroughly before washing. Then scrub lightly with the cleaning mixture, using a natural-fiber or nylon brush. Wire brushes can damage sand-coated, hand-molded, or historic brick and leave small metal deposits that can cause rust stains. Oil-based paint stains must be wiped immediately with paint thinner, then rinsed thoroughly with water, or they will be nearly impossible to remove.

Moss does not damage brick, but for aesthetic reasons, you may want to remove moss or algae from shaded brick surfaces. To do so, you may use an organic herbicide, following the package instructions, or you may douse the algae or moss with a mixture of half chlorine bleach and half water instead. Rinse thoroughly with plain water. Then let the area dry, brush away the moss or algae, and follow the same cleaning method as above. Reworking poor drainage or cutting down on shade will keep moss and algae from returning, Trimble advises.

Sometimes brick gets a chalky white stain in patches. This is caused by waterborne salts that have worked their way to the surface of the brick and dried. Usually, these marks will wear away on their own over time. Persistent marks may indicate a drainage leak around your home that should be fixed.

Speed tips: You may rent a pressure washer to clean brick, but make sure that it's one that can be set for 700 pounds per square inch or less, to avoid damage to the bricks or mortar. Be especially careful on sand-coated brick, where pressure washers set too high may leave "bald spots" on the surface.

Caution: You may hear that muriatic acid is good for cleaning brick; professional bricklayers use it to remove fresh mortar. But, Trimble warns, "indiscriminate use can cause staining, kill plants, and etch glass. It's just not something I'd recommend the average homeowner to be doing."

Briefcases

Like a good pair of shoes, a briefcase should be regularly conditioned to prepare it for the outdoor pounding it will take.

Technique: The easiest way to clean a briefcase made of finished leather (as opposed to suede or nubuck) is with a damp sponge and some mild liquid dishwashing detergent or Woolite, says George Mooers, manager of a Tandy Leather and Crafts store in Torrence, California. Squirt a little of the detergent onto the sponge and rub the surface. Then wipe away soap residue with a sponge dampened only with water. If this method fails, try a cleaner specially made for leather, available at most leather stores.

Every three to six months, depending on how often you use the briefcase and whether it is frequently exposed to harsh weather, you should treat the briefcase with a leather conditioner. You can use any good-quality conditioner. Follow the instructions on the container. "Even a boot cream would work," says Mooers. "If you don't treat the leather, the oils will dry out of it."

For briefcases made of vinyl or other imitation materials, use the liquid dishwashing detergent or Woolite. But instead of applying a

How to Get a Handle on Your Briefcase's Contents

Think of your briefcase as a "mini-desk" rather than as a general repository for all your stuff. That's the advice of Barbara Hemphill, an organizational consultant who has appeared on *Good Morning America*, *The Today Show*, *This Morning*, and other national television shows, and author of *Taming the Paper Tiger*. Hemphill, president of Hemphill and Associates in Raleigh, North Carolina, offers these tips so that your briefcase doesn't turn you into a head case.

- Open your briefcase next to the wastebasket whenever possible. Continually ask yourself, "What's the worst possible thing that would happen if I didn't have this piece of paper?" If you can live without it, toss it.
- Carry a file folder labeled "File" for papers you want to file back at the office. Inside the folder keep an index of your files so that you can determine quickly where you or your assistant should put the papers once you return.
- Carry a set of "action files" with labels such as "Call," "Discuss with _____," "Read," or "Write" for papers that require your action.
- Keep in your briefcase a well-organized store of office supplies that you may need on the road. For example, a small stapler, self-stick removable notes, highlighting marker, stationery, envelopes, and stamps. Keep a supply of return address labels on hand in case you need to mail things to yourself while on the road.

leather conditioner, protect the surface with an automotive tire and vinyl protectant like Armor All.

Detergent should not be used on suede or nubuck, both of which have a softer brushed feel. Instead, use cleaners and protectants made specifically for those surfaces.

Clean the handle and other fixtures of the briefcase according to the material of which they're made. (See Brass on page 33 and Chrome on page 61, for example.)

Speed tips: You can remove ink marks caused by ballpoint pens quickly and easily from a finished leather surface by rubbing with a cloth or sponge sprayed with a little hair spray, says Mooers. The chemicals in the hair spray break down the ink. Ink marks may be impossible to remove from suede or nubuck.

In a pinch: You can mask small scrapes or nicks in finished leather by dabbing the area with a magic marker of a color similar to your briefcase's. For tiny scratches that haven't gone through the surface color, you can simply rub them out with your fingertips. The natural oils in your hands will make these disappear. For scuff marks, try rubbing on some shoe polish that is similar in color.

Caution: Never use harsh cleansers or abrasive pads to clean leather.

Brocade

Brocade refers to fabric that has been decorated with a raised woven design, often in an intricate floral pattern. Brocaded fabrics range from silk to synthetic materials and may be used for clothing, drapery, and upholstery. Because of the complex weaves, the best bet is often to leave the cleaning of brocaded fabric to the professionals. "Cleaning brocade yourself is an iffy task at best," says Leon Moser, extension specialist and fabric expert at North Carolina State University's College of Textiles in Raleigh.

Technique: For light cleaning of brocaded upholstery or drapes, vacuum gently using a brush attachment. For heavy soil or stains, take the item to a dry cleaner whom you trust. This is especially advised if the item is old or prized.

Caution: If the brocaded item is an heirloom, be sure to let the dry cleaner know.

Bronze

A cousin of brass, bronze is an alloy of copper and tin, used since ancient times in sculptures and other objects. Left unpolished and unlacquered, bronze quickly develops a greenish patina through oxidation. That's not always bad. In fact, in older pieces patina is considered an important part of the beauty of the object.

Technique: General cleaning of bronze objects is easy and should be done gently. The main thing you want to avoid is scratching the surface. For routine maintenance, just dust with a soft dry cloth such as an old T-shirt. If grime from the air has built up on the piece, dampen the cloth before rubbing the piece. Dry the object right away to prevent water spots.

A Yard of Prevention

A bronze statue of a seated John Harvard has gazed down on generations of Harvard University students passing through the Yard in Cambridge, Massachusetts. Conservators cite the statue as being particularly well-maintained. That's quite a feat, considering that during football season the statue is a perennial target for pranksters from Yale, Dartmouth, or Brown, who are known to give John Harvard an unwanted coat of paint in their team's colors (blue, green, and brown, respectively).

To prepare the statue for the expected onslaught, workers give it a pre-football season coating of melted beeswax mixed with gum turpentine, explains Merle Bicknell, manager of Harvard Yard. They stir in some burnt umber and burnt sienna coloring to match the statue's dark patina. The mixture is then applied with paintbrushes, and the excess is patted off with cloths. "Basically, that prevents damage from vandalism, even when someone throws paint on it, or whatever," Bicknell says.

When an attack does occur (usually late at night), the university's 24-hour maintenance team springs into action. Workers wash the paint away before it has a chance to dry, using pressure washers and a water-soluble solvent.

Some bronze objects are lacquered to protect them from oxidation. Lacquered bronze does not need to be polished until the lacquer begins to wear away. When lacquered bronze does finally begin to tarnish, it must be completely removed before you polish or relacquer it. You can use any commercial lacquer thinner, available at hardware stores. Be sure to follow the directions carefully. Stubborn lacquer that has been baked on may have to be removed by a professional metalworker. Relacquering should also be done by a professional. Check your phone book for metal finishers, antique dealers, or even lighting repair shops to find a professional.

Unlacquered bronze will have to be polished as necessary to maintain its shine. Commercial brass polishes such as Brasso work well on bronze, says James W. McGann, vice president for quality at Virginia Metalcrafters in Waynesboro, which creates all the brass and bronze pieces used at Colonial Williamsburg. Home polishes will restore a shine, but getting them to like-new condition may require the skills of a professional metalworker using a buffing wheel and jeweler's rouge.

Speed tips: To add a quick shine to a small piece of bronze or copper, try rubbing it with a little ketchup. "If you want to see how this works, squirt a little bit on a penny," suggests McGann. "It'll brighten it up." Wipe away residue with a damp cloth.

In a pinch: You can make your own polish, says McGann, by mixing 1 tablespoon salt with 1 tablespoon flour. Stir in 1 tablespoon white vinegar. Apply the paste with a soft damp cloth, rub gently, rinse, and wipe dry with a dry soft cloth.

Caution: Never use harsh cleansers or abrasive pads to clean bronze. These can scratch the metal. Handle pieces as infrequently as possible. Oils from your fingers can leave permanent marks. If you have a piece of bronze that you think may be valuable or historically significant, don't polish it until you've had it examined by a professional conservator. If you use moisture when cleaning a bronze piece, dry it thoroughly afterward with a soft dry cloth to prevent spots from forming. Don't use spray waxes or furniture polishes. They'll just dull the shine.

Brushes—Hair

Periodic cleaning will keep your hairbrush from turning into a bird's nest of tangled hair and styling residue.

Technique: Whether your brush has natural or synthetic bristles, the best thing for it is a bath of warm soapy water. First, though, you will want to remove as much hair as possible. The best way to do this is to run a comb through the bristles. "Start pulling hair away from the base of the brush, working out to the tips," says Rebecca Viands, executive vice president of the Potomac Academy of Hair Design and a commissioner of the National Accrediting Commission of Cosmetology Arts and Sciences, both in Falls Church, Virginia.

Then, soak the brush in your sink in a sudsy mixture of warm water and mild liquid dishwashing detergent for 10 to 20 minutes, or long enough to remove hair oils and residue from styling products.

In most instances, particularly if you're the only one using the brush, the above cleaning method should suffice. If you're really finicky, or the brush has been used by multiple people, you may want to sanitize it by soaking it in a commercial bactericide or fungicide solution. These are available at professional beauty supply stores. Be sure to follow the instructions carefully.

Speed tips: Since brushes, combs, and curlers all do well in a warm soapy bath, you can save time and water by washing all these items together.

In a pinch: If a brush has become seriously fouled but you still want to save it, you can disinfect it by soaking it for about 15 minutes in a 10 percent solution of liquid household bleach and water. Then rinse thoroughly with plain water, says Viands.

Caution: Most brush handles are made of plastic, hard rubber, or coated metal and can stand up well to soaking. If you have your doubts, or if the brush is a prized item with a handle made of silver or some other valuable substance, try suspending the brush over a bowl of warm soapy water so that only the bristles are submerged.

Burns—Cigarette

Stains from cigarette burns may be reversible as long as the damage from the burn itself isn't too severe.

Technique: On clothing, "if it hasn't actually burned a hole in the fabric, a blot of water may take it out," says Jane Rising, instructor in the education department at the International Fabricare Institute in Silver Spring, Maryland. If plain water doesn't work, blot with mild laundry detergent and water. Rinse thoroughly with water. As a final step, try blotting the stain with a small amount of hydrogen peroxide.

For cigarette burns on carpet, mix ¼ teaspoon liquid dishwashing detergent per cup of lukewarm water. Use it to blot the stain with a white absorbent cloth or white paper towels. As a second step, rinse the area with lukewarm water and blot until dry, changing towels as needed. If these steps don't work, your next alternative is a professional carpet cleaner.

Speed tips: The quicker you attend to this or any stain, the better your chances of removing it.

Caution: Always test-clean an inconspicuous corner before attacking the stain to ensure that the cleaning method is safe for the material. When cleaning carpets, never use a stronger concentration than ¼ teaspoon liquid dishwashing detergent to 1 cup water. Residues of cleaning solutions may cause the carpet to get dirty faster. The stronger the concentration, the more likely residues will remain after rinsing. Never use laundry detergent on carpet. They contain optical brighteners that may dye the fiber. Blot carpet—don't scrub. Scrubbing may distort the pile.

Butcher Block

Like chapped hands, butcher blocks are susceptible to changes in humidity. In addition to regular cleaning, keep butcher blocks well-oiled to extend their life.

Technique: When you are finished preparing food on a butcher block, use a steel scraper or spatula with a wide blade to scrape away any scraps of food. Use a cloth to brush away remaining particles. Then dip a clean dishcloth in hot water mixed with soap or mild liquid dishwashing detergent and rub the surface of the wood. Rinse the cloth thoroughly in clear water, wring it out, and rub again. Use a different dry cloth and go over the surface until it is thoroughly dry, says Ken Ballard Jr., safety and quality engineer for John Boos and Company, a butcher block manufacturer based in Effingham, Illinois.

To prevent stains, clean butcher blocks immediately after using, and don't leave food sitting on the wood for extended periods. If stains do occur, you can gently rub them with a light-grade sandpaper or fine steel wool. Rub with the grain and then re-oil the board as explained later. Any remaining stain marks will eventually dissipate into the wood grain with regular cleaning and maintenance. Don't panic if dark streaks appear in the wood over time. These are caused by natural discoloring of the wood due to mineral

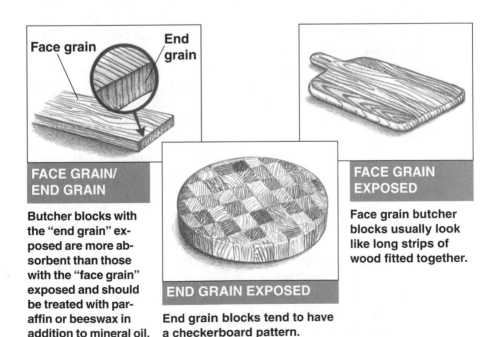

Face grain   End grain

FACE GRAIN/ END GRAIN

Butcher blocks with the "end grain" exposed are more absorbent than those with the "face grain" exposed and should be treated with paraffin or beeswax in addition to mineral oil.

END GRAIN EXPOSED

End grain blocks tend to have a checkerboard pattern.

FACE GRAIN EXPOSED

Face grain butcher blocks usually look like long strips of wood fitted together.

deposits in the tree and simply add to the character and individuality of your piece.

Excessive dryness is bad for butcher blocks and, in serious cases, may cause the wood to split. Before the first use and once every several weeks (depending on how often you use the block and how dry the air is), coat the block with a layer of mineral oil. This will help keep the natural moisture in the wood and will also help prevent the wood from absorbing bacteria from raw meat and other food, according to Ballard. Do not use vegetable oil.

Butcher blocks with "face grain" wood on the surface need only mineral oil. Surfaces of "end grain" wood are more absorbent and need mineral oil mixed with melted paraffin. End grain refers to the top or bottom of a board that has been cut lengthwise from a tree. (For example, when a tree is cut down, the circle of exposed wood on the stump is end grain). Face grain refers to the sides of the boards. You can tell the two apart in butcher blocks because face grain surfaces tend to be made of long strips of wood fixed together, while end grain looks more like a checkerboard of wood squares.

To apply mineral oil to face grain, warm some oil by heating it in a microwave oven for 20 to 30 seconds or less. Or you can place the container of oil in a saucepan of very warm water. The amount of oil required depends on the dryness of the wood, but you will need at least six to eight ounces of oil for every two-foot-square section of block. Pour the warm oil over the block and spread it around the entire surface with a horsehair brush or a heavy cloth. Let it sit for four to five minutes. "If it soaks in real fast, you want to apply a second coat," Ballard says. "It's really a judgment call."

For end grain wood, melt some canning wax, or paraffin (available at grocery stores), in with the mineral oil in a ratio of about four parts oil to one part wax. Or buy premixed block oils, which are much easier to use and are available at your hardware store, a chef store, or through a chefs' products catalog. Pour the oil and wax over the block and spread around with a brush. If it soaks right in, add more. When the oil and wax have dried, some of the hardened wax will bead on the surface. Scrape this away with your scraper or metal spatula. To clean the brush, hold it under hot running water for about five minutes or until the oil and wax are removed.

Speed tips: You can help your butcher block stay young and lessen the frequency of oiling by using a humidifier in your home during dry winter months.

Caution: Always be sure to clean your butcher block thoroughly shortly after preparing food. As an added precaution against bacteria, use one block or section of a block for cutting meat, fish, and poultry, and another for cutting vegetables and other foods. Never use harsh detergents or cleansers to clean a butcher block, says Ballard. If your butcher block is installed near a stove or other heat source, be sure that there's proper insulation between them. Don't cut continuously in the same place. Spread your cuts around to even the wear. If you have to alter your butcher block or wooden cutting board by cutting it, immediately oil the cut end to prevent it from drawing in moisture and cracking, says Ballard.

Cabinets—Kitchen

Most solid wood and veneer kitchen cabinets are finished with a protective varnish that makes cleaning straightforward. Laminated surfaces are even easier.

Technique: For general cleaning on solid wood or veneer, simply wipe cabinets with a damp cloth and dry them with a soft dry towel. For grease or heavier grime, dip a cloth lightly in a solution of 1 gallon water mixed with ¼ cup mild soap such as Murphy Oil Soap. Clean up spills as quickly as possible to prevent permanent stains. After cleaning, wipe dry with a clean soft cloth.

Immediately after installation and once every six months, wood cabinets should be waxed. First, wipe with a damp cloth and then dry with a another soft dry cloth. Then give them a light coating of liquid or paste furniture wax that does not contain abrasive cleaners. Working on small areas at a time, rub the wax into the wood quickly (before the wax sets) applying in the direction of the wood grain. If you use a spray wax, spray the wax onto the cloth rather than directly onto the cabinet. "This treatment helps resist excessive moisture and prevents damage to the finish," says Jean Butler, vice president of marketing at Yorktowne Cabinets, a Pennsylvania cabinet manufacturer.

Laminated cabinets should be washed with the water and mild soap solution and a clean soft cloth, as with wood cabinets. Unlike wood cabinets, laminated ones don't need to be waxed.

Caution: Avoid harsh detergents and abrasive soaps or cleaners, all of which may damage the surface. Don't use your dishcloth to wipe cabinets. It may contain residues of detergents or grease. Excessive moisture is the primary enemy of wood products. Spills should be wiped up as quickly as possible. Check areas near sinks and major appliances regularly. Avoid mounting or placing appliances such as coffeemakers or toasters on counters directly under cabinets. Heat from these appliances could damage the cabinets.

Camcorders

Sure, camcorders are meant to be used indoors and out. But they're delicate machines that must be protected from dust and moisture as well as extreme heat and cold. Leave the rough stuff to Bruce Willis.

Technique: The casing of the camcorder may be wiped with a soft dry cloth, but don't use any household cleaning products, especially liquids that may seep into the electronics. Wipe the lens periodically, especially if you're filming outdoors. Use a commercial lens cleaner made for cameras or camcorders. To clean the heads (the taping apparatus), use a head cleaner. This is a special cassette that cleans as it runs; it can be purchased at electronics stores.

Speed tips: "One thing every camcorder owner should have is a plastic bag," says Lisa Fasold, spokeswoman for the Consumer Electronics Manufacturers Association in Arlington, Virginia. Wrap the camcorder loosely to keep rain or other moisture from getting in. Thin clear bags such as those that come from the dry cleaner are good. But don't close tightly and leave for extended periods—that will trap moisture inside.

Caution: Never use a spray glass cleaner such as Windex to clean the lens. Never blow into the camcorder to clean out dust. Moisture from your saliva may rust components.

Cameos

True cameos are made of carved shell. Other materials such as coral, agate, or synthetics are sometimes substituted. Cameos, particularly if they are antiques, should be cleaned lightly and with care.

Technique: For general cleaning, rub the cameo gently with a soft damp (not wet) cloth to remove dust or other light dirt. If the item is prized and has a stain that won't come off with the damp cloth, take it to a conservator. "Don't go at it yourself," says Joyce Hill Stoner, Ph.D., professor of art conservation at the Winterthur/University of Delaware Program in Art Conservation in Newark. (For tips on finding a good conservator, see "Not Just Any Old Conservator Will Do" on page 10.)

Caution: Avoid using cleaning solvents of any kind on cameos. Don't confuse cameos with painted ivory pieces, which may be about the same size and, like cameos, usually depict a woman's face. Cameos are carved, while painted ivory is, as the name indicates, a painting. If you mistakenly rub a watercolor-painted ivory piece with a damp cloth, you may ruin it.

Cameras

You can buy all kinds of fancy (and expensive) stuff for cleaning your camera, but keeping your tools and your methods simple will cut costs and prevent you from damaging your gear through overcleaning. "Avoid high-markup items," says Chuck DeLaney, dean of the New York Institute of Photography, the nation's oldest photography school, based in New York City. Four basic tools will arm you for just about any camera cleaning task. These include:

- A sable watercolor paintbrush (number 2, 3, or 4) with a fine point, available at art or hobby stores
- A palm-size, rubber bulb–type ear syringe, available at drugstores
- Microfiber cleaning cloths, available at camera stores: soft cloths with an ultrafine weave that will clean effectively without leaving lint behind; can be machine-washed and reused many times
- Camera lens cleaning fluid, also available at camera stores

You can buy combination blower-brushes at camera shops, but these are much more expensive than a simple ear syringe and sable paintbrush and are less effective. "They have too little blower and too much brush," DeLaney says.

Technique: Start with the exterior of the camera. Look it over carefully to see what is dirty. Always clean your camera under a bright light. Under a dim light, dirt and grime can easily hide in the shadows of crevices. Examine the lens and viewfinder for dust, dirt, grease, or fingerprints. If your camera is an automatic point-and-shoot model with a built-in lens, use the microfiber to wipe the en-

HOW I DO IT

Camera Care on the Road

Professional photography assignments have taken Chuck De-Laney all over the world. As dean of the New York Institute of Photography in New York City, he offers some tips for caring for your camera when traveling or shooting outdoors.

Hit the beach with a decoy. A camera's two biggest enemies are excessive moisture and fine gritty sand. If you're going to be taking pictures at the beach, or in places with extreme humidity or dust, leave your expensive camera at home. Instead, take along a disposable camera or an inexpensive, waterproof point-and-shoot model. Even the disposable cameras take fine pictures these days, and an accident or damage won't break the bank.

Rescue it from salt. Should you drop an expensive camera in water, you may be able to save it. If it falls in salt water, remove the camera immediately and submerge as quickly as possible in a container of freshwater. Keep it submerged and take it to a camera repair shop quickly. You want to prevent salt water from drying and leaving corrosive deposits on the delicate parts. If it falls into freshwater, remove the camera from the water, dry it with a towel, then open it and allow the interior to dry with the back open. When it's dry, take it to a camera shop to be checked and relubricated.

Keep cool. Cameras hate heat almost as much as they do moisture and sand. Don't stick a camera or film in the glove compartment of your car, where the summer sun beating down raises temperatures to intolerable levels. Cameras sitting in the sun also can become too hot to handle. Keep them shaded whenever possible.

Skip the flashy cases. Whenever possible, use an old, beat-up looking case to hold your camera supplies, especially when traveling. "One that just says 'Steal me' is a big mistake," DeLaney says. "Those buffed aluminum bags say, 'Come and get it.'"

tire exterior, excluding the lens. If the lens is removable, take it off before wiping the exterior. The cloth should get rid of most dust and dirt along with oils from your fingers and face. For heavier grime, you may dampen the cloth slightly with water.

In cleaning the lens, make sure not to scratch it by rubbing a speck of sand or dirt across it. Your first step involves the blower. Holding the tip about one-eighth inch from the lens, blow off any loose dust or dirt. Then use the sable brush to flick away stubborn dirt lodged in crevices. Once the dust and dirt are gone, wipe the lens with the microfiber cloth. For stubborn grime, you may breathe lightly on the lens to create a haze, then wipe. If that fails, try a couple of drops of lens-cleaning fluid on the cloth.

Once you're satisfied that the exterior is clean, make sure that there's no film inside and open the camera. Most cameras are well-sealed, and the interior should require light cleaning only. "Once you're inside the camera, the key word is *gentle*," DeLaney says.

Use the blower and the brush to gently clear away dirt and dust from the film chamber and the take-up reel (which rolls the film as it's used). Clean the back of the lens in the same way that you clean the front. Don't forget to wipe the pressure plate with the cloth or brush. This plate is attached to the camera door and presses the film in place. Blow or brush away dirt and dust from the trough where the door fits into the back of the camera.

Speed tips: A good waterproof camera cover (or even a plastic bag) will help prevent major cleaning jobs by keeping dust and dirt away from your camera and by blocking out moisture.

In a pinch: As a low-budget alternative to microfiber cloths, you can use sections cut from old T-shirts. Older T-shirts work best because the more times they've been washed, the softer they are. But even the oldest, softest T-shirt will leave some lint behind, which is why microfiber cloths are preferable. If you use a T-shirt, follow up with the blower.

Caution: Never use harsh cleaning solvents or soaps to clean your camera. Avoid using lens cleaners made for eyeglasses. These often leave a coating that is perfectly good for glasses but gunks up a camera lens. Some camera stores sell "canned air" to blow-clean your camera. These should be avoided because the air pressure is enough to damage delicate parts if used improperly, says DeLaney. The simple handheld blower is best.

Can Openers

Paper from labels, metal shavings, and food can get jammed up in the cutting assembly.

Technique: If your electric can opener has a removable cutting assembly, the assembly can be placed in the dishwasher. If it's not removable, use a toothbrush or a light scouring pad and some liquid dishwashing detergent to degunk the cutter. A toothpick is the best tool for removing paper labels that get wadded up in the cutter, says Fay Carpenter, manager of home economics at Black and Decker Corporation in Shelton, Connecticut. Wipe the plastic case with a soft damp cloth as part of your regular counter cleaning.

Caution: Be certain that the opener is unplugged before you begin to clean it.

Carpets

The dirt that you can't see can be even more nettlesome to carpets than visible dirt. Bits of dry soil and other debris love to hunker down in the pile of your carpet, where they go to work trying to ruin your investment. To keep carpets in great shape, you will want to establish a long and intimate relationship with your vacuum cleaner. Modern carpets are designed to reflect light and resist stains, making soil harder than ever to see. That's a positive feature, but it means that you should vacuum regularly even if the carpet does not appear to be dirty.

Technique: The Carpet and Rug Institute, based in Dalton, Georgia, recommends vacuuming entryways daily because this is where outside soil is deposited. If you can eliminate the soil before it spreads to other areas, you can lighten your housekeeping load. If that kind of routine won't fit your busy schedule, it's a good idea to take your vacuum cleaner for a spin at least a couple of times per week. Vacuuming frequently will catch more soil while it is still near the surface of your carpet. Once embedded, it is much more difficult to remove. Under foot pressure, the sharp edges of embedded particles will scar or even shear off fibers, distorting the light reflection and dulling the carpet's appearance. "It's just like scratching glass," says Michael Hilton, the institute's carpet-cleaning expert.

Vacuuming protects more than just your carpet. "Cleaning carpets regularly cuts down on indoor air pollution," says Leyla McCurdy, director of indoor air programs for the American Lung Association in Washington, D.C. "You want to get rid of dirt particles. If there's activity on a dirty carpet, you make them airborne. Then, you're inhaling them."

Vacuuming frequently is especially important if people with allergies live in the house because it will help protect against allergic reactions to dust mites. Vacuuming won't suck up the mites themselves—they're great at clinging fast to fibers. But it will remove mite

Air Out That New Carpet

New carpets give off gases known as volatile organic compounds. These may result from chemicals used to glue the carpet to its backing, dyes, stain-resistant treatments, or other sources. The American Lung Association says that few people become seriously ill from these fumes but that they can cause temporary eye, nose, and throat irritation; headaches; skin irritation; or fatigue.

When you install new carpet, the American Lung Association recommends that you:

- Vacuum your old carpet before it's removed (to cut down on dust and other pollutants being kicked up into the air)
- Ask your carpet dealer to allow the carpet to rest unrolled in a well-ventilated area for at least 24 hours before it's installed
- Ask your carpet dealer about newer, "low-emitting" carpets that have become available with the awareness of indoor air pollution
- Ventilate your room or rooms, if weather permits, by opening windows before and after installation or by using mechanical ventilation systems for two to three days if you have them in your house
- Consider having the carpet installed when family members are likely to be away from the house

droppings and body parts, and that's more important than getting the live ones. "Those are the pieces that become airborne and cause allergic reactions," says Thomas Platts-Mills, M.D., Ph.D., head of the division of asthma, allergy, and immunology at the University of Virginia Health Sciences Center in Charlottesville and director of its Asthma and Allergic Disease Center.

When vacuuming, it's best to use slow steady strokes, both pushing and pulling. Pulling the vacuum cleaner against the grain of the carpet stands the fibers up and exposes embedded soil. Repeat several times over each area. Each stroke removes more particles. Make all of your final strokes in the same direction to leave a uniform appearance. A vacuum with rotary brushes is best for loosening soil. Keeping your vacuum cleaner well-maintained increases its effectiveness.

Regardless of how often you vacuum, your carpet should be deep cleaned at least every 18 months, or more frequently if it's in a high-traffic area, by you or a professional cleaner. Always vacuum before deep cleaning. There are several reliable deep cleaning

Carpet Stains: Out, Out Darn Spots

No carpet, not even modern carpet designed to resist stains, is entirely stainproof. Your best chance for removing stains is to attend to them as quickly as possible.

Always blot liquid stains with dry, white absorbent cloths or white paper towels with no printing on them. With semi-solids, remove as much as you can with a rounded spoon before using stain-removal procedures. The Carpet and Rug Institute, based in Dalton, Georgia, offers the following methods for dealing with specific stains. In each case, call a professional if your own efforts fail or if the stain seems too serious to handle yourself.

Alcoholic beverages: Mix ¼ teaspoon liquid dishwashing detergent in 1 cup lukewarm water. Blot the stain area with the solution, then rinse thoroughly with warm water. You may have to rinse several times to fully remove the solution. If the stain persists, try blotting it with a mixture of 2 tablespoons household ammonia per cup of water. Rinse thoroughly. Then blot the stain with a solution of 1 cup white vinegar to 2 cups water and rinse thoroughly with warm water.

Banana: First blot the stain with a commercial spot remover such as Carbona Stain Devils, available at supermarkets or discount department stores. Pour fluid onto a cloth rather than directly onto the carpet and blot the stain. Rinse thoroughly. If the stain persists, try the dishwashing detergent solution above, then rinse with warm water.

Cola: The methods are the same as for alcoholic beverages. If those steps fail, try using a spot-removal kit, available from most carpet retailers. Follow the directions carefully. These kits often contain a stain-resisting solution to be applied after using a detergent solution that is also included. Applying the stain-resisting solution before the stain is completely gone may make it permanent.

Egg: Same as for alcoholic beverages.

Fruit, fruit juice, jam, jelly: Same as for cola.

Ice cream or milk: First, blot the stain with a commercial spot remover such as Carbona Stain Devils or K2r, available at supermarkets, hardware stores, or discount department stores. Rinse thoroughly.

methods, some of which require special equipment that can be rented at appliance rental centers. The simplest methods include dry extraction (brushing in an absorbent cleaner, then vacuuming it out) and dry foam extraction (spreading a layer of foam on the carpet, then vacuuming it out). Dry extraction powders are widely available under brand names such as Host and Capture. Woolite, Shout, and Resolve are some of the major dry foam brands. The dry extraction

Next, try the dishwashing liquid solution described for alcoholic beverages. Rinse thoroughly. If the stain persists, try blotting it with a mixture of 2 tablespoons household ammonia per cup of water. Rinse thoroughly. Then blot the stain with a solution of 1 cup white vinegar to 2 cups water and rinse thoroughly with warm water.

Iodine: Same as for ice cream or milk.

Ketchup: Same as for cola.

Lipstick or lip gloss: As a first step, blot the stain with some nail polish remover. Be certain to rinse thoroughly. Next, blot the stain with a commercial spot remover such as Carbona Stain Devils or K2r, available at supermarkets, hardware stores, or discount department stores. Rinse thoroughly. Next, try the dishwashing liquid solution described for alcoholic beverages. Rinse thoroughly. If that fails, blot with the ammonia solution described for alcoholic beverages. Rinse thoroughly. Try the solution of 1 cup white vinegar to 2 cups water. Rinse thoroughly with warm water. As a final step before calling a professional, try the spot-removal kit described under cola. Then find out who has been kissing your carpet.

Peanut butter: The first step is to blot with commercial spot remover such as Carbona Stain Devils or K2r, available at supermarkets, hardware stores, or discount department stores. Rinse thoroughly. Next, try the dishwashing liquid solution described for alcoholic beverages. Then rinse thoroughly with warm water.

Note: For more information on spot removal, or for tips on hiring a professional, you can write to the Carpet and Rug Institute at P. O. Box 2048, Dalton, GA 30722.

Caution: Always test cleaning methods on an inconspicuous section of carpet before using them on the stain to be certain that your carpet can withstand the given method or solution. Never use laundry detergent on a carpet. These contain optical brighteners that may dye the fibers. Don't use automatic dishwasher detergent, which may contain bleaching agents. Be sure to rinse thoroughly between each step when removing stains. Different cleaning solutions don't always mix well. Carefully read product labels for proper usage and safety precautions.

or foam methods are good medium steps between vacuuming and deep cleaning and should be used as needed.

"I have a white carpet in my great room with a marble kitchen next to it. The marble gets dirty easily, and the soil tracks to the nearest carpet surface," Hilton says. "A three-foot-square area gets especially dirty. I use a dry absorbent compound about once a month. I sprinkle it on, scrub it in with a brush, and vacuum it up."

For more thorough cleaning, you can buy or rent a steam cleaner. They can be found at appliance rental centers and even some supermarkets. They're fairly easy to use, but be certain to follow instructions carefully to avoid overwetting the carpet or applying too much cleaning solution.

Even if you vacuum and deep clean regularly, it's a good idea to call in a professional at least every two to three years, more frequently if you've skimped on your own cleaning routine, says Hilton. Most professionals use hot-water extraction or steam cleaning. "Rotary shampoo" and "absorbent pad" methods involve machines that work something like a floor buffer to whisk soil away and only should be used by a professional. The rotary shampoo machine injects a cleaning solution through brushes. The absorbent pad method lifts soil into a pad. For any deep cleaning, it's best to choose whichever method the manufacturer of your carpet suggests. Some warranties will become void if other methods are used. It's also time to call a professional if your own efforts to remove a spot or stain fail.

Speed tips: A simple floor mat placed at each door to the outside can trap much of the soil that would otherwise find its way into your carpet. But it's important to keep these mats cleaned regularly themselves, if only with a good stiff beating outdoors. Otherwise, the mats will fill with soil just like a sponge with water and will actually become a source of soil spread to your carpet.

In a pinch: Place furniture glides or cups under heavy furniture to prevent depression marks from permanently marring your carpet. Also, move the furniture a few inches periodically. If you already have depression marks, work the pile back into place with a coin, then apply steam with a steam iron held two to four inches above the carpet for a few minutes. But don't allow the hot iron to touch the carpet directly.

Caution: When deep cleaning the carpet yourself, follow all instructions carefully, including the recommended strength and dilution for cleaning solutions. Remove furniture from the room until the carpet is completely dry to avoid furniture stain or rust from bleeding onto the carpet. If the furniture is too heavy to remove, place foil or plastic wrap under and around the legs.

Cleaning solutions that are not completely rinsed from carpet can attract dirt. Use ventilation, fans, and heating and air-conditioning units to help dry carpet. If left wet for more than a full day, mold or mildew may develop.

Vacuuming your carpet is bound to kick up some soil. If you are allergy-prone, wear a dust mask.

Cars

There's no set timetable for washing your car. A lot depends on where and how you drive it and whether it sleeps in a garage or under the stars—not to mention, of course, how finicky you are. Are you a car snob or a car slob? For the former, washing a car is an act of love worthy of endless hours of elbow grease. For the latter, a good hard rain suffices. Wherever you fit on the scale, it's important to remember that cleaning your car regularly can extend its life, boost its resale value, and possibly prevent costly repairs.

Manufacturers offer a dizzying array of cleaning products allowing you to get as detailed in your car cleaning as you wish. But for the average car owner, there are a few procedures you need to know.

Body

Wash your car's exterior as needed, and wax or polished it at least twice a year, or when water stops beading on the surface. Wash it frequently enough to "keep the car from becoming so dirty that cleaning becomes a major job," suggests Danny Cooke, a car maintenance and repair specialist with the American Automobile Association in Richmond, Virginia.

Technique: Automotive supply stores sell soap solutions specially made for cleaning car bodies. These are a good safe bet because they are certain to be effective and gentle, says Cooke. As an alternative, make a solution of mild liquid dishwashing detergent and water. Add enough soap to generate good suds, and add more as needed during the cleaning process to keep the suds going. Before washing, hose the car down thoroughly. This not only will make cleaning easier but also will help prevent dirt and debris from scratching the car.

Using a clean cloth or towel dipped frequently in the suds, carefully wash the entire exterior of the car, moving from top to bottom. Be sure not to neglect the out-of-the-way places. For example, open the doors and wipe down the door posts. This will help prevent corrosion, and will also prevent those annoying dirt marks on your clothes when you brush the posts getting into your car. Lift each windshield wiper and run the cloth along the blade.

One of the most important steps in washing a car, particularly if it's parked outdoors for extended periods, is to remove leaves and other debris that work their way into crevices. Open the trunk and clean out the trough that runs around the edge. The trough diverts water from the trunk interior, but if it gets backed up, you may find

HOW I DO IT

My Ugly Old Beauty

As a noted automobile historian, James A. Ward, Ph.D., would be the first to tell you that his turquoise six-cylinder 1965 Chevrolet Biscayne is not a car that serious collectors would fight over. But it was a wedding gift from his parents that year, and so the car has special significance. More than three decades and 180,000 miles later, Ward still drives the Biscayne daily and keeps it in pristine condition. Here's how.

"I don't wash my car more than once or twice a year because I never let it get dirty," says Dr. Ward, a professor of history at the University of Tennessee at Chattanooga. "I keep it in the garage at night and park in a covered space at work. Each morning, I dust the exterior to a shine before getting in. I use special dust cloths from a mail-order company called Kozak in Buffalo, New York, that come impregnated with a special cleaning oil.

"About once a year, I wash the vinyl upholstery with a solution of ammonia and water, applied with a sponge. The rest of the interior, which is also vinyl, gets an application of Armor All, the tire stuff. This keeps the vinyl from drying out.

"Chevrolets from the 1960s have a problem with water collecting under a chrome strip running around the base of the back window. Next time you see a Chevy from that era, look at the back, and you may see duct tape where the area has rusted out. I remove the water with a hypodermic needle inserted under the chrome.

"I'm a saver. I still have the original spare tire and the original windshield washer fluid stored away, though both are too old to use. The Biscayne wasn't exactly the cream of the General Motors crop. It's an ugly car. But I'm ugly, too," Dr. Ward jokes. "I have an affinity for things that look like me. I'm slow but I keep rambling along, just like my Biscayne. You are what you drive."

yourself with soggy luggage. Do the same for the troughs in your sunroof, if you have one, to prevent water from backing up and dripping on you when you drive.

When you've finished washing, be sure to dry the entire car using soft clean cloths or towels, or a chamois cloth. Don't let the car air-dry, as that may leave spots. Whenever possible, wash the car out of direct sunlight, to avoid having parts of the car dry before you've had a chance to dry them by hand.

Use a liquid or paste auto wax to finish the job. Each type has its devotees, but both work fine. Liquid wax is easier to apply. Either way, carefully follow the instructions on the container. Waxing is for more than just aesthetics—it adds a protective coating and dirt is more likely to slide right off your car.

Speed tips: The most obvious speed tip, of course, is to take your car to a car wash. But there are other timesaving measures you can take. To save time and effort during the buffing stage of waxing, you can buy an orbital power buffer at auto parts stores for less than $100. The professionals use rotary buffers, which spin in an exact circle at high speeds. In inexperienced hands, though, it's easy to mess up a paint job with a rotary buffer. The better choice is an orbital buffer, which rotates in an irregular pattern, more closely representing the hand-polishing motion. Even with an orbital buffer you must use a light touch to avoid damage.

Note: Use a toothbrush to remove excess wax from the nameplate, crevices, and other hard-to-reach spots.

Caution: Bird droppings and tree sap should be cleaned up as quickly as possible. They should come off easily if caught early. Over time, they'll eat into a paint job. Never use harsh detergents or abrasive cleansers to wash your car's body. These may scratch the surface or fade the paint. Never wash a car without wetting it down thoroughly first. If possible, wash the car out of direct sunlight. Wait two to four weeks after having body work done to wax your car. Paint jobs from a body shop may require time to properly cure.

Carpet

When vacuuming your car's carpet, tap the carpet firmly and frequently with the vacuum nozzle to dislodge sand and other gritty dirt that becomes embedded.

Engine

Today's auto engines are governed by sophisticated electrical systems and onboard computers that make cars more reliable than ever before. Unfortunately, their complexity means that weekend tinkering just isn't what it used to be. Dislocate the wrong gadget and you could throw the whole system out of whack. The same goes for cleaning an engine. Unless you're an experienced mechanic, any cleaning you do under the hood should be careful and light.

Technique: The best thing you can do under the hood is to clear out leaves and other debris. "You're not worried about appearance here. You just want to keep the crud out," says Cooke. Debris collects in the cowl area, just below the windshield wipers, where fresh

How to Spot a Good Car Wash

Sure, there's satisfaction in doing things for yourself, and that includes staring at your own smiling reflection in the shiny hood of the car you just spent hours washing and buffing. Still, there are many times when paying a professional is the best way to go. One of the main reasons that car wash customers cite is convenience, says Tina Gonsalves, spokeswoman for the International Carwash Association in Chicago. "It saves a big hassle," she says.

Professional car washes also are bound to be more thorough than average car owners, says Gonsalves, particularly in cleaning such hard-to-reach areas as the undercarriage, where salt and other corrosive substances can hide unseen.

As a third benefit, professional car washes offer environmental advantages, Gonsalves says. When homeowners rinse their cars off, the dirty soapy water runs untreated into storm drains or the surrounding land. Professional car washes are required under the Clean Air Act to dispose of wastewater into the sanitary sewer system. Increasingly, car washes are recycling and reusing water in a voluntary effort to reduce water consumption.

So, how do you choose a good car wash? Most professional car washes today use "touchless" or "soft cloth" methods that are gentle on your car's finish. Still, the array of choices as you drive in can seem vast. Don't allow yourself to be rushed, Gonsalves advises. "The operator should be able to tell you about every piece of the car wash package," Gonsalves says. "If the operator is not able to explain those things, choose another car wash."

Take a good look at the appearance of the business. If it's dirty, that's a good sign they're less than vigilant in washing cars. If the staff is unfriendly, they may be equally unfriendly to your car. Finally, don't be shy about bringing poor service to the attention of the manager. He or she should be courteous in resolving any questions or problems you have with the way your car was handled.

air is sucked into the cabin of the car. This should be removed. Also brush debris away from the water troughs on either side of the engine. If your car's radiator (located just behind the grille) is fairly accessible, use a low-pressure garden hose to wash debris away. You may also turn the hose on the firewall, which separates the engine from the passenger compartment.

Caution: Never spray a high-pressure hose directly on the engine. Water could work its way under seals and damage delicate electrical systems. Never dislodge an engine part in order to clean it. Any heavy-duty engine cleaning should be done by a professional.

Tires

Using the same solution for washing the body, scrub tires with a stiff-bristle nylon brush until clean. For whitewalls that have become particularly dirty, you may scrub with a product specially made for cleaning tires or a stronger household detergent or a cleanser such as Comet. This is the only part of the car where such cleansers are recommended.

You may want to give your tires a shine by applying a commercial tire dressing such as Armor All. These products are largely cosmetic. But hey, if the rest of your car is sparkling, why not have tires to match?

Windows

Any spray-on window cleaning solution will do a good job on car windows. You can make your own solution by filling a plastic spray bottle with an ammonia-water solution: 1 tablespoon ammonia per gallon of water, says Cooke. Rub inside and outside windows with clean paper towels. Some car buffs insist that old newspapers are best for wiping windows because they don't leave a lot of lint. Others, such as Cooke, say that it's just a good way smudge your fingers with ink.

On hot summer days, use one of those cardboard sunshades that fit between your window and your dashboard, even if it makes you feel like a prima donna. It'll do more than just keep the driver's seat from singeing your bare legs. A shade will help keep the windshield clean. How? When plastics—such as those used in modern dashboards—get hot, they emit solvents that can leave a haze on the inside glass. To remove that haze, pour some isopropyl alcohol on a clean soft cloth and rub.

Ceilings

You don't walk on them and you rarely even touch them, but still they get dirty. Tiny bits of dirt, dust, and other floating particles attach to a ceiling and make it look dim or dingy. For light cleaning jobs, the dry method is best. Heavy-duty dirt may require a detergent solution.

Technique: For conventional cleaning of smooth ceilings, simply dusting may work fine. "I'm a big believer in lamb's wool dusters," says Cliff Zlotnik, owner of Unsmoke/Restorx, a property restoration and cleaning company in Braddock, Pennsylvania, and a member of the Association of Specialists in Cleaning and Restoration in Millersville, Maryland. "They remove dust, particulate, and loose soil very effectively." Lamb's wool dusters can be purchased at cleaning supply stores, with extension poles that will reach most ceilings.

If the duster doesn't do the trick, or for ceilings stained by soot, you may need to get on a ladder and rub by hand. Rub grime-darkened areas with a putty wallpaper cleaner or a dry, foam-rubber sponge (available at hardware stores, janitorial supply stores, and paint stores) that is specially designed to rub dirt away from walls and ceilings. Place a drop cloth under the ladder to catch debris.

For more serious cleaning jobs, mix 2 to 3 ounces of a household detergent such as Spic and Span in 1 gallon water, and then rub the ceiling with a sponge dipped in the solution. A drop cloth is essential here because you're bound to drip. To prevent bead marks on the ceiling, dry thoroughly with a clean cloth or towel.

Textured ceilings present more of a challenge. You don't want to rub them, or else you may break small pieces of the ceiling off. And they're too absorbent to use a lot of water on. Dust gently, or vacuum using a brush attachment. You may also try lightly spraying dirty spots with a mixture of hydrogen peroxide and water, using mixture amounts recommended on the container. You don't need to wipe this away. If textured ceilings become seriously stained or dirty, the best option may be to paint over them, using a paint sprayer.

In a pinch: If you can't get to the paint store for a foam-rubber sponge or putty wallpaper cleaner, you may rub the ceiling with a hunk of stale crumbly bread, which will scrub without doing damage. Or pat the area with tape.

Caution: Always use a drop cloth when washing or scrubbing ceilings. Use goggles to protect your eyes from drips. Professional cleaners sometimes use harsh chemicals when cleaning ceilings, but these should not be used by inexperienced cleaners.

Chandeliers

Don't forget to glance upward once in a while during your regular cleaning routine. Chandeliers attract a lot of dust and will shine brighter if attended to regularly.

Technique: For light cleaning, run a feather duster lightly over the chandelier, or use a blow-dryer to blow the dust away from delicate parts. For more extensive cleaning, see listings elsewhere in this book for cleaning the metallic parts (Brass on page 33 and Chrome on page 61, for example). To clean glass or crystal prisms, you may want to remove the individual prisms, being careful not to twist or snap the wires that attach them to the chandelier. Use a spray glass cleaner and a clean soft cloth to wipe them down. Or make your own spray mixture using 90 percent distilled water and 10 percent rubbing alcohol. Distilled water is preferable to plain because it contains fewer minerals that can leave spots.

Speed tips: As an alternative to removing the prisms—a time-consuming task—try giving them the white-glove treatment. Put on a soft, white cotton glove. Then, spray the prisms and gently rub them with your gloved hand. "Cotton gloves allow you to grab the prism without straining the wire loop that attaches it," says Martin L. King, a restoration consultant in Arlington, Virginia, and technical advisor to the National Institute of Disaster Restoration in Millersville, Maryland. "It's a very efficient way to clean them."

Caution: Be sure to move around the chandelier as you clean it rather than staying in one place and twisting it. Even if you're working on a ladder, reposition the ladder periodically. Twisting the chandelier might unscrew it from the ceiling, causing it to crash to the floor. Place soft blankets on the floor or table beneath the chandelier to prevent prisms from shattering if they drop.

China

It's always best to wash china dishes by hand, although newer china will do well in the dishwasher.

Technique: To wash by hand, first place a rubber guard, available at housewares stores, on the faucet to prevent chipping. Place a rubber mat or double-folded towel on the bottom of the sink. If it's a divided sink, drape a rubber mat over the divider. Wash in a sinkful of warm water, using any liquid dishwashing detergent and a nonabrasive pad or sponge. To wash figurines or sculptures, use mild soap and warm water, and gently pat dry with a soft cloth.

When cleaning a figurine or sculpture with a wooden base, you don't want to get it wet. Instead of soap and water, just dust it lightly and often as part of your routine chores.

Speed tips: Most china made within the past 25 years will stand up to washing in a dishwasher. But you need to take some precautions. Each item should be loaded carefully but securely to prevent chipping. Use a mild automatic dishwasher detergent such as Cascade. For machine-washing, powders are preferable to liquids because they tend to be more gentle. Avoid detergents that contain lemon because they tend to cause spotting. Make sure that the dishwasher racks haven't worn through the rubber coating, exposing metal. The metal could chip the dishes or leave rust stains. Use the china setting if your dishwasher has one. If not, use a normal cycle. Allow china to cool to room temperature before unloading.

In a pinch: If you have no plate protectors (quilted pads that are sold in department stores), paper towels will do the trick.

Caution: When placing china items in a dishwasher, make sure that they are separated from metal objects that could chip them during washing. China that is 25 years old or older should always be hand-washed. Avoid abrasive cleaners when hand-washing china.

"When storing your china, always use plate protectors between the pieces to prevent scratching," says Alice Kolator, spokeswoman for Lenox, the china and crystal manufacturer in Lawrenceville, New Jersey.

Chocolate Stains

When chocolate melts on your clothes, not in your mouth, quick action is your best hope for coming out clean.

Technique: Milk chocolate and dark chocolate are different types of stains. For milk chocolate, first, blot the stain with cold water. If you can't get it out that way, blot with mild laundry detergent and water. Rinse thoroughly with water. If the stain persists, blot it with the detergent and water solution, with a few drops of ammonia added. Rinse thoroughly with water. If the stain persists, try blotting with an enzyme-based detergent such as Tide.

For dark chocolate, perform the first two steps. Rinse thoroughly with water. If the stain persists, then mix some white vinegar with the detergent and water, and blot. Rinse thoroughly with water. As a final step, try blotting the stain with a small amount of hydrogen peroxide.

Note: Rinsing thoroughly with water between steps is necessary to prevent mixing potentially incompatible solutions.

Speed tips: If you don't have the time or the patience to clean a stain slowly and deliberately, your best bet is a dry cleaner. This is also a good idea if the stain is particularly large or stubborn, or if the garment is one you adore. "If they're precious items, items of value, take them to a dry cleaner," says Jane Rising, instructor in the education department at the International Fabricare Institute in Silver Spring, Maryland.

In a pinch: If the stain happens at work or someplace else where you can't get to cleaning supplies, flushing immediately in cold water may do the trick.

Caution: Be sure to test any cleaning method on a small obscure corner of the fabric before attacking the stain, even if you've used the method before, to make sure that the colors and the fabric can withstand the cleaning. If you can't completely remove a chocolate stain, don't just decide to "live with it." An incompletely cleaned stain may well attract insects. If your methods fail, it's time to get professional dry-cleaning help.

Chrome

Chrome, found in everything from bathroom fixtures to decorative car parts, is not a solid metal like aluminum or steel. Rather, it's the result of a plating process. That's why cleaning must be gentle. Pitted or otherwise damaged chrome is difficult or impossible to repair and must be replaced.

Technique: For routine cleaning, use a spray glass cleaner and a soft clean cloth. "You don't want to use anything abrasive because it will eventually wear through the surface," says Randy Robinson, owner of Robinson's Chrome in Hughson, California, which makes customized chrome and metal products. Chrome can be brought to a shine (and protected) with an application of carnauba wax, available at automotive stores. Before applying the wax, clean the chrome with a solution of ¼ cup liquid dishwashing detergent to 1 gallon water. Wash with a soft cloth and dry. Then wax according to the product's directions.

In a pinch: As a substitute for commercial window cleaner, you can fill a spray bottle with club soda or a teaspoon of baking soda mixed with a quart of warm water. These are slightly less effective than the commercial cleaners but work nicely for routine jobs, Robinson says. To remove tough spots such as paint or tar, apply some paint thinner or lacquer thinner sparingly to a cloth and wipe the spot. To add a shine to chrome fixtures, try rubbing them with a little toothpaste.

Caution: Never use gritty abrasive cleansers on chrome. Over time, these will wear down the plating. Once that happens, the chrome is a goner.

Clocks

Hickory dickory dock, don't mess with the insides of your clock. Modern timepieces with automatic movements hardly require cleaning at all. Mechanical clocks, which *do* require periodic cleaning, should be cleaned by professionals. So confine your own efforts mainly to keeping the outside looking good.

Technique: The best tool in cleaning the exterior of a clock is a clean soft cloth. Rub the clear glass, plastic, or acrylic piece covering the face gently to wipe away dirt without scratching. If the covering is glass, you may use some spray window cleaner, but be certain to spray this onto the cloth rather than directly onto the clock.

Rub the rest of the exterior with a clean cloth. If the case is made of wood, you can use a spray-on cleaner and polish, like Endust, on the cloth. Again, spray onto the cloth rather than onto the clock. Most brass on a clock will be covered with lacquer, meaning that it only needs the soft cloth.

About the most you'll have to do with a battery-operated clock is change the battery as needed. Since the movement is usually stored in a compartment inside the clock, it is unlikely to get dusty. "Very seldom does the consumer have to deal with cleaning or repairing the movement," says George Gibson, horologist and manager of clock services for Bulova Corporation in Woodside, New York. If it is dusty, Gibson adds, you can wipe the outside of the movement with a soft cloth sprayed with a little dust-remover. Grandfather clocks and other mechanical clocks should be cleaned and inspected by a professional every two to three years.

Caution: Don't use Windex or other glass cleaners on acrylic or plastic face covers, as these may damage the surface. Never spray cleaners directly at the clock; you don't want the solution getting into the wrong places.

Coffeemakers

Mineral deposits in water can clog a drip coffeemaker. The brewing mechanism should be cleaned thoroughly about once a month, or more often if you use it all the time or if the water in your area is hard. The harder the water, the more deposits.

Technique: After each use, the filter basket and the glass carafe and lid should be cleaned with hot sudsy water or placed in the top rack of the dishwasher. If the parts appear faded from the dishwasher, rubbing them with a soft dry cloth should restore the shine. Wipe the coffeemaker and the heating pad with a soft damp cloth. "It's easy to do when you're wiping off the counters, and it will keep the coffeemaker looking nicer for a longer time," says Fay Carpenter, manager of home economics at Black and Decker Corporation in Shelton, Connecticut.

To clean the brewing mechanism, pour a quart of white vinegar into the carafe, then fill to the 10-cup level with cold water. Pour the mixture into the water reservoir as though you were about to make a pot of coffee. Place a fresh paper filter in the basket and turn the machine on. When about half of the mixture has brewed into the carafe, turn the machine off and let it sit for 15 minutes. Pour the mixture back into the reservoir and this time let all of it brew. Before making coffee again, brew a carafe of plain water.

Caution: Be sure that the coffeemaker has been turned off, unplugged, and allowed to cool before you wipe it down. Never use abrasive scouring pads; scratches will weaken the glass of the carafe and mar other parts.

Coffee Stains

EMERGENCY ACTION
If you spill coffee on yourself at work or some other place where you can't get to cleaning supplies right away, flush the stain immediately with cool water. That's the first step in conventional cleaning of a coffee stain anyway, and it may be all you need to do.

How you take it affects how you take it out. Coffee with milk or cream, because it contains animal products, becomes a "protein-based" stain that requires a different treatment than black coffee.

Technique: For black coffee on fabric, blot the stain with cool water. Rinse thoroughly with water. If the stain persists, try blotting with some mild laundry detergent and water. Rinse thoroughly with water. Still there? Blot that stubborn stain with detergent and water, this time mixed with a few drops of white vinegar. Rinse thoroughly. As a final step, try some hydrogen peroxide. The reason for rinsing thoroughly between steps is to prevent potentially incompatible cleaning solutions from being mixed.

For coffee with milk or cream, use the first two steps for black coffee. Then blot the stain with mild laundry detergent mixed with a few drops of ammonia. Rinse thoroughly. Finally, blot with an enzyme-based detergent, such as Tide.

Speed tips: If you don't have the time or the patience for a thorough cleaning job, it's a good idea to take the garment to a dry cleaner you trust. This is especially recommended if the garment is old or prized.

Caution: Never put a garment into the dryer until you're sure that the stain is gone. "Tumble it and it may be impossible for you to get the stain out," says Jane Rising, instructor in the education department at the International Fabricare Institute in Silver Spring, Maryland. Be sure to test any cleaning method on a small obscure corner of the fabric before attacking the stain, even if you've used the method before, to make sure that the colors and the fabric can withstand the cleaning.

Combs

Most combs are made of plastic, nylon, or other material that stands up well to a good bathing.

Technique: Before washing a comb, first pull off any hair that is attached to it. Then soak the comb in your sink in a sudsy bath of warm water and mild liquid dishwashing detergent for 10 to 20 minutes, or until there are no more oily deposits and residue from hair gel, styling creams, and such. Then rinse the comb in clear water and lay it on a towel to dry.

If you have a scalp condition such as dandruff, cleaning the comb may be a bit more complicated. "The white flakes sometimes adhere to the teeth, especially with fine-tooth combs," says Rebecca Viands, executive vice president of the Potomac Academy of Hair Design and a commissioner of the National Accrediting Commission

A CLEAN STORY

Keeping Combs Clean: The Story of Barbicide

As barber poles go the way of cigar-store Indians, a more enduring symbol of the tonsorial art has emerged: Barbicide, the blue comb-and-scissors disinfectant in the tall glass jar.

Invented more than 50 years ago by Maurice King, a chemical engineer from Brooklyn, New York, the ubiquitous sterilizing liquid is now sold to barbers and beauticians around the globe at a rate of 18,000 gallons a month. A jar of Barbicide even stands in the Smithsonian Institution in Washington, D.C.

Early in his life, King developed a healthy skepticism of barbers' practices. As a teenager suffering from scalp sores, he endured the painful pricks of many a dirty comb. Later, appalled that barbers cleaned combs and brushes only by running water over them, he set out to create his germ-busting concoction. The key to his breakthrough was a new type of disinfectant, an ammonium compound strong enough to kill germs but mild enough for everyday use.

King decided to dye the concoction blue because of the color's freshness and purity. The idea for the tall glass jar with the liftable platform came from soda fountain straw holders.

And then there's the name.

Because of his aversion to barbers, King called his creation Barbicide—which does *not* refer to the killing of germs—as a secret joke.

of Cosmetology Arts and Sciences, both in Falls Church, Virginia. You can solve this problem by running the bristles of an old toothbrush through the comb while you soak it, Viands says.

In most cases, especially if you are the only one using the comb, the above methods should suffice. If you want extra sanitizing, rub the teeth with a little rubbing alcohol.

Speed tips: Since combs, brushes, and curlers all do well in a warm soapy bath, you can save time and water by washing all of these items together.

In a pinch: In rare cases you might want to take extra steps to disinfect a comb—say, for example, you have combed a child's hair to remove lice eggs, but you don't want to discard the comb. Soak it for about 15 minutes in a 10 percent solution of liquid household bleach and water. Then rinse thoroughly with plain water.

Caution: If you are washing a metal comb, be sure to dry it thoroughly after washing it to prevent rust.

Comforters

Most comforters are easily cleaned in a washing machine and dryer—once you find washing machines and dryers big enough to handle them, that is.

Technique: Whenever possible, closely follow the cleaning instructions on your comforter's label. As a general rule, most comforters with a printed cotton cover and synthetic or down filling are machine washable. Because of their bulk, these items should be washed separately from other items in warm water on the gentle cycle, then machine-dried. Be certain that your washing machine and dryer are big enough so that the comforter fits easily in without cramming. If not, take it to a coin-operated laundry that has king-size appliances.

In a pinch: If the cleaning label has been torn away but you know where the comforter was purchased or who made it, contact the store or the manufacturer for instructions. If not, you may want to discuss your options with a professional cleaner. Comforters made from heavy upholstery-type fabric should be dry-cleaned, but dry cleaning may damage the colors of other comforters.

"Generally, printed fabrics should not be dry-cleaned," says Joan Garrison, manager of consumer relations for the bedding and linens company Fieldcrest Cannon in Kannapolis, North Carolina.

Caution: Never cram a comforter into a washer or dryer. In a washer, the comforter will clean unevenly. In a dryer, you risk scorching the portions jammed against the barrel while the portions turned inward remain wet.

Compact Discs (CDs)

Dust, fingerprints, grease, and oil can make a CD skip, almost like an old-fashioned vinyl record.

Technique: Holding the disc by the rim and center hole, wipe the surface with a clean, soft, dry lint-free cloth. Instead of wiping in a circular motion—which may leave residue on the disc—use straight strokes from the center of the disc to the outer edge, or vice versa, says Lisa Fasold, spokeswoman for the Consumer Electronics Manufacturers Association in Arlington, Virginia. This is called radial cleaning. For more thorough cleaning, you may want to buy a CD-cleaning kit, available in music stores. You can also buy a CD lens cleaner, which is a disc you insert in the player to clean dust that has gathered on the laser pickup.

Caution: Never use an alcohol-based cleaner or a household cleanser or solvent on a CD. These can damage the surface or destroy the CD altogether.

Computers

Dust is public enemy number one for computers. Keeping the air in your home clean and reducing dust in the computer room will go a long way toward keeping your computer free of costly maintenance and repairs. For general tips, see Air on page 3 and Dust on page 95.

Technique: The keyboard should be cleaned occasionally with a soft static-free cloth dampened with cleaning fluid made for computer cleaning. Both are available at computer or electronics stores. Be sure to apply the fluid to the pad rather than to the keyboard. You can also buy pads that are presoaked. For cleaning lint and dust from between the keys you can buy a small vacuum cleaner for computers that comes with a specially designed nozzle and brush, says Lisa Fasold, spokeswoman for the Consumer Electronics Manufacturers Association in Arlington, Virginia. For a less expensive alternative, use a cotton swab dipped in cleaning fluid. Use the same fluid and cloth to gently wipe the screen of your computer monitor. Don't use spray window cleaners. These can create a film on the screen that will even attract more dust. In combination with cigarette smoke, this film may yellow the screen.

Speed tips: Dust covers will lessen the need for dusting. You can buy dust covers to fit just about any computer component, from the monitor to the keyboard, to the printer to the disk drive.

Caution: Don't use household cleansers, ammonia, powders, or other abrasives to clean the outside of your computer components. These can scratch or otherwise damage the plastic. Don't use household cleaners on keyboards either. "You never know what's in them that could corrode the circuitry," says Fasold. "Never blow on the keyboard," Fasold adds. "You're blowing water into the keyboard. That could make components rust out."

Concrete

Dust and other airborne pollutants can turn concrete surfaces into victims of grime. "Concrete is not totally maintenance-free," says Mary Hurd, an engineer in Farmington Hills, Michigan, and consulting editor of the trade journal *Concrete Construction.* "People think, 'Oh, we never have to do anything to concrete.' " In fact, periodic cleaning can vastly improve the appearance of concrete and also expand its useful life.

Technique: For light cleaning, scrub the concrete with a dry, stiff fiber brush. A good stiff brushing periodically will go a long way toward thwarting grime. "Once every year or so will probably prevent a buildup," Hurd says.

For stubborn grime or stains, mix trisodium phosphate (TSP), which is available at hardware stores, in a bucket of warm water. Use whatever proportions the TSP container recommends for heavy cleaning. Scrub with a stiff fiber brush.

For old or fragile surfaces, first rub gently with a soft brush. Next, brush with warm water and soap. If the grime or stain persists, add some vinegar to the soap and water mixture.

It's best to attend to paint spills and other stains as quickly as possible. Untreated stains may soak into and become part of the concrete.

HOW I DO IT

King of the Road Spills

Andy Bailey, the top maintenance engineer for the Virginia Department of Transportation's 50,000 miles of highways, has cleaned his share of nasty fuel spills on concrete.

"The biggest immediate concern is fire. But spilled fuel can also damage roads, pollute the environment, and pose a safety hazard for drivers, so cleanup has to be done quickly.

"The first thing we do is spread sand or other absorbent over the entire area. Then a truck-mounted machine called a vactor sweeps and vacuums the sand and fuel. The next step is to blast the stain away. We used to use sandblasters, but for environmental reasons we've switched to waterblasters, which kick up a lot less dust.

"The problems are even worse on asphalt. Because asphalt is an oil-based product, diesel fuel left over time will act as a solvent and deteriorate the road. Sometimes the only option is to resurface the area."

Caution: Don't use metallic brushes. They may leave metal particles in the concrete that will rust. Always test-clean a small obscure section of the concrete with whatever method you're planning to use. This way you'll be sure not to make a big noticeable mistake. Read product labels carefully for proper usage and safety precautions.

Containers—Plastic

You finally finish off the leftover spaghetti sauce and you rinse out the plastic container. Uh-oh. Foods high in carotenoids (carrots, tomatoes, sweet potatoes) may be great for the body, but they can sure stain.

Technique: Rubbermaid Consumer Services in Wooster, Ohio, recommends Dawn liquid dishwashing detergent for cleaning their plastic food storage containers. Soak containers that have a greasy film in hot soapy water, remove any residue with a dishcloth, and rinse. To remove any adhesive residue from stickers, use vegetable oil or peanut butter. Stains may be removed by soaking in a solution of 1 tablespoon liquid chlorine bleach per cup of water. Do not mix detergents with bleach, advise experts at Rubbermaid. As a general rule, you can help prevent stains by rinsing containers after each use in cold water, followed immediately by warm sudsy water. To remove stubborn odors in food containers, Rubbermaid suggests placing a slice of lemon in the container, cover, and refrigerate for 6 to 12 hours. Then wash with warm suds. Store containers unsealed to allow air to circulate.

Coolers and Jugs

Stains and mildew are the big enemies to coolers. But since they carry food and drink, you must be careful how you conduct the battle.

Technique: To clean the outside of a plastic or composite-material cooler or jug, mix a weak solution of a household cleaner that doesn't contain bleach, such as Spic and Span and warm water, adding ½ cup cleaner to 1 gallon water. Use a clean soft cloth or sponge dipped in the solution to wash the outside surfaces. Stronger cleaning solutions or abrasive cleansers may cause the exterior color to fade.

The inside will require a different approach. "Don't ever use anything inside a cooler or jug that you wouldn't put in your mouth," says Sandy Hobbs, a consumer service representative for the Coleman Company in Wichita, Kansas.

The best material for cleaning the inside of a cooler or jug is baking soda. Sprinkle baking soda liberally onto a wet cloth or sponge, or directly onto the surface, then apply the elbow grease. To remove a stain, mix baking soda with just enough water to create a thick paste. Spread the paste over the stained area. Let it sit for a half-hour. Then rub the area with a cloth or sponge. Your chances of removing any stain are better if you attend to it quickly. Some stains become impossible to remove if not treated right away. "Nothing's going to take that grape juice out after it has sat there for a while," Hobbs says.

For persistent odors, mix 1 teaspoon vanilla extract in 4 cups water and use the solution to wipe the surface with a soft cloth or sponge.

Speed tips: You can save yourself a lot of cleanup time in the long run by preventing mildew from forming in the first place and by taking care of spills and stains quickly. After using a cooler or jug, don't just stick it back on the shelf with the lid closed. Wash it right away and dry the inside thoroughly with a towel. Then let the cooler or jug sit for two days with the lid off. After that, you can replace the lid and store it.

Caution: Avoid harsh cleaners or abrasives on the exteriors. Don't use chemical cleansers or bleach on the interiors. Never use a chemical mildew remover. Remember, if you wouldn't put it in your mouth, don't put it in your cooler or jug.

Copper

Methods for cleaning copper objects are the same as for bronze, which is an alloy of copper and tin. Left unpolished and unlacquered, it quickly becomes tarnished through oxidation.

Technique: General cleaning of copper objects is easy and should be done gently. The main thing you want to avoid is scratching the surface. For routine maintenance, just dust with a soft dry cloth such as an old T-shirt. If grime from the air has built up on the piece, dampen the cloth with water before rubbing the copper surface. (For tips on treating lacquered and unlacquered copper, see Bronze on page 37. For tips on cleaning copper pots and pans, see Pots and Pans on page 208.)

Unlacquered copper will have to be polished to maintain its shine. Commercial brass polishes such as Brasso work well.

Speed tips: To add a quick shine to bronze or copper buttons and other small pieces, try rubbing them with a little ketchup.

In a pinch: You can make your own polish by mixing 1 tablespoon salt with 1 tablespoon flour, says James W. McGann, vice president for quality at Virginia Metalcrafters in Waynesboro, Virginia, which creates all the brass and bronze pieces used at Colonial Williamsburg. Stir in 1 tablespoon white vinegar. Apply the paste with a soft damp cloth, rub gently, rinse, and wipe dry with a dry soft cloth.

Caution: Never use harsh cleansers or abrasive pads to clean copper. These could scratch the metal. Handle pieces as infrequently as possible. Oils from your fingers can leave permanent marks. If you have a copper piece that you think may be valuable or historically significant, don't polish it until you've had it examined by a professional conservator. If you use moisture when cleaning a copper piece, dry it thoroughly afterward with a soft dry cloth to prevent spots from forming. Don't use spray waxes or polishes. They'll just dull the shine.

Cork

People didn't have much use for cork until the sixteenth century, when they figured out it was great for stopping up glass bottles. These days you can find it any number of places in the home. Your cleaning approach depends on whether the cork is sealed.

Technique: "Cork floors are almost always going to be sealed, in which case you're dealing with the sealant rather than the cork," says Martin L. King, a restoration consultant in Arlington, Virginia, and technical advisor to the National Institute of Disaster Restoration in Millersville, Maryland. They can be mopped using whatever cleaning materials are appropriate for the sealant, King advises. Untreated cork, including many walls, is quite porous and should not be exposed to much water. Instead, try a dry method such as rubbing the cork with a putty wallpaper cleaner or a dry, foam-rubber sponge (available at hardware stores, janitorial supply stores, and paint stores). This sponge is specially designed to rub dirt particles away from walls and ceilings. Common kitchen sponges shouldn't be used because they will smear dirt instead of rubbing it away.

Cork walls may be lightly sanded to remove spots, but be sure to try this on a small area first to be certain that you don't damage the cork or wind up with unsightly patches where you sanded.

In a pinch: If you can't get to the paint store for a foam-rubber sponge or putty wallpaper cleaner, you may rub cork with a hunk of stale crumbly bread, which will scrub without doing damage, or pat the area with tape.

Caution: Even when washing sealed cork floors, don't overdo it with the moisture. If you're mopping, for example, don't pour the water from the bucket directly onto the floor. Never use bleach on untreated cork, which will create a spot.

Cotton

It's comfortable. It's cool. It's durable. It leaps tall washing machines in a single bound! "Cotton is a strong rugged fiber. It's very resistant to alkali, which means that it can stand up well to laundry detergent," says John D. Turner, Ph.D., senior chemist for Cotton, a cotton growers trade group based in Raleigh, North Carolina. Optical brighteners in modern detergents help make colors in cotton fabric bolder. Since just about any laundry detergent will work, your main concerns when washing cotton are shrinkage and discoloration of the fabric.

Technique: When washing cotton fabrics, it's always best to follow the instructions on the manufacturer's care label. The old rule about washing whites separately from colored laundry is a good one, even if the colored laundry has been washed many times before. "There's always some that bleeds off," Dr. Turner says. A white shirt washed repeatedly with colored items will gradually darken. "You don't see it until you buy a new white shirt and lay it down beside the old one," Dr. Turner adds.

Shrinkage

Many people assume that shrinkage occurs when the cotton fibers themselves shrivel as a result of heat in the drying process. Actually, only a fraction of the shrinking process takes place within the fibers. About 95 percent occurs when the weave is mashed and compacted during washing and tumble drying. So don't assume that low heat or air-drying will prevent your new cotton trousers from shrinking. Fortunately, shrinking occurs only once per garment.

The best way to avoid the problem altogether is to buy the increasingly common preshrunk garments. If you have a garment that is not preshrunk and that you desperately don't want to shrink, you can prevent it. But the process is laborious and must be repeated with each washing. First add ¼ cup laundry detergent to a tub of water. Then let the garment soak while gently pushing it up and down in the water. Refill the tub with plain water and repeat the process to rinse. Remove the garment dripping wet. Lay it on a towel and blot it with a second towel. Then pull the garment to its original form, tugging gently on the sleeves or trouser legs. Let it dry in a ventilated room.

Ironing

Cotton can withstand a hot iron. Iron garments while still moist, or spray them with a mist sprayer. This will lubricate the fibers, and they'll respond better to ironing.

Stains

For tips on removing specific stains, see individual listings of stain types elsewhere in this book. As a rule, though, you have the best chance of removing a stain if you attend to it immediately. A dry stain, particularly one that has been tumble dried, may be impossible to remove. If you can't attend to the stain right away, at least try to keep it wet until you can. Always test stain-removal methods on a small section of the garment to make sure that you don't damage it.

Caution: Never leave a hot iron facedown on the fabric for more than a few seconds. Even the most heat-resistant fabrics may scorch. Cotton is vulnerable to acids, which may destroy the fabric. Avoid spilling harsh acids such as battery acid or sulfuric acid on cotton. Even milder acids such as vinegar and fruit juice should not be allowed to linger.

Counters

You want clean kitchen counters for two important reasons: They're a highly visible feature of the kitchen, and they're the site of much of your food preparation. So your cleaning methods should be aggressive enough to get rid of potentially harmful bacteria but careful enough that you don't damage the surface.

Technique: Each time you handle food on a counter, wash the counter afterward with hot soapy water and a clean cloth or sponge. Liquid dishwashing detergent works fine. "It's the sudsing action that lifts the debris," says Bessie Berry, manager of the U.S. Department of Agriculture's Meat and Poultry Hotline in Washington, D.C. Then rinse the counter with clear water and pat dry with clean paper towels.

Each time you handle raw meat, poultry, or fish, take sanitizing an extra step. First, carefully wash the surface to remove debris. Mix 1 teaspoon liquid chlorine bleach per quart of water. Pour enough on the counter to cover it, and let the solution sit for a minute. Then rinse thoroughly with clear water and pat dry. Or use one of the commercial antibacterial products. Read the label for instructions on how to clean kitchen counters.

To keep counters looking good, wipe up spills as soon as possible. How you deal with stains will depend on what type of surface you have. For polished or laminated surfaces (a thin surface layer over a wood base), avoid using any type of abrasive cleanser or pad that could scratch them. "You dull the finish. You dull the sheen. You just take away from the beauty of the product," says Nick Geragi, director of education and product development for the National Kitchen and Bath Association in Hackettstown, New Jersey.

Some counters are nonporous, with a matte finish. These allow you to scour away stains and burn marks with powdered cleansers such as Comet or to use scouring pads such as Scotch-Brite. To ensure a uniform appearance, you might want to scour the entire surface of the counter after taking care of a spot. The Nevamar Corporation, a manufacturer of decorative surfaces, based in Odenton, Maryland, recommends using a wet Scotch-Brite pad on the surface, then cleaning thoroughly with soap and water and letting it dry.

Corian is a particularly tough counter material. It is stain-resistant because it is nonporous, and will stand up to the kind of scouring that will dull plastic laminate. So use of abrasive pads and powdered cleansers is fine. Because Corian, made of acrylic and natural materials, is solid all the way through rather than a thin layer, you can even rub out burns and scratches with fine sandpaper.

For details about cleaning other specific countertop materials, see Butcher Block on page 41, Plastic Laminate on page 205, Stone on page 260, and Tile—Ceramic on page 276.

In a pinch: Burn marks on laminated or polished surfaces are likely to be permanent. If the burn mark is especially noticeable, consider having the affected section removed and replaced with a section of butcher block or glass.

Caution: Never place hot pots or pans directly on counter surfaces. Harsh acidic cleaners such as oven, toilet, and drain cleaners, should be kept away from counters. If they do spill onto a counter, wipe them immediately. When using the bleach-water solution to sanitize a counter, make only enough for the single use. Don't try to save it. The chlorine evaporates and the solution weakens.

Crayon Marks

Yes, you want your budding Edward Hopper or Georgia O'Keeffe to create lasting works of art. You just don't want them on the furniture, walls, and carpeting.

Technique: Binney and Smith, which has been supplying children with crayons since 1903, found that the auto part cleaner/lubricant WD-40 is effective for removing crayon marks from many surfaces. "WD-40 is a penetrating agent that gets between the crayon material and the surface," says Patrick Morris, a spokesman for Binney and Smith in Easton, Pennsylvania. "It makes the crayon easier to remove."

To get crayon off brick or concrete, for example, spray the stained area with lubricant and brush with a stiff brush. Then re-spray and wipe with a soft cloth. For crayon marks on smooth surfaces such as glass, porcelain, metal, unwaxed vinyl floors, painted walls or painted wood, tile, or marble, spray the surface with WD-40 lubricant and wipe away with a soft cloth. If the stain persists, use a sponge to wash the surface with a mixture of warm water and liquid dishwashing detergent. Work in a circular motion and rinse. In all cases, stains should be treated as soon as possible.

But beware of using lubricant on fabric, warns Jane Rising, instructor in the education department at the International Fabricare Institute in Silver Spring, Maryland. "I can't get it rinsed out, and it leaves a residual odor," she says. Instead, Rising says, try pretreating the stained area with a laundry prewash spray, then running the garment through the hottest water that is safe for that type of fabric. If the stain doesn't go away, blot the stain with a generally available spot remover, such as Carbona Stain Devils or Energine.

Caution: Test-clean a small obscure portion of the surface before cleaning the entire surface. This will help prevent damage to the surface during the cleaning process. Never mix spot removers with water because the two will not dissolve into each other. Let the kids make the crayon stains; you clean them up. Having the offender work on his own stain may be tempting, but it's not a good idea for small children to handle cleaning supplies, especially chemicals.

Crystal

The lead in crystal gives it sparkle, brilliance, and clarity. It also makes the glass soft. Crystal should always be washed by hand. "Putting it in a dishwasher regularly will cause tiny scratches that will cloud up over time," warns Alice Kolator, spokeswoman for Lenox, the china and crystal manufacturer in Lawrenceville, New Jersey.

Technique: To wash by hand, first place a rubber guard (available at housewares stores) on the faucet to prevent chipping. Place a rubber mat or double-folded towel on the bottom of the sink. If it's a divided sink, drape a rubber mat or towel over the divider. Wash using any liquid dishwashing detergent and a nonabrasive cloth or sponge. Hold glasses by the bowl rather than the stem, to avoid dropping.

In a pinch: To remove dried-on food or stains that won't simply soak off, try rubbing with a little baking soda.

Caution: Avoid abrasive cleansers, even for dried-on food. Do not overfill the sink with items that could chip or break.

Cupboards

Keeping your cupboard clean and well-organized not only will make cooking easier and more pleasant but also will reduce your chances of harboring insects or rodents. Household pests require three main things: food, water, and a cozy place to live. A dirty kitchen cupboard, with crumbs, moisture, and dark recesses, is like a dream come true.

Technique: Clean your cupboard at least twice a year, during your spring and fall cleaning. The more often you do it, the easier it will be to remove any grease that has built up on it.

Starting at the top and working a shelf at a time, remove all of the food and other items. Pull up any old paper or shelf liners, and wipe down all surfaces.

Use a sudsy sponge or an all-purpose kitchen cleaner and a sponge on plastic, plastic laminate, and similar surfaces. Rinse by wiping it down with a clean moist sponge or cloth. For wood, either dust with a lightly dampened cloth or use a spray-on cleaner and polish, like Endust. Wipe dust off cans and jars with a lightly dampened cloth.

Make sure that the shelves have a chance to dry before you replace the cans and other items. "If you fill the shelves before they dry, they might stay moist and lead to bacteria growth and bad odors," says Michael Beglinger, executive chef at Deutsche Bank in New York City. If you use shelf liners, lay down fresh ones. For shelves that hold glasses, consider putting down mesh mats, which are available at housewares stores. "It keeps glasses steady and raised off the surface a bit," Beglinger notes.

Speed tips: To cut down on dust—and the amount of time that must be spent removing it—keep the cupboard door closed as much as possible.

Curling Irons

Get as wild as you like when you're putting that curling iron to use—that's your business. But when it comes to cleaning them, the simplest cleaning method is also the best.

Technique: Unplug your curling iron and allow it to cool before cleaning. Then wipe it down with a soft damp cloth. Hair-care products are water-soluble, so even a curling iron gunked up with hair spray or mousse should come off relatively easily with this method.

Caution: Avoid using any abrasive cleaners that could scratch or mar the surface of the curling iron. Never clean it while it is plugged in. Never immerse a curling iron in water.

Curtains

Think of your curtains as more than just pretty window dressing. They become a part of the airflow system in your home, filtering dust out of air moving in and out of windows. Cleaning helps prolong the curtains' life expectancy, which is about five years for lined curtains, four years for unlined curtains, and three years for sheers.

Technique: Always clean matching draperies at the same time. "You can use your vacuum cleaner to get the dust off them," says Maria Ungaro, program director of the Window Coverings Manufacturers Association in New York City. Once a month, vacuum them where they hang using a dusting brush or upholstery attachment. Work from top to bottom, taking care to clean the tops and hems, where dust tends to gather. Hold the curtains taut from below and reduce the vacuum pressure if possible to avoid sucking the fabric into the nozzle. If necessary, attach an extension tube to reach the top of the curtain.

At least once a year, wash your curtains—either in a washing machine or at a professional dry cleaner, depending on the material. Follow the curtains' washing instructions, which should be found on a flap inside the hem. If you machine-wash them, tumble until damp and hang to lessen the wrinkling and the need for ironing.

Speed tips: If curtains are not heavily soiled, instead of washing, simply freshen them by tumbling them in a dryer set on "Air-Fluff" with no heat.

In a pinch: If you don't have time to go over each curtain with the vacuum cleaner, simply beat them lightly or use a feather duster to get the dust out.

Cushions

On the couch, you want to be at ease—and not sneeze. The best strategy for cleaning cushions is to remove accumulated dust regularly so it won't stain when ground in or moistened. Dust also harbors microorganisms, like dust mites, which can cause allergies.

Technique: Remove dust—and dust mites—from cushions about once a month by vacuuming with the appropriate attachments, like an upholstery brush and crevice tool, says Rajiv Jain, laboratory manager for the Association of Specialists in Cleaning and Restoration in Millersville, Maryland. If you don't have a vacuum cleaner with attachments, gently brush away the dust using a soft-bristle brush.

If your cushions need washing, follow the upholstery manufacturer's suggestions, usually found on a tag attached to the cushion. If there is no tag, try to determine what type of fabric covers your cushions. Some fabrics should not get wet, while others, like nylon, can be cleaned using small amounts of soap and water. To remove stains on dry-clean-only fabrics, blot with a spot remover, like K2r or Carbona Stain Devils. Read product labels carefully for proper usage and safety precautions.

Prevention tip: Use armrest and headrest covers to protect those areas against buildup of greasy soil from skin and hair.

Here are some general cleaning tips, according to cleaning experts.

- Promptly scrape off excess solids or blot up spills using a clean white cloth.
- Do not remove the fabric cover from the cushion because it may be difficult to properly fit back on.
- Always pretest a cleaning solution in an inconspicuous area before using it to make sure that colors won't bleed.
- Never soak the cushion, either in water or in solvent. Moisture trapped inside the cushion can attract dirt.
- For soap-and-water cleaning, mix up a solution of 1 cup cool or warm water and ½ teaspoon mild liquid dishwashing detergent. Whip up a head of suds, and work small amounts of those suds into the soiled area using a clean white cloth. Rinse by blotting with a damp cloth. Let the cushion dry in the air or sun.

Caution: Don't vacuum down-filled cushions if they are not lined with down-proof ticking. Instead, brush them to avoid sucking out the feather quills.

Cutting Boards

Cutting boards are the perfect home for microorganisms. Whether you use wood or plastic, cleaning cutting surfaces is especially important for health reasons.

Technique: After each use, scrub the board vigorously with a scrubber or brush and soapy water. The friction ruptures the cells of microorganisms, and the detergent helps lift and remove the debris that may harbor pathogens. Rinse and air-dry or pat dry with clean paper towels. After each time you use a cutting surface to chop chicken, beef, fish, or any other meat, sanitize it by flooding the surface for a minute with a solution of 1 teaspoon chlorine bleach per quart of water. Rinse it well immediately afterward and dry. These steps are especially critical if you're going to reuse the

Cutting Boards: The Wood versus Plastic Debate

With all of the conflicting reports about bacteria growth, it's hard to know just which surface is safer. For many years, conventional wisdom held that nonporous plastic was less hospitable than wood to dangerous contaminants, like *Salmonella* from raw chicken. But a 1993 study done by University of Wisconsin scientists turned that thinking on its head. Trying to find a way to make wooden cutting boards as bacteria-free as plastic, they discovered that 99.9 percent of the bacteria they placed on wooden boards disappeared within three minutes, while none disappeared on the plastic ones.

Problem solved, right? Wrong. After conducting its own studies, the U.S. Food and Drug Administration's Center for Food Safety and Applied Nutrition is sticking with plastic. Its experts found that while bacteria may die on the surface of wood, microorganisms become trapped in the deep cuts common on wooden cutting boards and are hard to remove by washing. On the other hand, they say, these harmful pathogens are easily washed off plastic.

The bottom line is that whichever you choose, clean and sanitize it well, especially after cutting raw meat, says Bessie Berry, manager of the U.S. Department of Agriculture's Meat and Poultry Hotline in Washington, D.C.

board for cutting other foods that aren't going to be cooked. "You want to remove any bacteria left by the perishable product," says Bessie Berry, manager of the U.S. Department of Agriculture's Meat and Poultry Hotline in Washington, D.C. "The bleach kills the pathogens that cause people to become ill—*Salmonella, Listeria, Escherichia coli, Staphylococcus.*" Do not store the chlorine solution for future use; because chlorine evaporates, mix up only enough for one application. Because of sanitizing ingredients in automatic dishwasher detergent, machine-washing plastic cutting boards is a safe alternative. Wooden boards, however, warp in dishwashers.

Decks

If you remove the dirt, mildew, and tannin stains from your deck regularly, the wood will last longer and look new longer. The job doesn't take long, so you can get right back to your chaise lounge.

Technique: Occasionally sweep or hose foliage and other large debris off your deck. The longer that decaying leaves and sticks sit on the wood surface, the more chance they have to stain the wood.

Twice a year, give your deck a light scrubbing using a solution of warm water and a few squirts of liquid dishwashing detergent. Scrub with a stiff-bristle brush, preferably one with a long handle. "There are deck brushes that have broom handles so that you don't have to do this down on your hands and knees," says Charlie Jourdain, vice president of technical and inspection services for the California Redwood Association in Novato, California.

Once every two years or so, give your deck a more thorough cleaning. You have a couple of choices: using a two-step scrubbing process or power-spraying the deck.

The scrubbing process is generally less expensive than renting a power sprayer or hiring a professional to do the spray job. And power-spraying can damage a wood deck. But the downside to the scrubbing process is that it involves using chemicals—trisodium phosphate, liquid household bleach, and oxalic acid. When used correctly, none will hurt your lawn or other yard plants.

First, the two-step scrub: Begin with a solution of 1 cup trisodium phosphate (available at hardware stores), 1 cup liquid household bleach, and 1 gallon water. Mix it up, scrub it around your deck using a deck brush, and rinse it off using a garden hose.

Note: A phosphate-free alternative to trisodium phosphate is a product that contains sodium metasilicate, such as TSP-PF, available at hardware stores.

The bleach takes care of any mildew. The trisodium phosphate helps remove surface soil and sticky substances. "You're left with a pretty clean, mildew-free deck," Jourdain says, "but you may still have some darkening and discoloration as a result of weathering and the accumulation of tannins on the surface of the wood."

To remove these stains, clean with oxalic acid or a deck cleaner. Both are available at hardware stores or stores that sell wood deck supplies.

To clean with the oxalic acid, dissolve ½ cup of the crystals in a gallon of hot water, using a plastic bucket or some other non-metallic container. Apply the solution to the deck using a mop or sponge. Do not scrub. Just coat the wood, let it sit for 20 to 30 minutes, and then rinse it well with the garden hose. The diluted runoff will not harm the plants around the deck.

To clean using a power sprayer, either rent one at an equipment rental shop and do it yourself, or hire a professional. Keep in mind

HOW I DO IT

Quick Deck Maintenance

Bob Hanbury knows his way around a deck. He's a remodeler and the former host of *House Calls*, a home-repair call-in radio show in Newington, Connecticut. Here's what he has to say about cleaning decks.

"If you don't clean the debris that collects in the gaps in your deck, you're going to have a problem with the wood. It's like tooth decay. You want to make sure that the joints are open and clean so that the sun and air can get in there and keep the wood as dry as possible. If it's pressure-treated wood, it can darken it and cause mildew. And if it's not, then the wood can actually rot.

"A high-pressure water sprayer is a quick way to clean out the gaps—up against the house, around the posts and steps, wherever debris can accumulate. But if you're not careful, you can take the finish off the wood. I use an air compressor and nozzle, which is much safer. A leaf blower might do the same thing.

"My mother bought a pressure sprayer. The first time she used it, it was so powerful and had such a concentrated bead that she cut grooves into the wood."

that power-spraying can damage wood decks. "I've seen a number of cases where it has caused excessive erosion on the surface of the wood," Jourdain says.

If you decide to spray your own deck, here are some tips for preventing damage.

- Don't use too much pressure. "Many rentable power sprayers offer water pressure of 3,000 psi (pounds per square inch) or higher," Jourdain says. "I recommend the minimum pressure needed to accomplish the goal—usually 800 to 1,200 psi."
- Use a 45-degree nozzle instead of a needle or pinpoint nozzle.
- Hold the nozzle at an angle, 12 to 18 inches away from the deck's surface.
- Do not concentrate the nozzle in one area for more than a split second.

Caution: When using bleach, trisodium phosphate, or oxalic acid, wear goggles, rubber gloves, and other protective clothing.

When using oxalic acid, remove any potted plants and cover any other plants that could be splashed with the solution. It can burn foliage. (The solution you rinse off the deck will be diluted enough not to harm surrounding plants.)

When operating a power sprayer, use protective eyewear.

Always read the instructions for proper use and safety precautions.

Deodorant Stains

You had the best intentions in using deodorant—making the world safer for sensitive noses. But what you get in return is a dingy eyesore on your clothing. Depending on the type of deodorant you use, some stains can be worse than others. All, however, will eventually yellow and turn permanent if left untreated.

Technique: For washables, apply a liquid laundry detergent (or a paste made from a granular detergent and water) directly onto the stain. Lay the garment on a hard surface and pat the stain lightly with the back of a spoon. "You're trying to get in between fibers and inside fibers because that's where the stains are," says Ann Lemley, Ph.D., chairman of the department of textiles and apparel at Cornell University in Ithaca, New York. Don't rub the material together; that will abrade the fibers. Next, wash as directed either in a machine or by hand in the hottest water safe for the fabric. If your garment is bleachable, first try a color-safe bleach and then a chlorine bleach, both of which work against deodorant stains.

Dry cleaning works very well on deodorant stains; consider it even for clothing you normally would not take to the cleaners. "You'd be amazed," says Dr. Lemley. "Hand-washable silks get a lot of these kinds of stains. If once a year you dry-clean them, it works like magic."

Note: Before using cleaning solutions, always test them on an inconspicuous section of the stained item.

In a pinch: Blot using cotton balls and a spot remover, like Carbona Stain Devils or K2r, available at supermarkets, hardware stores, or discount department stores. Blot from the inside of the garment to push the stain out. Wear protective rubber or latex gloves, and use these products in a well-ventilated area.

Caution: Always rinse out one cleaning solution before trying another. Mixing chemicals, especially ammonia and chlorine bleach, can create noxious fumes. Always read the product label for proper use and safety precautions.

Dish Drainers

Think about it: The job of the dish drainer is to hold clean, drying dishes. A dirty dish drainer simply defeats the purpose. And since it is exposed to moist areas in the kitchen, a dish drainer is a potential breeding ground for bacteria.

Technique: Once every couple of weeks, soak the drainer in a sink or dishpan filled with hot water, a tablespoon of liquid household bleach, and a squirt or two of liquid dishwashing detergent. Clean off any deposits with a sponge soaked in the solution. "The bleach has wonderful germicidal properties," says Marry Keener, assistant director of facilities management at the University of Arizona in Tucson and a member of the technical advisory committee for *Executive Housekeeping Today* magazine. "It will kill any bacteria, mold, or mildew and leave the drainer visibly clean."

In a pinch: Put the drainer in the sink and spray it down with hot water to remove soil. Dry it well with a dry cloth afterward.

Caution: Wear protective gloves when cleaning with the bleach and hot water. Always read the product label for proper use and safety precautions.

Dishes

You want dishes to be sanitary, to be spotlessly clean, and to make it through the washing process in one piece. Plus, since you have a lot on your plate these days, you want to keep this daily chore from consuming too much precious time.

Technique: From a cleanliness standpoint, machine-washing your dishes has a definite edge. But that's not always possible or practical. Here's how to do a top-notch job, whichever route you take.

Hand-Washing

Fill the sink or a dishpan with water as hot as you can stand. "It kills bacteria and cuts grease better," says Kari Kinder, assistant director of food and beverage at the renowned Culinary Institute of America in Hyde Park, New York. While the water is running, add one or two squirts of liquid dishwashing detergent to produce a thick layer of suds. Wear rubber gloves to protect your hands against hot water, to minimize nail damage, and to give yourself a better grip when washing breakable pieces. Begin by cleaning the least-soiled pieces—typically glassware and flatware—followed by plates and bowls, then serving dishes, and finally pots and pans. Depending on your preference, you may clean the dishes underwater or out of the water using a variety of scrubbers: plastic mesh, metal mesh, rough-surfaced sponges and cloths, fine steel wool pads, and brushes. Just make sure that the scrubber is not too abrasive for the item you're cleaning. Change the dishwashing solution if it gets too greasy or too cool or if the suds disappear.

Next, fill a clean basin or sink with hot rinse water and dip the soapy dishes, or stack them in a drain rack on top of a drain tray and spray them with hot water. Be sure to rinse the inside of all bowls, cups and glasses. Air drying is easiest, but wiping with a clean, dry dish towel will remove spotting and filming.

Using a Dishwasher

Loading the dishwasher correctly is important. Most new dishwashers do not require prerinsing. If you plan to load dishes into the machine and wash them later, use the rinse-hold cycle. In terms of positioning, your main goal is to allow the machine's sprayers to get to the heavy soil. "Depending on how the wash arms in your dishwasher spray, your machine could actually miss the face of the plates," notes Kinder. Although you should consult your machine's manual for its optimum dish placement, here are some general tips.

- Place the soiled side of dishes toward the center or source of the water spray.
- Don't let large items shield small ones.
- Keep cups, glasses, and bowls bottoms up.
- Do not crowd flatware in its basket.
- Make sure that delicate items are secure so that they don't topple and chip or break.
- Don't overload the machine, which prevents proper water circulation.

Water temperature should be at least 130°F. To check it, place a food thermometer in a glass in the kitchen sink and let the hot water run until the temperature stabilizes. (Hint: Before turning on your dishwasher, clear the cold water out of the line by running the hot water in the kitchen sink for a minute or so.)

The only detergent you should use in the dishwasher is automatic dishwasher detergent. This tip may sound too simple to mention, but it's important. Those blue or green granules might look just like laundry detergent, but they are specially formulated to create a minimum of suds. Other detergents and soaps can inhibit the washing action or even overflow, damaging the machine and the floor around it. Make sure the detergent dispenser is clean and dry before adding detergent. Otherwise, granular detergents can get caked in the dispenser. Never sprinkle or pour detergent directly onto flatware or other metals. It could cause spotting or pitting.

Hard water contains minerals that can cause spotting and filming on dishes. The average water hardness is from 61 to 120 milligrams of calcium and magnesium per liter. To find out if the water in your area is hard, contact your water utility or your county Cooperative Extension Service. If your water is hard (above the average rating) and causes spotting, either increase the amount of dishwasher detergent or use a rinse agent, like Jet-Dry, to cause the water to sheet off and evaporate more quickly.

To improve dishwasher efficiency, avoid bathing, running the washing machine, and other activities requiring continuous water use while the dishwasher is running. Insufficient water pressure can leave dishes dirty.

Speed tips: Make sure that you scrape and rinse dishes thoroughly before hand-washing. Otherwise, food will end up in your wash water, making grease removal more difficult. Add a capful of vinegar to the dishwater in your sink or dishpan to reinforce the detergent and help it cut grease better. "As far as drying," says Kinder, "hot water definitely speeds things up because it beads up and steams off." Or use a rinse agent, like Jet-Dry, in your dishwasher to help water sheet off dishes and dry more quickly and without spots.

Caution: Do not put stainless steel and silver flatware in the same dishwasher basket. Direct contact between these metals can cause permanent damage to the silver. And because the blades of many silver-plated knives are stainless steel, point all of the blades in the same direction when loading them in the flatware basket.

Dishwashers

Dishwashers do a good job of cleaning themselves while they clean your dishes, so keeping them in good shape is fairly straightforward.

Technique: For general cleaning of the exterior, a clean, damp sponge is the best bet. "You don't want to use anything too harsh," says Eugene P. Krausz, supervisor of the quality engineering lab for Whirlpool Corporation in Findlay, Ohio. If more than plain water is required, add a dab of liquid dishwashing detergent to the sponge. Then rinse the sponge and go over the exterior again to remove the detergent. For caked-on grime, use a glass cleaner, but be sure to spray the cleaner onto the sponge rather than directly onto the dishwasher. Otherwise, liquid could work its way into the console and damage the electronics. Or, more likely, the cleaner will work its way into crevices between controls. Once there, it will be hard to remove and will attract grime.

The inside of the dishwasher is pretty much self-cleaning. Inspect the area where the lower inside lip of the door meets the washer from time to time for signs of discoloration. This can happen if the water in your area is particularly hard and leaves mineral deposits or if you habitually use too much automatic dishwasher detergent. The detergent will accumulate in spots and eventually cause discoloration. (Tip: Don't just automatically fill the detergent compartments all the way when you wash a load. Try filling them halfway for starters, and adjust from there according to need. You'll know if you've used enough if your dishes come out clean.) If discoloration does occur, rub the area with a damp sponge sprinkled with the same automatic dishwasher detergent you use for regular loads.

Speed tips: Occasionally, mineral deposits from hard water may discolor the rest of the interior casing of the dishwasher. When this happens, run your dishwasher through a regular cycle using an automatic dishwasher detergent like Glisten or Glass Magic, which contain citric acid. In case you cannot find either one, Krausz suggests an alternative: Place a clean cereal bowl containing ½ cup white vinegar in the upper rack of your empty dishwasher. Run it on a regular cycle without detergent. The acid in the vinegar should take care of the problem. If you still have discoloration, use more vinegar, says Krausz.

Caution: Never clean the inside of a dishwasher using any type of detergent not specifically made for automatic dishwashers—not even the liquid dishwashing detergent you use at the kitchen sink. "Any other detergent will suds up all over the place," Krausz says. "You'll wind up with a kitchen full of suds."

Don't use any abrasive cleansers or scouring pads on any part of your dishwasher, inside or out. And remember, if you use a spray cleaner on the exterior, never spray the cleaner directly at the dishwasher.

Disposals

In medieval times, you could just pitch your table scraps to a pack of semi-domesticated mutts. Vets frown on that nowadays. The beauty of the in-sink garbage disposal is that it conveniently grinds and discards food waste that might otherwise sit in your kitchen's garbage container, smelling and attracting insects. But unless you clean the disposal itself, food residue can grow rank, creating bad odors and possibly health risks.

Technique: To cut down on buildup, only grind small amounts of waste at a time and make sure to run the disposal each time you put waste in it. Run the disposal for a few seconds after grinding to make sure that it is empty of food. Once every week or so, after finishing the dishes in the evening, fill the sink about one-third full with lukewarm water and mix it with ½ cup baking soda. Turn on the disposal and pull out the stopper. The mixture will flow through the disposal and help remove odors. At least once every two weeks, flush the garbage disposal by stopping the sink, filling it halfway with cold water, then letting it drain while the disposal runs. "Grinding citrus peelings will help deodorize the disposal," says John Merrill, a doctor of architecture and housing specialist with the University of Wisconsin Cooperative Extension Service in Madison. Occasionally grind ice cubes, fruit pits, or cooked chicken bones to break up grease deposits on rotors. Do not, however, use steak bones or turkey bones, which are too big and too hard and can injure the motor. Always have the water running while your disposal is on.

Caution: Do not use harsh, drain-cleaning chemicals on disposals. They may harm the machine.

Dolls

There are many different types of dolls, from antique porcelain ones to lifelike babies. Some have hair. Most have clothing of some sort. Cleaning them is a matter of removing soil and stains without harming fabric, chipping the paint, or doing other damage.

Technique: The most common doll material—and the easiest to clean—is the rubbery vinyl used since about the 1960s to represent skin. Before you clean the vinyl, remove the doll's clothes.

Clean vinyl with a nonabrasive, nonbleach cleanser. Nonbleach

HOW I DO IT

Getting Dolled Up after a Bath

Susan Fritz is co-owner with her mother of Denver Doll Hospital, a doll-cleaning and restoration business. Here's how she puts the finishing touches on a freshly shampooed doll.

"We treat doll hair just like a person's hair," Fritz says. "If a doll had curly hair to begin with, we set it after we wash and comb it. We use perm rollers since they're so small. One of our drawers here looks like it belongs in a beauty shop. It's loaded with different sizes of perm rollers, perm wrapping paper, and hairpins.

"In the late 1940s, there was a doll on the market called the Toni Doll, sold by the same company that makes Toni home perm kits. She came with perm rollers, perm solution—which was sugar water—wrapping papers, the whole bit. Little girls could set the doll's hair. She was hugely popular. Today, she's a collector's item."

formula Soft Scrub works well, as does a paste of baking soda and water. Using a clean white cloth, gently rub the cleanser on the vinyl until it is clean. Rinse by wiping it off with a clean damp cloth. Avoid overscrubbing painted-on features like eyes, lashes, and mouths. They could rub off.

Some dolls have vinyl arms, legs, and heads, but their bodies are cloth and are stuffed with a fill material. "You can ruin the cloth if you try to spot-clean it," warns Susan Fritz, co-owner of Denver Doll Hospital, a doll-cleaning and restoration business. "If you get the cloth body wet, it leaves yellow water rings." Instead, have a professional doll cleaner dismantle, unstuff, and clean the doll. Look for a doll restorer in the yellow pages, or ask the owner of a shop that sells dolls for a recommendation.

Composition dolls, which typically date back to the early twentieth century, are also tricky to clean without damaging. Usually made of sawdust, chipped wood, and glue, composition dolls deteriorate and their painted surfaces blister when exposed to water.

"Water on a composition doll is deadly," says Fritz. Try rubbing gently with a white vinyl eraser, available at art and office supply stores. Do not rub with a pencil eraser, which is too abrasive. And be careful not to rub away any of the doll's painted features.

Some of the oldest antique dolls are made of bisque porcelain. Because it has been fired, you can clean it with water—but very carefully. Wipe it gently with a cloth dabbed with a nonabrasive, nonbleach cleanser. Avoid overwetting, and do not get any cloth parts wet. Even though the painted-on features are generally fired as well, take extra care with them.

Most doll clothing, unless it is old or deteriorating, is easy to clean. "It's like normal clothing, just smaller," Fritz says. "Some people are afraid of washing doll clothes, but if you treat them the same way as your own clothing, only more gently, they will be fine."

If the cloth is washable, first test for colorfastness by wetting a corner of the material and squeezing it between the folds of a white handkerchief. If it bleeds, use cold water. If not, use lukewarm water. Soak the clothing for an hour or less in a solution of 2 tablespoons of laundry detergent and 1 gallon of water.

Rinse the clothes by soaking them in clean lukewarm water. Empty the rinse water and repeat the process until there is no soap residue left in the water. To dry them, gently roll the clothes up in a towel. Then, lay them flat on the towel and let them air-dry. If the clothes are wrinkled, carefully iron them on a low setting, using starch, as necessary.

Caution: "When washing the clothes of older dolls, liquid household bleach is a no-no, even with white clothes," Fritz says. Old fabrics are usually delicate. The bleach can deteriorate them even further.

If the clothes are made of silk, taffeta, velvet, or some other non-washable fabric, take them to a dry cleaner. You might get a funny look, but the cleaner should be able to handle the job. Otherwise, send them to a professional doll cleaner.

Most doll hair, like most doll clothing, is washable. Use any standard shampoo. "Wash it the same way you would wash a small child's hair," Fritz says. Do it beside a sink, and try to only wet the hair. Avoid getting the bodies wet. Do not use a conditioner; it leaves a residue, attracts dirt, and can damage the synthetic hair. Once you have finished, comb the hair and reset it, if necessary, using small perm rollers. "You can let the hair air-dry," says Fritz, "but if you're in a hurry, a blow-dryer on a low setting is fine."

Doormats

Doormats serve an important function—to catch dirt and sand from shoes so that it does not get tracked through the house, where it can scratch floor finishes and abrade carpet and rug fibers. Besides, why welcome someone to your home with a dirty mat?

Technique: Clean doormats as often as possible. If you let them go, they fill up with soil and stop doing their job.

"There are many different varieties of doormats," says Marry Keener, assistant director of facilities management at the University of Arizona in Tucson and a member of the technical advisory committee for *Executive Housekeeping Today* magazine. "If it is an exterior mat, chances are that you can simply hose it off because it is already exposed to the elements."

For mats that can't handle the hose, vacuum the dirt and dust up with a carpet attachment. Try to use a vacuum cleaner with a good beater bar. That helps the machine suck up deeply deposited particles. "I vacuum the one by my back door because my dog brings grass onto it," Keener says.

Doors—Aluminum, Wood

A doorway is like a funnel inside your home. Not only does it get all the people traffic through that one little space but it's also part of your home's airflow system. All of this makes a door vulnerable to dust, grease particles, and smudges.

Technique: Wood is one of the most common door materials and is relatively easy to clean, especially if it is painted or finished with a coating of polyurethane or varnish.

Dust wood doors regularly to prevent particles from adhering to the surface. Clean them, when needed, using a cloth lightly dampened with a solution of warm water and a couple of squirts of liquid dishwashing detergent. Work from the top down. Rinse the solution completely from the door using a cloth dampened only with water.

If your doors are made of raw wood with a penetrating finish (in other words, if they are not protected by a surface coat, such as paint or polyurethane), simply dust them with a lightly dampened cloth, and then apply boiled linseed oil or tung oil, both available at hardware stores, says Douglas Gardner, Ph.D., associate professor of wood science at the School of Forestry and Wood Products, Michigan Tech University in Houghton. Work on a small section at a time. Use a clean cloth to rub in the oil in the direction of the grain until the wood absorbs no more. Fold another cloth into a pad and rub the area until it is dry.

Clean aluminum doors the same way as surface-finished wood doors: Dust them with a damp cloth, and then wash them with a detergent solution or a spray-on, all-purpose cleaner. "You're usually just removing dust particles that are clinging due to the accumulation of oil or pollution," says Marry Keener, assistant director of facilities management at the University of Arizona in Tucson and a member of the technical advisory committee for *Executive Housekeeping Today* magazine. "The all-purpose cleaner does a good job at cutting the grease."

If your aluminum door has a screen, remove it occasionally and spray it clean with the garden hose. Use a nylon or vegetable scrubbing brush to remove any heavy deposits.

Caution: When applying linseed oil, wear rubber gloves and work in a well-ventilated area. Always read the product label for proper use and safety precautions.

Down—Comforters, Jackets, Pillows

Down is a delicate—and expensive—gift from nature. It's one of our best insulating materials. Caring for it is relatively simple but important.

Technique: Clean down items twice a year: once during the wearing season and again before they are put in storage, says Jane Rising, instructor in the education department at the International Fabricare Institute in Silver Spring, Maryland. Most down- and feather-filled comforters and jackets are machine washable. The safest advice is to follow the care and cleaning instructions of the manufacturer.

If there are no instructions, wash in warm water on a gentle cycle and tumble dry on a gentle cycle, according to the American Down Association in Sacramento, California.

Down items must be tumble dried to fluff up completely, says Rising. And they must be dried thoroughly to avoid mildew. That can take up to several hours in the home dryer, she says.

Because down has a distinct odor when wet, wash down-filled items separately from other laundry to avoid transferring the smell. Treat down items like delicates; use a mild detergent and avoid those with enzymes. And never use liquid household bleach, which can break down the organic material that gives down its loft, or insulating quality. To help distribute the down and feathers evenly while drying, which improves loft, dry the down along with a couple of clean tennis balls. Once or twice a year, air out things filled with down outdoors in the shade to keep them fresh.

Down pillows are the exception to these rules. Unless the manufacturer gives you specific instructions to do otherwise, you shouldn't attempt to machine-wash a down pillow, according to Rising. "The down itself is not always the main problem. It's actually the pillow covering that causes turmoil in your washer. Most pillow coverings are made of water-souble material that can break down in the washing machine and allow the down to leak out of the pillow," says Rising.

The safest way to clean your pillow is to take it to a dry cleaner who is experienced in cleaning down, recommends Rising.

In a pinch: To freshen and remove humidity, place down-filled pillows, comforters, and jackets in a dryer on low heat for about 10 minutes.

Drains

You want drains to be speedy, one-way thoroughfares. Maintaining clean drains not only allows you to continue using sinks and tubs but also keeps water from backing up in the sink, a potential health hazard since bacteria and other contaminants breed in those dark moist recesses.

Technique: "Drains often get clogged because of slow buildup, and the problem suddenly becomes acute because you clean your hairbrush or something," says John Merrill, a doctor of architecture and housing specialist with the University of Wisconsin Cooperative Extension Service in Madison. In bathtubs and sinks, remove hair and lint from the drain strainers whenever you clean the bathroom. Avoid pouring grease down kitchen sink drains; it builds up on the walls of the pipes, eventually clogging them. Dr. Merrill suggests using a water-activated biological cleaner, as opposed to a chemical-based cleaner, once every month or two as a preventive measure. Some health food stores carry a product called Earth Enzymes Drain Opener. "These cleaners set up a bacterial culture in the drain that eats soap scum and grease and keeps hair masses from forming," he says. "They're an alternative to harsh cleaners. As far as I know, they're completely safe and biodegradable," he says. What they won't do is clear the drain if it stops up completely.

For clogs, start with a plunger (also known as a plumber's helper). First, fill the problem sink or tub with water and immerse the plunger sideways to capture as little air under the bell as possible. Plug the overflow, usually found above the drain on tubs and underneath the lips of sinks, with a rubber ball or damp cloth so that it does not weaken your suction. Also, the plunger has to fit completely over the drain to work correctly. Move the plunger up and down a few times over the drain to build up the suction, then pull it away quickly. Try it a few times until either it works or it's clear that you're having no impact at all.

Remember the volcano your kid built in science class? To create the eruption, he probably poured vinegar onto baking soda hidden in the crater. If plunging fails, try the same mixture as a nontoxic alternative to drain cleaners. Bail out as much water as possible from the clogged drain, then pour ¼ to ½ box of baking soda down the drain. Add ½ cup white vinegar, cover the drain tightly for a few minutes, then flush with cold water. The acidic vinegar reacts violently with the basic soda, creating pressure and eating away at the scum lodged in your drain.

In a pinch: Pour boiling water down drains regularly to keep them free of debris.

Caution: If you just can't stay away from a commercial drain-cleaning chemical, follow directions carefully. If the drain remains clogged after use, call a plumber immediately; the water backing up in the sink will now be contaminated with dangerous toxins. Whatever you do, don't use a plunger after unsuccessfully using a drain cleaner. You're just asking for a toxic splash in the face.

Drawers

Removing drawers means putting them back. Since refitting the drawer roller into the runner can be a hassle—and most drawers these days come on runners—this is one of those cleaning jobs that usually gets done only partially or gets skipped altogether.

Technique: The easiest way to clean your drawers is with a hand vacuum or a vacuum cleaner brush attachment, says Marry Keener, assistant director of facilities management at the University of Arizona in Tucson and a member of the technical advisory committee for *Executive Housekeeping Today* magazine. Remove the contents of the drawer and then suck up the dust and debris. That's as much of a cleaning as most drawers need.

If, however, your drawer needs a more thorough cleaning—to remove a spill, for example, or during your spring cleaning overhaul—wipe the inner surface with a sudsy sponge, says Keener. Rinse by wiping with a damp sponge. Dry the drawer completely before replacing the contents.

Dust

Think of every speck of dust you wipe up as the gunk that *didn't* make it into your lungs. Dusting is not simply getting rid of that unsightly layer that builds up on household surfaces. By removing dust, you improve indoor air quality, which is important, considering that the respiratory symptoms of asthma (which affects approximately 15 million people in the United States) are often provoked by dust or other airborne allergens.

Technique: Dust from the top down, using on most surfaces a soft cloth, lightly dampened to help it pick up more particles. (For draperies and upholstery, use a feather duster or vacuum using a brush attachment.) Go over hard surfaces—bookshelves, tables, chairs—and other items, like picture frames, books, stereo components, and knickknacks, until everything from the floor up is dust-free.

Next, vacuum hardwood floors using a brush attachment, says Carol Seelaus, a speed-cleaning instructor at Temple University in Philadelphia and owner of Somebody's Gotta Do It, a professional cleaning service. Don't use a broom or a dust mop, she adds; they only spread the dust around and embed the particles in cracks and crevices. If the floors are covered in carpet or rugs, vacuum them— daily for heavily trafficked areas and at least once a week for other areas. For rugs vacuumed weekly, flip them at least once a month and vacuum the backsides. For rugs in heavily trafficked areas, vacuum the backsides once a week. Use a quality vacuum cleaner with a good filter system and a rotating beater bar for stirring up particles.

"Today's technology means better multistage filtering systems on vacuum cleaners," says Claudia Ramirez, former executive vice president of the Association of Specialists in Cleaning and Restoration in Millersville, Maryland. These exhaust filters keep the finer dust particles that aren't caught by the vacuum bag from kicking back

Where Does Dust Come From?

"Anything and everything makes up dust," says Claudia Ramirez, former executive vice president of the Association of Specialists in Cleaning and Restoration in Millersville, Maryland. That can include minute soil particulates, fabric fibers, shed skin, animal dander, insect parts, smoke and ashes, pollen and plant spores, fungi, bacteria, dust mites—you name it. Some particles originate inside; others migrate in through windows, doors, and air vents and can increase in quantity if there is nearby construction work.

Sounds horrible, doesn't it? It can be, especially if you have asthma or allergies, or if certain parts of your house act as a breeding ground for the bacteria and other tiny critters floating around in the air. Take mildew, for example. It originates as a fungus present naturally in dust. When this fungus finds a hospitable location to dwell—a dark moist basement, for instance—it quickly settles in and begins munching on cotton, leather, and other organic materials.

Other microbiological beings, like dust mites, for example, live off the dead skin and hair particles they share dust space with. They hole up in upholstered cushions and bedding and wreak havoc among those who are allergic to them.

out into the air. But it's important to always clean or replace the filters. "It's like the dryer," she says. "After a while, the dryer doesn't like working with an inch of lint on its filter." Also, don't wait for the vacuum bag to fill completely. It removes dust from the air more efficiently if you empty it when it's between one-half and two-thirds full. After every third emptying, turn nondisposable collection bags inside out and sweep off excess lint and dirt. That way, it does not overwork the machine, and it does a much better job of collecting dust.

Your air-conditioning and heating systems do more than just heat and cool the home. They also circulate and filter air. To cut down on the amount of dust in your home, it's important to keep their filters clean. Ramirez jokingly calls the old fiberglass filters used in heating and air-conditioning systems boulder-catchers. They miss the smaller particulates, which tend to set off allergies or are loaded with potentially harmful living organisms.

A better choice is one of the electrostatic or pleated panel filters available today, says Cliff Zlotnik, a professional duct-cleaning instructor and owner of Unsmoke/Restorx, a property restoration and cleaning company in Braddock, Pennsylvania. No matter which filters you have, clean them regularly—in general, once a month—and replace them when they wear out. Those simple steps will also make your heating and air-conditioning more efficient, saving energy costs and increasing the life span of the equipment.

Don't forget the air conditioner drain pan. "It's moist, dark, and warm from the coils—a wonderful little breeding ground for microbiological agents," Ramirez says. Clean it regularly by removing it from the unit, draining the excess water, and washing it with a sponge or cloth in a mild soap and water solution.

Speed tips: To cut down on static electricity, which helps dust cling to objects, moisten a cling-free dryer sheet and wipe over plastic surfaces

Egg Stains

EMERGENCY ACTION
Rinse or blot away egg with cold water.

So a waiter slid a plateful of over-easies right into your lap? Don't fret. It's a protein-based stain and not that tough to get out. As with all stains, however, you should attack it as soon as possible to increase your chances of removing it entirely.

Technique: Scrape away any excess egg. For washables, first soak the stained item in cold water to remove as much of the egg as possible. The older the stain, the longer you should soak it—up to several hours.

"Then pretreat it," says Ann Lemley, Ph.D., chair of the department of textiles and apparel at Cornell University in Ithaca, New York. "That's the trick with most food stains." Begin by mixing ¼ teaspoon clear liquid dishwashing detergent and several drops of ammonia with ½ cup warm water. Apply it directly to the fabric, then lay the garment on a hard surface and pat the stain lightly with the back of a spoon. This allows the solution to get in between the fibers, where stains hide. Don't rub the fabric together; that will abrade the fibers. Next, wash as directed either by machine or by hand in the hottest water safe for the fabric. If the stain does not come out completely, follow the same pretreatment procedure, but this time with a liquid laundry detergent containing enzymes (or a paste made from a granular detergent and water). Apply it directly to the stain, pat, then wash.

For fabrics that cannot be washed, either have them professionally dry-cleaned or blot them with a clean white towel and a spot remover, like Carbona Stain Devils or K2r, available at supermarkets, hardware stores, or discount department stores. Blot from the inside of the garment to push the stain out. Read the label before using these products, and use them in a well-ventilated area while wearing protective latex or rubber gloves.

For carpets and rugs, first blot with the detergent and ammonia solution using a clean white towel. Then rinse by blotting with a clean towel and water. Do not blot with laundry detergent because it often contains optical brighteners that can bleach carpet and rug dyes. Instead, if the first solution doesn't work, blot with a solution of 1 cup white vinegar and 2 cups water.

Note: Before using cleaning solutions, always test them on an inconspicuous section of the stained item.

In a pinch: In the case of washable clothing, skip to pretreat step two: Apply an enzyme detergent directly to the stain, then wash.

Caution: Always rinse out one cleaning solution before trying another. Mixing chemicals, especially ammonia and chlorine bleach, can create noxious fumes.

Eyeglasses

Is your vision getting blurry? The answer might be right in front of your nose. Body oils and dirt constantly build up on eyeglasses. Regular cleaning will improve your vision and make glasses last longer.

Technique: Once a day, wash the lenses—front and back—in warm soapy water using a soft cloth. Before rubbing with the cloth, run water over them to remove large particles. A mild liquid dishwashing detergent is best; bar soap is fine, too. Blot them dry with a soft cloth. Never use abrasive materials or cloths. And avoid cleaning the lenses dry. "The problem is that small particles, perhaps not even visible to the eye, might be present on the lens surface and may scratch the lens as you move the cloth across it," says Stephen Miller, O.D., director of the Clinical Care Center of the American Optometric Association in St. Louis.

Once a month, clean the frames in soap and water. If they are really dirty, carefully scrub the nosepiece and hinges with an old toothbrush. You want to make the frames last at least as long as the lenses do.

In a pinch: "Cleaning them with a handkerchief is certainly an option if you don't have another choice," says Dr. Miller. Be careful, though. First, blow on them to get off as many of the loose dust and dirt particles as possible.

Fabric—Old

Found some clothing treasures in Grandma's attic? Watch your step. When you clean soils and stains on old fabric, your biggest concern is dry rot, which begins as water damage and eventually deteriorates fabric from the inside out. "The fabric may look okay," says Claudia Ramirez, former executive vice president of the Association of Specialists in Cleaning and Restoration in Millersville, Maryland. "But the minute you put stress on it, it begins crumbling."

Technique: When it comes to cleaning antique dresses, rugs, and other old fabric, the cardinal rule is simple: Be careful. If there is ever a time to seek professional cleaning help, even beyond a dry cleaner, this is it. Because of dry rot, you may ruin an heirloom, like an old wedding dress or an antique quilt, when trying to clean it. A professional, on the other hand, might be able to repair or restore the fabric, then clean it. For a fresh spill on old fabric, simply blot it with a clean white cloth; if the stain remains, contact a professional textile cleaner. (For a referral in your area, write to the Association of Specialists in Cleaning and Restoration at 8229 Cloverleaf Drive, Suite 460, Millersville, MD 21108.)

Fans—Ceiling, Exhaust, Floor

By their nature, fans attract dirt. As air passes through them, particles attach themselves to the blades and other parts. Remove this grime and you have a better-looking, and more efficient, appliance.

Technique: Dust window fans and floor fans regularly to cut down on buildup. Run the vacuum cleaner brush attachment over both sides of the fan grille to remove loose particles. To dust the blades and inner parts, use compressed air or a blow-dryer. Cleaning the blades keeps the fan running smoothly.

Two or three times a year, remove the grilles (if possible) and clean them with a garden hose and a nylon or vegetable brush. Wipe down blades and other plastic parts with a cloth and a little all-purpose cleaner. Spray a bit of lubricant, such as WD-40, at the base of the blade shaft.

Likewise, dust exhaust fans regularly using whatever method works best—a vacuum cleaner or a damp cloth. If possible, remove the fan covers twice a year or so and wipe down the blades and other nonelectric parts with a cloth dampened with a little all-purpose cleaner.

Range hoods collect cooking grease and require a more extensive cleaning. Wipe them down weekly with a sudsy sponge to reduce grease buildup. Every few months, soak the removable, nonelectric parts in a sink or dishpan filled with warm water and a few squirts of liquid dishwashing detergent. Gently scrub grease deposits with a sponge or plastic mesh scrubber. Wipe down the permanently installed parts with a damp sudsy sponge. Do not use steel wool. It can scratch stainless steel, enamel, and plastic.

If your range hood is a ductless one, replace the filter with a new one every three to four months. Or wash the filter as recommended by the manufacturer.

Ceiling fans gather just as much gunk as other fans, sometimes more when they are exposed to rising smoke from cigarettes, fireplaces, or kitchens. Unfortunately, ceiling fans can be difficult to clean. Dangling from a 10-foot ceiling, they make a formidable foe for any dust warrior.

Long-handle brushes designed to clean both sides of a fan blade at once are available. The brush head is shaped like a thin U and the fan blade fits in the slit. You can buy them at home supply stores or wherever they sell ceiling fans.

Dust your ceiling fan monthly. Then, two to four times a year, give it a more thorough cleaning. Wash the blades and housing with a damp cloth and an all-purpose cleaner or a solution of warm water and a couple squirts of liquid dishwashing detergent. Dry them well. Otherwise, they'll pick up more dust.

Caution: Unplug and turn off all fans before cleaning. Do not get any type of cleaning solution into the motor of a fan.

Fiberglass

Not all that glistens is rock hard. Work carefully when cleaning fiberglass, which you find in fixtures, windowpanes, and one-piece showers, tubs, and sinks. It scratches easily, and once its finish is gone, it stains easily, too.

Technique: Clean molded fiberglass using a nonabrasive sponge or cloth and either an all-purpose cleaner or a tub-and-tile cleaner, says Mary Meehan-Strub, Family Living agent at La Crosse County University of Wisconsin Cooperative Extension. Scouring powders or other abrasives will dull, scratch, and discolor the surface and make it vulnerable to staining. Rinse well and dry with a soft cloth.

Since abrasives can't be used, wipe molded sinks and tubs dry after each use to avoid mineral and soap deposits. If these deposits do occur, use baking soda as a gentle abrasive. Apply a paste of baking soda and cool water, leave for an hour, then rub off, rinse, and dry. For stubborn stains and deposits, apply cloths soaked in an all-purpose cleaner and let them stand for at least one hour. Rinse with a clean sponge.

Fireplaces

Because of the nature of what's happening inside a fireplace—and the porous quality of brick—you have to be realistic about how clean-looking you can get it. "Some people expect their fireplaces to look brand new, and that's just not going to happen," says Ashley Eldridge, director of education for the Chimney Safety Institute of America and technical director for the National Chimney Sweep Guild, both in Gaithersburg, Maryland. Keeping the fireplace working efficiently is your main goal. That means removing ash on a regular basis.

Technique: Remove the ashes from your fireplace when the pile gets as high as the fire grate or andirons. But for maximum efficiency, leave an inch-thick layer of ash. It insulates the floor, helping the firebox retain heat and keeping coals burning longer. To remove ash, wait at least two days after your last fire to make sure that all the coals are cool. Set aside the fire screen, andirons, and grate. Using a fireplace broom and shovel, sweep up the ashes and put them in a metal bucket—preferably one with a lid to keep the ashes from floating out. Immediately empty the bucket outdoors away from the house, in a metal trash can with a lid. If the fireplace has an ash pit, open it and sweep the ashes into it (then empty the ash pit from the clean-out door, usually located in the basement or outside the house). Do not vacuum the ashes. Most vacuum cleaners designed for home use will not pick up the finest ash. Instead, they suck it up and shoot it out into the air.

Once a year, give your fireplace a thorough cleaning. Make it part of your annual spring cleaning—after the fire season has ended—and do it first so that the dust it stirs up does not fall on already-clean surfaces. Begin by sweeping up all the ashes. Scrape creosote from the firebox walls using a stiff-bristle wire brush. You can buy them at hardware stores and fireplace-equipment stores, says Eldridge. Use a soap solution of ½ cup liquid dishwashing detergent per gallon of lukewarm water to wash the brick. Apply the solution with a sponge or cloth and scrub with a stiff-bristle fiber brush. (When scrubbing with both the wire brush and the fiber brush, wear protective eyewear.) Rinse the surface with a sponge or cloth and clean water.

For glass doors on enclosed fireplaces, use either a commercial glass cleaner, like Windex, or a homemade solution, like a squirt of liquid dishwashing detergent in a bucket of warm water or 1 cup vinegar per gallon of water. Let the glass cool before cleaning. Spray or sponge the cleaner on, and then wipe it off with newspaper to avoid leaving lint. Scrape off thick gunk deposits using a razor blade. For an old-fashioned chimney sweep's trick, take a moist cloth and lightly dip it in the fluffy ash that sits on top of the ash pile. Rub the ash on the dirty window in a circular motion. "It polishes the glass like a jeweler's rouge," Eldridge explains. Wipe it clean with a paper towel.

Use the same soap and water solution and fiber brush to clean fireplace accessories, like andirons, pokers, and shovels. Then wipe them clean and dry with a cloth. Remove rust or soot deposits from iron or steel tools by rubbing gently using a very fine (#000) steel wool. Then polish by rubbing with a superfine (#0000) steel wool. For brass surfaces, rub on a brass cleaner using a lint-free cloth.

At least once a year, hire a professional to inspect your chimney. Based on the thickness of the buildup, he can determine whether it needs cleaning. This is a necessary safety precaution against the buildup of creosote, gummy resin deposits that can cause dangerous chimney fires. For a referral in your area, contact the National Chimney Sweep Guild, 16021 Industrial Drive, Suite 8, Gaithersburg, MD 20877.

In a pinch: You can't expect to remove all the black coloring from the brick inside the fireplace. "Sometimes it's easier to clean the residual deposits from the surface of the brick, and then paint it all black. Then at least it's uniform," says Eldridge. Use a high-temperature (1,200°F minimum) paint, and be sure to leave the damper open for good ventilation while painting, says Eldridge.

Caution: Wear a dust mask when removing ashes from the fireplace. When sweeping ashes, be extremely careful to avoid still-hot coals. Wait at least two days after your last fire before cleaning ashes. Put them in metal containers only.

Fireplace Screens

Since the fireplace is the centerpiece of many rooms, it is important to keep the fireplace screen that covers it clean and presentable.

Technique: Make cleaning the fireplace screen part of your regular household cleaning routine. To remove dust, vacuum each side with the vacuum cleaner brush attachment.

Once or twice a season (or when necessary), use a cleaning solution of ⅛ cup liquid dishwashing detergent per quart of water to remove caked-on dirt. Gently scrub the screen with a soft-bristle fiber brush. Rinse by wiping the screen with a wet lint-free cloth. Dry thoroughly with a lint-free cloth to avoid rusting. Polish brass sections with a brass cleaner and a lint-free cloth.

Speed tips: To prevent creating extra messes that you'll have to clean up, lay the screen on its side on a drop cloth—in the garage or on a deck, not in the middle of your living room.

In a pinch: After dusting the wire mesh, paint it black using a high-temperature (1,200°F minimum) satin spray paint. Do it outside on a drop cloth or similar ground cover. Spray one side from all angles, let it dry, and then flip the mesh and spray the other from all angles.

Fishing Gear

Clean gear simply makes you fish better. "If you're fishing in salt water, removing salt from your gear is your most important goal," says Mark Sosin, host of *Mark Sosin's Saltwater Journal,* a television

HOW I DO IT

The Ultimate Casting Call

Mark Sosin makes his living as a sport fisherman. The author of more than two dozen books and countless magazine articles, Sosin is the host of *Mark Sosin's Saltwater Journal*, which ran on ESPN for 12 years and is now on the Nashville Network. "I depend on my tackle. We have big dollars flowing when we shoot our television show, and if the tackle fails, that's a very costly mistake.

"To get the salt and grime off my rod and reel, I use one of those car-washing mitts. I dip my hand in liquid dishwashing detergent and water and run it over the whole thing. I then rinse off with freshwater. It's quick, and if there are any sharp edges, my hand is covered."

program on the Nashville Network, and author of more than two dozen books and countless magazine articles. "But even in freshwater, dirt gets tracked into boats and finds its way into reels." Keeping equipment clean means smoother-spinning reels and other performance benefits, plus added years of use.

Technique: After each time you use your rod and reel, wash them with lukewarm water and liquid dishwashing detergent. Mix the solution in a bucket until sudsy, and then use a sponge or cloth to wipe off all dirt, fish slime, and salt. "You must have detergent to take salt off," Sosin emphasizes. "The detergent floats the salt. If you just rinse it with water, a salt residue remains." Either let the gear air-dry or dry it with a soft cloth. Then apply a coat of demoisturizing compound, like WD-40, by spraying it on a cloth and wiping the cloth over the metal parts. Never spray it directly on the reel. Too much can get sticky and actually attract dirt.

Most rods made today use foam rubber in the handle, but if you have a rod with a cork handle, gently scrub the cork with steel wool to remove dirt and discoloration.

To remove salt and other grime, soak lures in the same bucket of soapy water used to clean the rod and reel, rinse them, then dry them off. Even though most are made of plastic, that will help keep the metal hooks from rusting.

Spray the metal parts of a tackle box with a demoisturizing compound regularly. At least a couple of times a year—more if you fish often—lubricate the inside of your reel with a spray or a light oil.

In a pinch: "If I'm traveling, and I don't have the facilities to properly wash my rod and reel," says Sosin, "I just take them in the shower and wash them off with a washcloth."

Fish Ponds

"You want to reduce the organic debris that accumulates in the pond, in order to maintain the pond's natural balance of life," says Keith Folsom, co-owner of Springdale Water Gardens, a mail-order supplier in Greenville, Virginia. "Excess debris causes pond pollution, turning the water pea-soup green and creating odors." The organic wastes also give off nitrogen, which is toxic to fish.

Technique: Remove leaves, sticks, and other debris from the pond periodically, especially in the fall. This makes an annual cleaning easier.

Clean your pond once a year, in the spring or fall when the tap-water temperature is cooler and better-suited for fish. Clean on a cool, cloudy day so that your pond plants don't dry out, advises Folsom.

Begin by filling a holding tank for fish—a five-gallon bucket, an aquarium, or a kiddie pool—halfway with tap water. Use a commercial dechlorinating agent, available at pond supply stores, to dechlorinate the tap water. Fill the holding tank the rest of the way with water from the pond. Use a siphon or pump to make the transfer easier. This mixture helps ease the transition for the fish from a dirty pond to a clean pond.

Using a net, transfer the fish to the holding tank. Keep the holding tank in a shaded area. Place a screen over the container to keep the fish from jumping out.

Mulm's the Word: An Organic Tip for Fish Ponds

Sometimes squeaky-clean is not the best kind of clean. Take fish ponds, for example. "You don't want to clean your fish pond so that it's spotless," says Keith Folsom, co-owner of Springdale Water Gardens, a mail-order supplier in Greenville, Virginia. "You want to maintain some of the natural bacteria that have grown on the side of the pond."

"Organic waste, known as mulm, settles on the bottom of fish ponds. The beneficial bacteria consume nitrogen given off by the mulm, helping prevent the growth of algae, which needs the nitrogen to thrive. It keeps your water from turning green and protects your fish since the nitrogen can be toxic to them. It's a good way of controlling the quality of your water without relying on chemical means."

Bottom Feeders: Ridding the World of Scum

Remember the Scrubbing Bubbles from that popular TV commercial? The ones that attacked the dirty tub with the cleaning zeal of Marines on inspection day? Think of pond scavengers as real-life scum-busters.

"A combination of snails, mussels, and tadpoles help strike an ecological balance in your fish pond," says Keith Folsom, co-owner of Springdale Water Gardens, a mail-order supplier in Greenville, Virginia. They feed on the organic wastes given off by fish and plants, reducing algae growth and keeping the water clear.

Japanese snails, which graze the muck on the bottom and sides of the pond, are one of the best pond scavengers because they do not overpopulate or escape the water. Tadpoles and mussels filter suspended algae from the water.

A good rule of thumb is to stock one scavenger per square foot of pond surface.

Continue draining the pond, releasing the nutrient-rich water around the plants in your yard. Gently pull up plants and set them aside in the shade. Cover floating plants, like water lilies, with wet newspaper and plastic to keep them moist.

Note: Plastic alone will cause them to overheat quickly.

As the water level drops, scrub the sides of the pond with a nylon brush. Rinse where you have cleaned by tossing water up onto it and letting it fall into the pond. The sediment will collect at the bottom, once the pond is empty.

Finally, scrape up the silt that has settled to the bottom. Remove it with a shovel, and spread it around the garden as mulch.

After cleaning your pond, dump half the water from the holding tank where you've stored your fish back into the pond. This helps inoculate the clean pond with beneficial bacteria.

Next, refill the pond with tap water and dechlorinate it. To help the fish adjust to the temperature difference, fill the holding tank with tap water, and wait 20 to 30 minutes. Again, empty half of the water into the pond, and refill the holding tank with tap water. Repeat this procedure until the water temperature in the holding tank is the same as that in the pond.

If your pond is filtered, clean the filtration equipment, following the manufacturer's instructions. Usually, this is simply a matter of spraying the filter element down with a hose. If soap and water is required, make sure that you rinse the filter completely before you replace it.

Speed tips: Keep scavengers like snails or mussels in your fish pond. They help keep it clean, making the year-end cleaning quicker and easier. When cleaning, transfer the snails and mussels to your holding tank before cleaning the pond. Replace them once you have finished.

In a pinch: Using a plastic rake, carefully rake up organic debris from the bottom of your pond. If you use mussels or snails as scavengers, be sure to pick them out of the debris and return them to the water.

Caution: Do not clean your pond more often than once a year. The beneficial bacteria need that time to grow.

Don't attempt to remove fish when the water level in the pond is still high. Chasing them can bruise them. Instead, let it get low enough so that the fish have trouble escaping your net.

Fixtures—Bathroom, Kitchen

Soap scum and grease love to dull a faucet's shine. And when left on the fixture, they foster bacteria growth like a petri dish. You want to get rid of this layer of gunk before it strengthens its hold against future scrubbing.

Technique: Clean faucets, knobs, shower heads, and other fixtures regularly, using an nonabrasive all-purpose cleaner or a tub-and-tile cleaner, like Comet Bathroom Cleaner, and a sponge or soft cloth. Never use abrasive cleaners or scrubbers in the bathroom. Spray it on, let it sit for a few seconds while the cleaning agents work on the scum, and then wipe it off. The cleaner should do most of the work. Clean cracks and crevices with a soft brush. Rinse by wiping everything down with a clean wet sponge or cloth.

Simplify your chores by using one product instead of several. "The commercial spray scum removers like Tilex Soap Scum Remover these days are almost magic," says Jim Brewer, executive housekeeper at the University of Texas at Arlington and a technical advisor to *Cleaning and Maintenance Magazine*. "You're trying to remove three things—oil, soap, and mineral deposits—plus the occasional mildew. People used to clean fixtures at least twice, but the new products are composites. They take all three things off as well as the mildew." While using any cleaning product, it's important that you ventilate the room well by opening the door and windows and turning on the exhaust fan.

Speed tips: Clean bathroom fixtures with your damp towel after showering, when they are slightly moist. Do it often and scum will not have a chance to build up.

Caution: "Rule number one is to never combine any cleaning products because they may contain reactive ingredients such as ammonia or chlorine," says Brewer. "Ammonia and chlorine make a mustard gas, a toxic chlorine gas, if they're combined. I nearly killed myself mixing those chemicals once. I was sick for weeks." Never sniff the bottle to see what's in it, and be sure to read the label completely for proper usage and safety precautions.

Flatware

If dinner guests notice your flatware at all, you want it to be because it shines so brilliantly. Smudgy forks, knives, and spoons won't do. So follow this cutting-edge advice.

Technique: Wash all flatware after use. When you're washing by hand, make it one of the first things you clean, along with glasses. Or, if you do it last, change the dishwater. Let the utensils presoak to loosen caked-on food. Wash them in hot soapy water using a sponge or cloth—never anything abrasive, even on stainless steel. Abrasives will dull the finish of metals. Rinse flatware with hot water. Place it handles-down in a silverware basket to air-dry, and try to leave as much room as possible for air circulation between each piece.

When loading the dishwasher, also place flatware handles-down. "That way, when water drips off of them, it doesn't leave stains on the bowl of the spoon, the tines of the fork or the blade of the knife," says Kari Kinder, assistant director of food and beverage at the renowned Culinary Institute of America in Hyde Park, New York. Never sprinkle automatic dishwasher detergent directly onto flatware before washing. That can cause pitting.

When machine-washing, do not place silver or silver-plate flatware next to stainless steel flatware. The steel will tarnish the silver. For the same reason, make sure that all silver knives are situated with their blades up. Even if the handles are silver, the blades are often stainless steel.

For that extra shine—in preparation for a dinner party, for example—polish flatware with a soft cotton cloth after it has dried.

Floors—Brick, Concrete, Hardwood, Terrazzo, Vinyl

Floors suffer. They hold up our monstrous dressers, pianos, and couches. They bear our shuffling, running, and stomping. And, unless you live in a space station, they catch virtually everything that spills. Still, we expect them to maintain their composure and good looks.

Not only does keeping your floors clean make them look better but also dirt and grit can scratch floors. So clean floors also last longer.

Technique: Vacuum or sweep all types of floors regularly—daily in high-traffic areas—to keep grit to a minimum. Do not use abrasive cleaners that will scratch floors.

Brick

Sealed brick is easier to keep clean than unsealed brick. Regardless of the surface, vacuum or sweep it regularly, and damp mop periodically with plain water. For cleaning heavier soil, mop with a moderately strong alkali solution, like Spic and Span or another cleaner that contains trisodium phosphate. Rinse the floor well to remove all of the cleaning solution.

Concrete

Poor lowly concrete. Common in garages and basements, it tends to be forgotten when it comes to upkeep. But it needs regular cleaning, just like finer floors. In fact, a simple scrubbing every once in a while will dramatically enhance the appearance of your concrete.

Sweep your concrete floor regularly. Wash it when needed by mopping or scrubbing with a squirt of liquid dishwashing detergent in a bucket of warm water. For heavier soil, use trisodium phosphate, available at most hardware stores. Follow the manufacturer's recommendations for determining what strength solution you need.

"Scrubbing is, unfortunately, often necessary, and you may have to apply it more than once," says Mary Hurd, an engineer in Farmington Hills, Michigan, and consulting editor of the trade journal *Concrete Construction*. Scrub with a stiff-bristle nylon or vegetable brush. Do not use a metal brush. Tiny filaments can break off and stain the concrete when they rust. Be sure to rinse the floor thoroughly after cleaning with a solution.

Caution: Wear protective eyewear, gloves, and long sleeves when using trisodium phosphate. Always read the product label for proper use and safety precautions.

Hardwood

Most wood floors are protected by a sealer, which penetrates the wood pores, and a coating of polyurethane, shellac, or varnish. Others are covered only by wax. As with all floors, vacuum or sweep often to keep dirt from grinding into the floor's finish. Wipe up spills and mud immediately using a damp cloth. Avoid wetting even well-sealed floors too much. Dry them with a clean towel.

Do not wax a urethane finish. The wax prevents future recoating, which is how you renew a dulled finish without stripping, sanding, and refinishing the floor. Likewise, choose cleaning products carefully. "If a customer just picks up something that says 'Hardwood Floor Cleaner,' it's usually a diluted solution of mineral spirits and wax," says Daniel Boone, technical director of the National Wood Flooring Association in Ellisville, Missouri. "It may look good on the floor, but using it would mean they could never recoat the floor and would void the manufacturer's warranty for a new floor."

Instead, Boone suggests, use a cleaner recommended by the manufacturer of your floor or your floor's finish. "If you use Brand A wood floor finish, then you want to use Brand A cleaner or what Brand A recommends for that specific finish," he says.

If you don't know the type of finish or its manufacturer, use a general cleaner, like Woodwise Floor Cleaner, available at wood flooring distributors or warehouse-style home supply stores.

For wax finishes, do the same. Use a wax recommended by the maker. Never use a water-based cleaner. It can stain the wood white.

To remove white water spots on a wax-finish floor, rub gently and in a circular motion with an extra-fine (#000) steel wool and a small amount of mineral spirits. Be sure that the area in which you are working is adequately ventilated. Then apply additional wax to the area and buff.

Caution: Read product labels completely for proper usage and safety precautions.

Terrazzo

Terrazzo is a mixture of cement and small bits of marble and granite. Because the cement is porous, it tends to absorb stains and is often coated with a penetrating sealer. Some modern forms of terrazzo, made with synthetic resins such as urethane or epoxy in place of the cement, do not stain as readily.

Sweep or vacuum regularly. Damp mop using a cleaner that is as close to neutral as possible—those which are neither acid nor alkaline. Try something mild, like Murphy Oil Soap, suggests Dick Bray, technical services manager for the Wood Floor Covering Association in Anaheim, California. In general, avoid all-purpose cleaners, detergents, and wax removers. With a wet mop, apply the solution and allow it to sit for several minutes. Then mop up the dirty solution, changing the rinse water often. This helps remove all soil and also does away with unsightly mop lines.

If your terrazzo floor contains stubborn dirt, consider renting an electric scrubbing machine from an equipment rental company. Use a stronger solution of the neutral cleaner.

Caution: Never use petroleum-based cleaners, like Endust or Pledge, for dust-mopping terrazzo. The oil can penetrate the surface and cause permanent staining. (Murphy Oil Soap is okay because it is made from vegetable oil.)

Vinyl

Most residential vinyl flooring today is what is known as no-wax flooring. Whether it comes in sheet or tile form, it is usually protected by a polyurethane-type coating that has a built-in shine. To help your floor keep that shine, however, clean it regularly.

For a lightly soiled floor, sweep or vacuum first, and then mop with a sponge mop using warm water and a no-rinse floor cleaner, following label directions. Clean one section of the floor at a time. Rinse the mop in a sink or second bucket before placing it again into the warm water and cleaner. That will keep the wash water cleaner. Be sure to wring out the mop thoroughly at every step. Rinsing is usually not necessary after a light cleaning. To be sure, follow the product manufacturer's recommendations.

If your floor requires a thorough cleaning, begin by sweeping or vacuuming loose debris. Then apply a heavy-duty cleaner, such as a polish remover specifically recommended by your floor's manufacturer. Mop the entire floor, wringing the mop occasionally. Next, using a clean mop and bucket of fresh cool water, rinse the floor to eliminate any remaining cleaning solution. Avoid one-step "mop and polish" products, liquid dishwashing detergents, and oil-based cleaners. They leave a residue that can attract dirt and dull your floor, says Brian Quigley, director of consumer affairs at Congoleum Corporation, a vinyl flooring maker in Mercerville, New Jersey.

Eventually, all finishes lose some of their shine as the no-wax coating dulls. Wear and tear may cause dulling of the shine in some floors. You can renew it by applying a manufacturer-recommended acrylic floor polish, which will help protect the floor against surface abrasions. For best results, apply polish very thinly, following label directions.

Spot-clean spills or scuffs as they occur to prevent them from becoming permanent. Use a clean cloth or paper towel dampened with floor cleaner. Lighter fluid, applied gently with a clean cloth, is suggested for difficult scuff marks or adhesives. Lighter fluid is a flammable solvent, however, so use it cautiously and following information on the label.

Flowers—Artificial, Dried, Silk

You want them to look as beautiful as, well, fresh-cut flowers from the garden. However, "the trouble with silk and other artificial flowers is that, because they are permanent, they collect dust and spiderwebs," points out Louise Wrinkle, a veteran horticulture judge for the Garden Club of America in New York City.

Technique: Dust the flowers from time to time using a can of compressed air or a blow-dryer set on the lowest, coolest setting. Be gentle with dried flowers, which are often brittle and can shed. If you find that yours are shedding, take them outside to dust them.

In a pinch: Simply shake or ruffle silk flowers to remove dust. Or if they're delicate, gently blow on them.

Licking the Competition

Flower shows may not offer much in the way of thrills, chills, and excitement, but they can be competitive. And, it turns out, cleanliness counts in the judging. Here's how *The Daffodil Journal*, published by the American Daffodil Society, recommends preparing a winning blossom.

"Thoroughly clean all dirt from the bloom. Use a cotton swab, moistened in your mouth with saliva. Saliva will pick up dust particles better than water.

"Check the back of the flower to see if the spathe (a leaf at the base of the bud) became wet and stained the back of the petals. The only effective way to remove the stain is to lick it off. For those of you saying, 'Yuck,' it's only plant juice, for heaven's sake, and no different from eating your asparagus."

Foam Rubber

Dust, body oil, and perspiration accumulate on foam pillows, cushions, and mattresses. These things harbor microorganisms, like dust mites, which can cause allergies. Take away their dinner and those microorganisms will go away.

Technique: There are different types of foam rubber—some washable, some not. Before you clean for the first time, always read the product care label.

If your foam rubber is a single piece, remove dust and dust mite droppings and body parts by vacuuming it with the appropriate attachment, like an upholstery brush.

As for washing single-piece foam, generally speaking, you should soak it first in cool water. If there are oily stains and perspiration in the foam, pretreat it with a commercial product, like Biz, or apply a liquid laundry detergent (or a paste made from a granular detergent and water) containing enzymes. Look for enzymes in the list of your detergent's ingredients.

Next, fill a sink, tub, or basin with warm water and a few squirts of liquid dishwashing detergent, enough to create a nice sudsy bath. Wash the foam by pushing down on it, releasing and pushing down again. Rinse the same way, using clean water. Empty the rinse water and refill the basin with clean water. Repeat this process until there is no more soap residue.

To dry foam rubber, gently squeeze out as much water as possible, blot with clean towels, and then let it dry in the sun or at room temperature. "The center of the foam rubber can take a while to dry," says Rajiv Jain, laboratory manager for the Association of Specialists in Cleaning and Restoration in Millersville, Maryland. "But foam usually has a good network of capillaries, and water will eventually evaporate."

If you have the kind of foam pillows that are filled with many small fragments of foam rubber, never take them out of their cover. They are hard to manage and can deteriorate easily. You can wash most types of these pillows in the washing machine. Use cold water, which is safer on the synthetic filling. Tumble dry on low heat or dry them in the sun on a patio chair.

Speed tips: Use an electric fan to speed up the drying process.

Caution: Never use solvents on foam rubber, and never tumble it dry on high heat. Both can damage it.

Food—Lettuce, Root Vegetables, Spinach

If you're going to put it in your mouth, you *really* want it clean. So you want to remove not only the big stuff—dirt and grit—but also any pesticide residue or bacteria clinging to the surface of your fresh vegetables. Even though the veggies themselves do not nurture the growth of pathogens, like meats do, the debris on them very well could, says Bessie Berry, manager of the U.S. Department of Agriculture's Meat and Poultry Hotline in Washington, D.C. Here we address a few vegetables that are famous for needing extra cleanup help.

Technique: To clean lettuce, spinach, and other greens, first clean out your sink or a similar-size basin and fill it with cold tap water. Separate the leaves from the stalk, put them in the sink, and swish them around. The dirt lifts off and sinks to the bottom, and the cold water crisps the greens. Dry in a lettuce spinner, available at kitchen supply stores, or by blotting with paper towels or a clean dishcloth.

"You don't need to run water over each leaf," says Elizabeth Aquino, a freelance chef and graduate of the New York Restaurant School in New York City. "That's a waste of water and a waste of time."

If your greens are really dirty, repeat the procedure after emptying and rinsing the sink and refilling it with freshwater.

Clean root vegetables—carrots, beets, radishes—by scrubbing them under running water with a vegetable brush.

Speed tips: "You don't have to thoroughly clean root vegetables that you're going to peel," Aquino says. Save your energy. Simply rinse them under tap water and peel. If you're cooking the vegetables, roast them in the oven first to make peeling easier.

Food Graters

As with all food-preparation implements, you want to clean off all food residue to avoid bacteria growth and the mixing of flavors.

Technique: Clean graters with a nylon or vegetable scrub brush and warm soapy water. Stroke inside and outside surfaces with the "grain" of the grater, not against it, which will damage the bristles of the brush. The brush fibers work much better than a sponge or scrubbing pad. They get down into the nooks and crannies of the grater to remove stuck-on particles. Dry the grater completely before putting it away.

Speed tips: Surfaces used for grating hard cheeses, ginger, and citrus rinds—the finest side of a box grater—tend to be hardest to clean. To make this task easier, wrap the grater with plastic wrap, grate, and then remove the plastic. "For example, when you're grating lemon rind for a cake batter, all the zest sticks to the plastic wrap and not the grater," says Michael Beglinger, executive chef at Deutsche Bank in New York City. "It makes holes where the grater tips poke out, but the plastic wrap does not rip apart or shred into the food."

Food Grinders

Now you know why the tough chores are called a grind. The most difficult parts of a meat grinder to clean are the dies, the interchangeable pieces that determine the thickness of the food you're grinding. With a meat grinder, for instance, "it's just plain hard to get the meat out of those little holes," says Michael Beglinger, executive chef at Deutsche Bank in New York City. You want to remove any residue to avoid bacteria growth.

Technique: Disassemble the grinder and flush the parts with very hot water. This gets rid of most food particles.

A common way to clean the holes in the die is to poke the meat or other food particles through with a toothpick, but this is time-consuming. "One trick is to fold a sponge in half, soak it with water and press the die on it fast and hard," Beglinger says. That pushes the particles out of the holes. "It works especially well on the really fine dies that are hard to clean."

Next, clean all the pieces in warm soapy water using a nylon or vegetable scrub brush and let them air-dry.

Speed tips: To make it easier to clean a meat grinder, grind a piece of bread after you have finished grinding your meat. As soon as the bread starts coming out, stop. This gets all the meat out of the die. The bread flushes more easily when rinsed with hot water.

Food Processors

"Most food processors have safety precautions that make cleaning tough," says Michael Beglinger, executive chef at Deutsche Bank in New York City. Any way you slice it, the key is cleaning your food processor right away to remove food before it sticks to hard-to-reach places or dries up and is then harder to clean.

Technique: Begin by reading the manufacturer's recommended cleaning instructions. Generally speaking, you should disassemble your machine and wash the removable parts in warm soapy water. Clean the blades, bowls, and other parts as soon after you use it as possible. Wipe down the base with a sudsy sponge or cloth. Rinse it by wiping with a clean moist sponge. Do not scrub with steel wool or other harsh scouring cleaners. That could scratch the appliance's surface and dull its appearance.

If the food in your processor does dry out and stick, soak the nonelectric parts in warm soapy water. Scrub with a small nylon or vegetable brush to remove residue.

Speed tips: Put the removable parts in the dishwasher. (Read the instructions first to make sure that the parts are dishwasher-safe.) To be safe, put the parts on the top rack. They might melt if they are exposed to the heating element below.

Caution: Unplug your food processor before cleaning. Do not try to sharpen the blades of your food processor unless the manufacturer recommends it. Most have been permanently sharpened by the maker. Food processor blades are extremely sharp, so handle them with care.

Fountains

A trickling fountain is a serene addition to any backyard, until white or green discoloration gets your blood pressure up. "Scale, the white mineral deposits caused by hard water, and algae are the main issues when it comes to fountains," says Keith Folsom, co-owner of Springdale Water Gardens, a mail-order supplier in Greenville, Virginia. Sticking to a cleaning routine will help prevent either from taking hold.

Technique: Both scale and algae build up over time. The more you prevent their buildup, the easier it will be to clean your fountain.

To prevent algae, use a commercial algae treatment, available at water-garden and fountain suppliers. Typically applied a few drops at a time once a month or so, these inhibit algae growth without the use of chlorine or other harsh chemicals.

You can buy a similar commercial treatment for inhibiting scale. It works the same way to keep scale from forming on your fountain, fountainhead, and filters. You use 2 to 4 ounces for each 10 gallons of water.

If you want to not use the commercial products, clean your fountain as needed, usually once a week. "For scale and algae, vinegar is one of the best cleaning agents you can use," Folsom says. Empty the fountain and, using a one-to-one solution of vinegar and water, scrub the surfaces with a nylon brush. "The vinegar will neutralize alkaline mineral deposits, plus it has good cleaning qualities." Rinse well by spraying the fountain with the garden hose.

Clean the pump and filter weekly as well. Remove the filter and spray it with the garden hose. If not, algae, especially the filament-shaped kind, can clog it. Wipe down the exterior of the pump with a wet cloth. If the pump has mineral deposits, wipe it down with the vinegar solution and rinse with clean water. If you need to scrape algae or mineral deposits out of the intake valve, use the bottle brush supplied with your pump kit, or use a wooden stick, like a Popsicle stick. Metal can scratch the surface.

Caution: To avoid the risk of shock, always unplug your pump before cleaning it.

Fur

Furs are literally dust magnets. "Furs build up a certain amount of static electricity and attract dust and pollutants in the air, especially when the humidity is low," says David Datlow, a Washington, D.C.–based fur cleaner since 1936. "The dust dulls the sheen and becomes abrasive, causing fine hairs to break." Regular cleaning of your furs removes these harmful particles and leaves the furs looking shiny and new.

Technique: Have your fur professionally cleaned at least once every other year; once a year is even better. It needs conditioning to keep it soft and fresh. Take it to a furrier, never to a dry cleaner, unless the dry cleaner sends furs out to be cleaned by a furrier. To remove dirt and oils, furriers typically tumble furs in a drum with a sawdust-like material that has been soaked in a specially formulated chemical solution. Then they apply silicone and comb the furs, a process called glazing, to bring out their luster and make them soft and fluffy.

For spills, simply blot and dab with a clean white towel. Never rub. Then, immediately take the fur to a professional cleaner. Time and heat can cause stains to seep into the hide of the fur. "Let's assume for a minute that a woman is wearing a $20,000 mink coat," Datlow says, "and she accidentally knocks a cup of hot coffee onto it. If the coffee penetrates the leather, the heat of that liquid will cause that skin to shrink. All skin has a natural moisture content, but unlike living creatures, whose skin can heal itself, a fur simply dries up."

If fur gets wet, shake it out and hang it on a broad-shouldered hanger, away from direct heat and sunlight, to dry.

Furniture

Chairs, dining tables, bookshelves, and other pieces of furniture are big investments, and you want them to last a long time (knock on wood). So keep them clean them as part of their upkeep. "You can increase the lifespan of your furniture by taking care of it," says Nancy High of the American Furniture Manufacturers Association in High Point, North Carolina.

Furniture comes in a wide variety of styles and is made of many different materials, including aluminum, chrome, glass, marble, wicker, and wood. Each of these materials is addressed in the pages that follow. For more details, see the individual entries for those materials elsewhere in this book.

While there are more complicated cleaning challenges, your main task with furniture is dusting. A general, but important, dusting tip is to always use a 100 percent cotton cloth, like an old T-shirt or a cloth diaper. Synthetic fibers will create minute scratches that are visible in good lighting and that build up over time. Paper towels are a no-no, too.

Aluminum

Dust aluminum furniture by wiping with a moist cloth. Clean it, if necessary, by wiping with a solution of warm water and a mild liquid dishwashing detergent and a cloth. Never use alkaline cleaners, like ammonia, trisodium phosphate, or even baking soda. (That means no ammonia-based window cleaners, like Windex.) They discolor aluminum.

If the aluminum surface is discolored, wipe it down with a one-to-one solution of vinegar and water. (Pretest first on an inconspicuous area.) The acid in vinegar will help restore the aluminum's shine.

Caution: Do not use abrasive cleaners, such as scouring powders or steel wool. They will scratch or dull the surface. Be sure to read the product label completely for proper usage and safety precautions.

Chrome

Chrome is the shiny metal plating applied to utensils, furniture, and other household items. It is easy to clean but susceptible to scratching.

Dust chrome regularly with a damp cloth. For heavier cleaning, wipe with a sponge or cloth and an all-purpose cleaner.

Caution: Never scour with steel wool or other abrasives, including powdered cleaners like Comet.

Glass

Clean glass tabletops and bookcase doors using newsprint and a glass cleaner, like Windex, or a solution of ¼ cup vinegar to a quart of warm water mixed in a spray bottle. Unlike paper towels and many types of cloth, newsprint will not leave behind traces of lint. (But be careful if you get newspaper ink on your hands—you could leave smudges around the house.)

Be sure to clean the underside of glass tabletops, which also get dirty. If the glass in your furniture is framed by wood, spray the cleaner directly onto the newsprint and wipe the glass down. Otherwise, you might damage the wood.

Caution: Carefully peel off wax, paint, and other stuck-on substances with a razor blade. Do not use a putty knife, which can scratch the glass.

Hardware

Fixtures on furniture are often made of brass. These days, most hardware on new furniture is coated with a surface finish, like lacquer. All you need to do is dust it with a lightly dampened cloth.

Untreated brass hardware, however, will tarnish. Polish it occasionally using a brass cleaner, like Brasso. Do it every year or two, or more often if you're motivated to. But do it right: Remove the hardware before polishing it, so that you will not damage the surface of the furniture. Lay the hardware out on the floor or a counter in the order that it came off to make replacing it easier.

Lacquer

Lacquer is a type of hardwood finish, like shellac. But it can also mean a style of furniture that originated in Asia. "When people talk about lacquer from a fashion standpoint, they are usually referring to wood furniture with a black or red high-sheen finish," says High.

This type of furniture typically has an extremely durable polyester finish that does not need polishing with furniture polish. Simply dust and clean it with a lightly dampened cloth.

Marble

Marble has a highly sensitive surface. So dust marble furniture often with a lightly dampened cloth to keep tiny particles of grit from scratching it. Never clean marble with furniture polish or oil. "Marble is nothing more than a sponge," says Fred Hueston, director of the National Training Center for Stone and Masonry Trades in Longwood, Florida, and author of *Marble and Tile: Selection and Care of Stone and Tile Surfaces*. By soaking into marble, these substances will cause staining.

For heavier cleaning, use a sponge or soft cloth and a neutral cleaner, like Murphy Oil Soap or a liquid dishwashing detergent, mixed with warm water.

To remove stains on marble, use a poultice, which will draw the stains out. For oil stains, mix ½ cup bleached flour, a small squirt of liquid dishwashing detergent, and just enough warm water to make a paste that has the consistency of peanut butter. Spread it over the stained area, cover it with plastic wrap, and tape down the sides with masking tape. Let it sit overnight. Remove the plastic, let the poultice dry, and scrape it away. For food stains (coffee, tea, and juices, for instance), substitute hydrogen peroxide for the detergent. Rub ink, crayon, or nail polish stains with a cotton ball dipped in an acetone-based nail polish remover. (Don't mix the nail polish remover into the poultice.)

Caution: Lemon, vinegar, other substances containing acid will eat into the polished surface of marble. Remember that many bathroom cleaners contain acid. Check the label for proper usage and any safety precautions. And avoid using abrasive cleaners because even the finest grit can dull marble surfaces.

Rattan and Wicker

Most rattan and wicker is coated with one of the same hard-surface finishes used to coat wood furniture. If so, simply dust it by vacuuming regularly with a brush attachment or wiping it down with a lightly dampened cloth. Once every six weeks, polish it with a spray-on furniture polish like Pledge. Spray it directly onto a clean cloth and wipe the surface. This way, you avoid getting the polish into hard-to-reach cracks.

If your wicker is painted, vacuum it regularly and wipe it down with a lightly dampened cloth. Do not use furniture polish.

Upholstery

A good place to begin is with upholstery, a common feature in many different types of furniture. Vacuum it weekly, using the vacuum cleaner upholstery attachment.

"Upholstery takes the most abuse in a living area and is most overlooked when it comes to cleaning," says High. "People fail to realize that there's as much dust on upholstery as on the wood furniture, floor, and other places where you can see it."

Because dust contains microscopic abrasives, like silica, it can damage upholstery if left to be ground in by squirming sitters. And the fabric of upholstery typically wears out sooner than the wood or other materials of your furniture. Regular vacuuming should do the trick.

Wood

Before you clean your wood furniture, you need to know what type of finish it has. Most wood furniture, especially if it is relatively new, has a hard finish, be it lacquer, shellac, varnish, or polyurethane. Some pieces, however, have what is called a soft, or oiled, finish.

To determine the type of finish on a piece of furniture, rub a few drops of boiled linseed oil, a type of linseed oil available at hardware and paint stores, into the wood. If it soaks in, the wood has an oil finish. If it beads up, the wood has a hard finish.

To clean soft-finished furniture, dust it regularly with a lightly dampened cloth. Once or twice a year, or if the wood dries out, apply boiled linseed oil. Using a clean cloth, rub in the oil in the direction of the grain until the wood absorbs no more. Fold another cloth into a pad and rub the area until it is dry.

If your soft-finished wood needs a deeper cleaning, apply kerosene or mineral spirits the same way you would the boiled linseed oil. Follow up by applying the boiled linseed oil.

Dust hard-finished wood at least once a week using a nonwax spray, like Endust. Avoid dusting with a dry cloth. Not only does dry-dusting spread rather than remove dust but also it can scratch fine surfaces because of the minute abrasives dust contains.

Once every four to six weeks, apply a spray-on wax polish, like

Pledge, to hard-finished wood furniture. "I don't recommend doing this more frequently because your furniture doesn't need it and you don't need the extra work," High says.

Read the product labels and choose the appropriate product for the type of finish on your furniture. For furniture with a high shine, choose a high-luster wax; for pieces with a flatter finish, choose a low-luster wax.

You don't have to worry about wax buildup. These spray-on polishes contain mild solvents so that as you apply a new coating of protective wax, you also strip old wax. For detailed furniture or pieces with a lot of hardware, spray the product directly onto the cloth instead of to the furniture to avoid getting it into cracks and crevices.

Once or twice a year, or for sun-damaged or dried-out wood, apply an oil, like Old English Furniture Oil, to the wood. Never saturate the wood with the oil. "This gives life back to tired wood," says Trish Bullock, customer service manager of Bassett Furniture Industries in Bassett, Virginia.

While it may be temptingly handy, do not wipe your dining-room table down with your kitchen dishcloth, Bullock says. "The traces of detergent on it can damage the wood finish," she says. Clean up dried food with a damp cloth, and then follow up by using a furniture polish.

To repair water marks, like rings left by sweaty glasses, rub the area lightly with wood oil, like Old English Furniture Oil, and a cotton cloth. Repeat a few times, if necessary. Do not let the oil sit on the spot, and do not repeat too many times. Otherwise, the white mark will turn black.

If no furniture oil is available for repairing water marks in wood, try mayonnaise instead. Wipe the mayonnaise over the spot with a clean cotton cloth, and then wipe it off.

For yellowing on white-finished wood furniture—caused by tobacco smoke, sunlight, or anything else—use a smoker's tooth polish. Because it contains mild abrasives, avoid rubbing it in. Just wipe it on and wipe it off. Follow up by wiping down the wood with a furniture polish.

If your furniture has odors, like mildew or smoke, wipe it down with a solution of one part vanilla to two parts water. Use only a lightly dampened cloth, and follow up by wiping down the wood with a furniture polish.

Buff out surface scratches. "If you scratch the surface of your car, you wax it out," Bullock says. "You can do the same for wood furniture." Using a cotton cloth, rub briskly with a furniture polish or oil. Do not rub too briskly, however, or you might cause what are known as buffer burns.

If your regular polish doesn't correct the slight imperfections, try a furniture paste wax.

For deeper scratches and dents, use a wax fill stick, available at hardware and paint stores. Rub it in and buff with a clean cloth. Avoid using touch-up markers and stains. "Fill sticks go on like crayons," Bullock says, "so if you mess up, you can wipe it out of the scratch and start over." There are a variety of fill-stick colors. Be sure to buy one that matches the color of your wood. Try calling the manufacturer of your furniture. Most keep matching fill sticks in stock.

In a pinch: If you can't get your hands on a wax fill stick, try paste shoe polish instead. Make sure that the polish matches the color of the furniture: brown for walnut, cordovan for mahogany, or tan for oak. Apply it with a cotton swab or toothpick, and then buff with a clean cloth.

Caution: When working with linseed oil or kerosene, wear rubber gloves and work in a well-ventilated area.

Garden Tools

Leave the mud and dirt in the ground, not on your metal garden tools. Soil holds moisture, which causes rust and shortens the tools' lifespan. Rust is also bad for another reason, explains Fred Hicks, past president of the American Nursery and Landscape Association in Washington, D.C., and president of Hicks Nurseries in Westbury, New York. "In time, rust causes pitting. Dirt sticks to a shovel or spade that is pitted, and that puts extra drag on the tool as it goes in and out of the soil." In essence, dirty tools make you work harder.

Technique: After using garden tools, wipe the mud off them with a cloth before putting them away. Spray them lightly with a lubricant/rust protectant, like WD-40. This is especially important for cutting tools, like shears and pruning saws, and for tools that won't be used for a while. It is essential for people with damp sheds or garages and in colder weather, when condensation tends to build up on surfaces. Before using digging tools, if the soil is relatively dry, work the tool in and out of the ground a few times. The sanding action will remove the light film of rust, leaving it smooth and in good shape.

HOW I DO IT

When It's Time to Throw in the Trowel...

Fred Hicks, past president of the American Nursery and Land-scape Association in Washington, D.C., and president of Hicks Nurs-eries, runs his own nursery in Westbury, New York. Here's how he keeps his tools clean. "I use a piece of burlap to wipe the mud and dirt off my tools. They don't need to be spit and polished, just free of moisture. As far as painting the metal goes, who has the time? Well-used tools generally don't need paint. But if I'm putting a tool away for a week or two, I spritz it with WD-40, and it's protected."

Keep wooden handles smooth, clean, and dry. Use a solution of mild soapy water and a cloth to remove soil. "If they get wet and dry, wet and dry, the wood starts to get rough," Hicks says. If it starts to splinter or if the wood grain rises—a sign of impending splin-tering—rub the wood with a fine-grade sandpaper. "It's like your baseball bat," Hicks says. "You don't do much to a bat but keep it clean and dry. The perspira-tion that soaks into the handle is probably the best thing for it because it puts that little bit of oil and mois-ture in there." Oil is okay for wooden handles, but avoid products that leave a sticky residue, which collects dirt. Boiled lin-seed oil, available at hardware stores and paint stores, works well. Wipe it on with a cloth, and then let it soak into the wood and dry.

After using garden sprayers, remove any excess solution. Flush them with water, and then pump a solution of water and liquid dish-washing detergent through to remove the remaining residue. (If you can't resist spraying with toxic chemicals, at least follow your local guidelines about discarding the wash water. Even though you will have diluted your solution even more, be careful about where you empty the sprayer.) Again, flush with water. Clean the outside with soapy water and a cloth or brush. No matter how carefully you clean a sprayer in which weed killer has been used, there's always the danger of lingering chemicals. Therefore, if you use a sprayer for a weed killer, label it clearly, and use another one for nontoxic spraying. Also, be sure not to use the same sprayer for weed killer and insecticides you may spray on your plants. Any weed killer residue left in the sprayer can kill your plants as well.

Speed tips: With most tools, you can just hose them off to re-move the dirt and mud and let them drip-dry.

In a pinch: If there's ever a time you can slack off, it's during June, July, and August. "It's the middle of the summer, the sun is out, it's dry. That's not when your tools rust, so cleaning them after every use is not as critical," says Hicks. You're probably using the tools more, too, which helps keep rust from building up on them.

Caution: Remember that there is a nontoxic solution for most weeds and pests. But if you must use dangerous chemicals, be careful cleaning up after yourself. When cleaning sprayers used for toxic substances, never let the chemicals come in contact with your skin. Always wear protective gloves, like those made of rubber or latex, safety goggles, and a mask over your nose and mouth.

When working with linseed oil, wear rubber gloves and work in a well-ventilated area. Always read product labels for proper use and safety instructions.

Glass

Because they're nonporous, "doing windows" is actually easy. And they should be cleaned regularly because, believe it or not, glass can stain. "Acid rain and other chemicals reacting with window glass can cause discoloration and can even etch it," says Jim Brewer, executive housekeeper at the University of Texas at Arlington and a technical advisor for *Cleaning and Maintenance Magazine*. Exterior glass that has not been cleaned for several years will probably not sparkle the way it once did.

Technique: Clean glass with a solution of one squirt of liquid dishwashing detergent in a bucket of warm water or with 1 cup vinegar per gallon of water. Ammonia-based commercial window cleaners have a tendency to streak, a condition that is especially noticeable in bright sunlight. To avoid leaving traces of lint, wipe away the liquid using a squeegee or newsprint. (If you get ink on your hands from the newspaper, be careful not to smudge the window frames.)

When cleaning vertical glass surfaces, like windows, start at the top and clean down. Apply the cleaning solution with a sponge or soft cloth, and then scrub caked-on grime with a long-bristle vegetable brush. If you're cleaning windows inside, put a towel on the windowsill to catch drips.

When cleaning glass tabletops, use newsprint instead of a squeegee. Make sure to clean the underside of the glass, which also gets dirty.

Carefully peel off paint and other stuck-on substances with a razor blade. "Paint is held on by a vacuum, and a razor blade will actually

HOW I DO IT

No Streaking on This Campus

Marry Keener is assistant director of facilities management at the University of Arizona in Tucson and a member of the technical advisory committee for *Executive Housekeeping Today* magazine. After tending to the 35,000 students at Arizona, here's how she cleans her own glass. "I don't use glass cleaner because I don't like ammonia, which streaks. Some glass cleaners say not to use them with direct sunlight. Here, we have direct sunlight 365 days a year. I use a mild solution of liquid dishwashing detergent. It's designed to clean the finest china and doesn't streak, is not abrasive, and doesn't harm your hands or anything else. It has wonderful soil-releasers.

"I use a squirt in a bucket partially filled with warm water. A little is better than making up real heavy concentrations. I use a squeegee to clean without leaving lint. Nine out of 10 professional window washers use liquid dishwashing detergent. It's wonderfully economical."

get under the edge of the paint and pop it off," Brewer says. Do not use a putty knife, which has a duller blade and can damage the glass.

Speed tips: When you are using a squeegee to clean glass, keep a couple of cloths handy. "You have two back pockets," notes Brewer, "one for a cloth to wipe the squeegee with and the other for one to wipe up the corners of the glass."

Glassware

People take it pretty personally when they find smudges on the glasses or cups they're using. "Stains seem to cling to glasses," says Kari Kinder, assistant director of food and beverage at the renowned Culinary Institute of America in Hyde Park, New York.

Technique: Glasses are usually the least-dirty items in your dish stack. When you're washing by hand, clean glassware first. Or, if you do it last, change the dishwater first. Clean glasses in hot water, which helps cut grease. Use a soft sponge, never an abrasive scrubber. Your rinse water should be as hot as is safely possible so that it beads up and steams off, leaving less of a film. If your wash water is greasy, rinse glasses with running water.

Air-dry glasses upside down in a rack on the counter. The rack is essential for avoiding the "greenhouse effect"—the fogging up of glasses from a lack of air circulation. "Fogging leads to film residue," Kinder says. "You want that clear crisp look that comes from proper drying."

If you get a lime buildup on your glassware after washing it in the dishwasher—usually a sign of hard water—try a rinse agent, like Jet-Dry. Rinse agents help water sheet off during the drying process and are typically available either as a tablet that hangs on the dishwasher rack or as a liquid that you add to a dishwasher's automatic dispenser at the beginning of the wash cycle. The less water that remains on your glasses, the less chance they have to spot and streak.

In a pinch: When it comes to washing glasses by hand, air-drying is preferable to towel drying because towels can get greasy and breed bacteria. If you're pressed for time or counter space, however, dry glasses with a soft clean towel.

Gloves—Baseball

Baseball is a grimy game—if you're doing it right. "A ball glove is going to get dirty and messy," says Carrie Fischer, communications manager of the Wilson Sporting Goods Company in Chicago. "That's the nature of the game." So after a day of diving catches, your goal is to remove the dirt and mud from your glove and keep it supple.

Technique: Brush away dry dirt and other debris with a stiff-bristle leather brush, available at leather and shoe stores. If your glove gets muddy, let the mud dry. It's easier to brush off that way. Do not use water to clean a baseball glove.

If your glove gets wet, let it dry at room temperature. Never place it near a radiator, hearth, or other heat source to dry. The heat will cause the leather to stiffen and crack. "Some people say that you're supposed to dry wet gloves in a microwave oven," says Fischer. "We do not recommend that."

To clean stains from leather, try a leather cleaner, available at leather and shoe stores. Follow the manufacturer's instructions for use.

Speed tips: "The best way to break in a glove—and keep it soft and pliant—is continual use," Fischer says. "If you don't have much time, we recommend lanolin." Rub shaving cream containing lanolin into the leather, and then shape it by pounding your fist or a base-ball into the pocket.

Gloves—Fabric, Leather, Rubber

For such a common item, gloves are uncommonly tricky to clean. "Gloves are not just one large flat surface," says Jay Ruckel, production manager of LaCrasia Gloves, a glove factory in New York City. "And you're not only cleaning dirt off the outside but also dealing with your own body dirt and oils, which can stain from the inside out." Add to that the fact that many gloves are made of leather, a sensitive and hard-to-clean material, and you have a challenge on your hands, so to speak.

Technique: We'll begin with washable gloves, those made of natural and synthetic fabrics, rubber, and washable leather. Many work, gardening, golf, and driving gloves are made of washable substances. Read the gloves' care label to make sure that you can get them wet.

The secret to efficiently washing gloves is to do it with the gloves on your hands. That way, it's easier to flatten out the creases and to get in between the fingers. Wash them with a mild detergent solution—a couple of squirts of a liquid dishwashing detergent in a sink filled with cool to lukewarm water. Then remove the gloves and rinse them in clean water. Empty the water and refill, repeating the process until there is no soap residue in the water.

To dry the gloves, roll them in a clean dry towel. Unroll them, blow into them as you would a balloon to recover their shape, and lay them out flat at room temperature. Do not squeeze or wring them. Never dry them on a radiator or near a heater. If you must iron them, do it between the folds of a clean towel.

Many gloves are made of unwashable leather or suede. There's not a lot the average person can do to clean leather. It's easy to damage the finish. Try using a commercial leather-cleaning product, like Lexol pH, available at leather and shoe repair shops.

If you spill a potential stain-causing substance on your leather gloves, the first thing you should do is blot it up with a clean white towel.

If it's a greasy stain, lay the glove out flat, sprinkle cornstarch on the stain, and let it stand overnight. It might absorb some of the oil. Another method is to place a clean white piece of tissue paper on the greasy spot and run a warm iron over it. Put the iron on the lowest heat setting for cotton. Replace the tissue several times with new tissue until there are no more traces of the stain on the tissue.

For a stain on suede, blot what you can and let the remainder dry for a couple of days. Try to restore the nap by rubbing gently with a soft brush or a dry kitchen sponge. By bringing back the nap, you might eliminate the stain.

For leather discoloration, look for a commercial leather spray like Nu-Life Color Spray, which comes in a variety of colors and is available at shoe repair shops. Choose the one that best matches the original color of your gloves, and then follow the manufacturer's instructions. Be sure to use in a well-ventilated area and always read product labels for proper use and safety instructions. For suede, mask stains and other discoloration in a similar way by rubbing lightly with a colored chalk that matches the original color of the suede.

For stubborn stains, take your gloves to a professional leather cleaner. But choose wisely. Most leather cleaning today is done by wholesalers who pick up from cleaners. If you use a dry cleaner, make sure it sends leather goods out to a leather specialist. Some dry cleaners try to clean the leather themselves—to avoid paying a wholesaler—and they could end up damaging it. For a professional leather cleaner referral in your area, contact the Leather Apparel Association, 19 West 21st Street, Suite 403, New York, NY 10010.

In a pinch: If your leather or suede gloves are wrinkled, take them off and put them on your knee. Pull the fingers tight, stretch them to their natural length, and gently rub your palm over the gloves. "The heat of your palm is almost like a gentle iron," Ruckel says.

Caution: Always test your cleaning solution or method on an inconspicuous part of the gloves.

Keep Your Gloves in the Dark

"When it comes to leather gloves, preservation and care are as important as cleaning," says Jay Ruckel, production manager of LaCrasia Gloves, a glove factory in New York City. Protecting them from direct light, he says, is essential.

"I have some fuchsia gloves that are incredibly faded just from hanging under a fluorescent light for six months. Half the glove is an off-white, and the palm is still a strong fuchsia. I like to keep those around as an example to show people.

"We normally think that only sunlight fades leathers, but interior lighting does the same. They used to make glove boxes and linen and silk envelopes. Some of the bureaus from the nineteenth century would have little glove drawers on top on either side of the mirror.

"You should protect your gloves from the light because correcting that discoloration is difficult. But don't use plastic bags. Leather has to breathe, and plastic just strangles it."

Gold

Gold does not tarnish the way silver does. However, when gold is less than 24-karat, or pure, the copper, silver, nickel, and other metals alloyed with it can tarnish and smudge. For example, says Julie Livingston, a New York City–based retail training consultant to the World Gold Council, "some people get black marks on their ears when they wear 14-karat gold earrings." And any gold, regardless of its purity, picks up oils from your skin and dust and dirt from the environment. Here's how to keep gold looking the way it should— shiny and beautiful.

Technique: Remove dirt and discoloration by swishing your gold item around in a solution of equal parts water and an all-purpose cleaner such as Mr. Clean. To clean crevices and intricately detailed jewelry, like a link bracelet, scrub lightly with a soft toothbrush. Rinse the item with warm water, and then dry it with a soft chamois cloth.

In a pinch: Just use a drop of mild liquid dishwashing detergent and lukewarm water. Apply with a soft toothbrush or soft cloth and rinse with water. Then dry with a chamois cloth. Or you can simply polish your gold with a dry chamois cloth.

Caution: Gold's worst enemy is chlorine. Repeated exposure can deteriorate gold. Never clean with chlorine, and remove gold jewelry before using chlorinated pools and hot tubs. Do not clean with toothpaste, even though some jewelers recommend it. Certain toothpastes contain harsh abrasives that can sand gold to a matte finish.

Gore-Tex

You probably do your job better when you're nice and clean. The same goes for your Gore-Tex, that waterproof/breathable membrane made by W. L. Gore and Associates that is found in outerwear. Cleaning dirt from the membrane improves both of its functions.

Technique: Gore-Tex itself is machine washable. If the outer shell is washable as well, wash on a regular, warm-water cycle using any type of standard laundry detergent. Dry on medium heat until completely dry. If the outer shell contains leather or some other nonwashable fabric, follow the instructions on the garment's cleaning tag. Gore-Tex can also be safely dry-cleaned. If the outer shell is a water-resistant nylon, however, multiple machine washings or even one trip to the dry cleaner will remove its water-repellent coating, which helps the Gore-Tex membrane do its job. If this happens, re-coat the outer shell with a spray-on water repellent, available at most camping and outdoors stores.

Graffiti

Unless you want "the word" to spread, remove graffiti as soon as possible. That way, you not only prevent it from soaking into porous surfaces but also discourage other graffiti vandals. "They don't get a chance to admire their work," says Frances Quill, director of car appearance and chemical materials for the New York City Transit Authority, which manages the graffiti-plagued New York subway system. "A wall with graffiti often attracts more people to put graffiti on it."

Technique: Since graffiti is usually in the form of paint, the most common approach is to use a chemical paint remover or solvent, such as Super Strip or Graffiti Remover, available at paint and wallpaper stores. Most of these also lift marks made by felt-tip pens, lipstick, and other substances. To use methylene chloride, a strong but common solvent, carefully brush it on, wait 2 minutes and rinse with water while continuing to brush. Because of concerns that methylene chloride may be carcinogenic, Quill prefers alkaline pastes like Peel-Away 1 that contain a caustic, such as potassium hydroxide or sodium hydroxide. It's available at paint and wallpaper stores. While Quill suggests following the manufacturer's instructions, here's how it typically works. Rub the paste on and let it sit for 5 to 10 minutes until it bubbles up; wipe or scrub it off; then rinse the surface with water and apply a neutralizer, like Peel-Away Neutralizer, usually sold separately. Repeat two or three times if one application does not remove the graffiti.

Two other methods for removing graffiti are waterblasting and sandblasting, both of which work better on brick, stone, and concrete than on wood. Only the finest-grade sandblasters work on metal without damaging the surface. You can usually rent waterblasting machines at a small-equipment rental agency. For sandblasting, however, you should hire a professional. (Look in the yellow pages under "Sandblasting.")

A CLEAN STORY

Painting the Town

In 1970, a Greek-American teenager sprayed "Taki 183," his nickname and street address, or "tag," on hundreds of subway cars and walls throughout New York City. Though not the first example of spray-paint art, it was copied by many teenagers and quickly led to a graffiti epidemic that has afflicted New York ever since.

To combat graffiti vandals, New York officials have adopted many creative solutions. They experimented with solvents, like Klout and DWR (Dirty Word Remover), which either didn't work or were so corrosive that the subway car manufacturers threatened to void their warranties unless its use was stopped, according to the *Encyclopedia of New York City*. They coated the cars, plus monuments and public facilities, with Hydron 300, a Teflon-like substance that wipes clean (but that proved too expensive to use). They even passed a bill that outlawed carrying open spray paint in public without a permit.

Today, most of New York's subway cars are stainless steel, which is graffiti-resistant. But the vandalism continues, mainly in the form of tags scratched in the cars' Plexiglas windows.

No matter which method you choose to remove the graffiti, first try it out on an inconspicuous test patch since it may alter the surface appearance.

Speed tips: If you anticipate a graffiti hit on a particular surface, apply an antigraffiti coating or sealer, such as Graffiti Barrier, also available at paint and wallpaper stores. As a preventive measure, this will save you cleaning time in the future, especially when it comes to porous surfaces, like brick and concrete, and painted surfaces that can be damaged by graffiti-removing chemicals. Among the best coatings are the aliphatic urethanes, which do not yellow and resist abrasion and the paint solvents used to remove paint. There are other coatings, like acrylics and epoxies, but acrylics dissolve when paint solvents are applied to graffiti and epoxies tend to yellow and discolor.

In a pinch: "If you can find the paint that matches, painting over graffiti is generally the cheapest and easiest way to deal with it," Quill says.

Caution: Always wear rubber gloves and long sleeves when working with paint-removing chemicals. If you'll be scrubbing the chemicals with a brush—or if you're sandblasting or using a pressure steamer—wear protective goggles. Do not inhale the fumes of toxic chemicals. Always read product labels for proper use and safety instructions.

Grass Stains

 EMERGENCY ACTION
Blot with rubbing alcohol. If the colors might bleed, dilute the alcohol with two parts water.

Grass is a tough stain, one that is especially common on the knees of children's jeans. But it's not unbeatable, especially if it is fresh.

Technique: Using a clean white towel or cotton ball, blot with rubbing alcohol, then rinse thoroughly. To find out if the color might bleed, first use the clean white towel with alcohol to blot an inconspicuous corner of the stained garment. If the color of the fabric comes off onto the white towel, or if the fabric is acetate, dilute the alcohol with two parts water. If alcohol does not work, try a color-safe liquid household bleach. If that doesn't work, try a chlorine bleach, but only if your garment is bleachable.

"Bleach will take it out, without question," says Ann Lemley, Ph.D., chairman of the department of textiles and apparel at Cornell University in Ithaca, New York. If it is washable, follow up by washing with regular laundry detergent and the hottest water safe for the fabric.

Caution: Always rinse out one cleaning solution before trying another. Mixing chemicals, especially ammonia and chlorine bleach, can create noxious fumes. Always read product labels for proper use and safety instructions.

Gravy

 EMERGENCY ACTION
Rinse or blot away gravy with cold water.

Relax. You may have really embarrassed yourself at the dinner table, but a gravy stain looks worse than it actually is. "Even though gravy usually contains some grease, which can be tough to get out, it is still categorized as a protein stain," says Jane Rising, instructor in the education department at the International Fabricare Institute in Silver Spring, Maryland. That means for washable fabrics, simple water-based solutions should do the trick.

Technique: Scrape away any excess gravy. If the item is washable, soak it first in cold water to remove as much of the stain as possible. The older the stain, the longer you should soak it—up to several hours. Start with a solution of ¼ teaspoon clear liquid dishwashing detergent, several drops of ammonia, and ½ cup warm water. Apply it directly to the fabric, then lay the garment on a hard surface and pat the stain lightly with the back of a spoon. This allows the solution to get in between the fibers, where the stains hide. Don't rub the material together; that will abrade the fibers. Next, wash as directed either by machine or by hand in the hottest water safe for the fabric. If the stain does not come out completely, follow the same pretreatment procedure, but with a liquid clothes detergent containing enzymes (or a paste made from a granular detergent and water). The enzymes eat away at protein-based substances like gravy. Apply it directly to the stain, pat, then wash.

For fabrics that cannot be washed, either have them professionally dry-cleaned or blot with a clean white towel and a spot remover, like Carbona Stain Devils or K2r, available at supermarkets, hardware stores, or discount department stores. Read the labels before using these products, and use them in a well-ventilated area while wearing protective rubber or latex gloves. Blot from the inside of the garment to push the stain out.

For carpets and rugs, first blot with a white towel and a spot remover. If that doesn't work, try blotting with a solution of ¼ cup clear liquid dishwashing detergent and 1 cup lukewarm water. Then rinse by blotting with a clean towel and water; blot dry with a fresh towel. Do not blot with laundry detergent because it often contains optical brighteners that can bleach carpet and rug dyes. Instead, if the two solutions don't work, try blotting with a solution of 2 tablespoons ammonia and 1 cup water. Again, rinse by blotting and dry.

In a pinch: In the case of washable clothing, skip to step two: Apply an enzyme detergent directly onto the stain, then wash.

Caution: Always thoroughly rinse out one cleaning solution before trying another. Mixing chemicals, especially ammonia and chlorine bleach, can create noxious fumes. Always read product labels for proper use and safety instructions. Before using cleaning solutions, always test them on an inconspicuous section of the stained item.

Grease Stains

EMERGENCY ACTION
Remove excess grease with a paper towel, being careful not to spread it. Next, blot with a paper towel dabbed with an acetone-based nail polish remover. Do not, however, use it on acetate. It will dissolve the fabric.

Petroleum-based products act as soil magnets. So petroleum jelly, hand lotion, and engine grease and such can ruin clothing and carpets if left untreated. Your goal here is to remove these stains—and to do it as soon as possible.

Technique: The best substance for removing greasy stains is spot remover. Either have the fabric professionally dry-cleaned or clean it yourself with a spot remover, like Carbona Stain Devils or K2r, available at supermarkets, hardware stores, or discount department stores. Read the labels before using these products, and use them in a well-ventilated area while wearing protective rubber or latex gloves. Lay the stain facedown on a soft absorbent cloth. Apply the spot remover to another clean white cloth, and then blot from the inside of the garment to push the stain out. As the spot remover dissolves the grease, the cloth beneath catches it. For carpets, always apply the spot remover to the towel, never directly onto the carpet. Otherwise, it can soak into the carpet backing or pad and attract more dirt.

In a pinch: If you don't have any spot remover in the house, use an acetone-based nail polish remover. Don't use it on acetate fabric. "It dissolves acetate," says Rajiv Jain, laboratory manager for the Association of Specialists in Cleaning and Restoration in Millersville, Maryland. "The stain will be gone, but so will the fabric."

Caution: Before using cleaning solutions, always test them on an inconspicuous section of the stained item.

Grout

Unlike the smooth steel fixtures and tile you find elsewhere in the bathroom, grout is rough and porous, a sticking place for soap scum and dirt. Remove this layer of grime before it becomes a permanent resident.

Technique: Clean grout regularly, using a gel or foaming bathroom cleaner, like Comet Bathroom Cleaner, and a long-bristle vegetable brush. Do not use abrasive cleaners or scrubbers. Even nylon or short-bristle brushes can wear down the grout over time. Spray on the cleaning compound, let it sit for a few seconds while the cleaning agents work on the scum, and then scrub it off. Clean hard-to-reach cracks and crevices with a soft toothbrush. Rinse by wiping everything down with a clean wet sponge or cloth.

"Always let the cleaning agent do your work," says Jim Brewer, executive housekeeper at the University of Texas at Arlington and a technical advisor to *Cleaning and Maintenance Magazine.* "If it takes to much handwork, it's the wrong product because it's not breaking down the dirt. Too much scrubbing tends to rub dirt into pores." Instead of scrubbing harder, for heavy soil, repeat the application.

Speed tips: Clean grout soon after you shower, while the grout is still moist.

Caution: Be careful about using ammonia or ammonia-based products when cleaning grout because many bathroom cleaning products contain chlorine. When combined, these two chemicals create a potentially fatal gas. Always read product labels for proper use and safety instructions.

Gum

Chewing gum is fine in its proper place—your mouth—but once you spit it out, it has a nasty habit of sticking around. Here's how to get it out of most textiles, including loose-fiber carpets and rugs.

Technique: Heat the gum with a blow-dryer set on "high" for 30 to 90 seconds, being careful not to bring the heat closer than six inches to the synthetic fibers. It is possible to melt some carpet fibers with high temperatures. Remove as much of the warm, softened gum as possible by picking at it with small squares of plastic film, cut from a sandwich baggie or other bag. (The gum sticks to the plastic and not your fingers.) Reheat the gum and pick at it with fresh squares of plastic several times to get most of it off. Then rub about ½ teaspoon of extra-strength deep-heating muscle rub, like Ben-Gay, into the remaining gum.

"Between the heat and the sliminess of the Ben-Gay, or equivalent rub, you're breaking the actual bonds between the gum and the fabric," says Claudia Ramirez, former executive vice president of the Association of Specialists in Cleaning and Restoration in Millers-ville, Maryland.

Again, heat it for 30 to 90 seconds and pick at it with a fresh plastic square. Next, blot the area with a solution of 1 teaspoon mild liquid dishwashing detergent in 1 cup warm water. Blot the area with a clean dry white toweling; then blot with water and repeat with a dry towel. Allow the fabric to dry. If a slight stickiness remains, carefully reheat the area with the blow-dryer and remove the last gum traces with a plastic square.

In a pinch: A quicker, if less thorough, way to remove chewing gum stuck in carpet, fabric, or other materials is to freeze it with an ice cube, then crack it off once it is brittle.

Caution: Before using cleaning solutions, always test them on an inconspicuous section of the stained item.

Gutters and Downspouts

Want to know if your gutters need cleaning? Look for discoloration on the lip of the gutter, says Bob Hanbury, a remodeler and the former host of *House Calls*, a home-repair call-in radio show in Newington, Connecticut. "That means that they're clogged and water is spilling over the side." Unfortunately, it also means that you're in for a big dirty job. Naturally, you'd be better off preventing such gutter backups by cleaning regularly. So spend a little time in the gutter now and then.

Technique: Clean your gutters at least twice a year—once in the spring and once in the fall. "In the spring, you have flowers and pollen falling off the trees, and in the fall, dead leaves," Hanbury says. Depending on how heavily wooded your yard is, you might have to clean them more often, especially in the fall.

Check your gutters by climbing up on a ladder. If the gutters have backed up, the best way to clean them out is to reach in and scoop up the sticks and leaves with your hands. Wear work gloves to protect your hands from sharp objects. Hose the gutters out once you have removed the gunk.

Also, shoot the hose down the downspout to clear it of sticks and leaves. If it clogs, try using a hose bladder, also available at hardware stores. Attach it to the end of the hose and insert the bladder as far into the clogged downspout as possible. As it fills with water, the bladder expands several inches. It then opens to emit a powerful stream that helps dislodge the debris. If this doesn't work and you just can't unclog the downspout, you might have to remove the downspout from the side of the house and work on the shorter sections on the ground. Or, call a plumber. He can use his drain snake to unclog it.

Speed tips: Consider using gutter guards or hoods. Quality hoods prevent debris from jamming the gutter. "Cheap, or poorly installed guards, however, can actually lead to quicker clogging," says Hanbury. In no time, leaves can cover mesh screens that simply lie flat over the gutters. Shop wisely and use common sense.

Caution: Be careful getting to the gutters. "Know how to use a ladder properly," Hanbury says. Stabilize it on the ground. Attach it to the gutter so that you won't fall backward and the wind won't blow the ladder over. If your roof is pitched, don't try to clean the gutters while standing on the roof above them.

Hammocks

Hammocks, especially those kept outdoors, collect airborne dust and harbor mildew when they are moist. Keeping your hammock clean prolongs its life and prevents you from getting dirty when you decide to kick back in it for a nap.

Technique: Lay your hammock on a nonabrasive surface, like a tarp. Hose it down and then scrub it using a soft-bristle brush or cloth and a bucket of warm soapy water. A mild liquid dishwashing detergent works best; use a squirt or two. Hose the soap off, turn the hammock over, and repeat the process. Again, hose it down. Never use any type of bleach. Bleach can deteriorate the hammock's fibers.

Next, hang it in the sun to dry. "The rot gets in when it stays wet," says Douglas Orians, vice president of sales and marketing for the Pawleys Island Hammock, manufactured by the Hammock Source, Pawleys Island, South Carolina, whose knotless, spreader-bar hammock design was developed more than 100 years ago by a South Carolina riverboat captain. "A white hammock hung outdoors will never be perfectly white again," he admits. "But the sun will help to bleach it naturally."

Speed tips: When you first buy your hammock, spray it with two light coats of a commercial water-repellent compound, like Scotchgard Heavy-Duty Water Repellent. That will protect the fibers and make cleaning easier.

Handbags

Like luggage, handbags can take a lot of abuse. Unlike luggage, however, they are often made of leather, which is hard to clean without damaging.

Technique: If your handbag is not made of leather, chances are that it is fabric or some type of synthetic material, like vinyl or nylon, which can usually be cleaned with a little water. Never get your bag too wet. Instead, spot-clean by blotting with a damp cloth. For stubborn stains, blot with a sudsy cloth, and then rinse well with a damp cloth.

Most handbags, however, are made of some form of leather, be it full-grained or patent leather, suede, or an exotic skin. Unfortunately, there's not a lot that you can do to clean leather. Try using a commercial leather-cleaning product like Lexol pH, available at leather and shoe repair shops. Wipe the cleaner off with a damp cloth and then apply a conditioner such as Lexol Conditioner. If the leather is light tan, test the conditioner on a small inconspicuous area for color.

For patent leather, use regular Pledge, says Henry Goldsmith, associate professor in the accessories design department at the Fashion Institute of Technology in New York City. Spray it on and wipe with a clean white cloth. Do not use Lemon Pledge. It leaves a film, Goldsmith says.

Polish alligator bags with a paste car wax, such as Simoniz. Apply it lightly with your fingers, and then buff it with a clean white cloth. "I used to make alligator bags that retailed for $3,000 to $6,000," says Goldsmith, a former handbag manufacturer. "A good simonizing paste really protects the bag and makes it shine."

How you clean the inside also depends on what it's made of. Most interiors are safe to wipe down with a lightly dampened sponge or cloth. Either open the bag as far as it will open or carefully pull the liner inside out. Do not use water if the liner is made of silk. Instead, simply shake out any dust and debris and wipe the liner with a dry cloth.

If you spill a potential stain-causing substance on your leather bag, the first thing you should do is blot it up with a clean white towel.

If it's a greasy stain, lay the bag out flat, sprinkle cornstarch on the stain, and let it stand overnight. It might absorb some of the oil. Another method is to place a clean white piece of tissue paper on the greasy spot and run a warm iron over it. Put the iron on the lowest heat setting for cotton. Replace the tissue several times with new tissue until there are no more traces of the stain on the tissue. "Leather is porous," Goldsmith says. "This technique will pull some of the stain out but not all. And it will remove wrinkles."

For a stain on suede, blot what you can and let the remainder dry for a couple of days. Try to restore the nap by rubbing very gently with a brass brush for suede, or fine sandpaper. By bringing back the nap, you might eliminate the stain.

For leather discoloration, look for a commercial leather spray, like Nu-Life. "It's like spray paint for leather," says Goldsmith. It comes in a variety of colors. Choose the one that best matches the original color of your bag, and then follow the manufacturer's instructions. For suede, mask stains and other discoloration by rubbing lightly with colored chalk that matches the original color of the suede.

For stubborn stains, take your bag to a professional leather cleaner. But choose wisely. Most leather cleaning today is done by wholesalers who pick up from cleaners. If you use a dry cleaner, make sure that it sends leather goods out to a leather specialist. Some dry cleaners try to clean the leather themselves—to avoid paying a wholesaler—and they could end up damaging it. For a professional leather cleaner referral in your area, contact the Leather Apparel Association, 19 West 21st Street, Suite 403, New York, NY 10010.

Caution: Always test your cleaning solution or method on an inconspicuous part of the handbag.

Hard-Water Deposits

Hard water contains minerals—namely, calcium and magnesium—that build up over time on sinks and fixtures. Unless you're interested in growing your own personal stalagmites, stay on top of this. The longer you allow these deposits to stand, the harder they are to remove.

Technique: Dissolve hard-water deposits on metal or porcelain enamel with a solution of 1 cup white vinegar per quart of water. Apply the solution with a sponge or soft cloth, and then rinse thoroughly with water, says Kay Weirick, director of housekeeping services at Bally's Las Vegas Hotel and a member of the technical advisory committee for *Executive Housekeeping Today* magazine. Or you can use a commercial preparation, such as Lime-a-Way or Lime Buster, available at some hardware stores, supermarkets, and discount department stores. Read the label because it may not be appropriate on some metals. Follow the product label carefully for proper use and safety precautions.

Speed tips: Repair leaky faucets and clean sink and tub basins regularly to avoid stubborn hard-water buildup. A little prevention can save you time and effort in the long run.

Hats—Felt, Leather, Straw

Dust is your hat's primary enemy in terms of appearance. It can turn to mud if a drop of water hits it. "Any time a hat gets wet, you have possible stain problems," says Scott Bengel, plant manager at Hatco, in Garland, Texas, the makers of Stetson and Resistol hats, and a division of Arena Brands.

Technique: Dust hats regularly using a clothes or hat brush. It must be soft-bristle; otherwise, it might scratch the surface. When dusting felt or suede hats, always brush with the nap, not against it.

If something stains your hat, first blot up as much of the substance as possible using a dry cloth. Never use water to clean a fine felt, leather, or straw hat. There are commercial hat stain removers, either spray-on foams or sprinkle-on powders. Both work by absorbing the stain. Ask for them at hat or western retail stores.

For problem stains, you may need the service of a professional hat cleaner. If you can't find a hat cleaner, try a shoe repair shop. Cobblers sometimes clean hats.

In a pinch: If you stain a felt hat, blot as much of the substance as possible using a clean dry towel. Let the stain dry. "Once it's dry," says Bengel, "you can try to cover it up." Gently work colored chalk into the stain to try to match it. If it's too light, use a bit of graphite pencil to mix in with the chalk. "You want to come up with a color that blends the stain into the color hat you have," he says.

High Chairs

As with other items that come into contact with food—and high chairs most certainly do—you want to wipe up spills as soon as possible to keep the food from sticking. Keeping high chairs clean helps prevent the growth of bacteria, a potential health threat to your child.

Technique: Clean the high chair with a sudsy sponge or cloth immediately after your child has eaten. Use a liquid dishwashing detergent, preferably one containing antibacterial agents.

Lay a wet cloth over stuck-on food for a few minutes, and then wipe it off once it has loosened. Rinse by wiping down with a clean moist sponge.

Periodically follow the regular cleaning by sanitizing the high chair tray and any other areas that come into contact with food and child. Wipe them down with a fresh 10-to-1 solution of water and chlorine bleach. Let the solution sit for a minute or two, and then rinse it off by wiping with a clean moist sponge, suggest infection-control specialists.

Also, periodically clean any seat padding or covers. Just wipe down vinyl padding. If the padding is covered in a washable fabric, consult the care label for washing instructions.

Once or twice a year, take your high chair outside, hose it off, and give it a good scrubbing with a bucket of sudsy water and a soft nylon brush. Rinse it with the hose, and let it dry in the sun. Or put it in the shower to scrub and rinse off. Let it air-dry.

Speed tips: When it's humid outside, put the high chair in a shaded area on a porch or in the yard and let it sit for a few hours. The moisture will loosen stuck-on food and make wiping it off easier.

Hot Tubs

Above all, keep your hot tub sanitized. "If you don't sanitize the water, bacteria can grow in the tub," says Jeff Kurth, director of the Spa Council for the National Pool and Spa Institute, headquartered in Washington, D.C., and chief executive officer of Marquis Spas, in Independence, Oregon. "Pseudomonas, bacteria that cause a skin rash, are common in hot tubs that aren't cleaned properly."

Technique: One of the most important hot tub cleaning duties is treating the water with chemicals, like chlorine and bromine. When deciding quantity of chemicals and how often to use them, follow the manufacturer's instructions for your particular hot tub.

Clean the filter on a regular basis. "Hair, fibers, body oils, and other soils get trapped in there and cut down the rate at which the water flows through the filter," says Kurth, "which can starve the pumps and lead to bacterial contamination." Most portable hot tubs feature cartridge filters made of nonwoven polyester, Dacron, or treated paper. Clean these once a week by spraying them with a garden hose, and replace them once a year.

For sand and diatomaceous earth (DE) filters, typically found on larger more permanent hot tubs, you should reverse the water pump on the hot tub once every week or two to agitate the filter bed and remove debris. Follow your hot tub manual for more specific instructions on exactly how often to backwash these filters as well as when to replace the sand or earth.

Drain the hot tub at least three or four times a year—once a month if you're using it heavily. Most tubs are made of cast acrylic, which is easy to clean. Wipe the shell down using a soft cloth or sponge and a solution of warm water and mild detergent, like liquid dishwashing detergent. Do not use abrasive cleaners or scouring pads. Rinse detergent before refilling.

Humidifiers and Vaporizers

Ignore your humidifier, and bacteria, mold, and fungi will thank you. They just love to be left alone in a moist environment like that, says Bill Staples, director of consumer sales at Emerson Air Comfort Products in Hazelwood, Missouri. Regular cleaning will retard such growth. Cleaning humidifiers and vaporizers also removes mineral deposits left by hard water, and that will extend the life of your appliances.

Technique: If you use a portable humidifier with a one- or two-gallon tank, empty the tank every day and refill it with fresh tap water. For larger portable humidifiers, change the water as recommended by the manufacturer.

At least once a week clean all surfaces that come into contact with water, using 1 cup undiluted vinegar, Staples suggests, or follow your machine's instructions. Use a nylon or vegetable brush to loosen deposits and a wire pipe cleaner to clean the intake tube. Let it sit for about 20 minutes. Rinse with warm clean water. Be sure to follow your manufacturer's instructions.

To disinfect the humidifier, use 1 teaspoon chlorine bleach in 1 gallon water and wet all surfaces. Allow the solution to sit for 20 minutes, sloshing the liquid around every few minutes. Rinse with water until the bleach smell is gone. Follow the manufacturer's instructions for how often you should disinfect the unit. At the end of the season, follow the cleaning and disinfecting instructions and make sure that your machine is dry before you put it away.

Consider using a bacteriostat or bacteriocide in evaporative humidifiers. These products, sold at home supply stores along with the humidifiers themselves, help prevent bacteria from growing inside water that sits in the machine. Most are liquids that you add straight to the water, making them easy to use. They also control odors caused by mold and mildew. "Sometimes," Staples says, "people don't know that there's anything wrong with their units until they smell a musty odor."

Follow the same routine for cleaning vaporizers. Also, periodically disassemble the heating element, following the manufacturer's instructions, and wipe clean the heating element. To clean mineral deposits off the heating element, soak it for several hours in a container of undiluted white vinegar. Be sure not to wet the wire or electrical connection points. Use an old toothbrush to scrub off deposits. Rinse and dry the heating unit well, and reassemble it.

If you have a central humidifier attached to your heating or cooling system, be sure to clean the filter and the evaporator tray. Begin by reading the manufacturer's cleaning instructions.

In general, however, to clean the filter, first shut off power to the heating or cooling system and turn off the humidifier's water supply. Remove the cover and lift out the filter drum. Take the filter pad off its frame and soak it in a solution of 2 quarts white vinegar per gallon of water for several hours. This should remove any waterborne mineral deposits. Rinse it thoroughly with water, and wring it until it is almost dry.

Remove the evaporator tray and soak it in the vinegar solution for a few hours. Wipe off any deposits with a cloth soaked in the solution. Rinse the tray thoroughly, and then wipe it dry with a clean cloth. When you reassemble the humidifier, turn on the water supply before turning on the power.

Speed tips: "You can wash some parts of the small tabletop units in the dishwasher if the instructions state that it's okay to do so," Staples says. Do not wash fan motors or other electrical parts. To make sure that the plastic basin and other plastic parts don't melt, put them on the top rack, away from the heating element.

Caution: To avoid possible shock, be sure to unplug the humidifier before cleaning. Wear rubber gloves when cleaning with the bleach solution.

Ice Equipment

Cleaning your ice-making equipment is a matter of taste—literally. Many ice-makers themselves do not require cleaning, says Martha Reek, a senior home economist with the Whirlpool Corporation in Evansville, Indiana. However, free-standing ice-makers need regular cleaning. It's important to follow the manufacturer's directions carefully no matter what type of ice-maker you have. In every case, what does need cleaning is the pan that collects the ice and even the ice itself. Even if your freezer is empty, ice that sits too long in the ice bucket can take on the flavors of food in your fridge—onion and garlic, for instance—because cold air circulates through both compartments. "Fresh ice just tastes better," says Reek.

Technique: Purge ice regularly if you do not use it up. "If your ice begins to take on funky shapes, that means it has been in there way too long and you need to throw it away," Reek explains.

Every six months or so, remove the pan that holds the cubes and wash it in the kitchen sink with warm soapy water. Dry it thoroughly, and then put it back in the freezer. Do the same with ice cube trays. Empty, wash, and dry them; refill them with freshwater; and return them to the freezer.

Tip: If you need a quantity of ice for a picnic or a party, save it in a sealable plastic bag to keep odors out.

Ink

EMERGENCY ACTION
Blot with rubbing alcohol. If the colors might bleed, dilute the alcohol with two parts water. To test for colorfastness, dab a drop or two of alcohol on the inside of a seam or hem, using a cotton swab.

This is one of the toughest stains to remove. Sometimes all you can hope for, especially in the case of felt-tip pen ink, is minimizing the spot.

Technique: For ballpoint pen ink, blot with a cotton ball or white cotton cloth soaked with rubbing alcohol. If colors might bleed or the fabric is acetate, dilute the alcohol with two parts water.

If it is a washable garment, rinse out the alcohol with cold water, then wash in the hottest water safe for the fabric. If it is a carpet or rug, blot clean with a white towel and water.

If that doesn't work, try blotting with a solution of ½ cup warm water, ¼ teaspoon liquid dishwashing detergent, and several drops of ammonia. Finally, after rinsing the ammonia completely, try a 10-to-1 solution of water and chlorine bleach, but only on fabrics that are white or colorfast. (Reminder: Ammonia and chlorine react to create noxious fumes, so make sure that all the ammonia is rinsed out of the fabric before trying the bleach solution.) If the stain remains, try a 4-to-1 solution. "There's a certain point at which you must decide what's worse—a permanently stained garment or a bleached garment," says Ann Lemley, Ph.D., chairman of the department of textiles and apparel at Cornell University in Ithaca, New York. "Sometimes you have to make those choices."

For felt-tip pen stains, blot with an all-purpose cleaner, like Fantastik. Rinse with cold water or, in the case of carpets, blot with a wet towel. Repeat until as much of the stain disappears as possible.

Note: Before using cleaning solutions, always test them on an inconspicuous section of the stained item.

Caution: Always rinse out one cleaning solution before trying another. Mixing chemicals, especially ammonia and chlorine bleach, can create noxious fumes.

Iron—Wrought

Wrought iron is a commercial form of the metal that's both tough and malleable. It does have an Achilles' heel, though: rust.

Technique: If you simply need to remove soil or bird droppings, wipe your iron with a damp cloth or scrub with a nylon brush and wipe it dry.

To remove rust, use a wire brush or medium sandpaper. Then scour it with a fine-grade steel wool, like #00 grade. "The steel wool will remove a very thin layer of iron and make it look like new," says Rajiv Jain, laboratory manager for the Association of Specialists in Cleaning and Restoration in Millersville, Maryland.

To protect your wrought iron from future rust, treat it with a rust-prohibitor, available at hardware stores.

In a pinch: For light rust on wrought iron, rub with silver polish.

Irons

If the surface of your clothes iron is dirty, you risk staining your clothes permanently since heat seals in stains.

Technique: Always keep your iron dry between uses. This will help you avoid rust, which can ruin clothing. Empty your iron while it's hot. That way, the heat will dry out the cavity. Then, before putting it away, allow the iron to cool.

To remove melted plastic and fabrics, heat at a low setting until the material softens, unplug the iron, and scrape off with a piece of wood, like a wooden spatula or half a clothespin. "Don't use anything made out of metal, because that can scratch the surface," says Cindy Hupert, a product manager at Sunbeam, a manufacturer of irons in Delray Beach, Florida. To remove any remaining residue, let the iron cool and then rub the surface with a paste of baking soda and water. Clean the paste off with a moist cloth.

If your iron is coated with a nonstick soleplate, rub it gently with a nylon mesh pad and suds.

For taking off melted polyester, rub with a cotton ball dabbed in acetone or nail polish remover.

If mineral buildup from the water supply clogs your steam iron, poke the spray nozzle hole with a fine needle. To clean mineral deposits from the steam vents on the bottom of the iron, fill the iron with a solution of one part white vinegar and three parts cool water. Set it on the hottest steam setting, and place it on a flat wire rack (such as a cooling rack for baking) over a heat- and moisture-resistant surface. Stay with the iron while it's hot. Let the iron steam until it is empty. If your iron shuts off automatically after 30 seconds when motionless in the down position, you may have to move it periodically until it's empty. To avoid further mineral buildup in steam irons, use only distilled water.

If lint clogs the steam vents, try steaming it free. Fill the iron with water and let it steam until it is empty, as explained above. Remember, never leave a hot iron unattended.

Speed tips: To quickly remove melted-on plastics or other substances, heat your iron on a low setting until the material softens, and then iron over an old cloth or some other piece of throwaway fabric. "The residue will transfer from the surface of the iron to the surface of the cloth," says Hupert.

Caution: If you are using acetone or nail polish remover to remove melted polyester from your iron's surface, do not get it on the iron's plastic parts. It can eat them away.

Jewelry

"Once mined and worn, gems are exposed to hardships and chemicals they never experienced underground," writes Fred Ward, a gem expert in Bethesda, Maryland, in his book *Gem Care*. Body oils, airborne pollutants, soap scum, and other substances dull the luster of jewelry and can cause permanent damage to what are some of our most valuable possessions.

Technique: Do not overclean. Most jewelry does not need cleaning after each use. The exceptions are softer gems, like turquoise, amber, and especially pearls, all of which should be wiped down with a chamois cloth after each use. Because these gems are porous, substances like perspiration, perfume, cosmetics, and hair spray can stain them. For this reason, always apply makeup, perfume, and hair spray before putting on pearls and other soft gemstones, and try to wear them against clothing and not your skin. Their porous quality also means that certain cleaning fluids can stain them. Every once in a while, wash pearls and other soft gems in lukewarm water and soap, creating very light suds with a white bar soap and gently cleaning the gems with a soft cloth. Anything harder, like a toothbrush, could scratch them. Do not let the gems soak. Rinse them in clean water and dry with a chamois cloth.

Crystalline gems, like diamonds, rubies, garnets, and emeralds, do not absorb moisture and should be cleaned periodically to enhance their luster. "While cleaning them, the only thing you need to be concerned with is that you use something softer than they are to rub with so that you don't scratch them," says Ward. Clean them several times a year, depending on how often you wear them. For all crystalline gems, except diamonds, the safest combination is warm soapy water and a soft toothbrush. Rinse them to remove the soap, and then let them air-dry. "Diamonds are magnets for soap and grease, which make them look dull," Ward explains. Clean diamonds in a one-to-one solution of lukewarm water and an all-purpose cleaner such as Mr. Clean, using a soft toothbrush. Or place your diamonds in a shot glass of straight vodka for a half-hour, brush with a soft brush, and rinse under running water. Make sure that there are no absorbent gems, like pearls, on the piece of diamond jewelry you plan to clean in this solution. If there are, simply use warm water.

Ultrasonic cleaners, which loosen debris by vibrating at thousands of pulses per second, work safely on diamonds and a few other gems. But soft stones, like amber and pearls, can crack in ultrasonic cleaners. Ask your jeweler before using this method.

How Hard Can It Be?

Hardness of minerals is measured using the Mohs scale, developed in the nineteenth century by a German named Friedrich Mohs. Diamonds, the hardest substance known to man, rate 10. Talc, at the opposite end of the scale, rates 1.

Because substances of higher Mohs ratings can scratch those of lower ratings, knowing the hardness of gemstones and precious metals is important in deciding how to clean jewelry. For example, some people, including jewelers, recommend using toothpaste to clean gold. "But certain toothpastes have sand in them," says gem expert Fred Ward of Bethesda, Maryland, author of the *National Geographic*'s gem series for 14 years and author of *Gem Care*, "giving them a hardness close to quartz. They can damage softer gemstones and sandpaper gold, silver, and platinum to a matte finish."

Here's a list of how some common substances rate in the Mohs scale.

Substance	Hardness
Talc	1
Amber	2–2.5
Silver	2.5
Gold	2.5–3
Pearl	2.5–4.5
Coral	3–4
Malachite	3.5–4
Platinum	4–4.33
Glass	5–6
Turquoise	5–6
Opal	5.5
Rhodonite	5.5–6.5
Nephrite jade	6–6.5
Tanzanite	6–7
Zircon	6–7.5
Jadeite	6.5–7
Peridot	6.5–7
Quartz (includes amethyst and citrine)	7
Garnet	7–7.5
Tourmaline	7–7.5
Aquamarine	7.5–8
Emerald	7.5–8
Topaz	8
Ruby	9
Sapphire	9
Diamond	10

In a pinch: Simply wipe jewelry with a soft moist cloth to remove body oils, makeup, and dust.

Caution: Do not use ultrasonic cleaners to clean emeralds. Even though they are hard crystalline gems, they can crack when exposed to ultrasonic vibrations.

Juice Stains

A stain that comes from a plant—whether it's from juice or anything else—is called a tannin stain, says Jane Rising, instructor in the education department at the International Fabricare Institute in Silver Spring, Maryland. That includes grape, prune, tomato, citrus, and other types of juice. Tannin stains are easier to remove from some fabrics than other fabrics. "When you're dealing with polyester," she says, "a juice stain can look horrible, but it will probably come out easily." Cotton can be more difficult. While some juices, like grape juice, stain worse than others, attack them all the same way.

Technique: If it's a washable fabric, begin by blotting with a clean white towel and warm water. Continue until you don't see any more of the juice coming out on the blotting towel.

Next, pretreat the stain before washing the item. Begin by mixing ¼ teaspoon clear liquid dishwashing detergent with ½ cup warm water. Apply it directly to the fabric, and then lay the garment on a hard surface and pat the stain lightly with the back of a spoon. This allows the solution to get in between the fibers, where stains hide. Don't rub the fabric together; that will abrade the fibers. Next, wash as directed either by machine or by hand in the hottest water safe for the fabric.

If the stain does not come out completely, follow the same pretreatment procedure but, this time, with a solution of 1 tablespoon vinegar and ½ cup warm water. Again, wash as directed.

For fabrics that cannot be washed, either have them professionally dry-cleaned or blot them with a clean white towel and a spot remover, like Carbona Stain Devils or K2r, available at supermarkets, hardware stores, or discount department stores. Blot from the inside of the garment to push the stain out. Use aerosol spot removers in a well-ventilated area while wearing protective rubber or latex gloves. Follow all product labels carefully for proper use and safety precautions.

For carpets and rugs, first blot with a clean white towel and water. Next, blot with a white towel dipped in the liquid dishwashing solution. Then rinse by blotting with a clean towel and water. If the first solution doesn't work, blot with the vinegar solution. Do not blot with laundry detergent because it often contains optical brighteners that can bleach carpet and rug dyes.

As a last-ditch effort, try blotting with hydrogen peroxide. But be careful: It will cause color dyes to bleed and fade.

Caution: Always rinse out one cleaning solution before trying another. Mixing chemicals, especially ammonia and chlorine bleach, can create noxious fumes. Read and follow label instructions carefully for proper use and safety precautions. Before using cleaning solutions, always test them on an inconspicuous section of the stained item.

Ketchup Stains

Ketchup is one of our most popular condiments. Unfortunately, the stain it leaves is also one of the toughest to remove.

Technique: Scrape away any excess ketchup. For washables, first soak the stained item in cold water to remove as much of the ketchup as possible. The older the stain, the longer you should soak it—up to several hours.

Then pretreat it before washing it. Begin by mixing ¼ teaspoon clear liquid dishwashing detergent with ½ cup cold water. Apply it directly to the fabric, and then lay the garment on a hard surface and pat the stain lightly with the back of a spoon. This allows the solution to get in between the fibers, where stains hide. Don't rub the fabric together; that will abrade the fibers. Next, wash as directed either by machine or by hand in the hottest water safe for the fabric.

If the stain does not come out completely, follow the same pretreatment procedure but, this time, with a solution of 1 teaspoon ammonia and ½ cup cold water. Again, wash as directed. If that fails, try a liquid laundry detergent containing enzymes (or a paste made from a granular detergent and water). Apply it directly on the stain, pat, and then wash.

For fabrics that cannot be washed, either have them professionally dry-cleaned or blot with a clean white towel and a spot remover, like Carbona Stain Devils or K2r, available at supermarkets, hardware stores, or discount department stores. When you use these products, wear protective rubber or latex gloves and work in a well-ventilated location. Blot from the inside of the garment to push the stain out.

For carpets and rugs, act immediately. If the stain is fresh, you may be able to remove it by blotting the stain with plain water and paper towels. If not, then blot with a solution made from ¼ teaspoon liquid dishwashing detergent per 1 cup of lukewarm water (use a clean white towel). Then blot with a clean towel and water. If the first solution doesn't work, blot with an ammonia solution made from 2 tablespoons of ammonia per 1 cup lukewarm water. Do not blot with laundry detergent.

"If the stain just won't come out, try blotting with a 3 percent solution of hydrogen peroxide," says Rajiv Jain, laboratory manager for the Association of Specialists in Cleaning and Restoration in Millersville, Maryland. It is available at drugstores. But be careful: It might alter the dyes in the fabric or carpet.

Caution: Always remove one cleaning solution before trying another. Always read product labels for proper use and safety precautions. Before using cleaning solutions, always test them on an inconspicuous section of the stained item. Don't make the solutions any stronger than specified, and use them as sparingly as possible.

Kettles

These hefty pots, usually made of cast iron, were once as common as cooking lard was. Today, olive oil has replaced the animal fat, and fancy, lightweight alloys have replaced the cast iron. Still, some people are rediscovering the joys of cooking with kettles, especially with the increasingly popular Dutch ovens. In terms of cleaning, your main goal is avoiding rust by keeping the cast iron well-seasoned.

Technique: When at all possible, just wipe the surface clean with a dry paper towel. If that doesn't cut the mustard (or grease), use boiling water and a brush. If you need to scour the kettle, first use a plastic scouring pad. And if you have to, contrary to popular belief, you *can* scrub cast iron with soap and water and even scour it with steel wool to remove stuck-on food or rust. But you must reseason the surface after heavy cleaning. After washing, dry it, lightly coating with a no-stick spray like Pam, and wipe it with a clean paper towel to remove the excess grease. Never store your kettle with the lid on.

To season a small kettle—one that will fit inside your oven— begin by washing it with hot soapy water, rinse, and dry. Melt a

Cleaning Kettles the Old-Fashioned Way

Billie Hill recalls how her grandparents used to clean and season their large wash kettle. "Back then they only used pure lard to coat their pot. Cast iron rusts when it comes into contact with water. Since they were using the kettle to wash clothes, they put lard on the outside, too," says Hill, who is customer service manager at the Lodge Manufacturing Company in South Pittsburg, Tennessee, where she has worked for almost 50 years.

"Next, they would heat the kettle over a fire in the yard. Because their pot had only three short legs, they would stand the pot on flat stones or bricks over the fire. The pores of the iron would open up when heated and absorb the grease. Then, once the fire had died down, they would wipe the grease up onto the sides with an old mop. The lard on the outside charred the pot to a degree, but that just gave it a nice blackened look.

"Later, it would be ready to wash clothes in. They would boil water inside the pot, and then add the clothes and old-fashioned lye soap. The clothes didn't get greasy because the pot only had a thin coating. Plus, the soap took care of any excess grease.

"When she finished washing clothes, my grandmother would wipe the pot down with a greasy cloth, dry it, and wait for the next wash day."

dollop of solid shortening, like Crisco, in a pan on the stove. Remove from the heat and put a small cloth, about the size of a washcloth, into the melted shortening. Apply melted shortening to both the inside and outside of the kettle and the kettle lid.

Next move the bottom rack of your oven to the lowest slot and place a baking sheet wrapped in aluminum foil on it to catch the grease. Preheat your oven to 350°F. Put your kettle upside down on the rack above it. Heat for an hour. Turn the oven off and let the kettle cool completely.

"Cast iron works like a vacuum," explains Billie Hill, customer service manager for the Lodge Manufacturing Company, makers of cast-iron cookware for more than a century, in South Pittsburg, Tennessee. "When the pores get hot and open up, they suck up a minute amount of grease and no more." You will need to re-season it after cooking beans or acidic foods or if you had to scour with metal pads.

You can also season small kettles on gas or charcoal grills. "You get the grill heated up, put the pot in there, and let 'er cook," says Hill, who has worked at Lodge for almost 50 years. "It'll smoke and it'll smell, but it's outside so it doesn't matter."

Make sure that the kettle is upside down so that the grease will carbonize properly. Feed a charcoal grill with enough coals so that it cooks for an hour or more. The result is a well-seasoned kettle that is also blackened, the way kettles should be. Leave it on the grill until the coals die down and the kettle cools.

Speed tips: Clean a cast-iron kettle while it's still warm from cooking. Stuck-on food will be easier to remove then.

In a pinch: If your entire kettle does not need re-seasoning, simply wipe a little shortening on the inside and heat it upside down for 30 minutes in a 350°F oven.

Caution: To avoid oven fires, make sure that you catch all dripping grease with an aluminum foil–covered baking sheet. Never use liquid dishwashing detergents to wash cast iron.

Knickknacks

Knickknacks are for display, right? So naturally you want them dust-free and looking their best.

Technique: Knickknacks come in a variety of shapes and sizes and are made of many different materials. Most need only regular dusting.

"You can wipe the majority of things with a damp cloth," says Marry Keener, assistant director of facilities management at the University of Arizona in Tucson and a member of the technical advisory committee for *Executive Housekeeping Today* magazine. "These days, so many surfaces are protected with plastics, vinyls, and paint. Wood is protected with polyurethane."

Use a dry cloth for objects that cannot get wet—unfired pottery, for example, or something that has been hand-painted.

For soft-surface knickknacks, like small pillows and dolls, you also want to remove accumulated dust. They don't necessarily need to be washed; in fact, water can ruin many of these items. Instead, put them in the dryer and tumble for 5 to 10 minutes on the "Air-Fluff" setting, which uses only cool air. (Make sure that they contain no hard or breakable parts.) This will loosen the dust and transfer it from the item to the dryer's filter.

Speed tips: Put glazed pottery, glass, and similar items in the dishwasher and run it on the fine-china cycle. "I let the dishwasher do the work for me," Keener says. The fine-china cycle is typically more delicate and shorter than other cycles.

Labels—Removing Decals, Stickers

Removing that old sticker from the back of your car can be a pain in the bumper. The same goes for decals and such on windows, walls, and other surfaces. Your goal is to get rid of the decal and all of the dust-gathering adhesive without harming the surface on which it is stuck.

Technique: Warm ½ to 1 cup vinegar. Fold a pad of cloth large enough to cover the decal. Soak the fabric in the warm vinegar and apply it to the decal. Hold it there for a few minutes. Once the sticker is saturated, it should peel off easily, says Kay Weirick, director of housekeeping services at Bally's Las Vegas Hotel and a member of the technical advisory committee for *Executive Housekeeping Today* magazine.

Acetone, available in hardware stores, is the main ingredient in acetone nail polish remover and is good for removing old adhesive stains. Dab a cotton ball with acetone, and paint it over the decal. But avoid using acetone to remove decals stuck on painted surfaces. The acetone will remove the paint.

Speed tips: To help the vinegar soak in better, make slits in the decal with a blade—but only if that won't hurt the surface that it's on.

Attach the vinegar-soaked cloth to the decal using masking tape, and go about your business. Come back after a few minutes and the sticker should be saturated.

In a pinch: For removing labels from glass, metal, or some other surface that can withstand heat, first saturate the label as described and then briefly direct warm air from a blow-dryer set on medium toward the label. The label should peel off easily.

Caution: To make sure that your removal method will not damage the surface containing the label, test it on an inconspicuous area first.

Lace

Cleaning lace is no tea party. Lace is fragile because of its structure, and you don't want to damage it or distort its shape. Also, a lot of lace trim, like the glossy kind you see on wedding dresses, is made of rayon. When wet, rayon can lose up to 70 percent of its strength.

Technique: Begin by reading the care labels. If your lace is a dry-clean-only type, then do not wash it. Water could shrink the lace dramatically.

If your lace is washable, the best way to wash it is to soak the lace in warm water and a mild liquid dishwashing detergent, like Ivory Liquid or Palmolive. "Water is a wonderful solvent," says Jane Rising, instructor in the education department at the International Fabricare Institute in Silver Spring, Maryland. "A long soak will take out a lot of things." Avoid scrubbing or other aggressive tactics.

For machine washable lace, such as table linens, wash on a gentle cycle in a net bag or a pillowcase with the end tied. The bag will protect the lace by reducing the potential for snagging.

Dry lace by hanging it on a line out of direct sunlight or laying it on a clean white towel on a flat surface. The flatter you dry it, the easier it will be to press it. Tumbling lace in a dryer leaves it impossibly wrinkled.

"When you're ironing large lace items, use a table covered with a towel," advises Rising. "With an ironing board, you'll end up with puckers in between sections because you're never going to get it totally flat." Set your iron temperature based on the fiber content of the lace. To reduce stretching and distortion, gently move the iron in a circular motion, rather than the traditional back and forth.

Speed tips: "Sometimes with large lace items, it's better to have a professional clean it," Rising says. The large presses used by cleaners are best because they come straight down on the fabric. "It will save you time and hassle, and you'll probably be happier with the results."

Caution: Do not try to clean antique lace. Have a professional fine-textile cleaner do it—not your corner dry cleaner. Look for a specialty cleaner in the yellow pages. Wedding-dress cleaners are often familiar with lace and other fragile fabrics.

Lamps—Electric, Hurricane

Lamps, because they are illuminated, show grime more than most things. Keeping them clean not only improves their looks but also helps them shine brighter.

Technique: There are countless varieties of lamps, made from many different materials—porcelain, blown glass, wood. Cleaning methods will vary, depending on the material from which your lamps are made. Dust them regularly, using either a plain dust cloth or, for detailed designs, a soft-bristle brush.

For heavier cleaning, begin by unplugging the cord, removing the shade, and unscrewing any lightbulbs, says Kay Weirick, director of housekeeping services at Bally's Las Vegas Hotel and a member of the technical advisory committee for *Executive Housekeeping Today* magazine. Fill a kitchen sink with suds using warm water and liquid dishwashing detergent. Place the lamp on the counter next to the sink. Lay it on a towel so that it won't slip. If the base is washable, wipe it with the suds using a cloth or sponge, without getting the cord wet. Rinse the cloth or sponge and wipe away the suds. Dry the lamp with a clean cloth. If the lamp has a reflector bowl, wash and dry it by hand like you would a dish.

If the lamp is not washable, simply wipe it down with a cloth lightly dampened with plain water and dry it.

To wash the cord, wring most of the liquid from a sudsy sponge and fold it in half. Pull the cord between the two layers of the folded sponge, and then wipe it dry.

Clean the bulbs by wiping them with a damp sudsy sponge. Rinse by wiping with a clean sponge. Dry with a cloth. Do not let the metal neck get wet.

For hurricane lamps and other types with glass globes or chimneys, remove the globe and wash it in deep suds. Scrub inside the chimney using a bottle brush. Rinse the glass with hot water and wipe it dry. Wipe the lamp base with a wet sponge. If you'd like extra-sparkling glass, add a few drops of ammonia or vinegar to the rinse water.

Caution: Don't let the cord or socket of the lamp get wet.

Lamp Shades

Lamp shades can be tricky. For one thing, they show dirt because they are so well lit. They also come in many different—and often tough-to-clean—styles. One thing is for sure: If you dust them on a regular basis, dirt won't have as much of a chance to set and stain, and the shades will require deep cleaning less often.

Technique: Dust shades regularly with a clean soft cloth or with the brush attachment of a vacuum cleaner.

Clean shades that are laminated, coated in plastic, or made of parchment or fiberglass with "dry" suds. Put ¼ cup mild liquid dishwashing detergent into a bowl, and add just a little warm water. Whip the mixture with an egg beater to make suds that look like whipped cream, or cover the bowl and shake it a few times. With a cloth or sponge gently rub a little of the suds on the shade. Don't rub or moisten any glued-on bindings or frills. Rinse the shade immediately by wiping it with a clean damp cloth, and then wipe it dry, says Kay Weirick, director of housekeeping services at Bally's Las Vegas Hotel and a member of the technical advisory committee for *Executive Housekeeping Today* magazine.

For shades made of silk, rayon, or nylon, dip the entire shade into a tub or sink filled with mild lukewarm suds (liquid dishwashing detergent is best). Scrub gently, if necessary, with a cloth or sponge. Empty and refill the basin with clean lukewarm water. Dip the shade again to rinse. Repeat the rinse with clean water, if necessary. Tie a string to the middle of the frame, and hang it over the bathtub or from an outdoor clothesline to drip-dry. Do this right away to avoid rust on the metal frame, which could stain the material.

Caution: Do not wash linen, cotton, or hand-painted shades or shades with glued-on trim or other parts in water. Don't try to spot-clean a fabric shade. The flame-resistant solution on it will leave a yellow stain if it gets wet.

Laundry

In the United States, 35 billion loads of wash are done each year—1,000 new loads every second. Indeed, laundry is such a common chore that many people take it for granted. Yet there's more to washing clothes than just filling the machines, turning a dial, and pressing a button. A certain amount of preparation will help clothes get cleaner and last longer.

Follow these suggestions from the Soap and Detergent Association in New York City, and it'll all come out in the wash just fine.

Machine-Washing

By law, garment manufacturers are required to stitch care labels into garments sold in the United States. They are your best guide on how to care for your clothing. Always read the labels before washing. Don't overload the machine. Overloading can cause tangling and prevents clothes from circulating freely.

Is Your Water Hard or Soft?

Soft water makes cleaning easier. Hard water, however, contains minerals—primarily calcium and magnesium—that react with soap and form a curd. This curd leaves a white film on clothes, stiffens fabric, and builds up on the inside of the washing machine. That is why detergents, which react less with hard water, are used for laundry instead of soap. Even though detergents do not form a curd, they are not as effective in hard water as they are in soft water.

What are the signs of hard water? There are several: Soaps and shampoos do not lather well, there is a noticeable ring around your bathtub, fabrics feel stiff, or a white residue forms around faucets and drains. To determine the hardness, or mineral content, of your area's water, contact your water company or the nearest Cooperative Extension Service. You can find your local branch by looking in the government offices section of the phone book. Then, if your water is hard, add a commercial water softener or detergent booster, available at most supermarkets, when you wash clothes, or add slightly more detergent to the wash than the label recommends. According to the Soap and Detergent Association in New York City, here's how the different degrees of hardness are usually defined. The numbers indicate milligrams of minerals (usually calcium and magnesium) per liter:

Soft: 0 to 60
Moderately hard: 61 to 120
Hard: 121 to 180
Very hard: More than 180

A few tricks of the laundry trade can save you time and money. First, sort your clothing into washer loads that keep similar items together. To prevent lighter clothing from picking up bleeding colors, sort articles by color, keeping whites, darks, and medium colors together. Next, separate heavily soiled pieces from lightly soiled ones to avoid dirt transfer. Then separate delicate fabrics and loose knits from tougher fabrics, and separate items that produce a lot of lint such as chenille robes, new towels, or flannels. Finally, mix together large and small items and distribute them equally to balance the load while washing. A typical load might contain one or two twin sheets, a few pillowcases, two to four shirts and blouses, plus underwear and socks.

If you have a new brightly colored item that you think might bleed when washed, or if the label says "wash separately," wash it alone or with similar colors for the first few times.

Once your laundry is sorted, prepare it for washing by checking pockets. One pen, tube of lipstick, or stick of gum can ruin an entire load of clothes. Close zippers and other fastenings to prevent snagging, and tie strings and sashes to avoid tangling. Take off any nonwashable items such as belts, and treat stains.

Stain Removal

For stains, follow a few general rules before washing. First of all, deal with the stain right away; the longer you wait, the more a stain can soak in, making it harder to clean. Identify the source of the stain, then follow one of the recommended stain-removal methods in this book. Never rub a stain, which can spread it or damage fibers. Instead, blot patiently using a clean white towel. If you are using a stain-removing solution, pretest it on a hem or other out-of-the-way part of the fabric. After washing a stained item, check the stain before you put the garment in the dryer. "Stains get set by heat," says Ann Lemley, Ph.D., chairman of the department of textiles and apparel at Cornell University in Ithaca, New York. If the stain is still there, try again to remove it. If it won't come out, let the garment air-dry, rewash it, or try the dry cleaners—even for a piece of clothing you wouldn't ordinarily dry-clean. Be sure to tell the dry-cleaner attendant the stain-removal methods that you have already tried.

Detergents

Several factors determine how much detergent to use: load size, soil conditions, water volume in washer, and water hardness. Detergent box instructions are usually based on the following conditions: five to seven pounds of clothing, moderate soil, 17 gallons of water in a top-loading washer or 8 gallons in a front-loader and moderately hard water. You may need to use more than the recommended amount of detergent for larger loads, heavy soil, harder water, or larger-capacity washers. For softer water, smaller load sizes, lighter soil, or smaller-capacity machines, use slightly less. But too little detergent can lead to poor soil removal and redepositing of soil on clothes.

You can cut down on lint and soften clothes by using a fabric softener or dryer sheet. "They cut down on static, so the lint will not be attracted to the fabric," explains Jane Rising, instructor in the education department at the International Fabricare Institute in Silver Spring, Maryland. "It's similar to using a hair conditioner: If you don't, your hair is full of static electricity; use a hair conditioner, and you're back under control."

When you load the washing machine, add your detergent and any other additives such as water softeners or detergent boosters first. Then fill the tub and, finally, add your clothes. Your machine needs room to agitate the clothing properly, so fill the tub loosely. Set the water level to match your load size and the temperature to match the composition of the load. In general, wash whites, colorfast, and heavily soiled clothing in hot water (106° to 122°F/41° to 50°C). Wash noncolorfast, permanent press, nylon, acrylic, and other man-made fibers and moderately soiled items in warm water (87° to 105°F/31° to 41°C). You can also do washable silks and washable woolens at this temperature. Check the care label first to make sure that they are washable. Wash extra-sensitive colors and lightly soiled items in cold water (65° to 86°F/18° to 30°C). Rinse in cold water.

HOW IT WORKS

They Gobble Pills

Do you ever wonder about the bold promises printed on the front of laundry detergent containers? For example, "Makes clothes look brand new!" Most people think that it's just marketing hype. But Ann Lemley, Ph.D., chairman of the department of textiles and apparel at Cornell University in Ithaca, New York, confirms that there is scientific truth to their claims. Most machine washable clothes are made from cotton, she explains, which is a natural fiber containing cellulose. "Some detergents contain cellulose-dissolving enzymes that take the little pills off cotton clothing," Dr. Lemley says. "That makes the clothes look new. It's amazing. And because they're slow-working, they don't eat away the rest of the fabric."

Machine-Drying

Properly dried clothing looks better and requires less effort to keep wrinkle-free. First of all, make sure that the dryer lint filter is clean. Clogged lint filters increase drying time, which increases energy costs. A clogged filter also causes more lint to collect on clothing. Also combat lint with a dryer sheet or use a fabric softener in the rinse water, which reduces static electricity on clothes.

Before placing an item in the dryer, shake it out lightly to unwad it. As with the washer, don't overload the dryer; clothes will take longer to dry and will wrinkle more easily. Dry like garments together—towels in a load, permanent press in another, and so forth. Dry delicates, like lingerie, separately. Many synthetics—acrylic, nylon, polyester, polyolefin—require a low temperature setting.

Tag Translation

Here's a guide to the clothing care symbols that manufacturers use in garments sold in North America. They were introduced in 1997. You will find four basic symbols in washable clothing—wash, dry, bleach, and iron—with elaboration that provides specific instructions for each category. Temperatures will vary slightly depending on your home equipment. For easy reference, photocopy this guide and post it in your laundry room.

WASH

Machine Wash Cycle

| Normal | Permanent press/ wrinkle- resistant | Gentle/ delicate | Hand-wash | **Do not wash** |

Water Temperature

| ••• | •• | • |
| Hot (50°C/120°F) | Warm (40°C/105°F) | Cold/cool (30°C/85°F) | | **Do not wring** |

DRY

Tumble Dry Cycle

| Dry | Normal | Permanent press/ wrinkle- resistant | Gentle/ delicate | **Do not tumble dry** |

Heat Setting

| ••• | •• | • | ● | |
| High | Medium | Low | No heat/ air | **Do not dry** (used with do not wash) |

Special Instructions

| Line dry/ hang to dry | Drip-dry | Dry flat | In the shade |

BLEACH

Bleach Symbols

| Any bleach (when needed) | Only non-chlorine bleach (when needed) | **Do not bleach** |

IRON

Iron— Dry or Steam

| Iron | High | **Do not iron** |
| Medium | Low | **No steam** |

DRY-CLEAN

Dry-Clean—Normal Cycle

| Dry-clean | Any solvent (A) | **Do not dry-clean** |
| Any solvent except trichloroethylene (P) | Petroleum solvent only (F) | |

Professionally Dry-Clean

| Reduce moisture | Short cycle |
| No steam finishing | Low heat |

SOURCE: *Produced by the Federal Trade Commission as part of Project CLEAN*

Read the labels and follow instructions. To avoid wrinkles, remove items from the dryer as soon as it shuts off, then fold or hang them immediately. Straighten fabric lines and creases and brush out wrinkles. Close clasps and button buttons. This will cut down on the amount of ironing needed.

Ironing

Keep your iron and ironing board clean to avoid staining what you iron. Sort items that need to be ironed according to the amount of heat needed. Silks and synthetics should be ironed at low temperatures, while cottons and linens require higher temperatures. To keep wrinkling at a minimum, iron collars, cuffs, sleeves, and other small areas first and larger areas last. Do not iron stains; contact with

The Phosphate Debate

Not long ago, most laundry detergents contained a compound called phosphate, a "builder" used to increase the efficiency of the detergent's soil-removing qualities, especially in hard water. Nontoxic phosphate also makes plants grow. But that led to a problem. When wastewater laced with detergent runs into lakes, ponds, and streams, it causes something called eutrophication, or a spurt in plant growth that reduces the oxygen supply for fish.

Some environmentalists argue that phosphates in detergent should be banned. Indeed, in some areas there are now laws against producing and selling detergents containing the compound. As a consumer, you should check labels to find out if the detergent you use contains phosphates. To make your laundry come out whiter, softer, and brighter without phosphates, follow these recommendations from Maytag Consumer Education in Newton, Iowa.

- Use a heavy-duty liquid detergent. These do not contain carbonate, a phosphate substitute that tends to leave a residue and may cause color loss, stiffness, and dinginess in white clothes.
- Use the hottest water that is safe for your laundry load.
- Predissolve granular detergent in hot water before adding it to the wash load.
- Add $1/3$ to $1/2$ cup of a nonprecipitating water softener or conditioner, such as Calgon or Spring Rain.
- Pretreat stains and spots, soak garments before washing, or both.
- Use bleach whenever possible.
- Use soft water.

a hot iron—like dryer heat—will set the stains. To prevent the fabric you are ironing from getting shiny, buy a pressing cloth at fabric stores or make your own from a single layer of an old sheet. Put the cloth on top of item you are ironing and iron over the pressing cloth.

Hand-Washing and Drying Fine Fabrics

Carefully follow the instructions on the manufacturer's care tag. Wash in warm or cold water, depending on the instructions, then rinse in cold water. Use a light-duty laundry detergent or a liquid dishwashing detergent. Follow label instructions for how much to use. To make sure that the fabric is colorfast, test it by applying a cotton swab dipped in the detergent solution to an inconspicuous

Laundry Troubleshooting

Here are some typical laundry problems and ways to solve them.

Overall grayness or yellowing: Increase the amount of detergent you use. Increase wash water temperature or use a bleach, if possible.

Blue stains: These stains can be caused when the blue coloring in detergents and fabric softeners does not disperse or dissolve. If caused by a detergent, add 1 cup white vinegar to 1 quart water in a plastic container; soak the item for one hour, then rinse. If caused by fabric softener, rub stains with bar soap, then wash.

Rust stains: Use a commercial rust-removing product recommended for fabrics, such as Whink Rust Stain Remover, which is available at hardware stores. Read the label for safe use. Wear heavy-duty household rubber gloves when you use these products, avoid contact with your skin and eyes, and use only where there is adequate ventilation. Do not use chlorine bleach, which may intensify discoloration. To prevent the problem, try a "nonprecipitating" water softener or conditioner, like Calgon or Spring Rain, in both wash and rinse waters. They prevent iron from depositing on your clothing and are available in supermarkets or discount department stores. Rust in the water supply or from rusty pipes or water heaters sometimes taints wash loads. Run the hot water for a few minutes before starting the wash cycle to clear the lines. Drain the water heater occasionally.

Caution: Always read product labels for proper use and safety precautions.

Detergent residue or stiff harsh fabrics: Add 1 cup white vinegar to 1 gallon warm water in a plastic container; soak item and rinse. In the future, add the detergent to the water first, let it dissolve, then add clothes. Or switch to a liquid laundry detergent.

section of the garment, like the seam. If the color runs, be sure to wash the fabric separately. Allow powdered detergent to dissolve completely before adding clothes. Carefully wring out excess water and roll the garment in a dry towel. Then unroll it and lay it out flat, away from direct sunlight. To avoid damaging the fabric, do not rub while washing or wring while drying.

Speed tips: Pretreat or presoak stains; you stand a better chance of removing them in one wash cycle. When you are drying clothes, don't add wet items to a partially dried load. With some dryers, you can take advantage of residual heat by reloading the dryer as soon as a cycle is finished. (This won't work if your machine has a cooldown cycle programmed in.)

Lawn Mowers

With lawn mowers, your most important task is removing the grass from underneath the mower deck. But there are a few other things to keep in mind as well.

Technique: Scrape off caked-on grass clippings after each use of your walk-behind power mower. "When you're working with fresh grass, a quick cleanup probably doesn't take more than a minute or two," says Ed Cole, service and support manager for Toro Company's consumer products in Bloomington, Minnesota. Use a wood shim or plastic scraper rather than something made out of metal. Sharpen the end of a wooden dowel to get into crevices. To access the area under the mower deck of gas-powered mowers, turn the mower off, remove the spark-plug wire (and the key from the switch on electric-start models), and roll the mower onto spread-out newspaper. Tilt the mower 30 degrees in any direction, and then prop it on something like a cement block or a log. "Don't turn it on its side, because leaking fuel can damage the engine," Cole says. An even safer alternative is to run out as much fuel as possible while mowing the grass before you do this. For electric mowers, unplug them and remove the key before you start.

Because the walk-behind models are often mulching or recycling mowers, which cut grass into finer bits, grass is more likely to stick to them than to riding mowers. Therefore, it's not necessary—nor is it practical—to clean below the mower deck on riding mowers and small tractors after each use. Instead, do it several times each season— more after it rains and in the spring and fall, when the grass tends to

A bit of spray from a hose will help remove grass clippings from underneath your walk-behind mower. Put the mower on a flat surface and remove the grass catcher. Start the engine. Shoot the water onto the ground just in front of the right rear tire (or the side opposite the discharge chute).

be wet. You'll have to remove the mower housing from the machine. When doing so, carefully follow the manufacturer's instructions. Sharpen the blades a couple of times each season as well—more often if your yard contains sandy soil, which can dull blades more quickly. Plan to sharpen blades and scrape caked-on grass at the same time. If your riding mower is a mulcher, however, inspect it after every use and clean it as needed, suggests Cole.

Once a season, give your mower a complete washdown, but don't use too much water. Water can damage certain engine parts and, on riding mowers, the control panel, lights, and other electrical elements. Set your garden hose nozzle for a fine mist, rather than a direct jet. Never use a pressure sprayer to clean a lawn mower. Remove caked-on dirt and grass from the exterior using a soft cloth and mild soapy water in a bucket. When you've finished washing a mower with water, let it run or drive it around for a few minutes to spin the water off of all belts and pulleys.

Also regularly clean the air filter on lawn mowers. While you should follow the manufacturer's instructions, most air filters need cleaning after every 25 hours of use—more frequently in dusty conditions. If your mower's air filter is a foam filter, remove it, wash it in a bucket filled with mild soapy water—liquid dishwashing detergent works best—and let it dry completely. Most require you to distribute a teaspoon or so of oil throughout the filter. Again, follow the manufacturer's instructions on the type of oil and amount.

Engine oil gets dirty, too. Follow the manufacturer's instructions for changing oil.

Speed tips: "Human nature being what it is, most people want to get to the refrigerator and get that beer after they finish cutting the grass," says Cole. "But cleaning the mower is much faster and easier if you do it when the grass is fresh rather than waiting two weeks and trying to take it off when it's like hardened concrete."

In a pinch: You can do a quick exterior cleaning with a leaf blower. To remove grass clippings from underneath your gas-powered walk-behind mower, put it on a flat surface near a garden hose and remove the grass catcher. Start the engine. Hold a running garden hose at hand level and direct water onto the ground just in front of the right rear tire (or the side opposite the discharge chute). The rotating blade will draw water under the deck and wash out the clippings. Do not use too much water. Let the mower run for a few minutes to dry out belts and pulleys, says Cole.

Don't do this if you have an electric mower. They are light enough to tip over and clean with a wooden shim or plastic scraper as described earlier.

Leather

Most leather goods are made of three basic skins—lamb, cow, and pig—and are finished in a variety of ways, from a soft-nap suede to a tough full-grain leather. Cleaning leather, therefore, varies greatly. The only bit of advice that applies to all leather is this: Be careful. Leather can be delicate, and the risk of damaging it if you don't know what you're doing is high.

Technique: There is not much the average consumer can do to clean leather apparel, like jackets, vests, and pants. Usually, when you spill a potential stain-causing substance on, say, your leather coat, you should simply blot it up with a clean white towel, and then take it to a professional leather cleaner. "Forget what the waiter says about using seltzer," says Ralph Sherman, a professional leather cleaner in Roselle, New Jersey, and board member of the Leather Apparel Association in New York City. "Seltzer is good with a little chocolate syrup and milk—when you're making egg creams—but on leather it's no good. You have to be careful about using unproven home methods."

For greasy stains, you may stand a chance. Lay the garment out, sprinkle cornstarch on the stain, and let it stand overnight. Like absorbents used to soak up oil from a driveway, the cornstarch might soak up the oil.

For a stain on suede, blot what you can and let the remainder dry for a couple of days. Try to restore the nap by rubbing gently

SCRUB THIS APPROACH

Five Important Don'ts for Leather Care

1. Don't rub or scrape a stain without testing your technique on an inconspicuous area, like a hem.

2. Don't ever put pressure-sensitive labels, such as "Hello, my name is Joe," on suede or leather garments. "You go to a party, someone slaps that on your garment, and it's ruined," says Ralph Sherman, a professional leather cleaner in Roselle, New Jersey, and board member of the Leather Apparel Association in New York City. "Leather has oil in it. The oil combines with the pressure-sensitive adhesive, and they become as one."

3. Don't get perfume or hair spray on a suede or leather garment. They contain alcohol and other chemicals that will run colors.

4. Don't store suede or leather at home in a plastic bag. "The bag is like a greenhouse," Sherman explains. "All kinds of harmful things build up in there—moisture, mildew, particles from your house's heating system."

5. Don't use heat to dry a wet suede or leather garment. That dries it to a crisp and can cause it to shrink. Hang it on a broad hanger, if appropriate, and dry it at room temperature. If you press the garment, never use steam.

with a soft brush or a dry kitchen sponge. By bringing back the nap, you might eliminate the stain.

When you have leather apparel professionally cleaned, clean matching garments at the same time since the process can cause a slight variation in the color and texture of the leather.

Choose a leather cleaner wisely. Most leather cleaning today is done by wholesalers who pick up from cleaners. If you use a dry cleaner, make sure that it sends leather goods out to a leather specialist. "Most dry cleaners are ethical and won't try to clean a suede garment," says Sherman. "But you have to be careful. Some of them try to clean the leather to avoid paying a wholesaler, and they could end up damaging it."

For a professional leather cleaner referral in your area, contact the Leather Apparel Association, 19 West 21st Street, Suite 403, New York, NY 10010.

When it comes to leather hiking boots or work boots, you have a little more leeway. Clean the dirt off them after each use by scrubbing them in lukewarm water with a long-bristle nylon or vegetable brush. Dry them at room temperature, never near heat, which can cause them to shrink and grow brittle. Condition them occasionally with a commercial boot cleaner/conditioner, like Nikwax, available at outdoor stores and some shoe stores.

Speed tips: To remove sweat and moisture from leather hiking boots, the quickest way is to remove the footpad, if possible, and stuff single sheets of newspaper in them. Replace the newspaper daily until the boots are dry.

Light Fixtures

Sure, you could keep switching to higher-watt bulbs. But why pay all that extra expense when a quick cleanup of your light fixtures will cast a bright new light on everything—without raising your utility bill? Apart from everyday dust buildup, you want to remove the insects that are attracted to the lightbulb and die in the fixture.

Technique: First, remove or unplug the fixture. Dust fixtures as often as possible using a dry cloth. After dusting, wipe them down with a damp cloth or sponge and either an all-purpose cleaner, a glass cleaner, or a squirt of liquid dishwashing detergent mixed in a bucket of lukewarm water. "Most of the insects drawn to lights are moths, whose wings carry a fine dust," says Marry Keener, assistant director of facilities management at the University of Arizona in Tucson and a member of the technical advisory committee for *Executive Housekeeping Today* magazine. "The key is getting rid of that dust before you wipe it down with the damp cloth. Once it gets wet, it streaks and smears and is really hard to remove." Rinse by wiping the fixtures with a clean moist sponge or cloth. Since most light fixtures are made of either glass, plastic, brass, or some other scratchable material, do not use abrasive cleaners or scrubbers.

Speed tips: Remove dust and insects using a vacuum cleaner brush attachment.

Linen

Ah, linen! It's wonderfully absorbent and strong, and it breathes. But this product of the flax plant has its disadvantages as well. It wrinkles easily and is not as simple to care for as cotton, another natural fiber.

Technique: Some linen items are washable, while others are dry cleanable only. Be sure to check the manufacturer's care label. Generally speaking, dry-cleaning is recommended for drapery linens, upholstery linens, and decorative linens as well as fine linen apparel. Handkerchiefs, napkins, and some linen apparel can be washed in warm water by hand or machine. Wash colors in cold water. Use a mild laundry detergent and only oxygen-type bleaches such as Clorox 2, when appropriate. Chlorine bleach can cause yellowing.

"Linen fiber has a natural pectin—like the pectin that makes gelatin solidify—and if you wash it out, it makes the fabric softer," says Pauline Delli-Carpini, director of operations for Masters of Linen, North America, a trade association in New York City. "It becomes a personal statement, whether you want crisp, crisp linen or you want something soft and drapey."

Another reason for choosing dry cleaning is to save on ironing time because linen is a notorious wrinkler. As for why it wrinkles, Delli-Carpini says, "if you look at one linen fiber, it's inelastic—unlike, say, a wool fiber, which has lots of curls in it." Some of the newer permanent press and stain-resistant finishes—65 percent linen, 35 percent polyester—make washing easier and reduce wrinkling.

If you do wash linen, dry it in a machine on low or delicate, on a line, or by rolling it in terry towels. But always remove it before it gets bone-dry to avoid drying the creases into the fabric. Plus, a hot iron glides more smoothly over damp cloth. Do not wring out linen.

Here are some other ironing tips.

- For dark-color linen, iron on the "wrong" side so that the fabric does not get shiny.
- Clean the soleplate of your iron for smoother ironing and to avoid staining linen.
- Iron linen until wrinkle-free but not dry, and then hang it to let it dry completely.
- Minimize creasing and bunching when ironing large tablecloths by hanging them over a table adjacent to your ironing board.
- Remove linen from the dryer before it is completely dry and iron it immediately.
- Put linen items in a plastic bag in the refrigerator or freezer for 6 to 24 hours before ironing. "When you pull the fabric out and start ironing, the contact between the hot iron and the cool makes it glide faster and more smoothly," Delli-Carpini says.
- Spraying on sizing, like Magic Sizing, with also make your iron glide more smoothly.

Linens

"Your linens represent a substantial investment," says Marry Keener, previously an executive housekeeper who once oversaw the washing of 2.5 million pounds of laundry per year at the Loews Ventana Canyon Resort in Tucson, Arizona. You want it to be fresh and crisp for each use and to remain that way as long as possible.

Technique: First, check the label to determine the recommended cleaning method. Most bed and bath linens are made of cotton or a cotton-polyester blend and are machine washable.

Launder them frequently—once or twice a week. "When most people check into a hotel, they expect their sheets to be washed once a day," says Keener, currently assistant director of facilities management at the University of Arizona in Tucson and a member of the technical advisory committee for *Executive Housekeeping Today* magazine. That's overkill, she admits, but washing them every fourth or fifth day keeps them sanitary and bright.

Pretreat stains as soon after they occur as possible. Use a commercial stain spotting agent or a simple bar of hand soap. The soap is economical and will remove most stains, even some of the toughest. So keep a bar handy in your laundry room. Wet the stain with cold water—hot water can set stains—and then rub the bar directly onto it and toss the sheet or pillow case in the washer.

If you have silk sheets, chances are that they are made of washable silk, or they are actually satin sheets. Satin sheets resemble silk sheets, but they are made of synthetic material, not natural silk from a silkworm. In either case, wash them in cool water on a gentle cycle. Tumble dry on low heat. But before you wash them, be sure to read the label instructions.

Dry-clean silk bedspreads twice a year or so. You can machine-wash many types of bedspreads. Follow the care label instructions carefully. "Because of the sheer volume of the material," Keener says, "most washers won't hold bedspreads for beds larger than full size." Make sure that whatever you put in your machine will be fully covered with water and will agitate properly. If your bedspread won't fit in your washer, make a special trip to a Laundromat that has extra-large machines. Or, send it to be dry-cleaned. Once or twice a year, it's worth it.

If someone has been ill in the family, wash all of their linens, including the bedspread, afterward to avoid the potential spread of germs.

In a pinch: To freshen up a tired bedspread without giving it a complete washing, tumble it for 5 to 10 minutes in a dryer set on

"Air-Fluff." The cycle will loosen dust and other particles and will transfer them from the spread to the machine's filter. Toss in a dryer sheet to give the spread a fresh smell. Or hang the spread on a clothesline on a sunny breezy day. The sun's ultraviolet rays will kill bacteria, and the breeze will remove surface dust.

Louvers—Doors

Louvered doors and windows can add a handsome design touch to your home and help out with air flow. But their shape creates a cleaning nightmare—scores of hard-to-reach nooks, crannies, and corners. "It's very time-consuming to clean each window individually," says Clint Sargeant, production coordinator of the J. J. Swartz Company, a remodeling and fire restoration firm in Decatur, Illinois. Unfortunately, sometimes that's your only option.

Technique: Before cleaning wooden door louvers, you must first know how the wood is finished. If it has been coated in a surface finish, like lacquer or polyurethane, dirt will come off easier. The coating protects the wood from the moisture and prohibits dust from penetrating the wood pores. To clean hard-coated louvers, simply wipe them with a lightly dampened cloth. Be sure not to use mineral spirits or kerosene on hard-coated wood.

Follow up by wiping the wood down with a commercial furniture polish, like Pledge. To avoid wax buildup in hard-to-reach cracks and crevices, spray the product onto a cloth, not directly onto the louvers.

If the wood is not coated with a surface finish but, rather, has a penetrating stain or oil finish, dust with a lightly dampened cloth. "On this type of wood, the dust can sink into the wood," Sargeant says. Dust these as often as possible to prevent the soil from penetrating.

To clean these unfinished wood louvers, use a cloth moistened with boiled linseed oil, or a solvent like mineral spirits (both available at hardware stores) or kerosene, available at gas stations. Read the labels for proper use. Be sure to use these products in a well-ventilated room. Test your solution first on an inconspicuous area. Then, rub the cloth over the surface, turning it occasionally as it picks up the dirt and grime. Once you have cleaned the entire surface, you may need to wax the area to restore the shine. Use a product suitable for wood surfaces and buff, if required.

Regardless of the type of wood finish, there are hard-to-reach spots on louvers. To get to them, wrap your cleaning cloth around a putty knife or old butter knife and work it in between crevices.

Luggage

In a sense, luggage is meant to get dirty. Its job, after all, is to protect what's inside—clothes, camera gear, or golf clubs. But proper care helps luggage last longer and look better, which can be important in public places like airports and gyms and on golf courses.

Technique: It is best to spot-clean most luggage. For garment, tote, and duffel bags and hard suitcases made of synthetic materials and canvas, first try a moist cloth and a simple detergent solution—warm water and a squirt of liquid dishwashing detergent. Do not soak the luggage; rather, dab and lightly rub the soiled spots.

To clean scuff marks—the kind left by black airport conveyor belts—use an all-purpose cleaner, like Fantastik. Spray it on a soft cloth or sponge, and then wipe the surface with the cloth. "I've never had to deep clean it any more than that," says flight attendant Sharon B. Wingler, the Chicago-based author of *Travel Alone and Love It*. (Wingler's travel tip: Black luggage hides scuff marks, making cleaning less necessary. "All of my bags are black," she says.)

Aluminum Luggage

Use a solution of warm water and a mild liquid dishwashing detergent and a cloth. Never use alkaline cleaners like ammonia, trisodium phosphate, or even baking soda. They discolor aluminum. If the aluminum surface is discolored, wash it with the detergent solution mixed with a dash of lemon juice or vinegar. (*Note:* Pretest first on an inconspicuous area.) The acid in those substances will help restore the aluminum's shine.

Do not use abrasive cleaners, such as scouring powders or steel wool. They might scratch or dull the surface.

Leather Luggage

Leather is sensitive to water and cleaning chemicals, so be careful when you're faced with a dirty leather bag. First, follow the recommendations of the manufacturer. Try a leather cleaner, available at luggage stores or shoe repair shops. Before using it, however, test it on an inconspicuous area to make sure that it does not cause the leather dyes to bleed or affect the texture of the hide.

For fine leather luggage or especially difficult-to-remove stains, you may want to contact a professional leather cleaner. Choose wisely. Most leather cleaning today is done by wholesalers who pick up from cleaners. If you use a dry cleaner, make sure that it sends leather goods out to a leather specialist. For a professional leather cleaner referral in your area, contact the Leather Apparel Association, 19 West 21st Street, Suite 403, New York, NY 10010.

Golf Bags

Most golf bags these days are easy to clean. "It rains on golfers every once and a while, or it's early in the morning and you lay the bag down in the grass. That's why the vast majority of bags are made with synthetic materials," says Ron Reczek, production manager at All-American Golf, a maker of bags and other golf equipment in Joliet, Illinois. He suggests spot-cleaning with a terry towel and a solution of warm water and a squirt of mild liquid dishwashing detergent. Use a stiff-bristle toothbrush for scrubbing the nooks and crannies.

"Not too many people use leather—even the professionals. It's so expensive," says Reczek. For leather trim, however, use a leather cleaner, available at most luggage or shoe stores.

Speed tips: Using a thin-tipped attachment, vacuum the dirt and grass out of your golf bag's pockets. Also, put a damp towel stored in a plastic bag in your golf bag before you play. That will make it easy to clean dirt and mud off the bag as you round the links.

Macramé

Unless you let your dog drag it around the backyard, cleaning macramé is simple—usually just a matter of keeping it free of dust.

Technique: Dusting your knotty artwork might not seem easy, but you can easily remove accumulated particles from most macramé items by tumbling it on the "Air-Fluff" setting of your dryer. This cool-air cycle loosens the dust particles and transfers them from the macramé's surface to the dryer's filter. Do it for 5 to 10 minutes or until the macramé is clean.

If your macramé is stained, spot-clean it only, first using a damp cloth, and then trying a solution of 1 cup water and a few drops of liquid dishwashing detergent. Most macramé is made of heavy nylon cord and will come clean relatively easily. Machine-washing macramé is not recommended, unless the manufacturer's instructions explicitly say so. It might unravel or shrink.

"I've seen some macramé that is made of imported fibers," says Marry Keener, assistant director of facilities management at the University of Arizona in Tucson and a member of the technical advisory committee for *Executive Housekeeping Today* magazine. "We're not really familiar with some of the products coming from around the world. You launder something like that, and it can disintegrate."

In a pinch: Instead of tumbling your macramé on "Air-Fluff," try vacuuming it. This might remove the dust, especially if it is a large piece.

Makeup Stains

Grease is a major ingredient in lipstick and other cosmetics. When removing most makeup stains, therefore, you first want to attack that grease, then deal with nongreasy residue.

Technique: The best substance for removing greasy stains is spot remover, says Ann Lemley, Ph.D., chairman of the department of textiles and apparel at Cornell University in Ithaca, New York. Have the item professionally dry-cleaned or clean it yourself with a spot remover, like Carbona Stain Devils or K2r, available at supermarkets,

HOW I DO IT

A Makeup Cure, Bar None

Before she became the assistant director of facilities management at the University of Arizona in Tucson, Marry Keener was director of housekeeping at the fashionable Loews Ventana Canyon Resort in Tucson, where she oversaw the washing of 2.5 million pounds of laundry per year—with plenty of makeup stains. Here's her personal tip for removing these difficult stains from washable fabric. "One of the best methods of pretreatment for makeup stains is bar soap. You don't need to wet the spot first. Just rub it with a bar that has had a chance to soften up in its dish, and then wash the item as instructed. It's a lot cheaper than the commercial spotting agents, and it takes off mascara and lipstick like you wouldn't believe."

hardware stores, or discount department stores. Wear protective rubber or latex gloves, and use these products in a well-ventilated area. Lay the stain facedown on a soft absorbent cloth. Apply the spot remover to another clean white cloth, and then blot from the inside of the garment to push the stain out. As the spot remover dissolves the grease in the makeup, the cloth beneath catches it.

To remove the last traces of the stain, says Dr. Lemley, blot with a solution of ¼ teaspoon clear liquid dishwashing detergent and ½ cup cold water, using a clean white towel. Then wash the item as directed. If that does not remove the stain completely, follow the same technique but use a solution of 1 teaspoon ammonia and ½ cup cold water. Again, wash as directed.

For carpets, always apply cleaning solutions to a towel, never directly onto the carpet. Otherwise, it can soak into the carpet backing or pad and attract more dirt.

Note: Before using cleaning solutions, always test them on an inconspicuous section of the stained item.

Caution: Always rinse one cleaning solution before trying another. Mixing chemicals, especially ammonia and chlorine bleach, can create noxious fumes. Always read the product label for proper use and safety precautions.

Marble

Talk about walking on eggshells! "Marble is a wonderful thing, but it is a pain to take care of," says Kay Weirick, director of housekeeping services at Bally's Las Vegas Hotel and a member of the technical advisory committee for *Executive Housekeeping Today* magazine. For a stone, it's fragile and porous. It's important to keep marble clean, but it is equally important that you not damage its beautiful surface.

Technique: To keep tiny particles of grit from scratching the surface of marble floors, dust them often with an untreated dust mop. Because marble is porous, a treated dust mop can cause staining.

Clean marble with a sponge, soft cloth, or mop and a neutral cleaner, like Murphy Oil Soap or a liquid dishwashing detergent, mixed with warm water.

"To remove stains in marble, you have to wick or suck them back out of the stone," says Fred Hueston, director of the National

SCRUB THIS APPROACH

Hold the Vinegar!

You can sprinkle vinegar on a salad. But if you pour it onto a marble floor, it'll eat that gorgeous stone for lunch. Fred Hueston, director of the National Training Center for Stone and Masonry Trades in Longwood, Florida, and author of *Marble and Tile: Selection and Care of Stone and Tile Surfaces*, debunks a commonly held marble-cleaning myth.

"There's an old tale that says that vinegar and water is the greatest thing for marble. It's not. Absolutely never, ever use vinegar and water on marble.

"It began with ceramic-tile installers, who have branched over into the field of marble tile and brought a lot of their practices with them. For years they have recommended vinegar and water as a cleaner, which is fine for tile but not for marble. Vinegar is acidic and eats away at the surface of marble. It's one of the most common questions we get here at the training center: 'Can't I just use vinegar and water? That's what the installer told me.' "

Training Center for Stone and Masonry Trades in Longwood, Florida, and author of *Marble and Tile: Selection and Care of Stone and Tile Surfaces*. The best way is with a poultice. For oil stains, mix ½ cup bleached flour, a small squirt of liquid dishwashing detergent, and warm water into a paste that has the consistency of peanut butter. Spread it over the stained area, cover it with plastic wrap, and tape down the sides with masking tape. Let it sit overnight. Remove the plastic, let the poultice dry, and scrape it away. For food stains—coffee, tea, juices—substitute hydrogen peroxide for the detergent. Rub ink, crayon, or nail polish stains with a cotton ball dipped in an acetone-based nail polish remover. (Don't mix the nail polish remover into the poultice.)

Speed tips: Sealing marble surfaces with a penetrating sealer, available at hardware and home supply stores, facilitates cleaning. "A stone sealer does nothing to alter the appearance," says Hueston. "It works on marble like a water seal works on a wood deck."

Caution: Lemon or anything else with any acidity will eat into, or etch, the polished surface of marble. Be wary of bathroom cleaners. They often contain acid. Check the label: Federal law requires the product to list all acid ingredients. Also avoid using abrasive cleaners. Even the finest grit can dull marble surfaces.

Mattresses and Box Springs

Think of it as sleeping with the enemy. Your bed collects dust and dander and harbors microscopic dust mites, all of which are major causes of allergies. Keeping your mattress and box spring clean not only helps them last longer but also improves the health conditions in the room where you spend at least one-third of your time.

Technique: Vacuum mattresses and box springs twice a year. Use an appropriate attachment, not the carpet sweeper. "Put a fresh bag in beforehand as a test," says Marry Keener, assistant director of facilities management at the University of Arizona in Tucson and a member of the technical advisory committee for *Executive House-keeping Today* magazine. "You'll be surprised at how much dander and lint are in there."

If you use a plastic mattress cover, wash it in the washing machine or wipe it down using a sponge and a mild solution of liquid dishwashing detergent. "If someone in the home is ill, clean it with a disinfectant, like Lysol," Keener suggests. "That helps prevent the spread of viruses and bacteria from family member to family member."

You should also turn your mattress twice a year—each time you clean it—to distribute the wear. Alternate which way you turn it: side-to-side one time, and then end-to-end the next.

If you're cleaning up after a bed wetter, blot up as much of the urine as possible using a clean white towel, and then extract the rest using a wet vacuum–style carpet cleaner with an upholstery attachment. If you do not have access to one of those machines, blot with wet towels and sponge in a little vinegar to neutralize the odor. Blot again using wet towels, and then dry the mattress in the sun. The sun's rays also kill bacteria.

Speed tips: To facilitate cleaning up after a chronic bed wetter, use a plastic mattress cover. After an accident, simply wipe up urine with a sponge or cloth, and then follow up with a disinfectant such as Lysol.

Microwave Ovens

Microwaves are a zap—er, snap—to clean, especially if you do it regularly.

Technique: Wipe up spills as they occur, especially those around the door seal. To remove caked-on food, fill a bowl halfway with water and boil it for two to three minutes at the microwave oven's highest power, says Cindy Cook, a trained home economist at the Michigan State University Extension in East Lansing and manager of its Home Maintenance and Repair Database on the Internet. Wipe away stains loosened by the steam.

To remove odors, clean the interior with a solution of 1 tablespoon baking soda to 1 cup warm water, rinse, and dry. Never use abrasive pads or powders on a microwave oven.

Mildew

Mildew is like the monster in a horror movie: It seems to spring out of nowhere. Indeed, it is a living organism, the by-product of a destructive fungus that feeds on cotton, wood, paper, leather, and other organic materials. Mildew exists in the air in a dormant state. Dampness, darkness, and warmth cause it to multiply rapidly, often in less than 72 hours. When allowed to flourish, mildew causes discoloration, a musty smell—the result of its digestive process—and irreversible deterioration of fibers. Overcoming this household fiend is a matter of preventing its growth and then effectively cleaning the items it attacks. Since you're referring to this section, you probably already have mildew, so we'll start with the latter.

Technique: Treat mildew immediately to avoid serious damage to whatever it has latched on to. "Mildew is not just something on the surface," says Martha Shortlidge, a home economics program leader and cooperative extension agent with the Cornell Cooperative Extension in Valhalla, New York. Left to grow, mildew eats away at the organic fibers of things like cotton and wool rugs, clothing, and books, causing permanent damage. When you discover mildew, first brush off the surface growth outdoors to avoid scattering the spores. Then, let the items dry in the air and sun. Follow the care instructions of the particular item you're cleaning. Send nonwashables to a dry cleaner and launder washables promptly with plenty of hot suds, which should remove light stains. To remove stains from golf bags, canvas awnings, and other nonwashables, wipe them with a solution of 1 cup hot water and ¼ teaspoon liquid dishwashing detergent, using a white cotton cloth. When possible, use liquid household bleach in the wash. Bleach not only whitens mildew stains but also kills any remaining spores.

"Mildew is usually a symptom of poor ventilation," explains Shortlidge. To prevent mildew, keep your home clean and moisture-free. Use fans to ventilate the house and basement. But be careful not to pull air inside on really humid days; you might actually increase the moisture level. Poor housing design—an incorrectly graded slope that brings rainwater into the basement, for example—is often a cause of moisture problems, which you may need to address.

Other tips: Before storing clothes, remove grease or soil, which provide food for mold to develop. Even synthetic fibers that are mildew-resistant can attract the fungus if they are wet and soiled. Don't let damp or wet clothing lie around, especially in dark places like a clothes hamper. Either wash them immediately or hang them to dry. In closets, hang clothes loosely so that air can circulate around them; avoid storing items in garment bags. Store shoes and leather goods on a shelf instead of on the floor. During hot, humid weather regularly check the clothes in your closets for mildew.

Note: Before using cleaning solutions, always test them on an inconspicuous section of the stained item.

Caution: Always rinse out one cleaning solution before trying another. Mixing chemicals, especially ammonia and chlorine bleach, can create noxious fumes. Always read the product label for proper use and safety precautions.

Mirrors

You want that face staring back at you from the mirror to look as good as possible, right? You don't need streaks and lint sullying your image. Fortunately, cleaning mirrors, like cleaning glass, is pretty straightforward. So let's reflect for a moment on the best and quickest strategies.

Technique: Clean mirrors with a solution of 1 cup vinegar per gallon of warm water or a squirt of liquid dishwashing detergent in a bucket of water, says Jim Brewer, executive housekeeper at the University of Texas at Arlington and a technical advisor to *Cleaning and Maintenance Magazine.* Ammonia-based window cleaners have a tendency to streak, a condition that is especially noticeable in bright sunlight. To avoid leaving traces of lint, wipe away the liquid using a squeegee or newsprint.

When cleaning vertical glass surfaces, like windows, start at the top and clean down. Apply the cleaning solution with a sponge, soft cloth, or spray bottle, then scrub caked-on grime with a long-bristle vegetable brush.

Carefully peel off paint and other stuck-on substances with a razor blade. Do not use a putty knife, which has a duller blade and can damage the glass.

Mites

Yikes—the unseen enemy! There are many kinds of mites, from those that invade your houseplants to the microscopic dust mites that live off discarded human skin and are a major cause of allergic reactions in humans.

Technique: Spray mite-infested plants with a solution of insecticidal soap, available at most home and garden centers. These relatively nontoxic substances contain potassium salts, sodium salts, or certain fatty acids. "Insecticidal soap is one of the least toxic treatments available," says Jerry Giordano, a horticulture consultant with the Cornell Cooperative Extension in Valhalla, New York. Typically, you mix it with water and use a standard spray bottle or pump-up pressure sprayer to apply it. Because of its makeup, the soap only works when mixed with soft water. To test your solution, mix a small batch and let it sit for 15 minutes. If a scum or "curd" of soap forms on the surface, use a water softener and remix.

Be sure to thoroughly clean the undersides of leaves, where the mites may also live. Treat when and where infestation appears, not as a preventive measure.

Dust mites, which you can't see, thrive in moist, warm conditions and live in dust, often in mattresses, carpets, and upholstered furniture. Get rid of them by avoiding overhumid conditions and keeping dust to a minimum. Vacuum carpets and upholstered furniture often, and empty the vacuum bag after each session.

In a pinch: Instead of spraying houseplants with an insecticidal soap solution, simply wash the plants with soapy water and a soft brush or cloth, says the Cornell Cooperative Extension. Use 2 teaspoons of a mild dishwashing detergent in a gallon of water. Or spray them with a jet of clean water to knock mites off.

Caution: When using insecticidal soaps, watch your plants for signs of phototoxicity, an adverse reaction. Symptoms are yellow or brown foliage spotting, "burned" tips, and yellow or brown scorching on the leaf edges. If symptoms occur, stop using the soap. Always read the product label for proper use and safety precautions.

Motorcycles

Like cars, motorcycles are a big investment. And like their four-wheel counterparts, they collect dirt, grease, grime, and bug gunk on the road and in the driveway. So cleaning motorcycles is essential, not only for helping them look their best but also for keeping their shells, frames, and engines in top working order.

Technique: How often should you clean a motorcycle? Well, how often do you ride? And where do you park—outside or in a garage? As a rule of thumb, clean weekly if you ride your bike heavily or if it's subjected to the elements. If you only ride on weekends and park in a garage, a good wash once a month is sufficient.

A complete cleaning is a several-step process. Begin by wetting the motorcycle with a garden hose. Do not spray it directly, but rather sprinkle the water on gently. Never get water in the exhaust pipe or in the carburetor. That could cause engine damage.

Spray the wheels and spokes, engine, and other areas where grease has collected with a commercial degreasing compound, like S100 Total Cycle Cleaner, available at motorcycle supply stores. "That gets in between the cracks, where we can't get, to take out some of the excess grease and brake dust," says Eladio Gonzalez, a mechanic at Brooklyn Harley-Davidson in New York City. Let it sit

HOW I DO IT

The Brown Badge of Honor

Oliver Shokouh is the owner of Harley-Davidson of Glendale in Glendale, California, and founder of the Love Ride, an annual celebrity motorcycle event that raises money for muscular dystrophy. Here's what he says about cleaning bikes. "A lot of people think of their motorcycles as works of art. They like showing them off to friends. They're motorheads, and they're proud of their motors. But there are some people who spend more time cleaning than riding the bikes. I like riding long distances, and when I'm on the road, my bike gets pretty dirty.

"I took my bike up to Alaska. When I got there, I loved the way it looked. The dirt was like a sign of experience. People knew I hadn't trailered the bike. But I had to clean it.

"I used a high-pressure cleaner, like the ones at a self-service car wash. You have to be careful. The pressure can be too intense. It can strip the paint and stripes right off. But after my Alaska trip, it really needed it."

for 5 to 10 minutes while it loosens the grease, and then wipe it down with a wet cloth.

Next, using a soft cloth or sponge and a bucket of warm water with a few squirts of liquid dishwashing detergent in it, wash off the degreaser, along with any grime and stuck-on bugs. Never use anything abrasive. That can ruin the painted or chrome finish. Dry the bike completely using clean dry towels. Water left standing can rust exposed metal parts.

Once the bike is dry, clean and glaze the chrome with a special metal-cleaning product, like S100 Spray Wax or Mothers Mag and Aluminum Polish, also available at stores where motorcycles are sold. Wax the tanks, fenders, and other painted surfaces with a rub-on car wax

Speed tips: "Once I've washed a bike," Gonzalez says, "I bring it in the shop and use the air hose to blow-dry the bike completely so that nothing will rust." You can use a leaf blower to do the same thing, he says, as long as you do it in a dust-free area.

In a pinch: Simply follow the first couple of steps: Wet the bike, spray on the degreaser, wash it with soap and water, and dry it. This will remove bug gunk and other grime before it has a chance to stick too much. Then, once every few washes, follow up with a detailed polishing.

Caution: Always read the product label for proper use and safety precautions.

Needlework

You want to clean needlework without harming it, of course. That means dusting, and then seeking professional help for anything more involved.

Technique: During your normal cleaning routine, vacuum the dust off of needlepoint pillows and other needlework. The brush attachment works best.

Don't clean needlework with water. In the case of a spill, blot up as much of the substance as possible using a clean white towel. Then have the work professionally cleaned, says Marry Keener, assistant director of facilities management at the University of Arizona in Tucson and a member of the technical advisory committee for *Executive Housekeeping Today* magazine.

In a pinch: Take needlepoint pillows outside and gently beat the dust out of them.

Nylons

The world is cruel to nylons—when you wear them and when you toss them in the wash, too. You want to clean them without snagging, running, shrinking, or stretching them.

Technique: Put nylons in a tightly sealed mesh laundry bag and wash them on a gentle permanent press cycle using regular laundry detergent. "If you don't use a mesh bag, they get tangled up with the stem of the machine," says Dorothy Cummings, wardrobe mistress for the New York City Ballet. Pretreat stains, especially makeup, by rubbing in a little mild bar soap, like Ivory or Dove.

Remove the nylons from the bag and tumble dry at a low temperature. For best results, remove them from the dryer after about 15 minutes and hang them to dry completely.

Speed tips: To minimize static electricity and make handling your nylons easier, use a dryer sheet when drying.

Odors

Sniff, sniff. Phew! What's that odor? Most nose-offending scents are caused by spills—either from the spill itself or bacteria growing on the spill. Other common odors are caused by pet accidents, cooking certain foods, mildew, and skunks. The bigger a spill or pet accident and the longer it remains untreated, the more difficult it is to remove the smells.

Technique: "There are two main ways of handling odors," says Rajiv Jain, laboratory manager for the Association of Specialists in Cleaning and Restoration in Millersville, Maryland. "The easy way out is to mask the smell with something like perfume. The best way, however, is to remove the source of the odor."

Dave Heberly agrees. He is technical service director at Steam Way International, a carpet-cleaner manufacturer in Denver that provides education to professional carpet cleaners, including seminars on odor control. "If you find a dead mouse, do you run to the grocery store and buy something to spray on it, or do you just throw it away?" he asks. "Even when the source of the odor is not so easy to remove, you have to get rid of it first."

Beating Odors the Old-Fashioned Way

Isn't canned freshness a contradiction in terms? Many commercial air fresheners either coat your nasal passages with an undetectable oil film or diminish your sense of smell with a nerve-deadening agent. Here are some time-tested recipes for odor-eating alternatives, says Cindy Cook, a trained home economist at the Michigan State University Extension in East Lansing and manager of its Home Maintenance and Repair Database on the Internet.

Ventilation: This is as simple as opening windows and doors in the house as often as possible. It helps dry up and clear away the sources that cause odors. (Of course, if it's very humid out, don't ventilate.)

Vinegar: Boil a solution of 1 tablespoon white vinegar and 1 cup water to eliminate unpleasant cooking odors. When cutting onions, rub vinegar on your hands before and after slicing to reduce odors.

Celery: This is another remedy for onion odor on hands. Cut a celery stalk and rub the ends on your hands before and after handling onions.

Cinnamon and cloves: Mix these spices together in a cheesecloth bag and boil the bundle. The bag makes cleanup quick and easy.

Vanilla: Moisten a cotton ball with pure vanilla and place it in a small saucer. Place the saucer in the car (while it's standing), in the refrigerator, or throughout the house to remove odors. (Keep it out of the reach of children, however. Vanilla has a high alcohol content.)

Borax: To prevent the growth of odor-producing molds and bacteria, sprinkle $1/2$ cup borax in the bottom of the garbage can.

Pet Urine

This is one of the most common odor sources. If pet urine seeps into carpet and carpet backing, urine can smell for long periods and can draw pets back to urinate on the same spot. It is also a breeding ground for bacteria, which give off their own particular odors.

First, absorb as much of the pet urine as possible using white cloths or paper towels. Then blot the area with a white towel soaked in a solution of 1 teaspoon white or colorless liquid dishwashing detergent in 1 cup lukewarm water. Soak up as much as possible using a clean towel. Next, blot the area with a solution of one part white vinegar to two parts water. Again, use a towel to soak up as much as possible. Cover the area with several white terry towels, place something heavy on them, and allow the area to dry for at least six hours.

HOW IT WORKS

The Science of Smell

Odor occurs when substances, usually organic, give off molecules that float through the air and find their way into your nasal passages. Higher temperatures make substances more volatile and, therefore, increase smells given off. Higher humidity increases odors, too, by slowing the molecules' rate of evaporation. There are six main odor qualities: fruity, flowery, resinous, spicy, foul, and burned.

The sense of smell is thought to be 10,000 times more sensitive than taste. For example, scientists have found that humans can smell ethyl mercaptan, an odor-causing substance in rotten meat, even in traces as scarce as $\frac{1}{400}$ milligram per liter of air.

Hunger heightens the sense of smell. Pain does, too, probably as a way of alerting the body to dangerous stimuli in the environment. And because pain endings are found on the nerves in the nose, certain odors, such as ammonia, can actually cause physical discomfort.

Cooking Odors

"If you leave a four-pound chicken on the stove, and it cooks down to nothing," says Heberly, "you'll end up with four pounds of burned meat on your walls, carpet, and ceiling." Those particles give off odors.

The same thing occurs—albeit to a lesser degree—when you cook with strong-smelling foods like fish, onions, and garlic. To remove the source of cooking odors, clean kitchen surfaces. Disinfect with a commercial cleaner, like Pine-Sol.

Heat rises and, in its effort to seek equilibrium, is drawn to cool areas. Concentrate cleaning energy, therefore, on high areas, metal surfaces (faucets, towel racks, door handles, hinges), and areas around windows and doors.

Smoke

Treat smoke the same way you would cooking odors. Try to wash away the smoke residue left on the surfaces of the affected room. Wash or dry-clean rugs, draperies, and other fabric. If you're cleaning up after a more serious smoke odor problem, such as a house fire, you'll probably need to call a professional odor-removal company. To remove stubborn smoke smells, professionals use a variety of techniques, including treatment with ozone gas, which oxidizes the odor molecule and renders it virtually fragrance-free. For a professional referral in your area, contact the Association of Specialists in Cleaning and Restoration at 8229 Cloverleaf Drive, Suite 460, Millersville, MD 21108.

Refrigerator Odors

To keep refrigerator odors at bay, give your refrigerator a regular and thorough cleaning according to the manufacturer's instructions, says Martha Reek, a senior home economist with the Whirlpool Corporation in Evansville, Indiana. Keep all foods covered to prevent odor transfer. And discard old unusable foods before they start to smell. As a preventive measure, place a small opened box of baking soda in your refrigerator and another in your freezer to absorb food odors. Replace them with new boxes every few months.

For especially bad smells, says Reek, spread a medium-size box of baking soda or organic based activated charcoal, available at aquarium supply stores, into a shallow pan and let it stand on a refrigerator shelf for a few days. Or do the same with freshly ground coffee in a cereal bowl.

Note: Freshly ground coffee may cause ice and ice cream to take on a coffee flavor. To avoid this, discard these items or seal them in a plastic bag.

If you're about to junk your refrigerator because of ghastly odors—the kind caused by rotten and forgotten meat—try the following first, says Reek. Empty your refrigerator and clean it thoroughly according to the manufacturer's instructions. Pack each shelf with crumpled newspapers. Set a cup of water on the top shelf or sprinkle the papers lightly with water, and let it stand for five to six days while the refrigerator is running. Replace the newspaper every two days. The refrigeration system will pull moist air across the newspaper surfaces, which will absorb odor molecules. It's inconvenient, but it works. So arrange for a backup refrigerator.

Mildew

When you discover mildew, first brush off the surface growth outdoors to avoid scattering the spores. Then, let the items dry in the air and sun. Follow the care instructions of the particular item you're cleaning. Send nonwashables to a dry cleaner, and launder washables promptly with plenty of hot suds. To remove mildew from golf bags, canvas awnings, and other nonwashables, wipe them with a solution of 1 cup hot water and ¼ teaspoon liquid dishwashing detergent, using a white cotton cloth. When possible, use chlorine bleach in the wash. Bleach kills any remaining spores.

To avoid mildew, ventilate your house well and control moisture. If you can't pin down the source of a mildew odor, check the evaporation pan under your refrigerator, if it has one. It's warm, dark, and dank under there—the perfect mildew-growing conditions.

Skunk Odor

Neutralize the skunk funk on a dog by washing the dog with tomato juice or vinegar. For decks, driveways, and other hard surfaces harboring a skunk smell, mix a quart of 3 percent hydrogen peroxide, ¼ cup baking soda, and 1 tablespoon liquid dishwashing detergent. Put it in a plastic spray bottle, and spray it on the surfaces. Leave the solution for a few minutes, and then hose it off.

Speed tips: If you have a heavy-duty vacuum cleaner—like a Shop-Vac, capable of picking up liquids—use it to remove urine and other odor-causing liquids from carpet and rugs as soon as possible. First, mist the stain with water to dilute it, and then suck as much as possible up with the vacuum. Repeat the process as many times as needed.

Oil Stains

 EMERGENCY ACTION
Remove excess oil by blotting with a paper towel, being careful not to spread it. Next, blot with a paper towel dabbed with an acetone-based nail polish remover. Do not use it on acetate. It will dissolve the fabric.

Oil is a tough stain, plus it is like a magnet for dirt. Remove oil stains as quickly as possible.

Technique: The best substance for removing oily or greasy stains is dry-cleaning solvent. Either have the item professionally dry-cleaned or blot with a clean white towel and a spot remover, like Carbona Stain Devils or K2r, available at supermarkets, hardware stores, or discount department stores. Lay the stain facedown on a soft absorbent cloth. Apply the spot remover to another cloth, and then blot from the inside of the garment to push the stain out. "It's important to have something underneath because what you want to do is send the stain somewhere else," says Ann Lemley, Ph.D., chairman of the department of textiles and apparel at Cornell University in Ithaca, New York. "As the spot remover dissolves the oil, you want to drive it away." For carpets, always apply the spot remover to a towel, never directly onto the carpet. Otherwise, it can soak into the carpet backing or pad and attract more dirt. Wear protective rubber or latex gloves, and use these products in a well-ventilated area.

Note: Before using cleaning solutions, always test them on an inconspicuous section of the stained item.

In a pinch: If you don't have any spot remover around the house, use an acetone-based nail polish remover. Do not, however, use it on acetate fabric. It dissolves the fabric.

Caution: Always rinse out one cleaning solution before trying another. Always read the product label for proper use and safety precautions.

Ovens

There's nothing worse than trying to scrape off spilled food that has attached itself like igneous rock to the inside of an oven. The secret—at least with most ovens—is getting to the grime quickly, preferably just after it spills. And generally speaking, the more often you clean your oven, the easier it will be to remove the food and grease.

Of course, preventing spills in the first place will save you a lot of grief. If you think a pie or casserole might bubble over, place a piece of foil that is just slightly larger than the cooking dish on a rack below. (Do not place foil directly on the entire bottom of the oven or cover a rack entirely with foil. You might cause an uneven distribution of heat.) "All those drippings will fall right onto that foil," says Beth McIntyre, a home economist for Maytag Appliances in Newton, Iowa. "It saves an extreme amount of cleanup."

In terms of cleaning, there are three basic types of ovens: conventional, self-cleaning, and continuous-clean. Each has its own requirements.

Conventional Ovens

A quick and easy way to clean standard ovens that are lightly soiled is to fill a small glass bowl with ½ cup ammonia, place it in the oven, and close the door. Do not turn on the oven. "The fumes will help loosen the baked-on food," McIntyre says. Let it stand overnight. Be careful when you open the oven door. Ammonia fumes can irritate eyes. Stand back and let the air clear a few minutes before wiping the loosened crud from the oven with paper towels or newspaper.

Note: If you have a gas oven with a continuous pilot light, extinguish the pilot light before putting ammonia in your oven.

If your oven is moderately to heavily soiled, that method probably won't get all the grime. You'll need more intensive measures. Wash the oven with a scrubber, like a nylon mesh ball, dipped in warm soapy water. Rub the surface gently and then rinse it with a sponge or cloth. Avoid scouring with steel wool, which can scratch the surface. That will help food cling to it and make it harder to clean the next time.

Commercial oven cleaners work well on standard ovens. However, they are strong and should be used with care. "Depending on how burned on the food is, it could be next to impossible to remove everything with just ammonia and soapy water," McIntyre points out.

Oven cleaners can damage other nearby surfaces that come in contact with the product. Protect these areas with layers of newspaper or other materials, and wear protective gloves. Follow the manufacturer's instructions carefully.

Wash removable racks and broiler pans by hand, soaking them first in soapy water and then scrubbing them with a plastic scrubber. Add a little ammonia to the water to loosen food while you scrub.

Clean glass doors by wiping them with ammonia. Wait a few minutes, and then wipe them with a moist sponge. If the gunk is heavy, scrape it off with a windshield ice scraper or a single-edge razor blade. Do not, however, scour the glass with steel wool.

Caution: Never spray commercial oven cleaner on a hot oven. It can become even more caustic and can corrode surfaces. Likewise, never spray oven cleaner on oven lights, electric elements, or gas pilot lights. (It's best to turn off the pilot light when using spray oven cleaner.)

Self-Cleaning Ovens

Self-cleaning ovens have a cycle during which the oven gets hot enough to disintegrate food spills and other soil. Oven models and brands vary. First and foremost, follow your oven manufacturer's directions.

To prevent food from being baked on, preclean the areas not exposed to the high heat during the self-cleaning cycle: the frame around the oven opening and the edge of the door outside the gasket. (*Caution:* Never clean the gasket with anything. Even water can corrode it, breaking the heat seal.) Use hot water and liquid dishwashing detergent or a paste of baking soda and hot water on harder-to-clean areas. Rinse well with water mixed with a little vinegar to remove all residue. Reclean these areas after you run the cleaning cycle.

To avoid etching or discoloration of the oven finish, wipe up food spills that are high in acid, like tomato sauce, fruit, or milk products. The porcelain enamel inside your oven is acid-resistant but not acid-proof.

Remove the oven racks and broiler pan before starting the cleaning cycle. Wash them by hand, soaking them first in soapy water and then scrubbing them with a plastic scrubber. Add a little ammonia to the soaking water to loosen food while you scrub.

When the cycle is finished, wipe out the small amount of fine ash left inside with a damp cloth.

Caution: Never use chemical oven cleaner in a self-cleaning oven. If residue remains, it can be changed by the high heat into compounds that etch the porcelain enamel.

Continuous-Clean Ovens

These are made with a rough, porous interior surface designed to resist stains and partially absorb grease. It also spreads spills out so that they oxidize more easily when the oven is hot. Keep in mind, however, that these ovens do not typically get squeaky-clean.

To help the oven catch up with accumulated grease and food, occasionally wipe out the inside of the oven with a nylon pad and plain water.

Wash the oven racks and broiler pan by hand, soaking them first in soapy water and then scrubbing them with a plastic scrubber. Add a little ammonia to the soaking water to loosen food while you scrub.

Sugar spills are the hardest for a continuous-clean oven to remove, so take precautions against fruit-cobbler boil-overs and other such spills.

If large spills do occur, they can seal the surface, preventing the oven's continuous oxidation process. While the oven is still slightly warm and the spill soft, blot up the food using paper towels or a sponge. Don't rub because the particles could clog the oven's pores.

Once the oven is completely cool, spray the spill with an all-purpose spray-on cleaner, like Fantastik. Work it into the porous surface by scrubbing gently with a nylon-bristle brush or nylon net pad. Let it stand 15 to 30 minutes, and then scrub the softened soil gently with the nylon brush or pad. Rinse the area thoroughly with cold water and a sponge, being careful not to let water run down into the burner assembly on gas ranges.

Speed tips: Are your oven racks really dirty? Put them in a heavy-duty plastic trash bag, add ½ cup household ammonia, and tie the bag up tightly. Let it sit overnight. When you open the bag, stand back and let the air clear for a few minutes before removing the racks. Then hose the racks down outside or rinse them in the sink.

Note: Ammonia can discolor racks with a high nickel content. Check with the manufacturer and ask if yours contain nickel. If you're unsure, test first by applying ammonia to an inconspicuous area.

Caution: Never apply all-purpose cleaners to a hot oven. Be sure to rinse away all cleaner residue. When heated, they can leave a chalky, hard-to-remove stain.

Never use oven cleaners or powdered cleaners on continuous-clean ovens. They will clog the pores. Likewise, never use any metal pads or abrasives. They can wear off the coating.

Paint

 EMERGENCY ACTION
If it is a latex paint, soak or blot it with water. For oil-based paints, blot up excess paint with a paper towel, being careful not to spread it. Blot with a spot remover or acetone. Don't use acetone on acetate fabric. It dissolves the fabric.

No need to change clothes, you thought, for a tiny little touch-up paint job. And now you've speckled your favorite dress shirt. You've just had a brush with paint stains, one of the toughest types to clean. But attacking paint stains before they have dried will improve your chances of removing them completely.

Technique: If possible, lay the stain faceup on white paper towels on a flat surface. Blot with a paper towel dabbed with a generally available spot remover, such as Energine. Use the spot remover in a well-ventilated area. After you have removed all you can by blotting, turn the stain over onto fresh towels and drop a few drops of the liquid onto the back of the stain with an eyedropper. This should force loose particles into the paper towels. "At that point, you've probably gotten rid of the plastic component," says Jane Rising, instructor in the education department at the International Fabricare Institute in Silver Spring, Maryland. If not, try the same technique using acetone, the main ingredient in one type of nail polish remover, available in drugstores and hardware stores. Be careful because acetone dissolves acetate fabric.

To remove the last traces of the stain, blot with a solution of ¼ teaspoon clear liquid dishwashing detergent and ½ cup cold water, using a clean white towel. Then wash the item as directed. If that does not remove the stain completely, follow the same technique but with a solution of 1 teaspoon ammonia and ½ cup cold water. Again, wash as directed.

For carpets, always apply cleaning solutions to a towel, never directly onto the carpet. Otherwise, it can soak into the carpet backing or pad and attract more dirt.

Note: Before using cleaning solutions, always test them on an inconspicuous section of the stained item.

Caution. "Do not reach for the paint thinner," Rising warns "Paint thinners are not colorless liquids. You might get the paint stain out, but then you have another stain."

Always rinse one cleaning solution before trying another. Mixing chemicals, especially ammonia and chlorine bleach, can create noxious fumes. Read all product labels carefully for proper usage and safety precautions.

Painted Surfaces

Walls and other painted surfaces collect dirt and grime like magnets. "Dogs rub up against walls, and children wipe greasy fingerprints on them," says Kay Weirick, director of housekeeping services at Bally's Las Vegas Hotel and a member of the technical advisory committee for *Executive Housekeeping Today* magazine. "How you clean painted walls depends on what type of paint was used."

Technique: First, remove loose soil by dusting or vacuuming the surface.

No matter what type of paint you have, always test your cleaning solution first on an inconspicuous area. Wipe it on and let it dry before inspecting. If the paint is gloss or semigloss, use an all-purpose cleaner or a solution of liquid dishwashing detergent and warm water. Start at the bottom and work up so that your cleaning solution does not run down the dirty wall and cause hard-to-remove streaks. Rub gently using a sponge or soft cloth. Rinse by wiping with a clean moist sponge or cloth. Dry the area with clean towels.

Try to avoid touch-up painting. Even if you have the matching paint color, touch-ups of paint older than a year tend to look splotchy.

If it is flat paint, try removing small marks with a white vinyl eraser, available at art and office supply stores. Water can remove and stain flat paint.

Painting Equipment

The key to cleaning up after a painting job is to do it sooner rather than later. The more the paint has a chance to dry, the harder it will be to remove. Let the chore slip and you may have to buy new brushes or rollers the next time you pop open a paint can.

Technique: The first consideration when it comes to cleaning painting equipment—buckets and pans, brushes and rollers—is the type of paint that you're using.

Water-based paint is much easier to clean than oil-based paint. For rollers, begin by scraping the excess paint back into the original can using a crescent-shape scraper, often found on 5-in-1 painters tools. Then wash the roller in warm soapy water until it is free of paint.

Wash brushes used with water-based paint in warm soapy water until free of paint. Use a paintbrush comb, available at hardware and paint supply stores, to clean between bristles. Pans and buckets come clean easily when washed with soapy water.

For cleaning oil-based paint off equipment, first remove any excess paint. In the case of rollers, again use the crescent-shape scraper. Next, use a brush and roller cleaner, like Kwikeeze, available at paint supply and hardware stores. "These products work better than the typical paint thinner," says Jim Westerman, president of the Carbit Paint Company in Chicago, "and they work on all types of paint."

Pour the cleaner in an old paint-free paint can or coffee can. Let the brush or roller soak for a while, and then rub and scrape the paint off. "Because brush and roller cleaners don't evaporate very quickly, they're reusable," Westerman says. The paint eventually settles to the bottom, and you can pour off the pure solvent for use later. Give the brush or roller a final rinse in clean paint thinner. Wrap it in aluminum foil and tightly seal the ends for storage.

Clean buckets and pans used with oil-based paint with the brush and roller cleaner. Or, just remove excess paint and let the rest dry. Keep pans clean in the first place by covering them in aluminum foil. Throw the foil away when you're finished.

Speed tips: Holding your brush head-down inside an empty bucket or can, with the handle between your two palms, spin it to remove excess paint and paint solvent. Holding it in the can keeps paint from splattering. Do the same with rollers by using a roller spinner, available at paint supply stores.

In a pinch: When you're planning to reuse a brush that has been used with oil-based paint, save yourself the trouble of a complete cleaning by simply standing it on its bristles in a half-inch of brush and roller cleaner. Then cover it with plastic wrap. "Through capillary action, the solvent will rise and keep the brush from drying out for a day or two," says Westerman. Do same with a roller by dipping it in the solvent and wrapping it tightly with aluminum foil.

Caution: When cleaning painting equipment with solvents, such as a brush and roller cleaner or paint thinner, use protective eyewear. Petroleum-based solvents are very flammable and dangerous to breathe. Ventilate the work area well. Keep the solvent away from open flame (like pilot lights) and sparks. Carefully read product labels for proper usage and safety precautions.

Paneling

To properly clean paneling, you must first identify it. There is real wood paneling, which comes in a variety of different wood species and finishes, and there is hardboard paneling, which features a baked-on plastic coating made to look like wood. While the faux-finish style is relatively easy to clean, you must be careful cleaning real wood paneling. Like wood furniture, it is sensitive to many cleaning materials and techniques.

Technique: Dust both types of surfaces regularly as part of your normal cleaning routine.

To clean hardboard paneling, wipe it down with a sponge or cloth dampened in a solution of warm water and a squirt of liquid dishwashing detergent. Rinse by wiping it down with a clean damp sponge or cloth.

If the wall is very dirty, use a stronger solution, such as an all-purpose household cleaner whose label says it is safe for painted walls. Test it first in an inconspicuous area to make sure that it does not damage the finish. Rinse the paneling thoroughly by wiping with a clean damp sponge or cloth. Do not use any solvents on hardboard paneling. It may strip the finish.

For paneling made from real wood, try to get by with the dusting alone. "It's best to try to avoid water as much as possible when you're cleaning real wood," says Douglas Gardner, Ph.D., associate professor of wood science at the School of Forestry and Wood Products, Michigan Technological University in Houghton.

If the paneling needs a heavier cleaning, however, you can use a spray-on product like Endust or Pledge. A nonemulsified polish like Pledge is clear and will remove grease and wax. An emulsified polish, which is milky-white, will clean water-soluble dirt as well as grease. Use a nonemulsified polish on old fragile wood to avoid damaging the finish. Or use a lightly dampened cloth and a neutral cleaner, like Murphy Oil Soap. Follow the manufacturer's instructions for mixing the solution. Again, pretest the cleaner on a small inconspicuous area first.

Speed tips: To dust paneling, especially that with detailed carving, use a vacuum cleaner brush attachment.

Pencil Marks

It's time to get the "lead" out. "Pencil is basically graphite, which has layers," says Rajiv Jain, laboratory manager for the Association of Specialists in Cleaning and Restoration in Millersville, Maryland. "Since the stain is on the surface, you must use regular mechanical

HOW IT WORKS

Pass Me That Basketball, I Made a Mistake

Think of erasers as the other way to dry-clean, says Jim Weissenborn, chief executive officer of the General Pencil Company in Redwood, California.

"Through adhesion, erasers pull substances like pencil graphite off surfaces," says Weissenborn. "If you really wanted to, you could erase with a rubber ball, like a racquetball or basketball—anything that's abrasive. For years, erasers, like the pink kind you used in school, contained rubber and pumice. The old gray typewriter erasers had loads of pumice because they had to take the typing ink out of the paper. Actually, what they did was remove half of the paper. But more and more erasers these days are made out of plastic or vinyl, without the pumice. They don't dig in as much. They actually remove whatever is on the surface of the paper or wallpaper without hurting the material. There are even erasers for taking pencil out of fabric."

means, like surfactants." In other words, there are no chemical solutions that dissolve it.

Technique: For pencil marks in fabric, blot with a white towel and a solution of 1 teaspoon liquid dishwashing detergent and 1 cup lukewarm water. Don't rub the stain. That could smear it. Wash as directed.

If it's a pencil mark on a wall, use the same soapy solution but scrub gently with a sponge. "The sponge has just enough 'tooth' to pull the stain off," says Jim Weissenborn, chief executive officer of the General Pencil Company in Redwood, California, which has been in his family since 1889.

For nonwashable surfaces, gently erase pencil marks using a white vinyl eraser, available at office and art supply stores. Avoid using normal pink pencil erasers, which tend to be abrasive. A white vinyl eraser will work on painted surfaces, wallpaper, and even fabric.

Perfume

What pleases the nose may not please the eye. "Perfumes contain oils that can oxidize and become very difficult to remove," says Jane Rising, instructor in the education department at the International Fabricare Institute in Silver Spring, Maryland. "They also contain alcohol, which can damage color." The sooner you attack a perfume stain, the better.

Technique: Pretreat the stain before washing the item. Begin by mixing ¼ teaspoon clear liquid dishwashing detergent with ½ cup warm water. Apply it directly to the fabric, and then lay the garment on a hard surface and pat the stain lightly with the back of a spoon. This allows the solution to get in between the fibers, where stains hide. Don't rub the fabric together. That will abrade the fibers. Next, wash as directed either by machine or by hand in the hottest water safe for the fabric.

If that doesn't remove the perfume completely, try rubbing alcohol. But be careful because alcohol can cause dyes to bleed. Lay the stain facedown on an absorbent white cloth. Apply the alcohol to another cloth or cotton ball, and then blot from the inside of the garment to push the stain out. If colors bleed or the fabric is acetate, try diluting the alcohol with two parts water.

For carpets, always apply the solvent to a towel—never directly onto the carpet. Otherwise, it can soak into the carpet backing or pad and attract more dirt. Rinse by blotting with a clean white cloth soaked in water.

Note: Before using cleaning solutions, always test them on an inconspicuous section of the stained item.

Caution: Always rinse a cleaning solution before trying another. Mixing chemicals, especially ammonia and chlorine bleach, can create noxious fumes. Carefully read all product labels for proper usage and safety precautions.

Perspiration

"Sweat equity" is fine if you're improving your house. But don't let it build up in your clothes.

"Perspiration contains chloride salts, which can damage both color and fiber," says Jane Rising, instructor in the education department at the International Fabricare Institute in Silver Spring, Maryland. "It starts out acidic and becomes alkaline with age, and alkalis can damage silk and other fibers." Perspiration also attracts clothes moths. Your goal is to remove perspiration stains as soon as possible.

Technique: If you have washable items with stubborn sweat stains, soak them for several hours in a solution of warm water and a pretreatment product containing enzymes, like Biz. Keep the water warm while soaking. Next, wash as directed either by machine or by hand in the hottest water safe for the fabric.

Take dry-clean-only garments, especially silks, to be cleaned as soon as you can.

Note: Before using cleaning solutions, always test them on an inconspicuous section of the stained item.

Pet Urine and Excrement

When you gotta go, you gotta go—and that applies even to house-trained dogs and the most domesticated cats. The key in cleaning up after them is to do it as quickly as possible to prevent staining, discoloration, and odors.

Technique: Urine is more problematic, especially on carpets and fabrics, because it can cause dyes to bleed and fibers to deteriorate.

First, absorb as much of the pet urine as possible using white cloths or paper towels. Then blot the area with a white towel soaked in a solution of 1 teaspoon neutral white or colorless liquid dishwashing detergent in 1 cup lukewarm water. Soak up as much as possible using a clean towel. Next, blot the area with a solution of one part white vinegar to two parts water. Again, use a towel to soak up as much as possible. Cover the area with several white terry towels, place something heavy on them, and allow the area to dry for at least six hours.

As an alternative, first, clean up urine or watery excrement with paper towels. "Then, saturate the spot with an enzymatic odor neutralizer, such as Nature's Miracle, sold at pet stores," says Jacque Schultz, director of Companion Animal Services for the American Society for the Prevention of Cruelty to Animals, in New York City. These contain living bacteria that eat the waste's protein base. They typically call for keeping the spot moistened for about eight hours, but you should follow the directions on the particular product you purchase. Afterward, clean the area by blotting with a towel soaked in water, and then blot dry with a towel.

For excrement, pick up solid deposits as quickly as possible using a plastic sandwich bag or tissue paper and discard. Clean the area with the same detergent solution used to clean urine, and blot dry. Rinse the area with water and blot dry again. Follow up with a disinfectant or one of the many odor removers available at pet supply stores. For less-than-solid solids, follow one of the procedures described for cleaning urine, then follow up with the disinfectant.

Note: Before using cleaning solutions, always test them on an inconspicuous section of the stained item.

Caution: Store cleaning products in a safe out-of-the-way place so that your pets don't chew on them. Read product labels carefully for proper usage and safety precautions.

Pewter

Although pewter does not tarnish as much as silver, over time it still develops a layer of corrosion that can be cleaned.

Technique: Simply polish it with a flannel cloth. "On the whole, I don't do much to pewter," says Ellen Salzman, an objects conservator at the Metropolitan Museum of Art in New York City. "I think the nature of the material lends itself to a more modest shine." On older pieces that patina is desired and may even add value.

If, however, the pewter has been sitting for a long time and is covered in a stubborn layer of tarnish, use a mild silver polish diluted with water to make it less abrasive. "Generally, you can feel if something is too abrasive. If you can't feel the grit, it's mild enough," Salzman explains.

Photographs

Simple mishandling is one of the leading causes of injured photos. "There's a reason that you should hold the prints by the edges," says Peter Halpert, an independent curator in New York City and contributing editor of *American Photo* magazine. "Your hands naturally carry oils, and when you rub them over your face and your hair, they pick up more oil." The oils and salt will eventually react with the photographic chemicals and cause color distortion and fading.

Technique: Color prints are very sensitive. They cannot be safely cleaned with water or a solvent. Instead, buff fingerprints and other

HOW I DO IT

Focus on Prevention

Because photographs are so sensitive and fragile, prevention is just as important as cleaning, says Peter Halpert, an independent curator in New York City and contributing editor of *American Photo* magazine. Here are a few strategies that he uses to keep from having to clean his prints and negatives.

"I never put prints in those photo albums with self-sticking pages, the kind that have the glue backing," Halpert says. "The glue seeps into the papers. It's the worst thing you can do to your family treasures, or even your fun snaps.

"I use the old system that everyone's grandmother had of tucking the photos into four little corners and pasting those corners onto black acid-free paper. That's the best thing that you can do for photos.

"I also separate the pictures from atmospheric conditions as much as possible. Humidity can cause the emulsion of one print to stick to another print. If that happens, and you pull them apart, it will damage the photos. I'm not talking about things that necessarily have great artistic value, but they may have a great deal of sentimental value."

stains with clean dry cotton. Do not use an eraser because it can abrade the surface and remove the glossy sheen.

Most contemporary black-and-white prints are made from gelatin bromide, which can be cleaned carefully with a solvent. Look for a film-cleaning solvent that does not contain a lubricant at your local photo laboratory. Moisten a cotton ball and gently wipe across the fingerprint. Although the fingerprint impression may not come off, this will remove the damaging oily residue. The same applies to black-and-white gelatin prints dating back to the 1920s, but treat older photos with even more care. Anything before that era should be cleaned by a professional. (For a photography conservator referral in your area, write to the American Institute for Conservation of Historic and Artistic Works at 1717 K Street NW, Suite 301, Washington, DC 20006.)

If your photos get wet, the best way to dry them is to carefully hang them on a line using clothespins. Prevent moisture, dust, and other atmospheric substances from harming photos by putting them in photo albums with acid-free paper and storing the albums in boxes. Do not store the boxes in damp basements or near heaters. Do not stack photos together in a shoe box.

The Low-Sodium Résumé

On his way to becoming one of this country's most respected photography conservators, José Orraca worked at the George Eastman House International Museum of Photography and Film in Rochester, New York.

"It was often said at the George Eastman House," says Orraca, "that when you applied for a job in the research laboratory at Kodak, the last thing they would do in the interview process was put your fingers on a piece of metal. If the metal did not rust, you were more likely to be hired. The reason is that some of us have more natural body oils and salts than others, which rust metal and can damage photographic materials."

Pictures and Frames

The whole point of display objects like framed pictures is to keep them looking their best. So make sure that any cleaning you do will not harm the frame's finish or what is under the glass.

Technique: Dust pictures and frames regularly to avoid dirt buildup. Use a feather duster or soft-bristle brush.

For harder-to-remove soil, wipe with a slightly moistened cloth. Use a solution of warm water and mild liquid dishwashing detergent, if needed, taking care to wring the cloth well to avoid wetting the frame too much.

"Be careful of shellac and other finishes," says Kay Weirick, director of housekeeping services at Bally's Las Vegas Hotel and a member of the technical advisory committee for *Executive Housekeeping Today* magazine. "Something like Windex can remove a fake brass finish." Avoid wetting antique or especially fragile or ornate frames. Simply keep them free of dust.

Never spray glass cleaner directly onto the glass. It might hurt the frame or run between the glass and frame and ruin the matting or picture. Instead, wipe the glass carefully with a cloth moistened with the mild detergent solution. "In the old days, we used vinegar and water and newspaper," Weirick says. That still works for cleaning glass, as long as you apply it carefully and avoid making ink smudges.

Speed tips: For hard-to-reach nooks and crannies, blow air over them by squeezing an empty plastic bottle with a small nozzle—an old shampoo bottle, for example.

Pilling

Your favorite sweater has broken out with a rash of minuscule pom-poms. This pilling is caused by short fibers that stick out of the fabric. The fibers fray and form ugly little balls. "Those little fuzz balls are really grounded into the fabric," says Darcy Crocker, quality control supervisor at the Wool Bureau in New York City. "Has your dog ever come home with burrs in its fur? Pilling is similar."

Technique: The best way to clean up large pills on a garment is to remove them manually, either with your fingers or with a de-pilling device. To get rid of the small pills that form on cotton fabric, simply wash the clothes in a laundry detergent that contains enzymes (check the list of ingredients on the box). The enzymes eat away at the cellulose of the exposed fibers, leaving the garment looking fresh and new.

Crocker recommends a product called D-Fuzz-It, which resembles a lint brush but has a coarse-grade sandpaper facing. When you

Pilling: Know Thine Enemy

By understanding the nature of those annoying balls of fuzz that collect on clothing, you stand a better chance of defeating them.

"To make yarn—regardless of whether it is polyester, rayon or wool—you spin fibers together," explains Darcy Crocker, quality control supervisor at the Wool Bureau in New York City. "When you wrap them around one another, some fiber ends protrude." The arm of your jacket brushes against your side, abrading the protruding fibers. They fray and join together, forming balls. "That's what causes pilling," she says.

Then the pills slowly work the fibers out even more and grow into even bigger pills.

"The shorter the length of the fibers, the more chance there is for the garment to pill," Crocker says. Silk is a continuous filament and does not pill. Wool, on the other hand, is a notorious piller made from fibers that are only ¼ inch to 4 inches long. A worsted wool suit, made from long wool fibers that are well-combed and tightly woven, does not pill as much as a Shetland wool sweater, which contains short fuzzy fibers.

To combat pilling, you must either depill or try to prevent it, which isn't easy. Look for garments, like silk, worsted wool, or cotton, that are made from longer, more tightly woven fibers. Or try to reduce the amount of abrasion you subject a garment to. If your favorite dress has a tendency to pill, don't wear it quite as often. And try to wear nonpilling items when doing active things.

In other words, "don't play touch football in your favorite wool sweater," says Crocker.

brush it over the garment, the brush picks the pills off. Another type of device is the battery-operated pill remover. It looks like an electric shaver and works much the same way. A rotating blade clips the pills and draws them into a compartment in the handle. When it's full, you simply open it up and discard the pile of pills. Fabric and department stores sell both types of devices.

"Don't do it too roughly," Crocker warns, "or do too much at once." When you pull pills, you also pull fibers, which can thin out your garment.

In a pinch: "If you have a large area of pilling but you don't have a lot of time, defuzz it randomly," Crocker says. "Pick off one here and one there to reduce the overall appearance."

Pillows

Here's a thought that will keep you awake at night: "Most people don't realize how much dead skin our bodies slough off," says Marry Keener, assistant director of facilities management at the University of Arizona in Tucson and a member of the technical advisory committee for *Executive Housekeeping Today* magazine. You want to remove that dander to keep pillows fresh and clean-smelling.

Technique: Clean pillows at least twice a year. You can machine-wash most fiber-filled pillows. Use cold water, which is safer on the synthetic filling. Tumble dry on low heat, or dry them in the sun on a patio chair.

Don't clean down-filled pillows at home, recommends Jane Rising, instructor in the education department at the International Fabricare Institute in Silver Spring, Maryland. "Many pillow coverings have natural starches that hold the fill in place," she says. "Washing them causes the starches to break down, and the down can begin to leak from the pillow." Your best bet for pillows is to take them to a dry cleaner who is an expert in cleaning down, says Rising.

Once or twice a year, air out down pillows outdoors in the shade to keep them fresh.

In a pinch: To freshen and remove humidity, place down-filled pillows in a dryer on low heat for about 10 minutes. "A lot of the dust and dander will be trapped in the lint filter," says Keener.

Plants

Cleaning plants is not like scrubbing bathroom tile. You want to keep plants looking dust-free and fresh—but rough treatment would grind them into pulp.

Technique: The bathtub is a convenient place to clean houseplants. First, put each plant's pot in a plastic bag and tie the bag loosely around the stem. This keeps the water from splashing dirt out of the pot and onto the plant and tub. Next, put the plants in the bathtub and let the shower run over their leaves for a few minutes.

"They get sprayed from overhead just like they're out in the rain," says Louise Wrinkle, a veteran horticulture judge for the Garden Club of America in New York City.

When the weather is nice, take plants outside and spray them with the hose. Be careful, however, about leaving them outside. The sudden change from inside to outside—and vice versa—can harm some plants.

In a pinch: Dust plants where they stand using a can of compressed air or a blow-dryer set on its lowest coolest setting. Do not blow plants with heavy gusts of hot air.

Plastic Laminate

Often referred to by the popular brand name Formica, plastic laminate was designed to be easy to clean. Hey, someone's watching out for you after all!

Technique: Wipe up spills with a moist sponge. Clean with a soapy sponge or a grit-free all-purpose cleaner—never anything abrasive. "Use a germicide on kitchen countertops because that's one of the main places germs are," says Kay Weirick, director of housekeeping services at Bally's Las Vegas Hotel and a member of the technical advisory committee for *Executive Housekeeping Today* magazine. She recommends reading the labels of kitchen-cleaning products and choosing one that specifically says that it sanitizes or kills germs.

To remove stains, such as mustard, grape juice, or coffee, sprinkle baking soda on a soft damp cloth and rub gently. For more stubborn stains, dampen the stained area and spray or sprinkle with a cleanser containing bleach, such as Comet with Bleach. Let it stand for about 10 minutes, and then rinse it off with clear water. If it stands longer, it may bleach the color out of the plastic.

Do not cut on plastic laminate. Soil gets into cracks and causes stains and breeds bacteria.

Plywood and Particleboard

As with other wood products, the cleaning method for plywood and particleboard depends on the finish. Either way, they do not pose a big cleaning challenge.

Technique: Most plywood and particleboard used in the home is covered in some type of surface—either vinyl or a plastic laminate, like Formica. Clean these water-resistant finishes with a moist cloth and warm sudsy water or an all-purpose cleaner.

For raw wood surfaces, try to avoid cleaning with water. Dust periodically with a dry cloth. If you must wipe away soil or residue, use a cloth lightly dampened only with water, and dry the wood quickly. Use a dry cloth or ventilate the room well. Otherwise, the moisture could seep into the porous wood or particleboard and cause warping or thickness swells.

Polyester

Polyester is relatively easy to clean because its fibers do not absorb water-soluble stains. "Oil stains in polyester are another ball game," says Jane Rising, instructor in the education department at the International Fabricare Institute in Silver Spring, Maryland. "Stains with grease or oil, even body oils, are hard to remove because the polyester absorbs them."

Technique: Always read care labels first. Most polyester can be machine-washed. Other types, however, like coated polyester draperies should be dry-cleaned only.

For machine washable polyester, wash on a cool- or warm-water cycle using regular laundry detergent. "The danger in washing polyester in hot water is that it wrinkles terribly," Rising explains.

Tumble dry at a low temperature and remove the articles as soon as the tumbling cycle is complete. If ironing is needed, use a cool to moderately warm iron. Look for a polyester setting on your iron.

For most stains, including light oil-based and perspiration stains, pretreat with a spray-on stain remover, like Shout. Or apply a liquid laundry detergent (or a paste made from a granular detergent and water) directly onto the stain. Lay the garment on a hard surface and pat the stain lightly with the back of a spoon. Don't rub the material together. That can abrade the fibers. Next, wash as directed either by machine or by hand in the hottest water safe for the fabric.

For stubborn oily or greasy stains, have your polyester item dry-cleaned.

Porcelain

Because porcelain is delicate, cleaning it requires know-how and a gentle touch.

Technique: For soap scum, light rust stains, and mold growth on porcelain surfaces—sinks, tubs, toilets, and some appliances—use an all-purpose household cleaner, a nonabrasive tub-and-tile cleaner, or warm water and plain baking soda. Scrub with a cloth or sponge, rinse, and dry. Avoid harsh scouring agents and scrubbers. They can scratch the surface and cause it to stain. Never use steel wool on porcelain.

For valuable vases, cups, and other objects, which often can't be submerged, use a solution of warm water and a few drops of a mild liquid dishwashing detergent. Dip a cotton cloth, ball, or swab into the solution and wipe it across the surface. To clean hard-to-reach areas, try a soft toothbrush. "Do it the same way the dentist tells you to brush your teeth," says Ellen Salzman, an objects conservator at the Metropolitan Museum of Art in New York City, "slowly and carefully as opposed to sawing back and forth." Never use metal, which can scratch porcelain. Bamboo skewers and wooden toothpicks are good for safely cleaning gunk out of cracks and crevices.

For those impossible stains, especially the ones that adhere to cracks and other rough spots where the glaze is gone, try hydrogen peroxide, but only as a last resort. And be careful. Rather than removing the stain, hydrogen peroxide bleaches it, so make sure that all paint and gilding is securely fired on. Lay a cotton poultice soaked in a 5 percent solution of hydrogen peroxide along the stained area. Cover it with cellophane to keep it moist. Check it after 10 minutes to make sure that it is not damaging the porcelain surface. Repeat this procedure until the stain is bleached. Afterward, soak the object in water or wipe it clean with a moist cotton cloth.

If you have a valuable porcelain heirloom that needs cleaning, consider hiring a professional. For a referral in your area, contact the nearest museum and ask for the objects conservation department. Or write to the American Institute for Conservation of Historic and Artistic Works at 1717 K Street NW, Suite 301, Washington, DC 20006.

Speed tips: "Spit works very well," says Salzman. "Saliva has an enzyme called amylase that aids in the cleaning process." Just spit on a cotton cloth or moisten a swab in your mouth, and wipe it across stains.

Pots and Pans

Ignore your pots and pans and they'll get back at you. "Any food left in a pot will absorb a soap flavor and will affect the next thing you cook," says Kari Kinder, assistant director of food and beverage at the renowned Culinary Institute of America in Hyde Park, New York. "And it can breed bacteria." It's also important to clean pots and pans thoroughly to remove grease from the outside surface. Otherwise, when heated that residue can cause a nasty, hard-to-remove carbon buildup.

Technique: Generally speaking, you should wash pots and pans by hand. Don't forget to clean the greasy bottoms of pots and pans. For burned-on food, bring a solution of water and ¼ teaspoon liquid dishwashing detergent to a boil in the dirty pan. Simmer until soil loosens.

Aluminum

Automatic dishwasher detergent and minerals in water can discolor aluminum finishes. Washing by hand helps avoid dulling of the sheen. Remove discoloration in pots by boiling a solution of 1 to 2 tablespoons cream of tartar or lemon juice to each quart of water for 10 minutes. Loosen lime scale—deposited by waterborne minerals—from teakettles by boiling a one-to-one solution of water and vinegar. Let the solution stand in the teakettle for several hours, then rub with steel wool. Do not store water or moist foods in aluminum because the moisture can pit the metal.

Brass and Copper

To remove tarnish from brass or copper, sprinkle on salt and a little vinegar or lemon juice, rub, rinse, and dry. Or rub gently with a paste made from flour, salt, and vinegar or lemon juice. The acid in the vinegar and lemon juice gives the metal a bright shine. "Don't use abrasive cleaners like Brasso," warns Kinder. "We have actually had to replace pots here at the Culinary Institute because students scrubbed away the brass."

Enamelware

This cookware is usually made from metal covered with porcelain enamel. Soften burned-on food by presoaking it in warm soapy water. Scrub with a nonabrasive scrubber, like a nylon net ball. Avoid using scouring powders or steel wool. As a mild cleaning powder, try baking soda.

The Pots and Pans Problem-Solver

Pot type	Problem	Cleaning substance	Technique
Aluminum	Discoloration	1 to 2 table-spoons cream of tartar or lemon juice per quart of water	Boil for 10 minutes
	Lime scale (in teakettles)	One-to-one vinegar and water	Let stand for several hours, and then scrub with steel wool
Brass/copper	Tarnish	Paste made from flour, salt, and vinegar or lemon juice	Rub gently
Enamelware	Stubborn stains	Baking soda	Scrub gently
Iron	Cooked-on food	2 teaspoons baking soda per quart of water	Boil for a few minutes to loosen
Nonstick	Lingering flavors (like onion or garlic)	1 tablespoon vinegar or lemon juice per pan	Let soak, and then wash with soapy sponge full of water
	Stubborn stains or cooked-on food	3 tablespoons oxygen bleach per cup of water	Simmer for 15 to 20 minutes
Pyrex	Burned-on foods, especially sugar and starch	Squirt of liquid dishwashing detergent, 1 tablespoon baking soda, water	Let soak and then clean with nonabrasive scrubber

Iron

One of the biggest issues with cast-iron cookware, like skillets, is avoiding rust. Store iron pots and pans in a dry place. Never leave the lids on because condensation can cause rust. Iron cookware needs to be seasoned occasionally to avoid rusting. To season it, clean it in hot soapy water, dry it, and then coat it lightly with shortening or vegetable oil and heat at 200° to 300°F in the oven for 30 minutes. Let the skillet cool, and wipe off the excess fat with a paper towel. After use, gently clean the pan in hot sudsy water (without heavy scrubbing), rinse, and dry it. (Hint: To get iron pans really dry, heat them briefly over a stove burner.) Finally, wipe them with a thin coating of oil before storing. Never scour with harsh powders or steel wool. To loosen cooked-on food, boil a solution of 2 teaspoons baking soda per quart of water. If the pot does rust, scrub it with steel wool, clean in hot sudsy water, and re-season.

Nonstick

Once these surface coatings are scratched, they lose their non-stick quality. Avoid using abrasive cleaners, such as steel wool and scouring powders. Instead, wash in hot soapy water using a sponge, rinse, and dry. For hard-water stains or baked-on food in a nonstick pan, simmer a solution of 3 tablespoons oxygen bleach (also called all-fabric bleach) and 1 cup water for 15 to 20 minutes. Wash the pan thoroughly, rinse, and dry. For lingering garlic, onion, or other flavors in a nonstick pan, mix 1 tablespoon vinegar or lemon juice into a full pan of water. Let it soak, wash with a soapy sponge, then rinse and dry.

Pyrex

Wash this sturdy glass cookware in the dishwasher or by hand in warm soapy water. For baked-on food in casserole dishes and other bakeware of glass or glass-ceramic material, soak in a solution of liquid dishwashing detergent and water to loosen soil. For burned-on sugar or starchy foods, add a little baking soda to the presoak solution. Then scrub using a mild product like baking soda. Do not use metal scouring pads, which may scratch the surface. To remove greasy stains, use ammonia or a cleaner that contains ammonia, such as Soft Scrub. For coffee and tea stains, soak in a solution of 2 tablespoons automatic dishwasher detergent per quart of warm water.

Speed tips: It's common sense, but it's worth reiterating. Scraping and presoaking pots and pans greatly speeds up the process.

Use a nonstick spray, like Pam, before cooking. These typically spread a thin layer of vegetable oil or lecithin on the pan and are especially useful on old pans whose nonstick surface is worn partially off.

Pottery

Cleaning glazed pottery is a fairly simple task. Unglazed pottery requires a different technique and a gentle hand.

Technique: If the pottery is well-glazed, then simply clean it with warm water, a mild liquid dishwashing detergent, and a gentle sponge or vegetable brush, like you would everyday china. "The less fired the pottery, the more fragile it is and the less water you should get on it," says Ellen Salzman, an objects conservator at the Metropolitan Museum of Art in New York City. "It can start to break apart. If it's chipped, pieces of the glaze can fall off."

Clean fragile pottery like you would porcelain. Dip a cotton cloth, ball, or swab into a solution of warm water and a mild liquid dishwashing detergent, then wipe it gently across the surface. If there are parts that are not fired at all, roll the cotton over them rather than rub it back and forth. Or give them a gentle dry cleaning by lightly rubbing stains with a white vinyl block eraser, available at stationery and art supply stores. Do not use a pink pencil eraser, which is too abrasive and can leave behind damaging residue.

Speed tips: Because it contains the enzyme amylase, saliva is a good cleaning compound. "Sometimes I think I went to school for four years to learn how to clean with spit," laughs Salzman, referring to how often she uses this simple technique. Just spit on a cotton cloth or moisten a swab in your mouth, and wipe or roll it across stains.

Pressure Cookers

Pressure cookers are basically pots with a screw-on, tightly sealed top and a valve for letting steam escape. So cleaning them is much like cleaning any other pot, except you must also clean the valve and the gasket around the rim of the top.

Technique: Begin by cleaning your pressure cooker like any other pot—with warm soapy water or in the dishwasher. Don't forget to clean any grease on the bottom. For burned-on food, bring a solution of water and ¼ teaspoon liquid dishwashing detergent to a boil in the dirty pan. Simmer with the top off until the food loosens.

Remove the valve from the top, take it apart, and clean the parts with warm soapy water and a kitchen scrubber. (If it is unclear how to take the valve apart, read the manufacturer's instructions.)

"The valve should not be difficult to clean," says Michael Beglinger, executive chef at Deutsche Bank in New York City. "Steam is all that passes through it." Still, you want to wash and dry it completely before storing the pressure cooker.

Also remove the rubber gasket from the pressure cooker's lid. Clean it in warm soapy water, and clean the surface of the lid underneath the gasket. Let them both dry completely before replacing the gasket.

Quilts

Quilt cleaning is no simple Sunday chore. There are several key issues: the type and strength of the fabric, the colorfastness of the dyes, the type of fill, and the quilt's age and condition. You want to clean your quilt but not at the risk of ruining it, especially if it is old or has sentimental value.

Technique: If your quilt is treasured or fragile, avoid cleaning when possible, or if you must clean it, have it cleaned by a professional cleaner who is experienced in cleaning fabrics for museums. Quilt appraisers do not recommend dry-cleaning quilts. Often, wedding-dress cleaners clean quilts and other fragile textiles. If you must dry-clean a quilt, ask that fresh solvent be used. Certain types of quilts, such as wool, silk, and combination quilts (such as crazy quilts), should be dry-cleaned only if they are so soiled that you cannot enjoy them, says Nancy O'Bryant, a national expert on quilt care from Austin, Texas, and a contributing author in *The Quilters Ultimate Visual Guide*. For really valuable pieces, contact your local museum's conservation department for advice.

Even cleaning newer quilts can be tricky. First, look for a care label and follow the instructions. If it has no label, proceed carefully.

Begin by testing for colorfastness. Use a clean white handkerchief and a solution of liquid dishwashing detergent and warm water. Dip a corner of the handkerchief in the solution, wrap a color patch from the quilt around it, and squeeze for about a minute. "If there is any color transfer, you should not continue," says Jane Rising, instructor in the education department at the International Fabricare Institute in Silver Spring, Maryland. "It means that you can't clean the quilt without causing damage." If there is no color transfer, continue until you have tested each of the different colors and different pieces of fabric.

If it passes the colorfastness test, you must next consider the integrity of the fibers. Age and exposure to light, moisture, and atmospheric gases can cause fabrics to deteriorate. "Since we have three layers of goodies here—the top of the quilt, the fill and the back—it could be that one or all have lost enough strength so that it comes apart like tissue paper when it's wet," Rising warns.

Another concern is the quilt's fill, which will vary depending on its age and where it was made. Since the fill is on the inside—and presumably you don't want to tear open your quilt to get to it—the more you know about the origin of the quilt, the better. For example, older quilts are often filled with cotton batting that was never completely cleared of sticks and other cotton-plant residue. This residue can bleed when wet, leaving brown spots. Other quilts contain wool batting, which can shrink when washed with high heat and heavy mechanical action.

If you decide that it's safe to clean your quilt, line a clean bathtub with a sheet. Fill the tub up with 6 to 10 inches of warm water, and add several squirts of mild liquid dishwashing detergent. Fold the quilt and lay it flat in the tub. Using a clean plunger, agitate the water, not the quilt. Let it soak for five minutes, and then agitate the water some more. Do not scrub the quilt or put any tension on it because the stitches might pop. The combination of warm water, detergent, and mild agitation should remove much of the surface soil.

To rinse the quilt, empty the tub and refill it with clean water. Continue agitating the water. Empty the tub and repeat this cycle until there is no longer any soap residue. Carefully lift the sheet up with the quilt in it to move it to a flat drying area.

Do not wring the quilt to remove the water. Instead, roll up the folded quilt and push gently. Unroll it and repeat this drying process several times.

For a speedier method, you can use the tub of your washing machine to "hand-wash" your quilt, says Becky Herdle, a quilting expert and instructor in Rochester, New York, and a contributing author in *The Quilters Ultimate Visual Guide*. Spin the water out after the soaking and gentle agitation. Spinning pushes the quilt against the walls of the machine, but it doesn't agitate. Rinse several times to get the soap solution out.

Finally, place it somewhere—away from direct sunlight—to dry. Do not hang a quilt on a clothesline. The stress and weight of the wet quilt can be too much for the seams. To dry, first place a sheet outdoors on a clean, dry flat surface, such as the lawn or a deck. Then lay the quilt on top and cover with another sheet to protect it from debris, insects, and fading. If you must dry the quilt indoors, lay it on top of a clean plastic sheet. Direct a fan slightly above it to help speed drying.

Most quilts can be vacuumed, which removes quite a bit of dirt. Use a screen made from a square of fiberglass or nylon screening (two by two feet square) with the edges covered with duct tape so that they don't snag the fabric. Place the screen over one section of the flat quilt. Use old pantyhose or several layers of cheesecloth or similar material to cover the opening of the upholstery attachment of your vacuum cleaner or of a handheld vacuum. Use the lowest setting on the machine. Hold the screen firmly and move the vacuum over the screen and the quilt. Vacuum both sides of the quilt in this manner.

Caution: When washing a quilt, do not use water hotter than 89°F. High temperatures can cause the fill to shrink.

Radiators

Trying to heat your home with a dirty radiator is like driving your car around with a trunkload of bricks all year. It's wasting energy. "The layer of dust that collects on radiators acts as an insulator," says John Morrill, director of operations for the American Council for an Energy-Efficient Economy in Washington, D.C., and co-author of *Consumer Guide to Home Energy Savings*. It keeps the radiator from doing its job—to radiate heat—as efficiently as it can. Regular cleaning, therefore, can help you get the most for your heating dollar.

Technique: Vacuum radiators and hot-water baseboards as part of your regular vacuuming routine. Use a brush attachment on top of the radiator and a long thin tube to get in between and behind the pipes. "The baseboards radiate heat, but they also work by convection," Morrill says. "Air circulates underneath them, is heated, and flows upward, which is why it's important to keep them clean." It is also important to keep the area around all types of radiators free from clutter and other objects so that heat will be well-distributed.

Bleed hot-water radiators (as opposed to those that circulate steam) a couple of times each heating season. "This lets trapped air out to ensure that the radiators are full of circulating hot water instead of air bubbles because there's not a lot of heat in air bubbles," explains Morrill. Using a radiator key, available at hardware stores, slowly open the small valve near the top of your radiator. Hold a heat-safe cup under the valve. When all of the air has escaped, water will trickle out. Retighten the valve.

If your radiator is rusty, put on some protective goggles and scrape the rust off with a wire brush and sandpaper. The rougher the rusted surface, the heavier-grade sandpaper you'll need. If there's no evidence of a leak, just follow the directions given here for painting. To prevent future rust, make sure that there is no rust residue. If there is, the metal can continue rusting even after it has been painted. Next, treat the metal with a rust-resistant primer, or paint, like Rust-Oleum. Use a spray can to coat the hard-to-reach areas. This is a project to do during a time of year when your heating system is not in use.

In a pinch: While it's best to vacuum your radiators year-round, it's most important during the winter months, when the radiators are in use.

Caution: Be careful when bleeding or cleaning your radiator. The water can be very hot.

Rayon

Rayon fibers may be man-made, but they're actually organic in origin—spun from cellulose extracted from tree pulp. Because of the many different rayon blends and treatments, how you clean it depends on the particular garment.

Technique: As a general rule, rayon should only be dry-cleaned. Even to remove small stains, it is best to dry-clean the whole garment. Because rayon is highly absorbent—even more so than cotton—it tends to ring and spot when it gets wet, so dabbing food spills with a moist dishcloth can worsen the situation.

"There are some garments on the market that have been resin-treated, which means that the fiber is not as liquid-absorbent," says Roman L. Horne, a technical service representative with the Lenzing Fibers Corporation in Lowland, Tennessee, one of the few rayon-makers in the United States. If a rayon garment has been resin-treated, it may be washable. Always read the clothing tag for washing instructions. If the fabric is washable, it usually means that you should wash on a gentle machine cycle or by hand. If washing by hand, gently squeeze mild lukewarm or cool suds through the fabric and rinse in lukewarm water. Do not wring it dry or stretch it while wet. Smooth or shake out the article and place it on a rust-free hanger to dry. Or, simply lay it out flat to dry. Iron the inside of the garment while it is still damp with an iron set at moderate. If you must iron the exterior, use a press cloth.

In a pinch: Because of possible chemical residues, it's best to let a professional dry-clean rayon. But keep your own spot removers, like Carbona Stain Devils or K2r, available at supermarkets, hardware stores, or discount department stores, around the house for emergency stains. Blot using the spot remover and a clean white cloth. Always check for colorfastness first on an inconspicuous area. If the spot forms a ring, take it to professional dry cleaner.

Caution: When using a spot remover, always read and follow product label carefully for proper use and safety precautions.

Refrigerators and Freezers

Cleaning your refrigerator and freezer is important for many reasons. Wiping up spills and removing old unusable foods before they start to smell cut down on bad odors. And dusting condenser coils helps the machines run more efficiently, saving you money and lessening the chances of compressor failure, which can amount to several hundred dollars to repair on most refrigerators and freezers.

Technique: Give your refrigerator a thorough cleaning according to the manufacturer's instructions about once a month. A good time to do it is just before shopping, when the food supply is lowest. Get rid of spoiled food. Take out all removable parts—shelves, drawers, egg trays—and wash them with warm soapy water, preferably using a mild liquid dishwashing detergent. Wipe down the inside walls with a solution of 2 tablespoons baking soda to 1 quart warm water. Rinse thoroughly and dry. Wipe off jars, bottles, and other containers.

"If you use the meat pan regularly, and juice leaks into it out of the meat packages, clean that out more often—basically, once a week or before you buy more meat," says Martha Reek, a senior home economist with the Whirlpool Corporation in Evansville, Indiana. Clean other compartments weekly, too, for safe storage. Then clean the folds in the gasket seal around the door with warm soapy water, rinse well, and dry. If your refrigerator has removable drain plugs, take them out and squirt warm water through the drain using a turkey baster.

The baking soda solution will help remove odors, but plastic walls and hard-to-clean crevices can absorb smells and sometimes require further effort. "Maybe a power outage occurred while you were on vacation," says Reek, "and the food in your refrigerator sat for a week." Spread a medium-size box of baking soda or a couple of inches of activated charcoal, available at aquarium supply stores, into a shallow pan and let it stand on a refrigerator shelf for a few days. Or do the same with freshly ground coffee in a cereal bowl.

Note: Freshly ground coffee may cause ice and ice cream to take on a coffee flavor. Discard these items or seal them in plastic bags to avoid an unwanted coffee taste.

If problem odors are making you consider replacing your refrigerator, try the following first. Empty your refrigerator and clean it thoroughly according to the manufacturer's instructions. It helps if you have another refrigerator to use as a backup. Pack each shelf of the smelly one with crumpled newspapers. Place a cup of water on the top shelf or sprinkle the papers lightly with water, and let it stand for five to six days while the refrigerator is running. Replace the newspaper every two days. It's inconvenient, but it works. How? The refrigeration system will pull moist air across the newspaper surfaces, which will absorb odor molecules.

Defrost freezers when the ice is approximately ¼ inch thick. This helps the motor work more efficiently. Remove the frozen items and either store them temporarily in a cooler or wrap them in several layers of newspaper to insulate them. Turn the freezer control knob to "off" or "defrost." Then let the freezer sit until defrosted. To speed up the process, place pans of hot water in the freezer. Don't chip off the ice with a sharp tool. It could damage the freezer compartment. Get rid of the melted defrost water, then wipe down the compartment with the baking soda solution, rinse, and dry. Wipe off any moisture before returning frozen goods to the freezer.

Cleaning the refrigerator or freezer's condenser coils is even more important to your appliance's well-being. Dust that collects on them acts as an insulator, causing the compressor to work harder to cycle refrigerant through the cooling system. At least twice a year—twice as often if you have pets—dust them using your vacuum cleaner's crevice attachment or a soft long-fiber bottle brush. Unplug the refrigerator before dusting. Determine what type of condenser your appliance has—a static condenser mounted on its back or a fan-cooled condenser mounted below. If the condenser is mounted below, remove the front grille cover, typically held in place by spring clips, and run the vacuum across it until the dust is gone. If it's on the back, pull the refrigerator out until you can access it fully, then vacuum up the dust.

When you put the refrigerator back in place, make sure that there is enough room in back for it to "breathe"—it needs proper air circulation to work efficiently. (Check your manual for the manufacturer's suggested amount of air-circulation space.)

Finally, if your refrigerator has a removable condenser drip pan—sometimes found beneath the appliance—wash it with warm soapy water. This kills any bacteria growing there and prevents other microscopic life forms from homesteading.

Speed tips: If you see a spill, clean it up. Regular spot-cleaning will save you time during thorough cleanings.

In a pinch: "If you don't have time one month for the thorough cleaning, use the swipe and wipe method," says Reek. Getting up spilled foods and liquids, keeping foods covered, and purging old foods will cut down on odors.

Caution: Before you clean the condenser coils on a refrigerator or freezer, unplug the appliance to avoid possible shock. Be sure to read and follow the manufacturer's instructions for cleaning and maintaining your refrigerator and freezer.

Resins

If you've ever raised a tree-climbing kid, you know all about resin. It's the sticky sap that some plants—most notably pine trees—produce to help them withstand rot and weather. It is not soluble in water, which makes washing resin out nearly impossible. A stronger solvent is required, says Ann Lemley, Ph.D., a chemist and chairman of the department of textiles and apparel at Cornell University in Ithaca, New York.

Technique: First, gently scrape off any large deposits of resin. Then blot with rubbing alcohol, but only if the fabric is colorfast. Lay the stain facedown on a soft absorbent cloth. Apply the alcohol to another clean white cloth, and then blot from the inside of the garment to push the stain out. As the alcohol dissolves the resin, the cloth beneath catches it. For small stains, soak a cotton ball or swab in alcohol and blot the stain. When cleaning resin from carpets, always apply the alcohol to a towel, never directly onto the carpet. Otherwise, it can soak into the carpet backing or pad and attract more dirt.

A CLEAN STORY

A Christmas Miracle

Ann Lemley, Ph.D., a chemist and chairman of the department of textiles and apparel at Cornell University in Ithaca, New York, explains how the perfect solution for cleaning tree resin just hit her out of the blue. "I was carrying my 11-foot-tall Christmas tree out of the house when this huge glob of tree resin dropped into my hair. I thought, 'What a pain—this isn't going to come out with shampoo.' Then I used my chemist's logic and grabbed some rubbing alcohol. Like dissolves like, and resin is similar in content to alcohol. The alcohol took the resin right out."

Note: Before using cleaning solutions, always test them on an inconspicuous section of the stained item. Always read and follow the product label carefully for proper use and safety precautions.

Rugs

Many people think rugs are merely decorative. Yet rugs also act as filters, trapping dirt and dust and keeping it out of the air you breathe. Cleaning them regularly, therefore, is also more than a matter of cosmetics.

"A rug is kind of like a sinkful of dirty dishes," says Claudia Ramirez, former executive vice president of the Association of Specialists in Cleaning and Restoration, in Millersville, Maryland. "When you run out of space, things start spilling over."

Technique: One of the biggest causes of rug damage is dry soil, which makes up 90 percent of the trash your rug collects. (In fact, an excessively soiled rug can contain up to one pound of dirt per square yard.) The grains of soil cut away at the fibers and eventually wear them thin. The best way to keep a rug clean is by vacuuming correctly and regularly—daily for heavily trafficked areas and at least once a week for other areas. Use a quality vacuum cleaner with a good filter system and a rotating beater bar for stirring up particles. Look for HEPA (high-efficiency particulate air), HEPA-type, or electrostatic filter systems on a vacuum cleaner. Terms such as rotating brush or power head indicate a rotating beater bar on the machine. For area rugs vacuumed weekly, flip them at least once a month and vacuum the backsides. For area rugs in heavily trafficked areas, vacuum the backside once a week. To pick up hard-to-remove ground-in soil, run the vacuum against the nap of the rug. Make six to eight overlapping strokes over the dirtiest areas.

When it comes to spot-cleaning, a few major rules apply. First, blot; don't rub. When the fibers are wet, the chance for distortion of fibers increases greatly. "Think about when your hair dries funny," Ramirez says. The same thing happens to a rug—it ends up looking disheveled. And when blotting a large stain, work from the edges in. People have a tendency to dive right in and tackle the stain's center, or darkest part, but that only spreads the substance even more. The stain's tendency is to wick outward; you should contain it and work inward. If the spot has soaked all the way through a rug that is not tacked down, put another white cloth beneath and work from one side, forcing it down through to the other side. Finally, have patience. If mere blotting only pulls a portion of the stain, try blotting with the following cleaning procedures in the order indicated until the stain is removed, suggests the Association of Specialists and Cleaning and Restoration.

- First, use a small amount of spot remover. Follow the directions carefully.
- If that doesn't work try a mixture of 1 teaspoon mild dishwashing detergent that doesn't contain any strong alkalis or bleaches with 1 cup lukewarm water. Rinse by blotting with a clean white towel moistened with water. Do not overwet.
- Still no luck? Make a cleaning solution with 1 tablespoon household ammonia and ½ cup of water. Blot to rinse as above.
- Follow this with ⅓ cup white vinegar and ⅔ cup water, which neutralizes the ammonia. Blot to rinse as above.
- As a last resort, prepare a solution of powered enzyme laundry detergent (that does not contain optical brighteners) and water

following directions on the detergent label. Allow the solution to remain on the stain for the time recommended on the detergent label. Blot to rinse and remove the detergent. Discard any leftover solution.

Do not overwet wall-to-wall carpeting—excessive wetting can cause the fabric backing to shrink. Sometimes this shrinkage can even cause tears in the carpet.

For many nonoil-based stains on water-treatable cotton and wool rugs, a good solution to begin with is ¼ teaspoon clear dishwashing liquid and 1 cup warm water. Pretest by dabbing a cotton swab soaked in the solution on an inconspicuous area. Try it on the various colors—if any dye bleeds onto the swab, do not continue; rather, contact a rug-cleaning professional, who might be able to set the dyes or control the bleeding. (For a referral in your area, write to the Association of Specialists in Cleaning and Restoration at 8229 Cloverleaf Drive, Suite 460, Millersville, MD 21108.) If there is no dye transfer, blot the shaded area with a white cotton towel soaked in the solution. When the stain is gone, blot with a clean towel and water to remove detergent residue, which attracts dirt and dust if left to dry.

Cotton rugs or wool rugs with lengthwise cotton yarns often shrink or ripple when treated with water. When spot-cleaning with water, never pour the solution directly onto the stain; always blot with a presoaked towel. By overwetting you also risk soaking the underlying cushion. Moisture that sits in a rug mat may wick back up later—and bring with it other soils that you didn't know were down there.

Dirt is a lot easier to get out than mud. That means if your kids track mud over your Oriental runner in the hallway, let it dry first. Then lift up as much as you can with a dull knife or the handle of a spoon and vacuum the rest. If there is still a residual effect, like a slight shading where the mud was, use the aforementioned detergent solution.

Deep clean your rug every 12 to 18 months, either by hiring a professional or doing it yourself. If you use a wet method, like shampooing, remove the furniture from the room beforehand. Or, to prevent rust or other stains from leaking into the rug, place plastic food wrap under and around the legs of chairs and tables. Follow all instructions carefully. Never exceed the recommended solution strength.

When you are finished, remove all shampoos, detergents, and

moisture, which cause dirt to stick to the rug. Follow the instructions on the product label for proper use and safety precautions. Send higher-quality rugs, such as Orientals, out to a professional for in-plant cleaning. (For either an on-site or in-plant rug cleaner, look under "Carpet and Rug Cleaners" in the yellow pages of your phone book.)

Speed tips: Well-maintained vacuuming equipment improves vacuum-cleaner efficiency and speeds up the cleaning process. Don't wait for vacuum-cleaner bags to fill completely; replace or empty them once they are one-half to two-thirds full. After every third emptying, turn nondisposable collection bags inside out and sweep off excess lint and dirt. Before each use, make sure that the vacuum-cleaner filter is free of lint and dust.

In a pinch: If your time is limited, make vacuuming the heavily trafficked areas a priority.

Caution: Beware of commercial spotting products that contain optical brighteners, sometimes referred to as blueing or whitening agents. These are actually fluorescent or ultraviolet dyes that cancel out the yellowing that can occur as a result of old stains or age. They make a rug look clean, but overapplication can actually bleach out color. With repeated use, the dyes will even turn yellow.

Rust Stains

The most common rust stains appear around the drain in porcelain sinks and on clothing because of iron particles in the water.

Technique: To remove the brown rings around faucets and other light rust stains, rub with a sponge and lemon juice or white vinegar. Rinse with water. If that doesn't work, use a cloth to rub with a little kerosene. Rinse well with soap and water.

For tougher stains—on clothing, vinyl flooring, and concrete driveways—use a 5 percent solution of oxalic acid, such as Bondex, available at hardware stores. To create this solution, mix 6 ounces oxalic acid powder with a gallon of warm water. Apply the solution to the rust stain using a cloth, let it sit for five minutes, and then rinse it well with water. Repeat the process if necessary.

Caution: Oxalic acid is a skin and eye irritant in both crystal and solution form. Wear long sleeves, rubber gloves, and protective eyewear when using. Read and follow the product label carefully for proper use and safety precautions.

Chlorine bleach does not remove rust stains. It makes them darker. "Bleach is an oxidizing agent, so it oxides the rust further," says Rajiv Jain, laboratory manager of the Association of Specialists in Cleaning and Restoration in Millersville, Maryland. Hydrogen peroxide does the same thing. "On rust-stained textiles it will eat away the fabric."

Scissors

Clean scissors cut better and more precisely. Most scissors these days are made of stainless steel, and cleaning them is a snip—er, snap.

Technique: Simply wipe down stainless-steel scissors with a damp cloth or sponge. If they are sticky, oily, or covered with stubborn soil, wipe them down with a sudsy sponge.

If your scissors are not stainless steel, you must dry them completely after wiping them down. Otherwise, they can rust, which can ruin their cutting precision. Spray them with WD-40 or some other rust protectant and lubricant. Open and close them several times to work the lubricant down into the joint, says Cam Wiegmann, manager of Henry Westpfal, a New York City–based scissors sales and sharpening business founded in 1874.

If your scissors do get rusty, rub the rust away gently with a nonsoapy steel wool pad. The finer the pad, the better. Be careful not to rub the cutting edge—you might dull it. Afterward, spray the scissors with WD-40.

Do not try to sharpen scissors yourself. Take them to a professional—either a hardware store that can sharpen scissors or a fabric shop.

Caution: Do not put scissors in the dishwasher. The heat might affect the temper or plastic handles.

Screens

Think of screens as air filters that stand between your living space and the outside. "Frankly speaking, most people never clean their screens," admits Charlie Brakefield, a marketing director of

HOW I DO IT

Garden-Variety Cleaning

Marry Keener is the assistant director of facilities management at the University of Arizona in Tucson and a member of the technical advisory committee for *Executive Housekeeping Today* magazine. Here's how she cleans screens on her aluminum doors.

"I use the garden sprayer—the kind that looks like a jar and attaches to the end of a hose—with a few drops of liquid dishwashing detergent. This works wonders. Detergent has special surfactants that release clinging soil, particularly if it's bound by any kind of oil, like air pollution and kitchen grease. The combination of the water pressure and the detergent makes cleaning them easy."

Phifer Wire Products in Tuscaloosa, Alabama. They should. While keeping bugs, birds, and large airborne debris out of your house, screens are exposed to the elements and collect a lot of dust and dirt in the process.

Technique: Clean your screens at least once a year. If they are the type with the vinyl-coated fiberglass mesh—commonly referred to as plastic screens—do it more often. Because of static electricity, they collect more dirt.

Remove the screens from the window frames. Usually, that involves lifting two loop latches at the bottom of the frame, pulling the bottom out, and then sliding the screen out of two U-shape grooves at the top. Dust the screens' mesh and frames with a soft-bristle brush or cloth. Mix up a sudsy solution of liquid dishwashing detergent and hot water in a bucket. Lean the screens against something outside—the side of the house or a railing. Wet the screens by spraying them with a garden hose. Scrub the grime off each side of the screen mesh with a soft-bristle nylon brush dipped into the sudsy water. Wash the frame with a sponge or cloth dipped into the suds. Rinse the screens with the hose. Wipe the excess water away with a clean cloth, and then stand the screens up to air-dry.

Before replacing the screens, clean the grooves that hold them in place. Scrub the dirt from inside the grooves using a toothbrush dipped in the soapy solution. Rinse the grooves with a cloth or sponge, then dry them with a cloth. As long as the screens are down, you might as well wash the windows and window frames.

Speed tips: To make it easy to keep track of which screens fit which windows, number each frame, then give the same number to the matching screen. (Scratch the number in a corner of the screen that will be hidden once it is replaced.) Put the screws or nuts that accompany the screen in a bag and write the same number on it.

In a pinch: Hose the screens down in place (with the windows closed, of course). "Most of the airborne contaminants that collect on a screen are on the outside," Brakefield says.

Sewing Machines

A clean machine sews better and lasts longer. So keep moving parts free of lint and other debris.

Technique: At the end of every sewing session, clean the lint out of the shuttle area with a small, semistiff-bristle nylon brush. Remove the retaining ring, the shuttle hook (if you can), and the bobbin. If there is a removable throat plate, take that off as well and clean beneath it.

Then, unless your machine is self-lubricating, put a drop or two of oil onto the moving parts when putting them back into the machine. (Follow the manufacturer's instructions for oiling your particular model.) "The standard three-in-one type oil is not good," says Richard Hartmann, a technical-support manager for Brother International Corporation in Somerset, New Jersey, maker of sewing machines since 1954. "It gums up when the machine sits in the closet for a while. I use WD-40, or some other silicone-based lubricant." Do not spray the lubricant directly onto the machine, which could damage the motor or electronic components. Instead, spray a little bit on a cloth, and then wipe the cloth on the moving parts.

Keep the exterior shell free of dust with a lint-free cloth. Although all sewing machines were once made of metal, most machines these days are plastic. "Benzene and other harsh chemicals are strictly a no-no," says Hartmann. A mild all-purpose household cleaner works well to remove fingerprints and other rubbed-on grime. Again, spray it on the cloth, and then wipe the cloth on the machine.

Speed tips: If the machine has not been cleaned in a while and is caked with dust, inside and out, use a blow-dryer (set on cool) or a hose attached to the exhaust outlet of your vacuum cleaner to blow the dust away.

In a pinch: Keep a can of compressed air handy. When you don't have time to clean the shuttle area, just give it a quick blast of air to remove any lint or leftover thread.

Caution: Before cleaning, unplug the machine. "You don't want to sew your fingers together," Hartmann says. If your wall outlet is hard to reach, simply remove the cord from the machine. Most connect there as well.

Shades

With window shades, a little light dusting will go a long way. Do it regularly, and you'll delay the need for a big cleaning job down the road.

Technique: Dust shades with a feather duster or with a vacuum cleaner attachment, like a wand or soft brush. "Do it once a week, unless you're in some place that's really dusty. Then you might have to do it more often," says Kay Weirick, director of housekeeping services at Bally's Las Vegas Hotel and a member of the technical advisory committee for *Executive Housekeeping Today* magazine.

Clean vinyl shades once or twice a year using a sponge or soft cloth and an all-purpose cleaner or solution of ¼ cup vinegar and 1 quart warm water.

There are many different types of fabric shades. Some can be washed and ironed. Others must be dry-cleaned. Read care labels or call the manufacturer for care instructions. Be careful when trying to spot-clean shades. Before cleaning, always test cleaning solutions on an inconspicuous section of the shade.

Shells

When you pick up a shell on the beach, clean it as soon as possible. Remove any decaying flesh which, besides smelling unpleasant, could discolor and ruin the shell. Many beautiful specimens have been tossed away because the collector didn't realize that the meat had to be cleaned out of the shell.

Technique: Freezing is one of the easiest ways to clean a shell. But you have to be patient because the freezing and thawing process is gradual and takes four days to effectively clean the shell and prevent it from cracking, according to R. Tucker Abbott in the book *Kingdom of the Seashell.*

Place your mollusks in a plastic bag, tied shut, in the lower part of your refrigerator for a few hours. Then transfer to the freezer for two to three days. To thaw, place the bag back in the lower part of the refrigerator for 12 hours or so, and then soak it in cold water. When completely thawed, which usually takes about 24 hours, the meats of most univalves can be removed by pulling on them in an unwinding corkscrew fashion, using a fork or a bent safety pin.

Once the flesh is removed from the interior, clean the exterior of shells by brushing with warm soapy water. Shell exteriors can also be cleaned by soaking them overnight in full-strength bleach. To give shells a brighter color, sparingly apply a coat of baby oil.

Speed tips: Clean new shells in less time by boiling in freshwater or salt water. Because rapid temperature changes will cause minute cracks in the surface of shiny shells, start with warm water, not hot water. Boil bivalves, such as clam shells, for 1 to 2 minutes and univalves, such as snails, for 6 to 10 minutes. Let the pot stand for an hour to bring the temperature down slowly. You may add small quantities of cold water to speed up the cooling process. Once cool enough to handle, follow the procedure outlined above for removing meat from the shell.

Commercial shellers dump live smelly shells in a solution of one part water to one part chlorine bleach to dissolve the flesh.

In a pinch: If you discover the specimen of a lifetime while on a trip to a remote island paradise but don't have access to a freezer or a stove, bury the specimen in a bucket of dry sand with the open end of the shell pointing down. The decaying matter will drain out without harming the shell.

Caution: Do not soak shells in plain water to clean them. Decaying animal matter circulating in the water will remove the natural color from the shell.

Using muriatic acid, a hydrochloric acid often used to clean up mortar spills on brick, is not recommended. Even a mild 10 percent solution is corrosive enough to damage shells.

Shoes

In the 8,000 steps that each one of us takes in an average day, our shoes take a beating. But whether it's your finest leather dress shoes or a $10 pair of canvas sneakers, shoe care professionals recommend applying a protective water and stain repellent to the uppers of all shoes when they are new. "This puts a protective layer between the dirt and the shoe," says Mitch Lebovic, editor of *Shoe Service* magazine in Baltimore.

Athletic

Technique: Remove laces and inserts and rinse shoes with water. Use a sneaker shampoo or any neutral cleaner, such as liquid dishwashing detergent, and a soft brush to remove dirt. Rinse and allow to air-dry stuffed with absorbent white paper towels. Use a cedar shoe tree to reshape the shoe.

If shoes are scuffed, apply shoe whitening product to restore the color. Dusting with baby powder after you polish will prevent it from rubbing off.

The biggest problem in caring for athletic shoes is controlling odor. Each foot has 125,000 sweat glands, which deposit up to ¼ cup sweat into each shoe every day. The foam construction of athletic insoles provides an ideal breeding ground for odor-causing bacteria. Lebovic suggests using over-the-counter products that will counteract the odor-causing bacteria, such as Dr. Scholl's Odor Destroyers Deodorant Spray. Such products also are available as powders and insoles. But read the label to be sure that you're not buying a product that will simply mask the odor.

In a pinch: To get scuffs off white leather, rub with nongel toothpaste, rinse, wipe, and let dry.

Caution: Shoe manufacturers advise against placing athletic shoes in the washer. The agitation breaks down the adhesives of the shoe and damages the leather. When cleaning, do not use solvents, harsh abrasives, or bleach on shoes.

Canvas

Technique: You can throw old fashioned canvas sneakers in the washer; however, shoe-care experts say that this isn't the best way to get them clean. It ruins their shape and often doesn't do the job of removing the dirt thoroughly. If canvas shoes are sealed properly when they are new, says Lebovic, dirt can essentially be sponged off. Upholstery cleaner works well to lift dirt from the fibers. Spray on and sponge off. For white rubber soles, use whitewall tire cleaner. Always allow shoes to air-dry. The heat of the dryer will shrink them.

Speed tips: Use putty-type wallpaper cleaner, available at home center stores, to lift dirt off canvas shoes.

In a pinch: Spray starch or an ordinary fabric protector, like Scotchgard, will protect your canvas shoes from dirt.

Leather

Technique: A good pair of men's leather shoes can be resoled seven times if you take care of the uppers properly. Follow this four-step process recommended by the Shoe Service Institute of America in Baltimore for cleaning and maintaining leather shoes.

1. Clean. Remove loose dirt from the shoe with a soft brush. Clean with a cream leather cleaner.

2. Condition. Once the leather is clean, apply a conditioner, which prevents cracking and puts oil back into the shoes to make them last longer.

3. Polish. Polishes renew pigments and cover scuffs, provide shine, and protect and condition the leather. They come in three forms: liquid, paste, and cream. Liquid is easiest to apply but has the least staying power. Pastes provide the best coverage and a superior shine, but are not available in a wide variety of colors. Creams offer a happy medium between the other two. Apply polish in circular motions. Buff with a cloth. Apply a second coat and buff with a

second clean cloth. For an all-out gleaming shine, apply an additional coat of paste wax with a wet cloth. Let shoes dry and buff.

4. Weatherproof. Mink oil, beeswax, and silicone are some of the choices available for weatherproofing sealants. While polish provides some sealing qualities, if you work in a wet, muddy, or oily environment, you should weatherproof your shoes.

In a pinch: If your shoes get soaked from the rain, the best thing to do is put in shoe trees and allow them to air-dry at room temperature. Never put them near a heat source. It will dry and crack the leather.

Caution: Never polish leather shoes before you have cleaned them. If you do, the polish will embed the dirt in the grain of the leather.

Shower Stalls

If you stick to a simple weekly cleaning routine and follow a few daily preventive measures, you'll keep those three shower-polluters—soap scum, mildew, and hard-water deposits—out of your bathroom for good.

Technique: Remove soap and shampoos from shower. Spray shower walls, fixtures, floor, and the curtain or door thoroughly with an all-purpose cleaner. "Let the cleaner do the work for you," says Margaret Dasso, owner of the Clean Sweep, a professional cleaning service in Lafayette, California, and co-author of *Dirt Busters*. Dasso recommends using Tilex Soap Scum Remover. Working from top to bottom, wipe the shower with a nylon scrubber pad. Use a toothbrush or grout brush on any stubborn stains or buildup. Rinse with warm water and dry with a soft cloth. Shine chrome fixtures with rubbing alcohol and a dry cloth. (See Hard-Water Deposits on page 140, Rust Stains on page 222, and Soap Scum on page 245 for specific cleaning techniques.)

To retard the formation of soap scum and mineral deposits, finish off by applying a coat of lemon oil furniture polish to the entire shower area. Pour lemon oil polish onto a cloth and rub evenly over shower walls.

Speed tips: Use a sponge mop reserved strictly for shower cleaning to avoid kneeling and bending.

Rinse the shower after each use to prevent soap film and hard-water deposits from forming. Before you dry off after a shower, dry the shower it-self, the doors, and chrome fixtures with a squeegee or chamois. This one-minute job will save you tons of time and aggravation by preventing mildew, soap scum, and hard-water de-posits. The benefits are twofold. Not only will your shower look cleaner but also it will actually be cleaner since keeping it dry also prevents germ growth. Germs will begin to die after two hours on a dry surface, while a wet surface provides a breeding ground for bacteria colonies.

If you can't bring your-self to squeegee in the nude, simply leaving the shower doors or curtain open after use will help to prevent mildew by allowing air to circulate. Let the shower curtain hang loosely enough that it doesn't trap moisture in the folds.

In a pinch: If you don't have lemon oil furniture polish, any type of furniture polish or car wax can be substituted.

Caution: Avoid slips and falls. Do not apply wax or polish to the shower floor.

MONEY-SAVERS

Your Secret Weapon against Mildew

You don't need costly special-ized cleaners to get rid of black grimy mildew growing in your shower. Household bleach works just fine and will kill mildew in minutes, says cleaning pro Margaret Dasso, owner of the Clean Sweep, a professional cleaning service in Lafayette, Cali-fornia, and co-author of *Dirt Busters*. But avoid these common mistakes when working with bleach.

- Never use full-strength bleach on tile showers. It will erode the grout. The Clorox Com-pany recommends using a so-lution of about ¾ cup bleach per gallon of water.
- Don't skip the rinse cycle when working with bleach. Bleach residue will damage the grout.
- Wear old clothes, and use care not to let bleach solution splatter onto carpets or towels.

Shutters

Once they get really dirty, there's no easy way to clean shutters. Essentially, each one of those of pivoting little louvers that look so charming on your window has to be cleaned.

Technique: It takes a lot of water and scrubbing to reach all the cracks and crevices of shutters, so, if possible, remove the shutters from the window—they should lift right off the hinges—and work at a towel-lined countertop or table. Spray the entire shutter with all-purpose cleaner, taking care to reach all the crevices. Let the solution soak for a few minutes before cleaning each slat. Working from the top to the bottom, scrub each louver with a terry towel or grout brush. "You need a little brush of some sort because as soon as you spray the shutters, all the dirt is going to flow to the cracks and crevices," says Carol Seelaus, a speed-cleaning instructor at Temple University in Philadelphia and owner of Somebody's Gotta Do It, a professional cleaning service.

Spray loosened dirt and cleaning solution away with clean water. Dry with a clean cloth. Dry hard-to-reach areas by applying a clean absorbent cloth wrapped around a wooden spoon handle.

Speed tips: Keep shutters well-dusted and you won't have to scrub, says Seelaus. The longer dust and dirt are allowed to sit on a surface, the harder it is to just suck it up in the vacuum. Once a month, dust front and back sides of the louvers with a canister vacuum. Using the dust brush attachment, go up and down the shutter as well as side to side to vacuum dust in hard-to-reach areas. City dwellers should dust more frequently.

In a pinch: Use an old toothbrush in place of a grout brush. If you don't have a wooden spoon, use a small plastic or wooden ruler instead.

Siding

Do you want to give your house a face-lift and maybe avoid a paint job in the bargain? Clean the siding. Dirt from pollution, dust, pollen, trees, and even rain accumulates on siding, especially on the underside. If a chalky look on your aluminum siding is your only complaint, a good scrubbing may eliminate the need to call in the housepainters.

If the siding is only lightly soiled, even a heavy rain may remedy the problem. But in most cases you'll have to clean it every year or so, especially if you live in an urban or wooded area.

Technique: Start at the bottom and work up to the top, says the Vinyl Siding Institute in Washington, D.C. For light soil and surface

The Dark Side:
Getting Rid of Mold, Mildew, and Moss

Mold, mildew, and moss are most likely to appear on the sides of your house where there's high humidity and little sunlight—the north side of the house in particular. Mildew and mold may appear as black spots on the surface of the siding, while moss will show up as patches of green.

To remove it and discourage new growth of this dirty plant matter on aluminum and wood siding, scrub with the following solution recommended by PPG Coatings, a Pittsburgh manufacturer of the factory finishes applied to aluminum siding: $\frac{1}{3}$ cup laundry detergent, $\frac{2}{3}$ cup trisodium phosphate, 1 quart liquid household bleach, and 3 quarts water.

Using medium pressure, scrub with a soft-bristle brush and rinse well with clear water. Follow the proportions exactly—a stronger concentration of ingredients could damage the painted finish on the siding.

Do not use solutions containing bleach or organic solvents on vinyl siding. They could damage the surface. Instead, the Vinyl Siding Institute in Washington, D.C., recommends using a solution of 30 percent vinegar and 70 percent water, or an all-purpose nonabrasive cleaner such as Fantastik.

dirt, spray a section of siding with the garden hose and then lightly scrub with a long-handle, soft-bristle brush. Be sure to scrub the underside where dirt tends to build up. Follow with a second rinse to remove the dirt loosened by the brush. Work in sections that are the size of a comfortable arm's reach.

If you live in an area where heavy industrial deposits dull the siding, scrub with a solution of household detergent and water, then rinse with the garden hose.

Speed tips: Skip the scrubbing and use a pressure washer to clean the siding in minutes instead of hours. Pressure washers, which connect to your garden hose, remove dirt with water that is propelled at a pressure of 1,000 to 2,400 pounds per square inch. You can pick one up at a rental store for less than $75.

In a pinch: If you don't have time to scrub the entire house, spot-clean the areas that are dirtiest. Look for soiled areas on a shady portion of the house, smoke residue around the chimney area, or dirt splatters around the base of the house.

Caution: If it's necessary to use a ladder to clean the house, wear nonslip shoes.

Cleaners containing organic solvents, such as chlorine bleach, liquid grease remover, nail polish remover, or furniture polish, can mar the surface of vinyl siding.

Silk

Silk has been a symbol of elegance and beauty since it was discovered 4,000 years ago. It is the strongest of all natural fibers. A filament of silk is stronger than a like filament of steel, according to the International Silk Association in New York City. So it seems strange that when these fibers are woven, they create a fabric known for its delicacy—a fabric that in some forms will wrinkle and pucker at the first drop of water. Many of us shy away from silk garments, believing that they have to be dry-cleaned (and silk is the most expensive fabric to dry-clean, aside from suede and leather).

But this is not always the case. In response to consumer demand, manufacturers are producing garments from many types of silk that can be laundered at home. Before you buy a garment, find out what type of silk it is. Spun silk, the fabric most often used for lingerie, and untreated crepe de chine, which has a soft flowing texture, are natural silks and can be hand-washed, according to the International Silk Association. On the other hand, chemically treated silks, such as taffeta and treated crepe de chine can be damaged by water and should be dry-cleaned.

The labels on many items of silk clothing say "Dry-Clean Only," even though some may be safe to wash. If you don't know whether to plunge that $80 blouse into a basin of water, test the garment for colorfastness. If the color runs or changes, do not hand-wash the item. How do you know if your garment is colorfast? Dab a cotton swab moistened with cool water on a small inside corner of a seam, says the International Silk Association. Then press the spot on a white cloth or paper towel using a warm iron. If the silk doesn't leave a color, it can be washed.

Technique: The International Silk Association recommends the following method for hand-washing silk. Make a thick suds in lukewarm water with mild white soap flakes. Gently agitate by squeezing suds through the silk. Don't scrub; silk fibers will abrade easily. Rinse two or three times in tepid water until the water is clear. Roll the garment in a bath towel to remove as much water as possible, and then hang it indoors to dry away from strong sun or heat until it is damp-dry.

Only soak natural silk for three to five minutes, and "washable" silk no longer than two minutes. Alkalies such as soaps, shampoos, detergents and even toothpaste can cause color change or loss in silks, according to the International Fabricare Institute in Silver Spring, Maryland.

Press silk garments with an iron on the lowest setting while the garment is still damp. Always press silks on the "wrong" side with a low iron. Finish seams and collars on the right side with a pressing cloth to protect the fabric.

MONEY-SAVERS

Storing Silks to Make Them Last

It's beautiful and it's expensive, so naturally, silk is an investment that you want to last.

"Silk is supremely lasting," says the International Silk Association in New York City. "The beautiful fabrics remaining to us from ancient days attest to silk's almost uncanny resistance to aging."

Follow these tips to get lasting wear from your silk.

- Always hang silk on padded hangers and cover with plastic. The continuous fibers of silk can be damaged by folding.
- Never use mothballs. Silk will absorb the odor, and it's impossible to wash out.
- Store silk away from light, which will damage the fibers and cause dyes to fade.

Spots and stains are best left to a professional dry cleaner.

Speed tips: Washable silk can be safely laundered in most home washers on the gentle setting in warm water with a nonalkaline detergent or mild soap, according to the International Fabricare Institute. Hang it right away to reshape and prevent wrinkles.

In a pinch: Localized areas of color loss caused by spot-cleaning can sometimes be remedied by treating the area with steam. Hold the spotted area over steam from a teakettle, or mist it lightly with a steamer for three to five seconds, says the International Fabricare Institute. But be careful not to get the fabric wet. Color should be restored within 30 seconds.

Caution: Regardless of the type of silk, experts recommend dry cleaning for very fine garments such as evening dresses, bright multicolored silks, embroidered silk, and those with a raised pattern. Here are other cautions about cleaning silk.

- Alcohol can cause fabric dyes in silk to bleed. Allow perfumes, hair sprays, and other toiletries containing alcohol to dry before you dress. Spills from alcoholic beverages should be removed as soon as possible by a professional dry cleaner.
- Salts from perspiration can severely weaken and stain silk. If you perspire heavily, wear dress shields with silk garments. Clean perspiration-stained garments as soon as possible.
- Never use chlorine bleach on silk. It will cause permanent damage to the fabric.
- Test crepe de chine for colorfastness on a small piece of hem or cuff. Untreated crepe de chine is safe to wash, while chemically treated crepe de chine will streak in water. Most labels won't tell whether the fabric is treated or untreated.
- Printed silk has a clarity and depth that other fabrics cannot match. Bleeding and dye migration is a common problem, however. Never wash light-colored silks with bright-colored silks. Always test multicolored garments for colorfastness before laundering. And don't allow them to remain in a damp or wet condition for prolonged periods.
- Dry and store silks away from any light source to prevent fading.

Silver

The villain here is silver sulfide. If that's too much of a mouthful, just call it by its common name: tarnish. It's the black film that forms when silver comes into contact with sulfur in the air, the carbon in rubber, or even the acids and salts in certain foods.

Technique: Using your silver regularly will help keep tarnish at a minimum. The best way to clean silver is the old-fashioned way—with a good-quality, antitarnish silver polish and a soft cloth, says Robert M. Johnston, a consultant in Baltimore who has worked in the silverware industry for more than 50 years. Silver is the most reflective of all metals, and buffing with silver polish produces a rich luster that enhances the beauty of the piece and retards the development of tarnish.

Apply polish with a soft damp cloth or a sponge. Rub vigorously to remove tarnish. You will see the cloth turn black as tarnish is removed. Polish thoroughly and rinse right away with soap and warm water. Dry with a soft towel to avoid water spots.

SCRUB THIS APPROACH

Skip the Dip

You've seen it hyped on infomercials. A coal-black silver teapot is dipped in an instant cleaner and—voilà!—it comes out gleaming. According to experts, though, instant chemical cleaners should not be used on fine silver.

"Most dips are a chemical process that eats away at the top of the silver. Repeated use will erode the finish," says Robert M. Johnston, a consultant in Baltimore who has worked in the silverware industry for more than 50 years.

And don't bother with electrolytic cleaning—a process that uses an aluminum plate or foil and a combination of boiling water, baking soda, and salt to lift tarnish off the silver, according to Johnston. The process tends to dull the finish and may remove antique shading.

When storing silver for an extended time, seal it from air and moisture, protect it from bumps and scratches, and remember to check it at least once a year for signs of tarnishing. Store it in flannel antitarnish bags, which are available at jewelry stores, to prevent the silver from oxidizing. Then place it in zippered plastic bags. This is the most important step in storing your silver because it isolates the metal from environmental factors that cause tarnish and corrosion, according to J. A. Wright and Company in Keene, New Hampshire, manufacturers of metal polishes.

Speed tips: If you use your silver frequently and rotate place settings, you will only need to polish it once or twice a year. Less polishing will spare the thin coating on silver plate from being rubbed away by too-frequent polishing. Cleaning cloths impregnated with rouge are good for touch ups, but not if the piece is heavily tarnished.

In a pinch: "If you have guests at your front door and a speck of tarnish on your silver serving spoon, you can usually buff it out with toothpaste," says Johnston. Apply it with a damp cloth and rub the spot. "This is good if you're in a bind but is not really a very efficient way to clean anything more than a spot here or there."

If you don't have flannel antitarnish bags, it is acceptable to store your silver in zippered plastic bags alone. Just make sure that the bags are protected from bumps and abrasions. Do not use plastic cling wrap, which can stick to the silver and can be tough to remove.

For black spots that are etched in, take the piece to a silver repair shop or a jeweler to be buffed.

Caution: Chemical dips contain thiourea, a cancer-causing chemical. The colorless and odorless chemical can be absorbed through your skin, so wear protective gloves if you choose to use these products. And completely rinse silver, countertops, and sink to remove any traces of the chemical. Besides being harmful for you, chemical dips can also damage the finish of your silver, says Johnston. Also keep these tips in mind.

- Wash silver that has come in contact with mustard, salt, or ketchup right away to prevent pitting and tarnishing.
- Don't wrap silver in newspaper or rubber bands. Both contain carbon, which reacts with the silver, turns it black, and eats into the surface if left on the piece.

Sinks

Chances are that when you think of household germs, you think of toilets. In turns out, though, that sinks—in particular, kitchen sinks, not toilets—are one of the most germ-ridden areas of the house. A University of Arizona study found that bacteria tend to be concentrated in the sink, its drain, and the sponge or dishcloth. Germs that you expect to find on a toilet rim, such as fecal coliform, were seldom found there. But in the kitchen, they were everywhere. The smooth surface of a sink is a landscape of nooks and crannies from a microbe's perspective. The trick to cleaning is to knock them loose and discourage them from remultiplying.

Technique: Ordinary scrubbing with a disinfectant will dissolve food particles and remove clinging microbes. Using a new or sterilized sponge, scrub the sides and bottom of sink. (Hint: You can sterilize your sponge in the dishwasher or by soaking it for five minutes in a solution of ¾ cup bleach in 1 gallon water.) Follow up with a sanitizing rinse with a similar solution of diluted household bleach, which will destroy even the most tenacious hangers-on. Let the solution stay wet in your sink for five minutes. For stains, porcelain and stainless steel can tolerate light abrasive cleaners such as liquid cleansers or baking soda.

Speed tips: For a quick cleanup, spray the entire sink with a disinfectant cleaner and wipe it off with a paper towel.

In a pinch: Rinse sink with plain water and dry with paper towels. Whenever bacteria find a site harboring moisture and food, they will set up housekeeping and grow, says Edmund A. Zottola, Ph.D., professor emeritus of food microbiology at the University of Minnesota in St. Paul. Resident bacteria can only survive a few hours on a dry surface.

To remove stains from a porcelain sink, fill it with warm water and add a few tablespoons of chlorine bleach. Let the solution stand for an hour and rinse. If the stain persists, line the sink with paper towels, saturate them with chlorine bleach and let soak for a half-hour. Wear gloves and make sure that the area is well-ventilated when using this technique.

Caution: Don't use abrasives on cultured marble, fiberglass, or plastic, which will scratch the sink and cause it to become porous and prone to stains and germ growth. Always read product labels for proper use and safety precautions.

Skylights

If you want to let the sun shine in, skylights need to be cleaned once a year or so. If neglected, skylights—in particular, the Plexiglas bubble type—can be permanently damaged by droppings from trees, the growth of mildew or moss, and even ordinary rain and airborne dirt that can bind to the glass after it bakes in the sun for a period of time. "Let it go long enough and you'll have to replace it," says Karen J. Blough, who, as owner of Blough's Cleaning Services in Reading, Pennsylvania, has been washing skylights since 1989.

While fingerprints aren't usually a problem on skylights, interiors need to be cleaned as well since they develop a dirty film from cooking, fireplaces, and dust in the home.

Technique: Inside, move any furniture out of the way and lay a plastic cloth under the skylight to catch any drips. Because they're most frequently installed in vaulted ceilings at an angle, skylights can be difficult to reach. Use a professional-quality washer-and-squeegee tool (available at janitorial supply stores) attached to an extension wand. Use a six- or eight-foot stepladder under the skylight to reach it with the extended squeegee. Climb the ladder and remove the screen, if necessary. Clean the screen with a vacuum or brush. Dip the tool in a solution of ¼ cup sudsy ammonia and a squirt of liquid dishwashing detergent in 1 gallon water, and squeeze out the excess. Apply the solution to the skylight with firm even strokes. Squeegee off. Wipe around the edges with an absorbent cloth draped over the end of your extension wand to remove any drips.

Outside, place a ladder at the lowest point on the house and climb onto the roof. With a handheld squeegee, use the same ammonia solution and cleaning technique. Rub any stubborn spots with a nylon scrubber. Mop up any drips with a soft cloth.

Plexiglas bubble skylights should only be cleaned with soft cotton cloths to avoid scratching.

Speed tips: New windows have a protective film on them from the manufacturer and may need a stronger ammonia solution if it's a first-time cleaning. "Otherwise you'll get streaks and may end up cleaning it two or three times," says Blough. She recommends adding small amounts of ammonia or detergent to the solution until the glass comes out streak-free.

If you can reach the exterior surface of your skylight with a garden hose, give it a quick spray if you happen to be watering the flowers or washing the car.

In a pinch: If you don't have a strip washer, apply cleaning solution with a sponge mop. Make sure that it's clean and free of soap residue.

An old broom handle can usually be used to extend the reach of your squeegee.

Caution: Use care when climbing ladders and cleaning windows on the roof. Avoid loose or flowing clothing, and wear shoes with nonskid soles. It's a good idea to wear safety glasses to protect your eyes from cleaning solution drips.

Slate

Slate is a hard dense rock formed from compressed shale or clay. Usually a medium gray, it has a tendency to split into long thin planes, which are then cut for use as roofing shingles, floor tiles, and billiard tabletops. Slate is an extremely durable easy-care material that looks best when allowed to develop its own lustrous patina without being coated with waxes or shiny sealants.

Technique: Slate should be protected from stains with a stone impregnator, which chemically closes the pores of the stone and

SCRUB THIS APPROACH

With Slate, Keep It Simple

People often put wax or shiny coatings on slate floors. But in the long run, this approach is going to make the floor look worse, not better, says Detlev Wolske, president of HMK Stone Care System in San Francisco.

Waxes and surface coatings do not adhere well to slate and will rub off quickly from ordinary foot traffic. The floor will look good initially, but after a week or so, scratches will begin to show where the coating has chipped off.

If you want a shinier floor, mopping with a neutral, no-rinse stone cleaner and occasional buffing will develop a natural scratch-resistant luster.

hardens the surface. Like water filling a sponge, the impregnator fills the porous cells of the stone so that stains will not penetrate. Apply the product in two coats with a long-bristle brush, as if you were painting it on the slate. Wait 5 to 10 minutes between applications. Remove any excess with a clean, dry terry towel.

Regular cleaning should include frequent dust mopping or vacuuming to remove dirt particles, which dull and scratch the surface. Damp mop occasionally with a neutral no-rinse cleaner designed for stone. These cleaners provide a conditioning action, which is important to maintain the natural beauty of the stone. Commercial cleaners, which are typically found on the grocery store shelves, have a pH between 8 and 9 and are designed for glazed tiles and vinyl flooring. They are too harsh for slate and, over time, will dull and discolor the natural luster of the stone.

Speed tips: "An entrance mat is the most basic requirement for any stone floor. Without it, even the best maintenance system will be unsuccessful," says Detlev Wolske, president of HMK Stone Care System in San Francisco. The entrance mat collects dirt and grit from the bottom of shoes and prevents them from scratching the floor. The less dirt and grit on the floor, the less you have to clean.

In a pinch: Plain water can be used to damp mop your floor occasionally. It won't leave a dulling film on the stone, although the chlorine, minerals, and salts in ordinary tap water are capable of staining a stone floor over time.

Caution: It's an old trade secret that's good to know: Don't use vinegar on slate floors. It will dull the floor overall.

Sleeping Bags

Sleeping bags are filled with either goose down or a synthetic down imitator. Down bags will need to be cleaned more often to keep the fill fluffy and insulating.

Technique: Clean only when necessary. Although they're made for roughing it in the great outdoors, they aren't cut out for the rigors of a normal household washer with an agitator. Take them to a Laundromat and wash in warm water on the gentle cycle in a front-loading, oversize commercial washer. Down bags should be washed with a mild detergent, according to the American Down Association in Sacramento, California. Run the bag through a second cycle without detergent to thoroughly rinse. Dry on a warm gentle setting. Be patient. Down bags dry slowly. If not dried thoroughly, a down bag will mat down and mildew.

Speed tips: To keep cleaning to a minimum, sleep with a folded sheet inside the bag and keep it off the bare ground. When camping, shake it out hard every day and hang it to air out. Store sleeping bags outside their stuff sacks to avoid overcompression of their fill. Spot-clean stains and spots before resorting to the washing machine.

In a pinch: A sleeping bag can be washed in a bathtub if a commercial Laundromat is not accessible. Care must be taken when handling the wet bag so that you do not rip the interior baffling. Be sure to rinse it thoroughly.

Caution: Do not dry-clean sleeping bags. The solvents will strip down feathers of their natural oils and are very toxic. If a care label insists on dry-cleaning, air the bag out for at least a week before sleeping in it again.

To avoid rips in the baffling, gently transfer wet bags to the dryer rolled in a ball.

Sliding-Door Tracks

A buildup of dirt and debris makes rough sliding for your door. And that's not all: It also attracts and holds water and moisture, which can damage the tracks of the slider or the door itself. To have a smoothly operating door, remember to clean the bottom and top tracks of the slider.

Technique: Vacuum any loose dirt out of the track, and spray with an all-purpose cleaner. Let it soak for a few minutes, then wipe loosened grime with a cloth. If your fingers are too big to get into the grooves comfortably, try wrapping a piece of cloth around a wooden spoon handle and run it back and forth along the tracks. You may have to repeat the process a few times to get sparkling results. Once clean, run the door back and forth a few times to dislodge any additional dirt from the glides or wheels. Then give the tracks a final wipe.

Speed tips: Clean regularly with the dusting or crevice tool of the vacuum cleaner, according to Caradon Doors and Windows, a sliding glass door manufacturer in Norcross, Georgia.

Caution: Lubricate the tracks after cleaning with a good silicone spray lubricant, which does not attract dirt and trash. Keep in mind that only a light coating is needed.

Smoke

 EMERGENCY ACTION
If there's a fire in your home, or if you don't know the source of the smoke, get everyone out and call the fire department. If there is no fire, open windows and doors to air out the house immediately. This will quickly lower odor levels and reduce the amount of smoke residue and the amount of cleanup necessary.

When the fire is out and the air has cleared, the filth that's left behind is called smoke residue. And while the dirt and damage will be most prevalent where the fire occurred, it usually permeates the whole house, requiring cleaning of clothing, drapes, carpeting, and upholstery to eliminate the foul odor. Depending on what has burned, the residue may be dry particles, smeary flakes, or even sticky liquids. Protein fires, such as a forgotten pot roast in the oven, leave a clear residue with a yellowish, pinkish cast and are typically characterized by their obnoxious odor.

Smoke and soot are often mistakenly lumped together as one problem. Smoke, however, is far more difficult to clean up since it is driven by heat, says Martin L. King, a restoration consultant in Arlington, Virginia, and technical advisor to the National Institute of Disaster Restoration in Millersville, Maryland. It permeates fibers and invades closed areas. Unless you're attempting a minor cleanup, smoke cleanup is best left to professional restoration specialists.

Even the smoke from a closed fireplace flue can cause enough damage to warrant professional attention.

Laundry

Shake loose particles from items. Soak or spray stains with pre-treater. Wash in the hottest water allowable for fabric and detergent. Add ½ cup washing soda to the load to cut through the oily residue.

Speed tips: Masking tape can help remove surface spots and residue from fabric.

Caution: Do not take smoked garments to an ordinary dry cleaner. Improper cleaning may permanently set stains and odors. Find a dry cleaner who is knowledgeable, and only take one or two things to be cleaned initially and see how they turn out.

Upholstery and Carpets

Carpets and upholstery can be shampooed or cleaned with a powdered cleaner such as Host or Capture (available at home centers), says King. Inaccessible smoke odor and residue trapped in the carpet padding and furniture stuffing materials, however, is likely to persist. Airing it out will help, but often the only solution is to have carpet and upholstery professionally cleaned and deodorized.

Caution: Avoid using upholstered furniture that has been damaged by smoke residue until it has been properly cleaned or restored. Using the furniture will further embed the residue in the textile fibers. Toxicity of the residue is also a concern if it is ingested by children or pets, says King.

Walls and Ceilings

Because of the numerous types of smoke residue, the Association of Specialists in Cleaning and Restoration in Millersville, Maryland, advises that you seek professional help to clean walls, ceilings, and other absorbent surfaces so that the appropriate cleaner can be used to neutralize odors. Cleaning smoke-damaged walls is a long tedious process, says King. If you only have an isolated amount of smoke damage, however, you can use the following technique to clean walls and ceilings.

Technique: Remove smoke with dry sponges (a specific type of smoke-cleaning sponge available at janitorial supply stores). Then wash with a solution of degreaser, such as Formula 409, and water. Dry with a cloth.

In a pinch: If smoke film or odor persists, repainting or refinishing may be required.

Smoke Alarms

If you keep in mind that the piercing shriek of a smoke alarm could save your life someday, it makes sense to give it some cleaning attention now and then.

Technique: The manufacturer of First Alert smoke alarms recommends that you gently vacuum the accumulated dust from the cover with a handheld soft brush attachment once a month. Make sure that the perforated sensing chamber isn't blocked by lint. Test the unit after vacuuming by following the manufacturer's instructions.

Caution: Don't use water, cleaners, or solvents on the unit because they may damage it.

Soap Scum

Do you have any insoluble precipitates lurking in your shower? No, don't call the vice squad. Insoluble precipitates are what you get when soap combines with mineral salts found in hard water, such as calcium and magnesium, says the Soap and Detergent Association in New York City. Of course, those of us who have attempted to scrub, scrape, and dissolve this tenacious gray film from the bathtub, the shower walls, or even clothing just call it soap scum.

Technique: You can purchase one of the numerous cleaners on the market specifically formulated to dissolve soap scum or use a variety of home remedies for ridding tile, showers and bathtubs from the dull gray film. Shower tile and doors can be cleaned by wiping on lemon oil furniture polish with a clean soft cloth. Allow it to soak a few minutes—longer if the film is severe. Then wipe clean with a dry cloth or paper towel. You may need to use a plastic scrubber in areas where there is a heavy buildup of residue. Lemon oil also retards future soap-scum buildup. For the shower curtain, rub a sponge soaked in white vinegar over the curtain to dissolve soap film. It will also kill mold and mildew.

On your laundry, soap residue makes fabrics feel stiff and shows up as white streaks or spots. To remove residue, add 1 cup white vinegar to 1 gallon warm water in a plastic container. Soak the item and rinse. To prevent future residue from forming, add a water-softening agent to your washer or use liquid laundry detergent. Make sure that textiles are adequately rinsed before drying.

Speed tips: The best way to save time cleaning up soap scum in the bath or shower is to prevent it from forming in the first place. "Try changing brands of soap," says Margaret Dasso, owner of the Clean Sweep, a professional cleaning service in Lafayette, California, and co-author of *Dirt Busters*. Some brands, such as Zest and Ivory, cause less film.

Clean a soap-scummed shower curtain in the washing machine. Fill the washer with warm water and equal parts of detergent and baking soda. Add the shower curtain and two large terry towels (the towels will help to rub the scum off the curtains during the washing process). Add 1 cup of vinegar to the rinse cycle. Remove the shower curtain before the spin cycle and hang to dry.

In a pinch: There are several household items that cut through soap film. Soap is alkaline, and acidic products such as vinegar or lemon juice will dissolve it.

Caution: Be sure to follow warnings on commercial soap-scum dissolvers. They may irritate the skin, eyes, or nose.

Soil

 EMERGENCY ACTION
If it's dry, brush or shake off as much of the soil as possible before laundering. If it's in the form of mud, let it dry before attempting to clean it. Trying to remove soil when it's wet will embed it further into the fibers. Once dry, most of the soil can be removed with a vacuum or a dry brush.

You'll find five basic types of soil dotting the backyards of America—sand, limestone, clay, silt, and peat. While scientists can't say for sure that Georgia clay has more staining power than Mississippi River silt, in general, soils composed of finer particles, such as clay and silt, stain more readily than coarse granular soils like limestone. "Smaller particles penetrate deeper into the fibers," says Beth McIntyre, a home economist for Maytag Appliances in Newton, Iowa. Regardless of the soil type, your cleaning technique is the same.

Technique: Brush unpenetrated dirt off the surface. Soak in cold water for a few minutes to loosen dirt particles. Then pretreat with a paste made of granular detergent and water. "Granular detergents remove soil and mud better than liquid detergents," says McIntyre.

Launder in the hottest water possible for the fabric. All-fabric bleach can be added to boost the cleaning action of the detergent. Check to make sure that the stain is removed before drying sets it.

Speed tips: Items do not need to be soaked for hours at a time. Most of the cleaning action occurs in the first half-hour, according to McIntyre. Use the presoak cycle on your washer to save time and effort. The 20- to 30-minute cycles on washing machines provide an adequate soaking time.

In a pinch: If stain persists, instead of water, make the paste with the granular detergent and ammonia, says Jane Rising, instructor in the education department at the International Fabricare Institute in Silver Spring, Maryland. Wash as directed above. (If the detergent contains chlorine bleach, don't mix it with ammonia. Toxic fumes can result.)

Caution: Use extra care when making a pretreat paste from granular detergent that contains all-fabric bleach. The bleach may fade the fabric, so only allow pretreat pastes of this type to sit on the stain for 5 to 10 minutes. Always read product labels for proper use and safety precautions.

Soot

EMERGENCY ACTION
Take these steps right away.

- Change your furnace filter. (Save the old one to show to the service technician.)
- Vacuum soot particles from upholstery, drapes, carpeting, and floors. Use the brush attachment with long soft bristles. The brush may have to be cleaned repeatedly during the cleaning process. Do not allow the metal vacuum tube to touch surfaces. It could cause the soot to smear and stain.
- Tape double layers of cheesecloth over air registers with masking tape to prevent further soot deposits.
- Cover upholstery with clean sheets.

Soot is a combination of oil and carbon, usually deposited in the form of fine homogeneous dust caused by unburned fuel from a malfunctioning furnace. Smoke and soot are often mistakenly lumped together as one cleaning problem. Smoke, however, is heat-driven and pushes its way into even closed-off places, such as drawers, while soot travels through the air currents and settles on surfaces. One way to tell them apart is that soot has no odor.

"Soot can accumulate because it does not have an obnoxious odor like smoke does," says Martin L. King, a restoration consultant in Arlington, Virginia, and technical advisor to the National Institute of Disaster Restoration in Millersville, Maryland. Soot also tends to be evenly distributed, while smoke damage is concentrated near the source of the fire.

Technique: If the problem occurred as a result of a furnace malfunction, cleanup may be covered under your homeowner's insurance policy, and your best bet may be to have a cleaning restoration specialist tackle the job. There's not much room for error when dealing with soot; an oily smear easily becomes a permanent stain.

Remove as much soot as possible from all surfaces through dry methods such as vacuuming. In places where a vacuum does not reach, try blowing the soot out with compressed air.

Once vacuumed, clean hard surfaces, such as wood furniture, countertops, sinks, appliances, light fixtures, hardwood and resilient floors, and windows with a towel dipped in a solution of degreaser and warm water. Use a lifting motion as you clean, not a circular rubbing motion.

You probably should leave walls and ceilings to a professional. "The average individual does not have the skills or patience because it's a long and tedious process," says King. "They might start out okay, but then they start looking for shortcuts." If you're determined to do it on your own, use dry sponges, which are available from janitorial supply stores.

Textiles are difficult to clean. Everything should be vacuumed or shaken out first. If it's washable, pretreat any stains and wash in the warmest temperature possible, preferably hot water. Adding ½ cup washing soda, a strong alkaline which boosts the water's cleaning ability, to the load can help battle the grease. Carpets should be vacuumed first and cleaned with a powdered cleaner such as Host or Capture, which are available at home centers.

Speed tips: When you're working with only a three-inch dust brush attachment on a vacuum cleaner, the task can seem endless. On large areas, a feather duster works well to lift soot off and push it to the floor where it can be quickly swept up.

In a pinch: If you don't have cheesecloth to tape over your air registers, any lightweight cloth that permits air circulation, such as handkerchiefs, will do. You want to prevent more soot from blowing into the house until the air ducts are cleaned.

Caution: Do not attempt to clean the following items. They should be cleaned by a professional restoration specialist, says King.

- Electronics (computers, televisions, and stereos need interior cleaning)
- Walls and ceilings
- Duct system
- Artwork
- Pianos and organs

Spills

Spill cleanup is the emergency-room duty of the cleaning world. Unlike regular cleaning, when you're trying to sparkle, sanitize, or even beautify, cleaning up spills and the unexpected mess they make is essentially damage control. You can prevent 90 percent of the spots and stains from liquid spills if you take immediate steps to absorb the mess, according to the Association of Specialists in Cleaning and Restoration in Millersville, Maryland.

Technique: Every spill is different—from candle wax on your tablecloth, to vomit on your carpeting, to a broken toner cartridge in your office, to a plate of spaghetti in your lap. So you need to know some basic techniques that prevent spills from becoming stains.

The time to take care of a spill is immediately after the mishap. Always remove as much of the spillage as possible before attempting any stain-removal techniques.

- If it's dry, keep it dry. Dry spills such as flour, sugar, or toner should be cleaned as thoroughly as possible by first using dry methods such as a vacuum cleaner, broom, or a dustpan and brush. Using water to clean up dry items will only liquefy the mess and make it harder to clean up and more likely to penetrate fibers and cause an annoying stain.
- Soak it up. Liquid spills should be blotted up with clean, white absorbent material such as paper towels, napkins, or tissues. The more of the spillage that's absorbed right away, the less residue is left to create a stain.
- After absorbing as much as of the spill as possible, sponge water-based spills such as coffee, tea, fruit juice, soda, milk, blood, or egg with clear water to remove residual spillage, which will even-

How to Beat the Drinks Jinx

Spilled drinks can come back to haunt you.

Beverages containing sugar are often the culprits when a brown discoloration appears days, weeks, or months after a spill on carpet or upholstery. Why? Because the liquid, containing colorless sugar, remains in the fibers after the spill is cleaned up. After exposure to air, the sugar causes insoluble brown stains.

To prevent this kind of damage from spilled coffee, tea, fruit juice, or soda, immediate action is necessary. Put a half-inch thickness of white absorbent towel on top of the spill and weight it down. As the stain is wicked into the towel, replace it with fresh material. When you have absorbed as much of the spill as possible, the Association of Specialists in Cleaning and Restoration in Millersville, Maryland, recommends blotting with small amounts of the following solutions until you remove the stain. Keep a supply of clean, white absorbent towels handy. You'll need a clean one to apply each solution in the order indicated below and to blot and rinse excess solution between applications.

- A commercial spot remover or alcohol
- 1 teaspoon mild (nonalkaline and nonbleach) liquid dish-washing detergent mixed with 1 cup lukewarm water
- 1 tablespoon household ammonia and $\frac{1}{2}$ cup water
- $\frac{1}{3}$ cup white vinegar (to neutralize the ammonia) and $\frac{2}{3}$ cup water
- A paste of powdered enzyme detergent and water

Always spot-check in an inconspicuous area to make sure that the fabric is colorfast, says Wm. (Bill) R. Griffin, president of Cleaning Consultant Services in Seattle. And refer to the instructions that came with your carpet or upholstery to be certain that you won't void the warranty by attempting to clean it yourself.

Be conservative with water. The Association of Specialists in Cleaning and Restoration warns against overwetting, which can cause carpet and upholstery to shrink. After you have eradicated the stain, blot away any lingering solution with a towel. Weight it down and allow it to dry for at least six hours, changing the dressing frequently. (Keep in mind that some stubborn stains may need professional attention.)

tually cause staining. If water does not remove the spill completely, a specific stain remedy will be necessary.

- Spills such as paint, oil-based paint, or grease should be blotted with spot removers, such as K2r or Energine (available at supermarkets, hardware stores, or discount department stores), instead of water.

• When working with carpets and upholstery, use small amounts of water and blot the area frequently to prevent discoloration from overwetting stuffing or backing materials. Blot from the outside edge and work your way toward the center to prevent the spill from spreading.

• Start with the mess, then work on the stain. When you spill a combination of liquid and solids, like a nice hearty bowl of minestrone soup, you have a combination mess. Spilled solids, such as food, should be lifted off first with a spoon or spatula. After you have removed as much solid matter as possible, soak up the liquid part of the mess with absorbent white towels and follow the tips for liquid spills.

Speed tips: A wet-dry vacuum cleaner will make quick work of wet, dry, and combination spills. They are especially useful in extracting liquids from carpeting and upholstery. One-gallon wet vacuums are available at hardware stores for small jobs. Clean and dry the equipment when you are finished with it.

In a pinch: If you don't have any cleaning tools handy, pull out your wallet. A credit card works great for lifting and scooping messes up and off surfaces.

Stainless Steel

An alloy of iron, chromium, and occasionally other metals, stainless steel is practically immune to rust and corrosion. It can stain, however—especially when exposed to high heat—and must be cared for.

Technique: Even though stainless steel resists corrosion, it is vulnerable to scratching. "Try to keep abrasives away from your stainless steel," says Kari Kinder, assistant director of food and beverage at the renowned Culinary Institute of America in Hyde Park, New York. "They will scratch and dull its shine."

Wash stainless-steel utensils and cookware in hot sudsy water or in the dishwasher. Wipe down stainless-steel sinks with a sudsy sponge or cloth. Brighten stainless steel by polishing it with a cloth soaked in vinegar. Rinse and buff items dry to remove water spots, which are caused by minerals in the water, a condition known as hard water.

How to Keep That Stainless Steel, Well, Stainless

With stainless steel, rust isn't a problem, and for the most part, neither are stains. Manufactured in different grades, the finish can be as shiny as a mirror or brushed. Here are a few tips from cleaning experts to keep your stainless looking its best.

Dry spots away. Washing in hot soapy water keeps pots and utensils clean. But make sure that you dry it right away with a cloth since stainless steel tends to water-spot.

Say goodbye to the blues. You can remove some of the blue discoloration that appears when stainless steel is overheated by scrubbing brushed surfaces with a mild abrasive cleaner like Bon Ami and polishing shiny surfaces with a cream silver polish.

Shine on. Surfaces that don't come in contact with food, such as appliance fronts, can be rubbed with lemon oil to shine and protect from fingerprints.

Water that has more than 60 milligrams of calcium and magnesium per liter is considered hard. If you have hard water and spotting is a major problem, increase the amount of dishwasher detergent that you've been using by one extra teaspoon for each 20 milligrams per liter of water hardness over 60. To find out the hardness of the water in your area, contact your water utility or your county Cooperative Extension Service.

Rub burned-on foods with baking soda or a paste made of ammonia, water, and a mild nonchlorinated scouring powder.

Discolorations caused by overheating are almost impossible to remove. Try rubbing them lightly with steel wool and a mild scouring powder. Otherwise, never use steel wool on stainless steel flatware.

Caution: Ammonia and chlorine, when mixed, cause noxious fumes.

Stains

Dealing with stains is a confusing maze of do's and don'ts for many of us. There are dozens of stain remedies, yet no universal rule applies to all stains. A remedy that works on one stain will set another. A good example is ordinary bar soap. It's great for getting out fabric softener stains but will set a fruit stain.

"It's not just the stain; it's what it's on and how long it has been there," says Carol Seelaus, a speed-cleaning instructor at Temple University in Philadelphia and owner of Somebody's Gotta Do It, a professional cleaning service. With the exception of mud and Play-Doh, stains that are treated right away are much more likely to be removed completely than stains that have had a chance to dry and penetrate the fabric or surface. This is the first rule of stain removal—act quickly.

But when it comes to stain removal, quickly is a variable term. Depending on the stain, you could have minutes, hours, or even days before it sets. Drinks like red Hawaiian Punch are some of the worst stain offenders, says Margaret Dasso, owner of the Clean Sweep, a professional cleaning service in Lafayette, California, and co-author of *Dirt Busters*. But if you treat it in the first few minutes, you may be able to remove the stain. The folks who make Hawaiian Punch suggest rinsing clothing immediately with cold water, then soaking the item in an enzyme prewash, such as Biz. Wash it in the hottest water allowable for the fabric. Check to make sure that the stain is gone before machine-drying. On carpets, flush the spill with club soda and then blot with clean white towels. If it's greasy salad dressing, you still need to act quickly, but you have a few days until the oils oxidize and permanently darken the fabric.

Technique: For the best results, follow these general rules for stain removal.

First, try to identify the stain. "You're miles ahead if you know what you have on it," says Beth McIntyre, a home economist for Maytag Appliances in Newton, Iowa. Look at the color of the stain. Look at

The Seven Deadly Stains

Watch out! These stains don't just work their way into the fibers; they permanently deface and discolor furniture, carpeting, flooring, upholstery, and clothing, says Carol Seelaus, a speed-cleaning instructor at Temple University in Philadelphia and owner of Somebody's Gotta Do It, a professional cleaning service.

1. Acids (tile cleaners, toilet-bowl cleaners, urine, vomit)
2. Benzoyl peroxide (acne medication, age-spot remover)
3. Bleach (automatic dishwasher detergent, chlorine)
4. Hair dyes
5. Herbal teas
6. Liquid plant food
7. Strong alkalis (drain cleaner, lye, oven cleaner)

Your Stain-Fighting Tool Kit

Be prepared. Keep these tools and cleaners on hand, advise cleaning experts.

Absorbents: Cornmeal, cornstarch, or talcum powder; can be sprinkled on a grease stain, allowed to sit to absorb it, and brushed or vacuumed to remove.

Ammonia: Use the plain kind when you need a mild alkaline solution. Use with caution. Never mix chlorine bleach and ammonia. This can cause dangerous fumes.

Bar soap: Rub on fabric softener stains to remove them.

Chlorine bleach: A powerful tool for removing stains if the fabric can tolerate it.

Denatured or isopropyl alcohol: Useful for removing stains on water-sensitive fabrics. Check for colorfastness first.

Digestant: Contains enzymes that eat tough protein stains such as food, vomit, and blood. Can be purchased in pure enzyme form from some health food stores or as a laundry presoak, such as Biz. Use warm water. Don't mix with other chemicals. Enzymes are sensititve. Also, you may need to apply several treatments.

Laundry pretreaters: Available in sprays, liquid, gels, and sticks. Different types work better on different stains.

Neutral detergent: A liquid dishwashing detergent works fine. Use a clear one that has a pH of 7. Mix a light solution of 2 or 3 drops in 1 cup water. Opaque or colored ones may contain dye or skin softeners.

Spot remover: A spot remover, such as Energine, Carbona Stain Devils, or K2r (available at supermarkets, hardware stores, or discount department stores), is good for removing oily stains from fabrics that can only be dry-cleaned. It can be used on most fabrics and will not set stains. Watch for flammability.

3 percent hydrogen peroxide: Provides a mild bleaching action for fabrics that can't tolerate chlorine bleach. Allow time for it to work.

Water: A spray bottle filled with water at room temperature is your best tool. "Most stains are water-soluble," says Carol Seelaus, a speed-cleaning instructor at Temple University in Philadelphia and owner of Somebody's Gotta Do It, a professional cleaning service. "Nine times out of 10, water will do the trick."

Use it to flush the stain and to rinse solvents from the fabric or stained surface.

White vinegar: Good for stains that call for acid or to neutralize alkaline stains. It will also neutralize smoke odor.

the surface. Is it soaked in or crusted on? Crusty stains that turn white when scratched are often sugar-based. If you can't identify the stain specifically, try to learn if it's a protein stain, a greasy stain, a water-soluble stain, a waxy stain, a chemical stain, or a combination stain. Certain stains can be set by the wrong treatment. If you can categorize the stain, proceed with an appropriate treatment.

Wait before you wet. Remove as much of the stain as possible before wetting it with water or cleaning solvent, which will immediately start to dissolve the stain and spread it to other fibers. So blot away liquids and scrape or lift away as much solid residue as possible.

Be wary of heat. The heat of the dryer or even hot water can set stains, so stick to cool or warm water when working on an unknown stain. After laundering, allow stained items to air-dry until you're sure that the stain has been completely removed.

"Anytime a stain is washed, not noticed, and dried, it is very difficult to remove because the dryer heat sets the stains," says McIntyre. The heat of the dryer will set sugar stains, protein stains, and a host of other stains. The iron will permanently set perspiration stains and bring out a lovely shade of yellow-brown in old sugar stains. There are exceptions, though. Grease and soil stains should be washed with hot water.

Lift the stain out. Never rub a stain. Rubbing abrades textile fibers and carpeting and drives the stain further into the surface. Use the following methods to effectively pull stains from some fibers and surfaces.

- Blot fresh stains with clean white cloths.
- Flush with cool or warm water, or with an appropriate cleaning solvent.
- Soak in cool water.
- Freeze the stain and peel or pick off.
- Tamp with a flat-bristle brush to break up stain particles so that they can be lifted off by cleaner. Tamping is a vertical striking motion, not a back and forth scrubbing motion.

Check the colorfastness before treatment. In an inconspicuous place, such as a seam or hem on clothing or a hidden corner on carpeting or furniture, test your fabric for dye bleeding. Apply cleaning solution or pretreater. Let it soak for a few minutes, then blot with a clean white cloth. Look for dye on the cloth or lightening on the fabric. Silk is extremely prone to dye migration. Commercial stain pretreaters may make neon dyes bleed.

HOW IT WORKS

The Chemistry of Laundry Pretreaters

Laundry stain pretreaters help you soften up the enemy before the battle even begins. They're available in aerosol and pump sprays and liquid, gel, and stick form. They work by suspending stains in the fabric so that they can be washed away.

But pretreaters are not created equal when it comes to stain removal. Although they are marketed as a general, cure-all stain solution, pretreaters are stain-specific, says Beth McIntyre, a home economist for Maytag Corporation in Newton, Iowa.

Liquids and sprays are derived from petroleum distillates and work best on oily and greasy stains.

"We have found that grease removes grease better. Grease takes grease out," says McIntyre. The liquid and spray forms should be applied a few minutes before laundering. It is important to remember that these products should not be allowed to dry out or else they lose their stain-removal power.

Gels and sticks, on the other hand, are enzyme-based and work well on protein stains, such as blood, grass, baby formula, dairy products, eggs, and chocolate, says McIntyre. Sticks can be applied up to a week before laundering.

Do not use pretreater for spot removal on items that cannot be laundered, such as upholstery, carpeting, or dry-cleanable items.

Pretreat stains. This can be done using a commercial prewash stain remover, such as Shout or Spray 'n Wash, or by making your own from a liquid laundry detergent, a paste of water and granular detergent, bar soap, or a laundry additive, such as borax.

Be persistent. It may take more than one try to get the stain out. If you see some lightening of the stain on the first attempt, try again.

Toss it in the washer. Always launder washable items after treating to remove residues of both the stain and the stain remover.

Speed tips: To save yourself time and aggravation when dealing with a stain, remember the first rule of thumb: Deal with it right away. It also helps to:

- Know where to look for stains. On clothing look at collars, underarm areas, elbows and knees, cuffs, and seams.
- Mark the spot. If you don't have time to attack a stain until laundry day, mark it with a piece of masking tape or a Post-it Note before putting it in the hamper.

- Use the soak cycle on your washer, recommends McIntyre. Soaking does not need to take hours and hours to be effective. The 20- to 30-minute cycle provides an adequate amount of cleaning action.
- Wash it on laundry day. If you don't have time to wash it now, laundry stain sticks do a pretty good job on most stains, says McIntyre. As long as it's not a grease or oil stain, a stick is effective. Keep one next to the hamper and train everyone in the household to use it.

In a pinch: If you just can't figure out what kind of stain it is, McIntyre recommends soaking the item in cold water for 30 minutes to loosen the stain, then applying a pretreater such as a paste made from granular detergent and water, and then laundering the item in warm water.

Caution: For the sake of your family's health as well as your clothing:

- Never mix chemicals together. They can give off toxic fumes. The classic example is chlorine bleach and ammonia.
- Work in a well-ventilated area, and don't smoke when working with chemical spotters. They're flammable.
- Prevent accidental poisoning. Keep cleaning chemicals in their original packaging stored out of the reach of children.
- Wear gloves when working with all cleaning solvents. Chemicals can be absorbed through the skin.
- When using any bleach (chlorine or oxygen), treat the entire item. That way, if the color is affected, at least it will change evenly.

Steel

Because it is so prone to rust, steel is usually coated with a protective finish. Its exterior coating determines how you should clean it. Steel appliances often have an enamel finish. Vinyl coated steel is used in items like dishwasher racks or appliance trim. In general, you'll need to guard against scratches and punctures, which would allow the steel to come in contact with moisture and rust. Rust can form in just four hours.

Technique: Clean surfaces with a nonabrasive all-purpose cleaner, such as Formula 409, and a sponge or soft cloth. Rinse with a separate sponge dipped in clean water, and dry with a soft cloth. You can also clean and protect appliances and cabinets with a painted or baked enamel finish with a creamy liquid kitchen wax, according to the Soap and Detergent Association in New York City. Wm. (Bill) R. Griffin, president of Cleaning Consultant Services in Seattle, suggests Jubilee. Apply wax to a damp cloth and rub onto the finish. Work in small sections, cleaning about one square foot at a time. This is necessary so that you can buff each area with a dry cloth while the wax is still moist. Appliances should only be waxed three or four times per year to avoid wax buildup.

Speed tips: Hardened spills on stove tops may need to soak in a cleaning solution for 15 minutes to remove without scratching the protective finish. Save yourself time by cleaning up spots and spills when they happen with plain water or a spray of all-purpose cleaner.

In a pinch: If rust develops at the site of a scratch on a painted finish, you may be able to repair the damage. Remove rust with sandpaper or a rust remover such as Duro Naval Jelly. If the steel is still in good condition, touch up the spot with a dab of appliance paint or enamel paint.

Caution: Never use abrasive cleaners, such as steel wool or powdered cleansers on coated steel finishes. It could scratch the surface and eventually cause the steel to rust. It's okay to use a white scrubbing pad.

Stereo Equipment

Your ears will tell you when it's time to clean your stereo equipment. Dirt, dust, and oxides gradually collect on the sensitive parts of your audio system and erode the sound. Telltale signs are crackling when the volume knob is adjusted, muffled or distorted sound, weak or dropped signals from the left or right speaker, or the compact disc (CD) player skipping tracks. You can have your audio system sounding as good as new by investing a few dollars and a few minutes.

Technique: Periodically dust the stereo components. Use a nonmetallic brush to loosen dust and a vacuum cleaner to remove it. "Don't move around any parts, such as wires or resistors. From the way they look, you say, 'Why is this thing sticking up in the air?' But moving them around can loosen connections and cause problems that you never had before," says Dave Barnes, service manager for Crutchfield, a mail-order audio equipment distributor in Charlottesville, Virginia. "As far as dust buildup, the only thing that's truly harmful is dust on the optic laser of the CD player."

But steer clear of manually cleaning the lens of the CD player; it can be damaged easily. You can clean lenses safely and effectively on single CD players by purchasing a commercial CD cleaner, which has a brush fused to its playing surface, for about $10.

Don't forget about the wires that deliver the sound to your system. About once a year unplug and wipe down all jacks and cables with denatured alcohol.

If you hear a crackling sound when you adjust the volume, you probably have a buildup of dust and dirt on the carbon tracks in the knob housing. Turn the unit off and unplug it. Remove the cover from the component and any shrouding around the knob until you can see where it meets the circuit board. There should be a hole visible. Spray a small amount of light silicone cleaner into the hole. It will remove the dust and prevent further buildup. Turn the knob back and forth about four times. Turn the unit on with the volume at a minimum level to see if the crackling has disappeared. Repeat the process if it hasn't. If you don't have a silicone cleaner, denatured alcohol will remove existing dirt, but it won't provide the protective coating to repel dust. This procedure can be used to clean

SCRUB THIS APPROACH

Don't Gum Up the Works

It makes audio service technicians shake their heads sadly— the common misuse of aerosol lubricants on stereo systems, says Dave Barnes, service manager for Crutchfield, a mail-order audio equipment distributor in Charlottesville, Virginia.

"It makes a mess out of stuff," he says. Sometimes a tape player or turntable runs slowly or appears to be sticking. Thinking that they'll just get things moving a little better, a person sprays a silicone-based cleaner or lubricant into the system.

"That ruins the felt drive clutches and impregnates the rubber, causing it to slip and swell," Barnes says. His advice is to stay away from aerosol lubricants. Unplug your unit and remove the outer cover. Use a vacuum cleaner reversed to blow air out instead. If you can't remove the dust by vacuuming, try blowing it out with compressed air. Wipe the rubber and clutch pads with a cotton swab moistened with a small amount of denatured alcohol.

all your function knobs—balance, bass, treble, tape monitor, and auxiliary. "When you have one dirty knob, you probably have a mess of them," says Barnes.

If the jacks on your equipment are badly corroded, rub them with fine sandpaper.

Even if you don't play records like you used to, don't ignore your turntable. It's a good idea to replace your needle after every 30 hours of use. A dull needle can damage your records, especially as they become brittle with age. It's a good idea to buy more than one replacement because you may not be able to find it in a few years. Store your vinyl records in an upright position (never leaning) away from sunlight. Use a velvet brush to clean them.

Speed tips: Keep covers and doors closed on stereo equipment to avoid dust buildup. Dirt on tapes, CDs, and records get deposited in your components. Store them in their jackets or cases to keep them clean and dust-free.

Caution: Make sure that the system is off and unplugged during cleaning, especially when you're removing the jacks. You don't want to send a damaging blast of noise through your speakers as you re-connect them.

Be sure to check with your manufacturer to make sure that opening the unit will not void the warranty.

Stone

Stone is being used in an increasing number of American homes for floors, counters, and walls. "Stone is becoming more affordable because of improving technology in the stonecutting industry," says Fred Hueston, director of the National Training Center for Stone and Masonry Trades in Longwood, Florida, and author of *The Stain Removal Guide for Stone.* Granite, marble, limestone, slate, and sandstone are easy-care durable materials that will last a lifetime if cared for properly.

Technique: The first step in maintaining a stone surface is to protect it from stains by sealing it with an impregnator, which is available from a floor-care specialist. Like water filling a sponge, the impregnator fills up the pores of the stone so that stains cannot penetrate.

New surfaces should be cleaned with a stone soap, allowed to dry thoroughly, and sealed. On older surfaces, make sure that all

To Clean Stone, Go Deep

You need more than a scrub brush to remove a stain from stone. You may scrub it away only to have it resurface days later.

"What most people don't realize is that the stain has permeated into the pores of the stone," says Fred Hueston, director of the National Training Center for Stone and Masonry Trades in Longwood, Florida, and author of *The Stain Removal Guide for Stone.* "You have to put something on the stain to draw it out."

Stain removal for stone requires making a poultice, a paste which is applied to the stained area, allowed to dry, and scraped off.

"Drying is very important. If it's not allowed to dry, it will not wick or draw the stain out of the stone," says Hueston.

Poultice Formulas
Ink, tea, coffee, wine, fruit and most food stains (excluding oil): Mix white bleached flour with hydrogen peroxide to form a paste the consistency of yogurt.

Cooking oil, copper stains: Mix white bleached flour and ammonia into a paste.

Mildew, algae, mold: Form a paste combining household bleach and flour. This works well on grout that has embedded stains.

Directions
Apply the poultice over the stained area, overlapping by at least one inch all around. Cover with plastic wrap and allow to sit for 12 to 24 hours. Remove plastic and test for dryness. If it is not thoroughly dry, allow it to dry uncovered. Once dry, scrape with wooden spoon or similar dull instrument and examine the area.

Don't give up after one try. If you see some improvement, try again. It may take two to five applications to completely remove some stains.

---

stains are removed prior to sealing. Once the stain is sealed in, it will never come out.

Sealers can be sprayed on or wiped on. Hueston recommends using a lamb's wool applicator to wipe the impregnator on because it doesn't streak.

Depending on the level of use, the stone can be resealed every six months to five years. "From practical experience, I think it's a good idea to go on a once-a-year basis," says Hueston.

If in doubt, Hueston says, you should perform the water absorption test. Drop several drops of water on the surface. "If you see signs of absorption (darkening of the stone) in under one minute, it's time to reseal."

Ordinary maintenance of stone floors should include daily dust mopping or vacuuming to remove scratchy grit and weekly damp mopping or scrubbing with a stone soap. Wipe countertops clean with nonabrasive cleaner after each use.

For tips on stone care, send a self-addressed stamped envelope to the National Training Center for Stone and Masonry Trades, 941 Longdale Avenue, Longwood, FL 32750.

Speed tips: Save steps by including your stone walls and floors in your vacuuming routine to remove excess dirt and dust. Frequent vacuuming will lessen the need for mopping. Prevention and cleaning frequency are key. Use exterior walk-off mats. Take off your shoes at the door, recommends Bill R. Griffin, president of Cleaning Consultant Services in Seattle.

In a pinch: If you don't have stone soap, use a mild vegetable-oil soap, like Murphy Oil Soap.

Caution: If you live in an area where it freezes in the winter, experts advise against sealing exterior stone. If stone is sealed improperly with water trapped in it, freezing will destroy the stone. Allow exterior stone to weather and develop its own patina.

Stoves

When *Woman's Day* magazine surveyed 1,000 women to find out the household chores that they absolutely hate, cleaning the stove came up number one. So if degreasing little knobs and scouring petrified food from once-shiny surfaces is a dreaded task in your house, take heart; you have lots of company. Since there are hundreds of different models in use, it makes sense to consult your owner's manual for any specific instructions. But basically, cleaning a stove—whether it's gas or electric—involves the same tasks: taking it apart, cleaning it, and putting it back together.

Technique: Make sure that all parts of the stove are cool. Remove control knobs and grates and soak them in hot soapy water. Clean with a nylon scrub pad or toothbrush and rinse well. Soak drip pans in a strong solution of automatic dishwasher detergent, says Margaret Dasso, owner of the Clean Sweep, a professional cleaning service in Lafayette, California, and co-author of *Dirt Busters.* Clean the stove top and backsplash with a degreaser, like Ultra Mr. Clean Top Job, and a white nylon scrubber. If it's not a sealed cooktop, don't forget to clean the area underneath the burners, where all the drips flow. Clean the underside of the stove top with a degreaser and white nylon scrubber. Rinse with a sponge. When all areas are clean, finish off with by polishing with window cleaner. Replace knobs, grates, heating elements, and drip pans.

Speed tips: Don't give food a chance to fossilize on your stove surfaces. Wipe spills up as soon as they occur. Or include a quick spray and wipe with all-purpose cleaner in your daily kitchen cleanup routine.

Clean drip pans in the dishwasher. Prior to cooking, remove drip pans and lightly spray them with nonstick vegetable spray; cleanup will be easier.

In a pinch: If you don't have a commercial degreasing solution on hand, make your own degreasing spray cleaner with these ingredients suggested by "green"-minded cleaning experts. Mix ½ teaspoon washing soda, 1 teaspoon borax, ¼ to ½ teaspoon liquid dishwashing detergent, 3 tablespoons vinegar or 2 tablespoons lemon juice, and 2 cups hot water. Spray and let soak on greasy area for several minutes before rinsing.

Caution: Harsh abrasives, green scrubbing pads, and steel wool will cause scratches on all surfaces.

Stuffed Toy Animals

Every year toy manufacturers flood the market with more than 110 million stuffed animals. When faced with a treasured collection of dusty, matted, stained critters as big as nature's own wild kingdom, many parents have faced the dilemma: Do I clean them or do I trash them? If you opt for cleaning, there are three basic techniques. Which method you use is determined by the age, construction, and stuffing materials.

Technique: Read the tag to see if the stuffed animal is machine washable. Some can be machine-washed in cold water on the gentle cycle. To protect the animal's "fur" and your washer should the animal disintegrate in the wash, place it in an old pillowcase tied shut before washing. Use mild laundry detergent. After washing, put it in the dryer on "Air-Fluff" for 5 to 10 minutes, then allow it to air-dry.

For collectible stuffed toys, toys with unknown stuffing contents, or toys with no care instructions, cleaning should be restricted to the surface of the animal. Saturation of the toy with water or other cleaners could cause an array of complications—from split seams to lost appendages. To clean, vacuum to remove surface dust and dirt, says Marjorie Merritt Darrah, owner of Mary Merritt's Doll Museum in Douglassville, Pennsylvania. Apply foam upholstery cleaner, or make your own with an electric mixer with 2 cups warm water with a squirt of liquid dishwashing detergent. Mix at medium speed until it foams. Using a circular motion, apply foam to the toy with a dry brush. Using a spray bottle, rinse with clear water. Alternately spray the animal with water using the "spray" or "mist" setting and blot with clean cloth. Continue this procedure until the animal is thoroughly rinsed. Wipe the surface with a dry white terry towel. Then allow to air-dry, and brush with hairbrush to fluff.

Speed tips: To dry shampoo your furry friends, rub cornstarch into the fur and vacuum.

In a pinch: Place the stuffed toy in the dryer on "Fluff" or "Air" setting for a few minutes to freshen.

Caution: Don't use harsh upholstery cleaners on toys that will be handled by young children who might want to put the toy in their mouths.

Suede

A simple preventive maintenance routine is the key to protecting your suede from looking flat and shiny.

Technique: Suede shoes and garments should be brushed with a plastic- or rubber-tipped suede brush after each wearing. Suede tends get shiny when it is dirty, and brushing fluffs up the nap, loosens and releases dirt, and restores the rich texture of the suede.

Remove spots and oily stains immediately before they have chance to penetrate the leather. You can use solvent-based cleaners (similar to dry cleaners) that are specially formulated for suede. Oil-absorbing blocks, which abrade the leather to bring back the nap and remove the stain, are also available at some shoe repair shops and some supermarkets.

Speed tips: The key to saving your time and saving your suede is preventive maintenance. Before you wear your suede shoes or clothing, always protect them with a water and stain repellent designed specifically for suede. "That way when you do encounter stains from day-to-day wear, they will be much easier to take off," says Mitch Lebovic, editor of *Shoe Service* magazine in Baltimore. "As soon as you notice that water is no longer beading up, treat again."

In a pinch: Use a terry towel or an old toothbrush to brush suede. A gum eraser or fine sandpaper can be used in place of a stone to remove dirt and stains.

To restore the color to faded suede, pass it quickly through the steam of a teakettle. Be careful not to let condensation form.

Caution: Suede and water don't mix. If suede becomes wet, allow it to dry away from heat sources, then brush to remove water spots. If spots remain, have the garment professionally cleaned.

Leather cleaners are formulated for the smooth finish of leather. Do not use them on suede. They will mat down the nap and ruin it.

Tablecloths

It's inevitable. Even the most careful diners eventually slop greasy gravy, dribble candle wax, or slosh red wine onto the table linens. Don't panic, advises Elizabeth Barbatelli, president of the Laundry at Linens Limited, a Milwaukee-based mail-order laundry that specializes in cleaning heirloom-quality linens. You don't need to whisk the tablecloth out from under your guests in quick-jerk magician fashion. "It takes about three weeks for a stain to set," says Barbatelli.

Technique: Prior to washing, treat and remove any known stains on the tablecloth. (See Stains on page 252 or specific stain listings.) Then determine whether the tablecloth (or napkins or place mats) can be machine-washed or needs to be laundered by hand.

For new items, read the care label instructions. For other items, follow these recommendations outlined by Michele Durkson Clise in her book *The Linen Closet: How to Care for Your Fine Linens and Lace.* Antique whites made of cotton or linen that are not trimmed in lace can be machine-washed in hot water on the gentle cycle using plain laundry soap without any additives such as bleach or blueing ingredients. Lacy or fragile items, containing embroidery or cutwork should be washed by hand in Liquid Tide or Orvus, which is available at most quilting stores, a nondetergent cleanser frequently used on antique textiles. Place items in a net bag or white pillowcase tied shut with colorfast material.

For heavily soiled items it is essential to presoak first in cold water, then in hot water to loosen stains and dirt.

Whether washing by machine or by hand, make sure that there is enough room for the water to adequately circulate around the cloth in order to wash effectively. A bathtub or utility sink is a good choice.

Rinse thoroughly in hot or cold water three times or until suds are no longer visible. Poor rinsing can leave a residue, which may scorch during ironing or turn yellow over time.

Sturdy table linens can be dried on a low-heat setting in the clothes dryer. However, air drying is preferred because it preserves the shape and dimensions of linens. For easier ironing, give it a quick shake before hanging. If linens are going to be stored for several months, put them away unstarched and not ironed. Roll them in clean white cloths or acid-free tissue until ready for ironing.

Speed tips: For quicker results once it's time to get the ironing board out, season your table linens. The process of sprinkling your tablecloth with hot water, rolling it up, and setting it aside for several hours—or seasoning—makes the linen fibers much more pliable and easier to iron. Lay table linens on a clean countertop or table. Sprinkle evenly with hot water to prevent a blotchy finish. Roll up in a clean white cloth for an hour or more. Putting the tablecloth in the refrigerator for several hours makes ironing even easier. Iron within a day to avoid mildew growth.

In a pinch: If you don't have a spray bottle to season your linens, use a whisk broom or your fingers. Dip in the hot water and shake fine drops over the linen.

Caution: Handle wet linens carefully. When line-drying, never hang a tablecloth by the corners. It could stretch or tear from the weight of the water. Instead, fold it over the clothesline and secure with clothespins. Also, storing table linens on bare wood shelves could cause yellowing.

Tape Players

Is your tape player emitting a pronounced hiss? Has the sound gotten muffled? Those are sure signs that a tape deck needs to be cleaned, says the Consumer Electronics Manufacturers Association (CEMA) in Arlington, Virginia. The dirt, dust, and oxide that build up inside the player cause these problems. As tapes move through the machine, bits of the oxide particle coating can flake off the tape and stick to the heads and tape path mechanism. Ordinary dust can also damage heads, decks, and tapes. Dust can build up in automobile

Clean Tapes, Clean Tape Player

Keeping your tapes in top-notch condition will keep your tape deck cleaner. Follow these tips, according to the Consumer Electronics Manufacturers Association.

- Keep tapes in their cases when not in use.
- Eject tapes after playing if your player doesn't do it automatically.
- Keep cassettes away from heat when not in use.
- Avoid storing cassettes on top of the TV, stereo speakers, or anyplace where a magnetic field can partially erase high-frequency sounds.

and portable tape decks even more than home decks. Dirty capstans are the leading cause of problems in car decks, according to CEMA.

If you ignore the problem, eventually the player will start to eat your tapes. But investing just a few minutes and a few dollars can keep your sound sparkling.

Technique: Isopropyl (rubbing) alcohol is the universal audio cleaning agent. But the kind you get in the drugstore is diluted and not very effective. Your best bet is to buy it in concentrated form at an electronics store, where it's typically labeled as a cleaner/degreaser.

Using a cotton swab dipped in alcohol, gently clean recording and playback heads, the capstan, the rubber pinch rollers, and any tape guides. Use enough cleaner to dissolve all the buildup, but take care not to drip it all over the tape player's interior. CEMA recommends that you clean your tape deck after every 15 to 20 hours of playing time.

Vacuum the cabinets, exterior, and ventilation grille of the tape player often to remove dust. Both plastic and metal exteriors should be cleaned by wiping with a cloth moistened with water or all-purpose cleaner. Don't use paper towels; they can scratch the plastic.

Speed tips: Popping in a tape head–cleaning cassette can be a time-saver. However, it will not clean the player as effectively. Some miss the cap-

Here's a look at the interior of a typical tape player. Use a cotton swab dipped in alcohol to gently clean the capstan, pinch rollers, recording and playback heads, and tape guide.

Excess Magnetism: The Invisible "Dirt"

An invisible kind of contamination can build up in tape players—excess magnetism. Because the playback heads rub against magnetic cassette tape, they can eventually become magnetized. In addition to causing a distinctive hissing sound, magnetized heads can also erase music from your tapes. To prevent this from happening, use a demagnetizer at least once a year, says the Consumer Electronics Manufacturers Association in Arlington, Virginia.

There are two types: wand demagnetizers, which generate their own magnetic field to neutralize the one on your tape head, and cassette-type demagnetizers, which utilize a filament brush and a field-discharge chip to demagnetize heads. Electronics retailers sell both types.

stan and the roller entirely, so only use them occasionally. Use a nonabrasive cassette—preferably the type that uses a cleaning solution. The dry cleaners clean by grinding dirt away and can eventually damage your tape player, says Gary Leiby, owner of Electronic Hardware Repair in Allentown, Pennsylvania.

In a pinch: Ordinary isopropyl alcohol can be substituted. However, since it is diluted, it is not as effective at dissolving built-up gunk and dirt.

Caution: Alcohol is extremely flammable. Do not smoke while using alcohol-based cleaners or use them near an open flame.

Tar

 EMERGENCY ACTION
Freeze with ice cubes until the tar becomes brittle, then carefully scrape with a plastic spatula. If ice is not available, gently pull as much tar off the surface as you can.

Remember that tar was made to be tough. When you try to remove a tar stain, keep in mind that you're up against a construction material highly valued for its imperviousness to water and its ability to stick where stuck.

Technique: After you've scraped as much tar as possible from the surface, treat the underlying stain as soon as possible. There are several methods. Before you begin, test a small part of the fabric for colorfastness. For a fresh stain, the Soap and Detergent Association in New York City recommends placing the stain facedown on paper towels and sponging it with white kerosene. Replace the paper towels frequently to absorb as much tar as possible and to avoid transferring the stain. Apply stain pretreater and launder the article in the hottest water possible with regular laundry detergent.

For a hard dry stain, apply petroleum jelly to soften it, then sponge with cleaning solvent.

Speed tips: The quickest way to get tar out is to act quickly. Old stains are nearly impossible to remove.

In a pinch: Try nonbutane lighter fluid to loosen and remove the tar stain. Test for colorfastness first. Use in a well-ventilated area away from heat or flames.

If you still can't get the stain out after several tries with kerosene or lighter fluid, apply and reapply laundry pretreater to keep the stain wet for 20 minutes. Follow with a rinse in warm water.

Caution: Do not apply water to the stain until you have removed as much as possible with solvents. Water tends to set tar and make the stain even worse. Do not launder until the stain is completely gone. Always read the product label for proper usage and safety precautions. Tar stains are some of the most difficult to remove without permanent damage to fabric surfaces, according to Bill R. Griffin, president of Cleaning Consultant Services in Seattle.

Tarnish

When it develops on a bronze statue, tarnish is called patina and is considered a beautiful part of the aging process. But on most metals regular removal of tarnish is recommended to prevent it from becoming embedded in the finish.

Tarnish is the discoloration that occurs when metals react with salts, acids, and even the oxygen in the air. Over time, tarnish will progressively dull and darken brass, silver, copper, and gold. On aluminum, which reacts with salt in the air, tarnish shows up as a white crust.

Technique: To keep your metals gleaming, wash and polish them regularly. Use a commercial polish formulated for the specific metal, or mix your own polish from household ingredients. (Also see specific entries for individual metals.)

There are four basic cleaning methods that naturally bring a shine back to metal.

- Abrasion, which combines a granular ingredient with elbow grease
- Soaking in an acidic solution
- Applying an alkaline paste, which is rubbed onto the surface, allowed to dry, and then rinsed off
- Submerging the item in an acidic solution

Pantry staples like lemon juice, vinegar, salt, cream of tartar, baking soda, toothpaste, and olive oil are the basis of various home-made metal polishes. Apply polishes or pastes with a sponge, cloth, or soft brush.

For brass and copper, which need a stronger abrasive than silver, mix 2 teaspoons salt, 1 tablespoon flour, and enough vinegar to make a paste. Vigorously apply the paste with a sponge and dry. Rinse in hot water and polish to a shine with a dry towel.

Although different metals require varying degrees of abrasion and rubbing, you can use an effective all-purpose metal cleaner. Rub some soft-grade blackboard chalk into a damp rough cloth and polish the surface. It will remove dirt and grease, yet it won't scratch.

Speed tips: Opt for the submersion method of cleaning if you want to save some time and elbow grease. Stains on aluminum, for instance, can be removed by stewing the metal piece on low heat for an hour or so in a water bath that contains an acidic ingredient, such as 2 halved tomatoes, 2 or 3 halved lemons, or 1 grapefruit cut in quarters, plus 1 to 2 cups freshly cut rhubarb.

In a pinch: The acidic qualities of lemon juice used full strength will remove tarnish on brass, bronze, and copper. The white of its rind will polish chrome.

Caution: Baking soda or washing soda are not recommended for cleaning aluminum.

Taxidermy

Keep dirt and dust from accumulating on your mounted tro-phies by following a few preventive measures. Display your stuffed creature away from sunlight or else your black bear may end up looking like a polar bear. A climate-controlled room free of the air-borne impurities of smoke (either fireplace or cigarette), kitchen fumes, and humidity from bathing and laundry is the best location for your display.

Technique: At least once a month, remove dust from the fur using a one-inch artist's brush. Carefully stroke in the natural direction of the fur.

Eyes, teeth, noses, horns, and other hard surfaces can be cleaned with a lightly dampened (not wet) cloth or with an anti-static cloth (the kind used to clean photographs). Be careful because water and moisture can stretch the skin or fur of preserved animals.

While the most common cleaning concern for your mounted treasures is dust, pests that feed on the organic matter of the animal

A CLEAN STORY

Happy Tails to You, Trigger

A star in his own right, Trigger appeared with Roy Rogers in 188 movies and television episodes. Although he died in 1965, the golden palomino legend isn't just a celluloid memory. You can visit all 15½ hands of Trigger, who is mounted at the Roy Rogers–Dale Evans Museum in Victorville, California.

"Never call him stuffed. He's mounted," says Roy Rogers Jr., president and executive officer of the family-run museum. After his death at age 33, Trigger's hide was stretched over a fiberglass mold that details his physical structure down to the last muscle and vein.

Over 100,000 people a year trek to the desert to visit him, so he has to look good.

"The mounts in the last few years are a lot easier to take care of," says Rogers. About once a year, he wipes Trigger's coat down twice with alcohol. "This removes airborne contaminants that could discolor the fur and keeps a sheen to the hair."

The mane and tail are gently shaken free of dust, which is swept up with an ordinary vacuum cleaner held about three inches away. To protect Trigger's coat from skin oils, Rogers wears gloves during the cleaning process.

As manager of the family museum, Rogers takes care of everything else, too, including 200 other mounted creatures and thousands of items of memorabilia. "I do a little bit of everything. If the toilet overflows, they call me for that also. And I wear gloves when I'm doing that, too."

can be a problem since arsenic is no longer used in the preservation process. Museums regularly freeze their taxidermy to kill any bugs or larvae. You, too, can use your freezer (if it's large enough) to get rid of infestation. If you've inspected your trophy and found evidence of infestation (such as bits of wings or shed insect larval casings), Catharine Hawks, a conservator in private practice in Falls Church, Virginia, recommends placing the taxidermy in the freezer. First, remove all the food from the freezer and put the taxidermy in a sealed plastic bag to avoid contact with any moisture, which could damage the fur or skin of the animal. Freezing is most effective at –4°F for a minimum of one week. If your freezer doesn't go that low, extend the freezing time. If your freezer only goes to 14°F, you may need up to 30 days of freezing to kill all stages of any insects. To properly measure the temperature of your freezer, put a candy thermometer in a glass of water into your freezer.

Speed tips: You can also blow dust off with a blow-dryer on a cool setting.

In a pinch: If you don't have an artist's brush, use any soft-bristle clean brush or a feather duster. Remember to clean in the direction of the nap, never against it.

Caution: Wear rubber or disposable surgical gloves when handling all taxidermy to avoid transferring skin oils onto the piece, which will act as a dust magnet. If you have a pre-1970s mounting that was preserved with arsenic, don't clean it by hand. The only safe way to clean mounts with arsenic is with a vacuum with a HEPA (high-efficiency particulate air) filter. The HEPA-filtered vacuum doesn't redistribute dust into the air. Electrolux makes HEPA-filtered vacuums, but you might find it more reasonable just to hire a professional conservator to care for your pre-1970s mounting. Call your local museum and ask them to recommend someone.

Don't brush or wipe birds with anything. You will ruin the feather patterns.

Telephones

Because we get up close and personal with the telephone every time we use it, skin oils, hair preparations, dirt, and plain old germs accumulate on it. So we really ought to try to keep them a little cleaner than we do.

Technique: A cloth soaked in ordinary rubbing alcohol will cut through dirt on plastic telephones. It will also serve as a disinfectant. Be sure to put the alcohol on the cloth, not the telephone, and wipe clean. Remove dirt between push buttons with a cotton swab dipped in alcohol, says William Ruhe, owner of Atlantic Telephone and Data Services in Whitehall, Pennsylvania.

The metal battery charger buttons on the base of cordless telephones should not be wet down with cleaner. Instead, rub clean with the tip of a pencil eraser, says Ruhe.

Speed tips: Don't neglect the coils of your telephone cord. Extra-long, walk-around-the-kitchen-while-you-talk versions can get particularly dirty from dragging on the floor. To clean, disconnect it from the base and handset, and then pull it through a folded cleaning cloth that has been generously sprayed with all-purpose cleaner.

In a pinch: If you don't have rubbing alcohol on hand, any spray-on disinfectant or all-purpose cleaner will also work.

Caution: Never spritz cleaner directly into the receiver holes or onto the button area. Plastic telephones are easily scratched by abrasive cleaners. Stick to soft cloths.

Televisions

The average American watches about three hours of television a day. And the more that it's on, the dirtier it gets since heat and static electricity generated by televisions make them natural dust magnets.

Technique: Dust accumulates on the entire television, not just the screen. Clean your television once a week with an antistatic dust cloth, says Carol Seelaus, a speed-cleaning instructor at Temple University in Philadelphia and owner of Somebody's Gotta Do It, a professional cleaning service. Polish the glass screen with a cloth or paper towel dampened with window cleaner. Be sure to reach all the nooks and crannies around knobs and buttons where dust can get stuck. And don't neglect the back of the television, where dust bunnies nest in the jumble of cables and wires that connect the VCR, video games, and cable television to the electronic command station. Wood cabinets can be polished with furniture polish.

Speed tips: If fingerprints aren't a problem, you can get a dust-free television by vacuuming. A few swipes with the dust brush at-

Cleaning for Couch Potatoes

Armed for a night of couch-bound relaxation, you have the remote in one hand and a bowl of popcorn in the other.

"Everyone I know has popcorn in their couch and grease on the remote," says Carol Seelaus, a speed-cleaning instructor at Temple University in Philadelphia and owner of Somebody's Gotta Do It, a professional cleaning service.

Remote controls fall into the same category of cleaning neglect as doorknobs and telephones—frequently touched and hardly cleaned.

Next time you're planted in front of the tube for an evening, take a bottle of rubbing alcohol, a couple paper towels, and a few cotton swabs and clean your remote.

Alcohol evaporates quickly, so it's the best cleaner to use on electronic items. There's less chance of getting them wet. Dip the swabs in the alcohol to clean the buttons and in between. Dampen the paper towel to clean the plastic casing. Never pour the alcohol directly onto the remote, or you may find yourself having to walk across the room to change channels from then on.

tachment of a canister vacuum while you're cleaning the rest of the room should do the trick.

In a pinch: If you don't have an antistatic cloth, any cloth dampened with a window cleaner like Windex will pick up dust just fine. Make sure that it's damp because a dry cloth will only scatter dust.

Caution: Never poke anything into the ventilation openings of a television for cleaning or any other reason. Never spray cleaner or polish directly onto the television. The wetness could seep into the electronic parts and ruin the set. Never clean the television while it is turned on.

Thermos Bottles

Cleanup of freshly used Thermos bottles is no problem. But the one that rolls around in your car for three weeks before making its way to the kitchen sink presents a challenge. Ask anyone who has tried to clean the dried-on goo from the bottom of a one-quart Thermos.

Technique: On all three types—glass, stainless steel, and plastic—a swish of dishwashing detergent and hot water will remove fresh food and drink residue. Rinse well, and turn the bottle upside down to dry fully before storing. Store the bottle with cup and stopper removed to discourage odors and bacteria growth.

To clean dried-on residue, fill the bottle with hot water and a few tablespoons of baking soda and allow to soak for several hours, says the Thermos Company, based in Batesville, Mississippi. If odors are a problem, soak in a solution of hot water and lemon juice or vinegar. On stainless-steel and plastic bottles a brush may be used.

Hard-water buildup and coffee stains can be removed with the coffeepot cleaner Dip-It, or by filling the bottle with water and dropping a couple of denture tablets in it (soak for up to eight hours, then rinse.)

Speed tips: For light dirt, fill stainless-steel bottles with boiling water, allow to soak for five minutes, and rinse.

In a pinch: Don't throw a broken glass Thermos away. You can replace broken glass liners. Write the manufacturer at Thermos Company, 355 Thermos Drive, Batesville, MS 38606 to order a replacement liner.

If mildew is a problem, soak the cup and stopper in a mild bleach solution or liquid dishwasher detergent.

Caution: Don't use bleach on stainless-steel bottles. It breaks the weld, and the bottle will no longer hold heat.

Glass bottles are fragile. Do not clean with a brush or any other cleaning tool. And do not remove the base of the liner.

Do not put Thermos bottles in the dishwasher. And avoid immersing the entire bottle since water could seep between the bottle and the insulating liner.

A CLEAN STORY

From the Lab to the Lunch Box

Patented in Germany in 1903, the household vacuum bottle was invented 10 years earlier—not for keeping your chicken soup hot but as a science apparatus for storage of vaccines. The winning entry in a contest to name the new household contraption was Thermos, the Greek word for heat. Though the original glass and metal design has remained handy for the past 100 years for keeping things hot or cold, two other types of vacuum bottles are also popular—stainless steel, which are sturdier and more expensive than glass, and plastic, which are only effective for keeping things cold, according to the Thermos Company in Batesville, Mississippi.

Tile—Ceramic

Ceramic tile is an extremely durable, low-maintenance surface. Used on walls, floors, and countertops, most tiles have a glazed glassy finish that protects the baked clay from stains and moisture. Unglazed tiles, such as quarry tile, may require additional care, such as more frequent cleaning and occasional sealing. But for the most part, tile is virtually carefree, requiring no waxing or floor finish. Most cleaning and maintenance headaches are related to the grout that holds it all in place (see Grout on page 135).

Technique: Sweep loose dirt with a broom or vacuum. Mop regularly with clear water or a mild soap solution. Change the water frequently—as soon as it gets cloudy—or you'll have streaks. If you use a soap solution, rinse with clear water or else your tile will have a dull sticky film. Walls and countertops should be wiped regularly with a damp cloth or sponge and all-purpose cleaner. In kitchen areas, a dose of antibacterial cleaner used regularly will disinfect countertops and prevent the spread of germs. (See Mildew on page 179 and Soap Scum on page 245 for tips on how to clean tile walls in showers.)

Stubborn dirt from spills and drips can be cleaned with a brush or nylon scrubber.

Speed tips: "Some tile floors streak no matter how carefully you rinse them," says Margaret Dasso, owner of the Clean Sweep, a professional cleaning service based in Lafayette, California, and co-author of *Dirt Busters*. A quick swish of a large bath towel will fix the problem. "Just step on the towel with both feet and boogie around a bit," says Dasso.

How Does Your Tile Rate?

You won't have to clean as often if you buy a high-rated tile, advises *Consumer's Research Magazine*. Most American tile manufacturers use a 1-to-5 rating scale for their floor tiles, with the highest rating indicating the most durable. However, you may find the 1-to-4 rating system used by European tile-makers more prevalent since most of the tile sold in the United States is imported.

Lower ratings may save a few dollars, but in the long run they add up to more hours swishing the sponge mop. The potential for scratches, chips, and breaks increases with lower numbered tiles, which are often fired at lower temperatures. This means that even small bits of gravel tracked in on shoes can scratch a low-grade finish and eventually lead to cracking.

Ventilating the bathroom is one of the easiest ways to cut on cleaning time for mildew-prone bathroom tile. Install a ventilation fan or simply open a window after showering.

In a pinch: If you crack a tile and don't have an extra to replace it, use one that you remove from an inconspicuous place, such as a closet.

Caution: Never use abrasive cleaners or scouring powders. They can scratch the finish.

Tile—Vinyl

The vinyl tile on your floor could be solid vinyl, which often has a soft resilient feel, or vinyl composition tile, called VCT, which is made of mineral fillers bound to a thin layer of vinyl. Care and cleaning of either vinyl tile is essentially the same as vinyl sheet flooring, but there are precautions to be aware of when cleaning VCT, some of which, if it was made prior to the mid-1980s, may contain asbestos.

Technique: To preserve the shine and finish, use the mildest cleaning method possible to make the floor clean again. Vacuum or sweep frequently to remove dirt before it has a chance to grind into the finish and abrade the shine. If a light damp mop with plain lukewarm water fails to remove the dirt, clean with a solution of warm water and a detergent recommended by the tile's manufacturer. Follow label directions for proper amounts. Use care not to let water stand on the tiles, as it may loosen the adhesive backing. Rinse well with cool clear water, no matter what the cleaner says about not rinsing.

Speed tips: Mopping with plain water when possible will preserve the shine and save you from having to rinse.

Caution: Unless you are sure beyond a doubt, as-

Causes and Cures for Yellowing

If your white or light-colored vinyl tile has yellowed, one of these reasons may be the cause.

- Too much sunlight. Hang window treatments to prevent further yellowing.
- Asphalt residue from driveway and road surfaces tracked in on feet reacts with vinyl and can cause permanent yellowing. Prevent it by using a doormat to wipe feet.

sume that VCT contains asbestos. If your floor is in good shape, leave it alone. Just keep it waxed and don't use an abrasive cleaner on it, which can remove the protective coating, says Ken Giles of the Consumer Products Safety Commission in Bethesda, Maryland. If the floor must be replaced, hire a professional to do the job, says Giles.

Tin

A soft crystalline metal with a silvery-white luster, tin is used as a thin, protective coating on pans and utensils and for decorative items. Tin darkens with age, which is beneficial on ovenware items since the dark color absorbs heat better, according to the Michigan State University Extension in East Lansing.

Technique: Wash tin in warm sudsy water and dry thoroughly. Do not use sharp tools or harsh abrasives, which may scrape off the thin plating and expose the rust-prone base metal. Remove rust by rubbing tin with superfine (#0000) steel wool dipped in vegetable oil.

Speed tips: Coat decorative tin items with a thin coat of paste wax containing carnauba or lacquer to help prevent rust. Waxed tin is also easier to dust.

In a pinch: Baking soda and water will remove food from tin without scratching.

Toaster Ovens

Most toaster ovens have a continuous-cleaning coating that keeps the interior looking good, but the rest of the oven parts require regular cleaning to remove crumbs, greasy fingerprints, and food splatters.

Technique: Empty the crumb tray regularly to avoid a fire hazard, and wipe up any food spills with a damp cloth. Baked-on crud can be removed with a nylon scrubber. The wire rack and the oven tray can be cleaned with a nylon scrubber and warm sudsy water, says Joanne Nosiglia, product manager for cooking at Black and Decker Household Products in Shelton, Connecticut. Clean the glass door with a nylon pad and sudsy water. Do not use spray glass cleaners. Exterior chrome and plastic should be cleaned with a damp sponge or cloth. Stubborn spots can be removed with baking soda, but avoid harsh abrasives, which will scratch the finish.

It's important to dry all parts of the oven thoroughly prior to use.

Speed tips: You'll save time in the long run if you wipe up spills, splatters, and crumbs after each use. A drip of melted cheese, which wipes away in seconds today, may form a fossilized crud that adheres to the oven with the tenacity of superglue after continued use of the appliance.

Save time and elbow grease by washing the wire rack, glass door, and drip tray in the dishwasher.

Caution: Make sure that the oven is unplugged and cool before cleaning any part. Avoid dripping water or cleaners inside the oven or poking around with utensils, which could damage the elements or heat sensor.

Toasters

Ever since the Egyptians started baking bread in 2600 B.C., people have been making toast. For more than 4,000 years, the family toaster was a skewer that held a piece of bread over an open fire. With the arrival of electricity around the beginning of the twentieth century, inventors began seeking convenient ways to enjoy a slice of toast. The first pop-up toaster for the home, the Toastmaster, introduced in 1926, solved that problem but created another—how to clean the crumb-filled contraption.

Technique: Unplug the toaster and allow it to cool. Hold the toaster over the trash can or sink and empty the crumb tray. Use a thin brush to clean out stubborn crumbs. Wipe the tray with a damp cloth or sponge, and dry it completely before closing. How often you need to empty the crumb tray depends on how often you use the toaster. If you use it every day, appliance manufacturers recommend that you clean it once a week.

Clean the outside of chrome toasters with a damp sponge and baking soda or a cloth dampened with window cleaner. Lightly rub stubborn stains with dry superfine (#0000) steel wool. Wipe plastic-sided toasters with mild liquid dishwashing detergent or baking soda and water. Do not use abrasive cleaning products, which could scratch the finish.

Speed tips: If your toaster regularly sits out on the counter, give it a quick wipe with a damp sponge or cloth while you're wiping up your countertops or cleaning fingerprints off the refrigerator.

In a pinch: Clean stubborn crumbs with a pipe cleaner if you don't have a brush handy.

Caution: Always unplug the toaster before cleaning it. To remove a piece of stuck toast from the toaster, first unplug it. Then, move the toaster carriage up and down while turning the toaster upside down and right side up until the toast gets dislodged, says Joanne Nosiglia, product manager for cooking with Black and Decker Household products in Shelton, Connecticut. Always be careful not to insert utensils into the toaster, for they will damage the fine wires, which do the toasting. Do not spray cleaners directly onto the toaster.

Toilets

It's not as bad as a root canal, but there are few household chores more thoroughly reviled than cleaning the toilet. "Most people are revolted by the idea of cleaning the toilet," says Kent Gerard, a cleaning consultant from Oakland, California. "They pinch their noses and get through it as quickly as possible."

Maybe that's why the manufacturers of toilet-cleaning products are always trying to show us a lighter side to toilet cleaning. Remember the startled housewife of the 1970s discovering a miniature speedboat floating in her toilet tank? Bobbing around in a sea of crystal blue toilet water, the Ty-D-Bol man—clad in his nautical duds—assured us that the repugnant task of cleaning the toilet could be solved by using an automatic toilet-bowl cleaner. He wasn't totally off base. In-tank toilet-bowl cleaners help sanitize the bowl, prevent stains, and can even stretch out the time between cleaning. But they're no substitute for regular scrubbing with a brush and some liquid cleanser such as Comet or Ajax with bleach.

The good news is that toilets aren't as dirty as you think. "The toilet is probably a safer place to eat a sandwich than the countertop," says Charles Gerba, Ph.D., professor of microbiology at the University of Arizona in Tucson, who has done several studies on household germs.

Technique: To thoroughly clean a toilet bowl stained by hard water, rust, or just plain neglect, you should drain the water out of the bowl. You can do this two ways. Force the water out by thrusting a plunger into the neck at the bottom of the toilet bowl, or turn off the water valve and flush the toilet. Bacteria and germs cling the sides of the bowl and set up housekeeping in the pores of the porcelain. To kill germs and open pores for a deep cleaning, pour boiling water in the toilet bowl and allow it to drain. "Like cleaning your skin, the hot water will open the pores of the toilet bowl, so you can get it clean," says Gerard. Using a small

A BETTER BRUSH

The metal wire in a traditional oval-shape brush (top) can cause black scratch marks in the toilet bowl. A better choice is a round toilet brush (bottom) with nylon bristles attached to a plastic handle.

brush and liquid cleanser containing bleach, scrub the toilet bowl and under the rim where rust and mineral stains are likely to build up. After you're done scrubbing, turn the water valve back on and flush once the tank is filled with water.

The best way to clean a toilet, according to Bill R. Griffin, president of Cleaning Consultant Services in Seattle, is with liquid cleanser, a white scrubbing pad, and a gloved hand. Further, he stresses the importance of doing it at least twice a week for best results.

Most of the germs that we come in contact with are on the toilet itself, so spray the entire fixture with disinfectant cleaner—the lid, the top and bottom of the seat, the rim of the bowl, around the hinges where billions of microbes like to accumulate, the base, the tank, and the handle. Allow the disinfectant to do its germ-killing work for a few minutes and then wipe dry with a clean cloth or paper towel. Beware of sponges, which could reinfect your sanitized toilet with their own thriving colony of germs.

Speed tips: If you're going away for the weekend, pour a cup of household bleach into the toilet, close the lid, and flush it when you come home. This is a good way to get rid of old built-up stains. "Letting it soak for a couple of days in bleach water does wonders for some stains," says Gerard.

In a pinch: Even if you don't have any toilet-bowl cleaner on hand, you can effectively get rid of germs in the bowl. When you flush, some bacteria cling to the sides and remain in the bowl. You can remove almost all of the bacteria from the toilet bowl by just scrubbing the sides with a brush and flushing, according to Dr. Gerba.

If you live in a hard-water area, your toilet will develop a raised ring at the water line from mineral deposits. If acid toilet bowl cleaner and brushing have failed to remove it, try using a pumice stone. Wet the stone in water and rub it on the ring. Make sure that the stone stays wet as you work your way around the bowl. Only use a pumice stone on white, vitreous china toilets. It will scratch the finish on colored, enameled, or plastic fixtures. Pumice is a last resort. Regular cleaning is the better approach.

Caution: Do not spray cleaners on the seat or rim at the same time you are cleaning the bowl with an acid toilet-bowl cleaner. Toilet-bowl cleaners often contain hydrochloric acid, which could cause a dangerous chemical reaction if inadvertently mixed with other cleaners. To avoid the possibility of a noxious mixture, use

Keep a Lid on Those Germs

If you want to keep your bathroom from being contaminated by a layer of airborne bacteria and viruses, close the lid when you flush.

"When you flush, the toilet spews a fine mist of whatever is in the bowl," says Kent Gerard, a cleaning consultant from Oakland, California, and advocate of lowering the lid.

Studies conducted by Charles Gerba, Ph.D., professor of microbiology at the University of Arizona in Tucson, show that when you flush, the toilet shoots out an invisible mist of tiny germ-infested water droplets that get all over everything. You can get infected with diarrhea or hepatitis A by touching the surfaces where the bacteria- and virus-laden spray lands—like your toothbrush, for example—or by inhaling the invisible mist into your respiratory tract.

Closing the lid is one way that you can prevent the mist from being propelled into the room. But Dr. Gerba advises that you keep the lid down until the toilet is used again. The germ-laden mist remains airborne in the bowl for some time after the flush, Dr. Gerba says. Opening the lid too soon will only draw aerosol up and out of the bowl—and usually directly into your face.

If you don't feel like hanging a sign in your bathroom that says, "Close the lid when you flush," automatic toilet-bowl cleaners—such as Ty-D-Bol or 2000 Flushes—are an effective way to reduce the number of bacteria that are propelled from the bowl during flushing.

Six Dirty Little Secrets about Toilets

1. The dirtiest part of the toilet is the bottom of the toilet seat. Second place goes to the base and the floor surrounding the toilet.

2. The average person uses the toilet seven times a day.

3. Older toilets need to be cleaned more frequently than new ones. "The older a toilet is, the more porous it is to stains. The older it is, the more you need to clean it," says Kent Gerard, a cleaning consultant from Oakland, California.

4. In public rest rooms, the first stall is most likely to have the fewest bacteria and the middle ones are likely to have the most because more people use them.

5. Women's rest rooms are dirtier than men's rest rooms. The floor of the stall and the hot-water tap were the most frequent sites for bacterial contamination, while the top side of the toilet seat, which nearly half of all women either wipe or cover before using, ranked as one of the least contaminated areas in public rest rooms.

6. The cleanest public toilets are found in national chain restaurants; the worst are found in gas stations.

acid toilet-bowl cleaners either before or after disinfecting the seat and rim. If used prior to cleaning the seat area, be sure that the acid cleaner is flushed and thoroughly rinsed away. In most cases, regular twice-weekly cleaning will eliminate the need to use harsh acid bowl cleaners, says Griffin.

Automatic toilet-bowl cleaners that contain bleach are great for killing germs, but they are hard on the working parts of the toilet tank—especially those made of rubber.

Toys

Most toys don't come with cleaning instructions. If they do, they're usually long gone by the time hours of play have left their mark. So you usually have to rely on common sense when figuring out how to clean kids' playthings. Rule number one: If it's not washable, don't give it to a child.

Technique: Toddler toys often have to pass the taste test and should be washed regularly to discourage the spread of germs. Most are plastic and can be washed in the sink with warm water and mild liquid dishwashing detergent. Rinse thoroughly and drip-dry on a dish rack. Harsh cleaners and vigorous scrubbing can remove painted facial features and decorative stickers.

Use a damp cloth to wipe off toys that cannot be immersed in water, such as wooden toys, battery-operated dolls, and electronic games. A cotton swab dipped in alcohol is handy for cleaning hand-held electronic toys.

The plastic skin on dolls can be cleaned by gently rubbing with a cloth dipped in cold cream. Board games can usually tolerate a quick wipe-down with a barely damp cloth. Wipe plastic toys with a mild disinfectant solution after use to help prevent the spread of germs to nonfamily guests, advises Bill R. Griffin, president of Cleaning Consultant Services in Seattle.

Speed tips: Many toys manufactured for children under the age of two years are dishwasher-safe. Since these toys often spend as much time in curious little mouths as they do the hands, it's a good idea to use the cleaning capabilities of the top rack of the dishwasher. It saves time, too.

In a pinch: Of course, there's another angle to cleaning toys: gathering them up when they're scattered all over the floor. Straighten up a toy-covered floor with a plastic rake, recommends Margaret Dasso, owner of the Clean Sweep, a professional cleaning service based in Lafayette, California, and co-author of *Dirt Busters*. "It will cut time and fatigue by two-thirds," she says.

Trash Compactors

If your municipality or collector limits the amount of trash that you can dispose of each week, a compactor can reduce your waste volume by 80 percent. Recycling can reduce waste volume by 40 to 50 percent.

Technique: Remove the compactor bucket or drawer, and wipe down the inside of the compactor with disinfectant. It's a good idea to wear rubber gloves because glass shards and sharp debris may be hidden in the recesses of the compactor. Hose down the bucket or drawer outside and scrub with disinfectant cleaner. While you have the compactor apart, change the odor filter, if necessary. Consult your owner's manual for instructions on how to clean the ram (the part that actually compacts the trash). Wipe down the outside of the appliance with all-purpose cleaner.

Speed tips: To keep the compactor clean and free of odors, avoid putting messy wet garbage such as food scraps in it. Save those for the garbage disposal or the compost heap. Also, don't put odor-prone trash such as disposable diapers in it.

In a pinch: If the compactor must be used to dispose of all your trash, place messy items such as food scraps in plastic bags before compacting.

Caution: Make sure that the compactor is in the "Off" or "Lock" position before cleaning. Consult your owner's manual for specific cleaning instructions.

Umbrellas

Both kinds of umbrellas protect you from the elements. But the two basic types—those that block the rain and those that block the sun—require slightly different care and cleaning procedures.

Rain Umbrellas

Technique: If you get mud-splashed while waiting for the bus next to a puddle, hose off your umbrella in the open position to clean it. Stubborn dirt can be removed by sponging on any water-based cleaner, such as ordinary liquid dishwashing detergent that doesn't contain bleach, which will discolor the fabric, advise experts at Totes Isotoner Corporation, a leading umbrella manufacturer based in Loveland, Ohio.

Speed tips: After use, allow your umbrella to dry in the open position to prevent rust from forming on interior hardware. To speed up drying, shake the water from the fabric by opening and closing the umbrella quickly a few times.

Caution: Do not use spot removers on umbrellas. They can remove the silicone water-repellency coating on the fabric.

Sun Umbrellas

Technique: Clean your patio umbrella once a year before storing it for the winter. The festive sun shade that looks so cheerful and fresh in the spring usually accumulates a gray film by fall, caused by dirt from rain, trees, and the air.

You can clean coarse fabric and vinyl umbrellas with a solution of mild liquid dishwashing detergent and water, according to experts at the Michigan State University Extension in East Lansing.

Sponge or brush it on, particularly in the folds of the umbrella where dirt tends to collect. Allow it to soak for several minutes and then rinse it with a hose. Dry thoroughly in an open position before storing.

Speed tips: Open sun umbrellas after it rains and allow them to dry in an open position so that dirt will not collect in the folds.

In a pinch: Use an automobile vinyl-top cleaner, such as Blue-Magic Convertible Top Cleaner, on vinyl umbrellas that will not come clean with detergent. Then apply vinyl protector for upholstery or automobiles, such as Armor All Protectant, for a finish that will resist dirt. This is easiest to do if the umbrella can be spread on a large flat surface, such as a driveway.

Caution: Always close a sun umbrella during storms and high winds to avoid damage.

Upholstery

You won't notice the dirt on upholstered furniture until it's really heavily soiled. So adopt a regardless-of-whether-it-looks-dirty approach in your vacuuming routine. If your furniture is dirty enough that it's readily visible, then vacuuming will probably not remove the dirt. You'll have to take cleaning to the next level.

Cleaning a piece of upholstered furniture is a complicated task that requires patience and skill. Because so many things can go wrong—dye bleeding, shrinkage, yellowing, browning, and water spotting—your best bet is to hire a professional.

There are a lot of unknowns when it comes to upholstery. You don't see what's behind the surface fabric. Stuffing materials may contain color that will wick to the surface if you overwet the upholstery during cleaning. Materials may turn brown or shrink after cleaning.

"The hidden sin can come to the surface," says Claudia Ramirez, former executive vice president of the Association of Specialists in Cleaning and Restoration in Millersville, Maryland. Sometimes during manufacturing, pens are used to mark cushions. "You may see a number one wick to the surface during the cleaning process," she says.

Upholstery fabrics are often blends of different fibers that react differently to cleaning. So test the fabric in an inconspicuous area before applying any type of cleaning solution. While man-made

How the Pros Clean Up Their Dirty Talk

Professional cleaners are trained to avoid certain words so that they won't alarm customers. But here are some translations so that you'll understand what's going on.

A client's furniture is never *dirty*; it's *soiled*. Testing for colorfastness is done with a *sour* solution, not with an *acid* one.

They never *scrub*, *wash*, or *bleach*; they *clean*, *restore*, or *brighten*.

A qualified professional will *preinspect* your furniture before cleaning to spot potential problems and point them out to you so that they are not held responsible. The Association of Specialists in Cleaning and Restoration in Millersville, Maryland, says that these are some of the things they look for.

- Color bleeding from previous cleanings or spills
- Color loss
- Deterioration of the foam rubber in cushions, or markings that will bleed through during cleaning
- Loose gimp—the decorative trim strip on furniture edges
- Rips, tears, or frays in fabric, particularly on the welting
- Odor
- Nicks in the wood trim
- Stains from hair oil, perspiration, or shoe polish
- Structural damage or weak joints

fibers such as olefin, nylon, and polyester stand up well to wet cleaning, natural fibers such as cotton, silk, linen, and wool are likely to shrink, spot, or bleed.

If you're determined to try your hand at cleaning a piece of upholstery yourself, there are two methods to choose from: hot-water extraction and wet shampooing.

Hot-Water Extraction

Sometimes called steam cleaning, this process extracts soils and residue from fabric with a machine that applies a solution of hot water and special detergent, not steam, to the fabric and then suctions it out. The method is effective, especially at removing residue from previous cleanings. Before you begin, test your fabric for colorfastness in an inconspicuous area by applying a small amount of water and blotting it with a white cloth. If it doesn't bleed, try the same procedure with the cleaning solution. If there is any color transfer in either test, consult a professional upholstery cleaner.

What Those Cleaning Code Labels Mean

Furniture purchased in the last few years may have a cleaning code on its label. Look under the cushions for a tag. Some manufacturers have voluntarily adopted uniform standards for furniture cleanability.

W: Use a water-based cleaner.
S: Solvent-based cleaners or dry cleaning are necessary.
W-S: Choose either of the above two methods.
X: Neither water- nor solvent-based cleaning can be used. Only cleaning by vacuuming is recommended.

One of the problems with the codes is that they are based on colorfastness, says Claudia Ramirez, former executive vice president of the Association of Specialists in Cleaning and Restoration in Millersville, Maryland. The codes don't have anything to do with shrinkage or browning, two of the most common problems with cleaning upholstery, especially natural fibers.

If the fabric passes the cleanability test, you can proceed with wet cleaning, but be careful not to overwet the fabric, advise experts at the Michigan State University Extension in East Lansing. Overwetting increases the likelihood of discoloration caused by liquid penetrating the colored stuffing materials or wood and wicking to the surface fabric. It also promotes the growth of mildew.

Once the piece is cleaned, open windows and use fans to speed drying. Upholstery should dry within 24 hours.

Wet Shampooing

Use a commercial upholstery shampoo such as Blue Luster, or make your own shampoo by mixing ½ teaspoon liquid dishwashing detergent per quart of warm water and making suds by squeezing a sponge through it, advise experts at the Michigan State University Extension. Test material for colorfastness first, then apply the suds to the fabric with a sponge or soft brush rubbing gently with the grain of the material. Work on a small area at a time, rinsing each area as you go along with a damp sponge dipped in clear water. Avoid soaking the fabric, but be sure to remove all the soap. If you leave a residue, it will attract dirt.

Speed tips: You can reduce or eliminate the need for costly and time-consuming cleaning procedures if you vacuum your upholstered furniture regularly—weekly for your favorite chair and monthly for any touch-me-not stuff in the living room. Dust doesn't show up on fabric the same way it does on wood furniture, but it's there along with a host of other critters.

SCRUB THIS APPROACH

Foam Cleaners: A Not-So-Bright Idea?

Some commercial foam upholstery cleaners contain fluorescent brightening agents that make the fabric appear cleaner initially but can yellow with age and exposure to ultraviolet light, according to the Association of Specialists in Cleaning and Restoration in Millersville, Maryland.

"Brighteners make the fabric look cleaner to your eye; the fabric looks brighter," says Claudia Ramirez, former executive vice president of the Association of Specialists in Cleaning and Restoration in Millersville, Maryland. "Perception is reality, so if it looks brighter, it's cleaner."

While foam cleaners may remove some of the dirt, they leave a residue that can cause yellowing. If that happens to you, talk to a professional upholstery cleaner.

"Vacuuming will take the surface soils out before they can damage the fibers," says Ramirez. Regular vacuuming will also take care of your upholstery from a health standpoint. "When you sit in your favorite chair, your body sheds its skin cells. The dust mites feed on them, and their feces and decomposing carcasses serve as allergens," explains Ramirez.

Use a canister vacuum with an upholstery attachment, and change the bag when it's one-half to two-thirds full. Vacuum the entire piece—both sides of the cushions, the back and sides, the arms, and the platform underneath the cushions.

In a pinch: If you don't have a canister vacuum, you can remove dust from upholstered furniture by brushing it.

Spot-clean stains as soon as possible. Scrape away excess spillage. Working toward the center of the stain, sponge with the dishwashing detergent suds solution on wet-clean fabrics or a solvent-based cleaner on dry-cleanable materials. Blot frequently, and be careful not to overwet the area or spotting could occur.

Caution: Cushions may appear to be removable because of their zippered construction. However, you should not remove the covers for cleaning. Shrinkage could occur, making it impossible to replace the cover.

Spot removers are intended for spot-cleaning only. Never try to clean an entire piece of furniture using these products, which could create a dangerous amount of fumes. Read product labels carefully for proper usage and safety precautions.

Varnished Surfaces

Unlike shellac or lacquer finishes, oil-based varnished surfaces will not develop a white ring from moisture. That's what makes it a durable finish for surfaces like dining room tables that are subject to spills and moisture, says Ian Turner, restoration expert for Garrett Wade Company, a professional woodworkers supply house in New York City.

Technique: To protect the finish, wax twice a year with a good-quality beeswax and carnauba wax blend, such as BriWax, available in home stores. Apply the wax in a circular motion with a soft cloth and allow it to sit for a few minutes. Then buff to a shine with a dry cloth. If you follow this procedure, wax buildup should not be a problem, says Turner. "People get this image of wax that it builds up on layer upon layer. But most of it is wiped off in buffing. Only a very minor layer remains to protect the varnish," Turner says.

To remove fingerprints and light soil, softly wash the surface with a barely damp cloth that has been dipped in a solution of warm water and a few drops of liquid dishwashing detergent and then wrung nearly dry. Buff the surface immediately with a dry cloth.

If the wood finish still seems lackluster after cleaning, gently wipe the surface down with a cloth that has been lightly soaked in mineral spirits. "Sometimes the grain of the wood becomes obliterated by years of dust and wax," Turner says. The mineral spirits will effectively remove dirt and wax without harming the finish.

What Kind of Finish Is It?

Many surfaces that appear to be varnished may actually contain lacquer or shellac. Here's a quick test recommended by Ian Turner, restoration expert for Garrett Wade Company, a professional woodworkers supply house in New York City, to find out if the surface that you're cleaning is really varnish. Knowing the finish can be important if you're working with a valuable or antique piece of furniture.

In an inconspicuous place, apply a dab of denatured alcohol. If the finish becomes tacky, it contains shellac. In a second inconspicuous spot, apply a drop of acetone (or nail polish remover). If the surface becomes tacky, it contains lacquer. If nothing happens on either spot, your surface is a varnished finish.

Speed tips: In between damp-cloth cleaning, which should be done only when necessary, buff the surface with a soft dry cloth to remove dust and restore the shine.

Dust regularly with a feather duster or dust wand attachment of the vacuum cleaner. Use a light touch to avoid scratching. Save a lot of time and elbow grease by using a small electric polisher when waxing varnished surfaces.

In a pinch: If you develop a white ring on a varnished surface, it may actually be caused by the wax, not the wood finish. Strip the wax using a cloth dipped in mineral spirits.

SCRUB THIS APPROACH

The Shine Is Left Behind

Wood-finish experts recommend that you avoid using the following items when cleaning varnished surfaces.

- Oil soaps, which can leave a gummy residue on the finish
- Spray furniture polishes, which often contain silicone to create a shine but will eventually cause a buildup that will streak and dull the wood

Use a superfine (#0000) steel wool to remove wax in recesses and other hard-to-reach areas. Be sure to rub with the grain of the wood.

Caution: Avoid using paper towels to clean varnished surfaces—they can scratch the finish.

Vases and Bottles

Dirt that you can't easily reach, like the residue that dries on the sides of vases and bottles, may seem impossible to clean. Before you toss it on the recycling heap, try some of these easy remedies.

Technique: Even if you can't get your hand (or even a finger) down the neck of a vase or bottle, you can scrub it using dried beans, uncooked rice, or sand. Fill the bottle halfway with hot soapy water, add a handful of your chosen scrubbing material, and shake vigorously. This action will remove the dirt. If the container is extra dirty, before you scrub it, let it soak overnight in ammonia water or in a solution of automatic dishwasher detergent and water. Use 1 tablespoon detergent for each cup of water.

HOW I DO IT

Vase Advice

Louise Wrinkle often brightens her Alabama home with flowers from her own splendid garden, which has been featured more than once in glossy decorating magazines. A veteran horticulture judge for the Garden Club of America in New York City, she offers these tips for keeping cut flowers—and gardening hands—clean and fresh.

"When you fill a dirty bowl with water, it grows algae, which stops up the stems and causes flowers to dry up sooner," says Wrinkle. "To keep bowls and vases really clean, use a denture cleaner, like Polident. Dissolve one or two tablets in a vase half-filled with water. Scrub the inside of the vase with the solution and it will be squeaky-clean.

"I also put three or four drops of liquid household bleach into the water to deter bacteria from growing. I fill an old eyedropper bottle with bleach and keep it on the shelf next to my vases. That way, I don't have to reach under the sink for the big heavy bottle.

"When you're finished cutting flowers, if you have green and brown grunge on your hands, wash them with the denture-cleaner solution. It cleans them and leaves them feeling smooth."

To remove stains, let a mixture of 1 cup strong, cold black tea and 3 tablespoons vinegar stand in the vase overnight.

If a vase or bottle is cloudy, it probably has a mineral film buildup on the sides, according to Robert Montgomery, who has unearthed and cleaned more than 250 antique bottles buried in southeastern Pennsylvania. Remove mineral buildup by filling the container with water, adding 1 to 2 tablespoons automatic dishwasher detergent, and soaking it overnight. Or fill it with water and a couple teaspoons of ammonia, or drop in a denture tablet and shake. If these remedies don't work, try using a commercial mineral and lime remover that contains phosphoric acid, such as CLR.

Speed tips: If you don't have a day to soak an encrusted container, bottle brushes are the most effective way to get right to the dirt. They are available in dozens of shapes and sizes and are generally sold in hardware stores. "The brushes are flexible and bendable. Get a range of sizes from small to large, bend them to the shape you need for a particular bottle, and then clean," says Montgomery.

In a pinch: Sometimes old bottles develop a milky-white haze that just won't come off. If you want to hide the stain, try an old trick used by bottle collectors. Clean the bottle as well as you can and dry thoroughly. Put several drops of vegetable oil in the bottle and roll it around to mask the cloudiness caused by magnesium and calcium.

VCRs

Because a VCR can play as good as new for 2,500 hours, or four films a week for seven years, one approach to cleaning it is this: Don't bother. If you buy a $200 VCR, the cost works out to about eight cents a day. On the other hand, regular cleaning will extend the life of your VCR, preserve your tapes, and keep your picture sharp. In an age where techno-obsolescence of electronics products is calculated in months instead of years, seven years of trouble-free service may seem like a fair trade-off for cleaning neglect. But for those of you looking for some extra mileage for your investment, here are a few cleaning strategies.

Technique: A VCR has more moving mechanical parts than any other consumer electronics product, according the Consumer Electronics Manufacturers Association in Arlington, Virginia. Most of the dirt and dust particles that build up are magnetic, so they are naturally attracted to your tape heads. If you don't clean them, eventually the dirt will begin to affect your video quality, translating into images full of white streaks, black lines, and snow. "In fact, most video problems with a VCR can be solved simply by cleaning the heads," says Lisa Fasold, spokeswoman for the Consumer Electronics Manufacturers Association.

They should be cleaned after every 20 hours of use with a good head cleaner—more frequently if you rent a lot of tapes. There are three types of head-cleaning tape cartridges on the market: dry, wet, and magnetic-based. All you do is place the cartridge in the VCR, push "Play," and let the head cleaner do its work.

Magnetic cleaning is the safest method. As you play the tape, on-screen video and audio signals tell you when the heads are clean. With wet cleaning cartridges, the ribbon is moistened with a cleaner and then placed in the VCR. As it plays, it swabs away dirt. Just be careful not to use too much cleaning solution. Dry systems, which use abrasion to clean and can wear down the heads, are not recommended.

Although the wet and magnetic cleaners do a good job at cleaning your tape heads, they don't remove dirt that builds up

MONEY-SAVERS

Tape Tactics

The Consumer Electronics Manufacturers Association in Arlington, Virginia, offers the following advice on tape maintenance.

1. Tape used over and over for timed recording and viewing will begin to shed its oxide coating and gum the heads. Discard them after about 200 recording/playback cycles.

2. Keep tapes in their jackets to prevent dust and dirt from accumulating. A dirty tape can transfer particles to the record and playback heads causing poor image quality and possible head damage.

3. Keep tapes away from strong magnetic fields, such as televisions, speakers, and electric motors.

4. Use your tapes at least once a year to prevent the magnetic particles and binder from sticking together. If you don't have time to watch the tape, simply fast-forward it and then rewind it. For longer tape life, store the tape in an upright position like a book with the fully wound spool of tape on the bottom to ease pressure on the hubs.

along the tape path. If streaks and snow persist, your VCR may need to be cleaned by a professional.

Don't neglect the outside of your VCR. Dust frequently and wipe with a damp cloth, if necessary.

Speed tips: You'll need to clean your VCR less frequently if you use good-quality tape. Low-quality tape can damage your VCR by shedding particles that clog heads and the tape path. Although letter designations indicate the grade level of tape within a brand, there are no standard designations, so relative quality of high-grade videotape varies from manufacturer to manufacturer. In other words, a bargain store's high-grade tape may not be as good as standard-grade tape from a high-quality supplier. The Consumer Electronics Manufacturers Association recommends buying your tapes from a high-quality, well-known supplier.

In a pinch: If you can no longer tell whether Dorothy is in Kansas or Oz and you don't have a head-cleaner system, cotton swabs and rubbing alcohol should clear up your image. Longer cotton swabs on wooden sticks—if you have them—will work better to reach inside the machine. Dip the swab in alcohol and rub on the audio and video heads to dissolve dirt and particle buildup.

Caution: Do not pour alcohol or cleaning solution directly onto or into the machine.

Veneer

To produce a wood product less expensively sometimes a thin layer of fine wood, called veneer, is glued to a base of lesser grade. Cut with giant blades, veneer manufactured today can be as thin as $\frac{1}{60}$ inch, while antique veneer cut by hand will vary in thickness. Whether it's thick or thin, you should clean veneer according to the finish that is on the wood, such as shellac, varnish, lacquer, or polyurethane.

Technique: Wax once or twice a year with beeswax, suggests Ian Turner, restoration expert for Garrett Wade Company, a professional woodworkers supply house in New York City. Clean fingerprints and dust with a damp cloth and buff dry with a cloth. Veneer is more susceptible to changes in heat and humidity than other types of furniture. The expansion and contraction caused by temperature and moisture variations can eventually cause veneer to bubble or pop. Position veneer away from heat sources and air conditioners. Do not store in damp areas such as basements.

In a pinch: Small pieces of loose veneer or small blisters in veneer can be reglued. Experts from the Michigan State University Extension in East Lansing offer the following advice: Lay veneer on a flat surface and scrape off the old glue. Do not get the veneer wet. Then scrape the old glue from the base wood or furniture. Put glue on both pieces, put the veneer in place, press the pieces together, and cover with a paper pad. Lay weights on it, making sure that there is pressure on all sections of the newly glued veneer. Use a thin knife blade or hypodermic needle to force wood glue into areas where the veneer is loose but still attached. Then weight the glued area down until dry.

Vents

Airborne dust and dirt that circulates through your home's heating and cooling system will eventually collect on the blades that channel air through the vent.

Technique: Vacuum loose dust with the handheld brush attachment. Wipe with a damp cloth following the pattern of the ridged air channels. Extremely dirty vents, such as those soiled by soot from a malfunctioning furnace, should be vacuumed and removed and then scrubbed with a nylon brush and dishwashing detergent solution. Be sure to dry it thoroughly. Most are made of painted metal and may rust if subjected to prolonged moisture.

Speed tips: Skip the scrubbing by vacuuming air vents regularly when sucking up dirt on floors or along baseboards.

In a pinch: If you don't use a vacuum with handheld attachments, a dusting wand works well to snare dust trapped between the ridges of a vent.

Vinyl

Vinyl made its debut in the plastics market in 1928 when it was commonly used for tablecloths, garment bags, and shower curtains. It's virtually maintenance-free, so in today's plasticized world it is found everywhere—from floors to upholstery. About 20 percent of new homes are now covered in vinyl siding. While it's known for its easy-care properties, vinyl can become hard and brittle over time if you don't take care of it.

Technique: According to experts at the Michigan State University Extension in East Lansing, for light soiling, wash vinyl with a mild cleaner, such as liquid dishwashing detergent, and water. Use a soft-bristle brush to loosen dirt from crevices and textured surfaces. Rinse with clear water and buff dry. The vinyl cleaners, such as Armor All Protectant (sold in auto supply stores), are useful for removing stubborn soil, and the conditioners in these products help to rejuvenate the plasticizers that keep the vinyl soft.

Speed tips: Unlike the leather that it simulates, vinyl does not like oil. Even a buildup of skin oils will eventually cause vinyl to harden. Instead of scrubbing down an entire piece of furniture, spot-clean headrest and armrest areas, where oil tends to collect.

In a pinch: To restore luster to dulled surfaces, the manufacturers of Naugahyde products recommend spraying the surface with a light coat of furniture wax. Allow it to soak for 30 seconds, and follow with a light buffing.

Caution: Some household cleaners and solvents remove plasticizers from vinyl, which will cause it to get harden and crack. Avoid the use of acetone, lacquer thinner, and dry-cleaning fluid to remove spots and stains.

Vomit

Act quickly. Like chlorine bleach, the stomach acids in vomit can permanently change the color of fabric. Scrape and blot up as much of the mess as you can, and then dilute the acids with water, advises Carol Seelaus, a speed-cleaning instructor at Temple University in Philadelphia and owner of Somebody's Gotta Do It, a professional cleaning service. On clothing or washable fabric, flush the spot with cool or tepid water. On carpet and upholstery, sponge with water and blot to remove.

Scientists believe that vomiting is one of our most important adaptive traits. It keeps us from getting sick or even dying from something we've eaten, all of which is small comfort to the poor souls who must clean up a chunky foul-smelling stew of stomach acids, enzymes, and partially digested food.

Technique: After you have scraped the spot and flushed it with water, soak washable items for 30 minutes to an hour in a solution of 1 quart warm water mixed with 1 teaspoon laundry detergent and 2 tablespoons ammonia. Rinse in cool water. If the stain remains, soak the item in an enzyme presoak, such as Biz, to digest the stain and then launder in warm water. If the stain is colored, it may be caused by dye in something you ate or drank. If the fabric appears to have lightened, the stomach acids in the vomit have caused a permanent color change.

On carpet and upholstery, flush with a solution of water and a bacteria/enzyme digester, such as Odormute, available in some pet supply stores, before applying any other cleaning solution. The natural enzyme formula chemically changes the source of the odor to eliminate it, not just mask it. And as anyone who has had the unpleasant experience of cleaning up tossed cookies knows, vomit has a lingering stench. Detergents or cleaning solutions that are applied before the enzyme digestant could set the odor permanently, advise the makers of Odormute.

Speed tips: Remember the kid who threw up in grade school? While everyone ogled the mess, the janitor came into the room and shook a pungent smelling sawdust material on the vomit to absorb the liquid so that it could be quickly swept up.

If vomit occurs on a hard surface, such as a floor, a brown powder substance called Z Goop, available in janitorial supply

A CLEAN STORY

What Happens When Your Lunch Is Lost in Space?

During the first few days of space travel, 40 to 50 percent of astronauts experience space motion sickness (SMS). Like motion sickness or seasickness on Earth, SMS can cause nausea and vomiting. Unlike Earth-bound motion sickness, with SMS vomiting can come on suddenly and without symptoms.

In the microgravity environment of space, the problem with vomiting is not how to mop it up but how to contain it so that it does not become a floating mess in the tight confines of the space shuttle. Astronauts are armed with airsick bags. But in the event that this method fails, the shuttle is equipped with a vacuum cleaner to snare space messes.

stores, will absorb the mess so that it can be easily scooped up and thrown into a trash can. Cat litter will also do the trick.

In a pinch: Borax, a naturally occurring mineral used as a laundry booster, can effectively neutralize some odors on carpets and upholstery. After sponging and blotting the area with water, sprinkle with dry borax to cover the entire spot. Allow it to dry, and vacuum. Test for colorfastness in an inconspicuous area by applying a paste made of borax and water.

Caution: Do not use ammonia to clean vomit from silk or wool.

Waffle Irons

Maybe the thought of scrubbing batter from a zillion nooks and crannies is keeping you from making a delicious waffle breakfast. Well, get out the syrup. All your waffle iron needs is a little seasoning. Properly seasoned grids will develop a nonstick surface that brushes clean in a few seconds.

Technique: After baking waffles, remove crumbs by brushing grids with a soft plastic brush while it's still warm. Do not wash grids or put any water on them, or they will have to be re-seasoned. Allow the iron to cool and wipe any spills or splatters on the outside while they're still fresh, using a damp sponge or all-purpose cleaner.

Speed tips: Proper seasoning of the grid surface is essential for quick cleanups. All waffle irons should be seasoned prior to first use and periodically after that if waffles begin to stick.

Brush unsalted fat or cooking oil on grids and heat until they begin to smoke. Bake a waffle, following the manufacturer's directions concerning time and temperature, to absorb excess fat. (Generally, the waffle is done when the iron stops steaming.) Discard the waffle. You now have a perfectly seasoned waffle iron.

Grids should be re-seasoned if they are washed with soapy water.

In a pinch: If you don't have a soft brush, wipe warm grids with a paper towel or dish towel to remove crumbs.

Caution: Unplug the waffle iron prior to cleaning to avoid burns or electrical shock.

Wallpaper and Wall Coverings

Although it tends to conceal dirt better than plain painted walls, wallpaper can last 10 years or more, so you'll have to clean it sooner or later. More than 75 percent of the wallpaper sold today is vinyl-coated, which means that it's washable and often scrubbable. Despite its easy cleanability, if you leave dirt on vinyl wall coverings too long the vinyl tends to absorb it.

Technique: Vacuum periodically with a brush attachment to remove loose dust and dirt, especially on textured and fabric covered walls that cannot not be easily washed. Use an upward motion to snare cobwebs; brushing down may cause streaks.

Washable coverings can be cleaned with a sponge dampened in a mild all-purpose cleaner or in ½ cup ammonia mixed in 1 gallon water. Scrubbable papers can be cleaned with the same solution applied with a soft-bristle brush. Be careful not to overwet the seams, or you may find yourself pasting them back down.

Nonwashable papers, such as uncoated papers and flocked and fabric coverings, can be cleaned with a commercial dough-like product called Absorene that is rubbed over the surface. Test behind a piece of furniture to make sure that it does not streak. After cleaning, brush or vacuum stray bits of cleaner from the wall.

Speed tips: Wash the wall in half the time by using a sponge mop reserved for walls only.

Stain Remedies on Wallpaper

Here's how to remove common stains and marks from wallpaper, according to cleaning experts.

Grease
• Blot spot with paper towels and sprinkle cornstarch on the stain. When the grease is absorbed by the cornstarch, remove gently and vacuum.
• Rub with a slice of white bread.

Crayon
• Apply WD-40 to the stain and wipe with a soft cloth. If there's still crayon remaining, add some liquid dishwashing detergent to water. Using a sponge, work in a circular motion to clean the area, and rinse. This is for scrubbable wallpaper. If yours isn't, test it on a small area before starting.

Felt-Tip Marker
• Spray with nonoily hair spray and wipe off.
• Apply rubbing alcohol and blot up.

In a pinch: If you don't have a vacuum, use a clean cloth tied around a broom or mop to remove dust from the walls. Change the cloth when it becomes soiled to prevent streaks.

Walls

Wall-washing rule number one is to start at the bottom and work your way up. "If you start at the top, the dirty water will drip down over the soiled walls and create streaks that are hard to remove," says Kent Gerard, a cleaning consultant from Oakland, California. Essentially, the clean streaks created by dirty water dripped on dirty walls are harder to clean than dirty water dripped on clean walls. "In general, you want to be careful. You want to enforce drip control," says Gerard. To do this, work in small overlapping sections.

Technique: Before washing, dust or vacuum walls to remove loose soil. Most painted surfaces can be cleaned with a mild solution of warm water and liquid dishwashing detergent and then rinsed with clear water.

You'll need two buckets—one for the cleaning solution and

one for the rinse water—two large cellulose sponges, and it's a good idea to have two rubber gloves to protect your hands, says the Michigan State University Extension in East Lansing.

Working in overlapping sections manageable for your arm length, apply the cleaning solution to the walls by rubbing gently with a sponge. Semigloss and gloss paints are less likely to be damaged by cleaning than flat latex paint. Rinse with a separate sponge reserved specifically

Before You Open That Paint Can...

Preparing your walls for a new coat of paint? Paint professionals use trisodium phosphate, a powdered cleaner sold in hardware stores, to clean and degloss walls. The alkaline cleaner doesn't disinfect; it smooths and levels the surface of the wall. If you decide to use it to clean your walls for better paint adhesion, be sure to wear protective eyewear, rubber gloves, and a long-sleeve shirt, and rinse the walls thoroughly afterward.

for the rinse water. After you're done with one section, proceed to the next area, making sure that the cleaning edges overlap. When you've done several areas, dry off the excess moisture with a soft absorbent cloth.

If the walls are very dirty, you can use a stronger alkali solution to dissolve the dirt. Add 2 tablespoons ammonia, 1 tablespoon trisodium phosphate (available in hardware stores), or 2 tablespoons powder laundry detergent to 1 gallon warm water, says the Michigan State University Extension. Stronger solutions may remove paint, particularly flat finishes. For greasy walls, dissolve ½ cup washing soda in 2 gallons hot water for your cleaning solution.

Speed tips: In seldom-used rooms or in bedrooms, you can get away with simply dusting and spot-cleaning the walls. Use an all-purpose spray cleaner, such as Fantastik, and wipe dirty areas like light switches and doorways. Test the spray cleaner in a small area before spraying the entire area. If it makes the wall feel tacky, don't use that cleaner.

You can work in larger overlapping sections by using a sponge mop on walls and ceilings. But make sure that it's not the same one that you use on the floor, or your walls could actually end up dirtier than when you started.

In a pinch: In between cleanings, rub smudges away with an art gum eraser (the brown crumbly kind from art stores).

If you have rough plaster walls that shred sponges, clean them with bunched up nylon panty hose.

To remove tape from walls, apply a warm iron over a protective cloth. Press the iron lightly to loosen the tape, and then peel it off slowly.

Caution: Test cleaner in an inconspicuous corner first to make sure that the paint color and finish are not damaged by cleaning.

When using trisodium phosphate, wear protective eyewear, rubber gloves, and a long-sleeve shirt. Always read the label for proper usage and safety precautions.

Watches

When you wear a watch day in and day out, lotion, perfume, skin oil, and perspiration eventually accumulate on your timepiece and watchband. If neglected, the buildup can cloud the crystal and corrode the case plating. In general, the more skin preparations you use, the more often you need to clean your watch.

Technique: Wipe the crystal and watch case with a barely damp cloth. "You have to be very careful. You don't want to get any solution moisture in the movement of the watch," says Gordon Engle, proprietor of Engle's Jewelers in Pottstown, Pennsylvania.

To thoroughly clean the band, remove it by releasing the spring action pins on each side of the case. Fine metal bands can be soaked overnight in a detergent-and-water solution—a couple of

Getting a Watertight Seal Is Worth Your Time

If you're a scuba diver, ask your jeweler to send your water-resistant timepiece to the manufacturer for battery changes, says Gordon Engle, proprietor of Engle's Jewelers in Pottstown, Pennsylvania. When the batteries are changed on a water-resistant watch, the original factory seal is broken. After resealing, the tiny gasket in the watch will not be as effective as before at keeping water out. And if water gets in, the watch will stop keeping time.

"When you're depending on that watch to tell you how much air you have in your tank, it's critical," says Engle, who has been repairing jewelry for more than 40 years. Sending the watch back to the manufacturer ensures a factory-quality seal that will stand up to the rigors of scuba diving. It will, however, take more time and cost more than having your jeweler do the job.

drops of Ivory Liquid in a regular-size coffee cup—or washed with a cloth dampened in ammonia. Leather bands can be spruced up by cleaning them with saddle soap, but they also must be replaced periodically. "After being exposed to day-to-day perspiration and dirt, they get to the point of no return," says Engle.

Save any cleaning or maintenance of the interior movement of the watch for the jeweler. Today's quartz watches have very few moving parts and don't require much maintenance beyond a periodic battery change. Windup watches, however, should be serviced and cleaned by a jeweler when their timing becomes sluggish.

Speed tips: For gleaming results with little effort, place a metal watchband in a nylon bag and run it through the washer. "Toss it in with a load of towels and it comes out really nice," says Engle. The ultrasonic cleaning devices used by jewelers have a vibrating action similar to the agitation in a washing machine.

In a pinch: If you don't feel dexterous enough to remove your watchband to clean it, you can prevent dirty buildup by getting in the habit of wiping your watch off with a dry cloth a few times a week. Good times to do it include when you take it off at night or before you shower.

Caution: Moisture will damage the movement of the watch, so use little or no wetness when cleaning. Even water-resistant watches are susceptible; the gasket that provides a barrier to moisture breaks down over time.

Water Beds

On a conventional bed, the oil and skin cells you shed burrow into the fibers of the mattress. But on a water bed, they build up on the surface of the vinyl mattress instead.

Technique: About once a month, sponge the top and the sides of the mattress off. Use a mild soap solution (any hand soap or liquid dishwashing detergent may be used, mixed with warm water). Use one bucket for the cleaning solution and one for the rinse water. Then rinse the mattress so that there isn't a soap residue left on it. Vinyl cleaners and conditioners really aren't necessary, says James Hauser, general manager of Specialized Plastic Sealing, a water bed mattress manufacturer in Carlsbad, New Mexico. The conditioners are applied to the surface to refresh the plasticizer.

A CLEAN STORY

Bacteria Can Make Waves in the Bedroom

Bacteria don't harm the vinyl of your water bed mattress, but they can cause an odor similar to the stench of rotten eggs.

"It will chase you right out of your bedroom," says James Hauser, general manager of Specialized Plastic Sealing, a water bed mattress manufacturer in Carlsbad, New Mexico. "It kept me out of my bedroom one time for a month."

When the rotten odor started, Hauser suspected that it was a dead mouse. When he finally determined that the smell was coming from the water bed, he drained it and tried twice to deodorize the mattress by refilling it and adding $\frac{1}{2}$ gallon chlorine to the water. He ended up draining it a third time and airing the mattress out for six months to dissipate the odor.

You can avoid this scenario if you make sure to use a conditioner when you fill the bed, especially if you have well water. Conditioners come in liquid, powder, and tablet form and cost from $4 to $30. Hauser recommends using the powder. It's easy to handle and comes in a bottle that you pour directly into the valve.

"The problem is that vinyl deteriorates from the inside out, not the outside in. The volatile chemicals escape, and eventually, it will harden. It takes 735 years for vinyl to turn back into its natural state," says Hauser. "Vinyl conditioners won't extend the life of your mattress except maybe by a few days."

Take care of the water inside your mattress by adding a conditioner approved by the Environmental Protection Agency that kills odor-causing bacteria (available at water bed stores) before you fill the bed. Adding it before the bed is filled will distribute the conditioner throughout the mattress.

Speed tips: Use a mattress pad to extend the life of your water bed and to keep it cleaner.

Water Stains

Exposure to plain old H_2O can damage or stain furniture, walls, carpets, upholstery, and certain fabrics. As with other stains, prompt action can minimize or prevent the damage caused by water.

Wood Furniture

Water rings or white marks on furniture are caused when moisture gets trapped under the finish, giving it a milky appearance. Even the condensation from a hot pizza box can cause discoloration. Water rings usually indicate that the finish contains lacquer; varnished finishes will not ring, says Ian Turner, restoration expert for Garrett Wade Company, a professional woodworkers supply house in New York City.

Technique: Some marks will fade by themselves, so allow the stain to sit for a couple of days to give the absorbed moisture a chance to evaporate. If it doesn't go away on its own, a white mark can usually be rubbed out by using a mild abrasive mixed with a lubricant. Rubbing with the grain of the wood, try one of these combinations.

- Paste wax or mineral spirits and superfine (#0000) steel wool
- A small piece of cheesecloth dipped in hot water containing a few drops of household ammonia; wring the cloth out thoroughly, and lightly rub the spot

Apply a protective coat of wax to the furniture after the mark has been removed.

In a pinch: Make your own rubbing compound from some of these household ingredients. Rub with a mixture of nongel toothpaste and water, then buff. Or rub in a little mayonnaise or salad oil mixed with cooled cigarette or cigar ashes. Let it sit for a while, and then wipe it off.

Caution: Don't be tempted to use stronger abrasives when dealing with water rings. They may scratch or even remove the finish.

Carpets and Upholstery

When carpet or upholstery fibers get overly wet and then dry slowly, dyelike material will dissolve from the backing or stuffing and wick to the surface. Spills, tracked-in rain or snow, floods, and even overwetting by do-it-yourself carpet and upholstery cleaners can cause brown discoloration, which usually goes unnoticed until a subsequent cleaning, says the Association of Specialists in Cleaning and Restoration in Millersville, Maryland.

Technique: You're going to need a carpet or upholstery professional for this. On synthetic fibers the brown discoloration can usually be removed by professional treatment. On some natural fibers, such as wool and cotton, the staining may be permanent. For the name and location of a certified technician, contact the Association of Specialists in Cleaning and Restoration, 8229 Cloverleaf Drive, Suite 460, Millersville, MD 21108.

Speed tips: If your carpet or upholstery becomes overwet, take measures to minimize water damage. "The harmful effect of water is sharply reduced by prompt action," says Martin L. King, a restoration consultant in Arlington, Virginia, and technical advisor to the National Institute of Disaster Restoration in Millersville, Maryland.

Immediately blot as much of the water as possible from the affected area with white paper towels to prevent soaking the backing or stuffing material. To prevent discoloration from wicking to the surface fibers, dry the area quickly. Remove upholstery cushions and prop them up. During the summer, turn on air-conditioning for maximum drying. To speed drying in the winter, alternate heat and open windows.

Ceilings and Walls

Water that leaks through walls or ceilings will leave a brown ringlike discoloration after it dries.

Technique: If a pipe has burst and the ceiling is sagging, punch a small hole in it and place a pan underneath to collect the water.

After the water has dried, try to bleach the stain out by spraying it with a solution of one part chlorine bleach to five parts water, or straight hydrogen peroxide.

If bleaching doesn't work, repaint the area. First apply a coat of sealer such as B-I-N Primer/Sealant, available at any paint store. Follow with a coat of paint to match the surrounding area. If you don't seal it first, the stain will bleed right through the fresh paint.

Speed tips: Dab spots on white ceilings with a little white shoe polish.

Fabric

Water stains occur on fabrics that contain sizing or finishing agents, which give a stiffer feel or a sheen. There are a variety of finishes; some may even have a waxy or plastic feel to them. The water-soluble, starch-based finishes—applied to new fabrics to give them added body—are the most prone to water spotting. When exposed to a drop of water, the sizing is displaced and forms a ring or wavy line where it is deposited. Water spotting often happens with taffeta, moiré, silk, and rayon.

Technique: Launder washables or rewet the entire garment and dry as you normally would. Dry-cleanable fabric can be rewet by passing it through steam from a teakettle spout. Press while the fabric is still damp. If the spot remains, have the garment dry-cleaned professionally.

Wax—Dripped

There are two methods of removing dripped wax—scraping it away or using heat to melt it so that it can be absorbed. Scraping is the best technique for removing wax from hard surfaces such as floors or wood furniture, while melting is the best method to remove it from textiles, such as table linens and upholstery. Colored candles complicate the wax-removal process because they create the potential for permanent dye stain, "Often the dyes used in candles can penetrate the fibers and create a stain," says Elizabeth Barbatelli, president of the Laundry at Linens Limited, a Milwaukee-based mail-order laundry.

Technique: Scrape away as much wax as you can with a firm plastic kitchen spatula. This procedure should remove all but a few traces of wax. To remove the last bits on wood, rub with a cloth dampened with mineral spirits.

Peeling, scraping, or pulling hardened wax can damage fabrics, says Barbatelli. Instead, for white wax, place several layers of clean white paper towels over the wax (and under it if you are working with a tablecloth) and press the towels with an iron at its lowest setting. Change the towels as the wax is absorbed, and keep ironing until all the wax is gone. Sponge wax residue and dye with a small amount of spot remover and blot dry. On carpet and upholstery, blot with a spot remover such as Goof-off, available at grocery stores. On washable items, launder as soon as possible using a laundry detergent, and add a bleach that is safe for the fabric in the hottest water allowed by the manufacturer, says the Michigan State University Extension in East Lansing.

The iron technique above won't work for colored wax. You may have to use bleach. Test the fabric in an inconspicuous area and bleach the entire item in a bleach that is safe for that material.

In a pinch: Plain kraft paper, like that used for paper bags, can be substituted for paper towels.

Before laundering, sponge dye stains with rubbing alcohol to help remove them.

Caution: Candle wax colored with red dye is the most difficult to remove and may require professional treatment. Always read product label for proper use and safety precautions.

Wax Buildup—Floors

Wax buildup is usually most evident in corners where the wax or polish isn't worn away by traffic. A vinyl or tile floor may begin to look yellow, while a wood floor that has been waxed too much may appear scuffed or white. Remove old wax and polish no more than once a year, or after six to eight coats have been applied.

Technique: Unless you're using a floor buffing machine, stripping wax typically takes a lot of time and elbow grease. There are commercial products for removing wax buildup, but a typical formula for removing wax finish from nonwood floors is ¼ cup nonchlorine floor cleaner and 1 cup ammonia mixed with ½ gallon hot water. Sweep or vacuum the floor to remove loose dirt. Apply stripping solution to a small workable section of the floor with a sponge mop and let it sit for 5 to 10 minutes.

The floor will begin to turn cloudy if the wax is softening. Scrub the softened area with a stiff brush, an electric scrubber, or very fine (#000) steel wool pads to lift the wax. You can squeegee the loosened slop into a dustpan and dispose of it. This is quicker than trying to mop it up. It is best to use a wet vacuum, suggests Bill R. Griffin, president of Cleaning Consultant Services in Seattle. Then thoroughly rinse the stripped section with clean water. Let air-dry and then move on to the next section. When done, refinish the entire floor with two or three thin coats of finish instead of one thick coat, says Griffin.

If you still see dark areas after rinsing the floor, or if you can still scrape up wax with the edge of a coin, you probably need to repeat the stripping process.

Wood that hasn't been covered in a surface finish, such as polyurethane, should be waxed with a solvent-based wax, such as paste wax. Never use water or commercial wax removers to strip wax from a wood floor, according to the National Wood Flooring Association in Manchester, Missouri. Instead, use a solvent-type material such as mineral spirits or paint thinner and fine (#00) steel wool. Be sure to rub with the grain of the wood when removing the wax.

Speed tips: Once you have about two coats of wax on the entire floor, wax only in high-traffic areas where it needs it. This way you'll prevent wax buildup from occurring.

On wood floors, try buffing with a floor polisher instead of waxing to restore the luster. Only wax when buffing the floor no longer makes it shine. Use a wet-dry vacuum to suck up the waxy goop as you scrape it off the floor.

In a pinch: If you don't have a squeegee, scoop up softened wax with a Teflon spatula from the kitchen.

Caution! Wear rubber gloves and work in a well-ventilated area when stripping wax because the fumes are strong.

Do not use self-polishing waxes on unsealed wood floors, says the National Wood Flooring Association. Most of these products contain water (which should not be used on wood) and plastic. The shiny coat of plastic will discolor the wood and require harsh chemicals to remove.

Whirlpools

Some people avoid using their whirlpools because they don't want to contend with the chore of cleaning an oversized bathtub with a dozen little jets along the sides. With price tags ranging up to $2,000 or more, whirlpools may just be one of the most expensive ways to get clean. But if you have one, you may as well enjoy it.

Technique: Clean acrylic, fiberglass, and cast-iron whirlpools with nonabrasive household cleaner, such as Comet Liquid Gel Cleaner with Bleach. Wipe down the sides of the whirlpool with a sponge and cleaner. Rinse with clear water and dry with a soft cloth.

Flush the whirlpool system at least twice a month to keep jets clean and functioning properly. You should adjust jets so that there is no air induction (that is, they're not drawing in air—check your manual). Then fill the bath with hot water to about three inches above the highest jets, and add 2 teaspoons of a low-foaming automatic dishwasher detergent such as Calgonite or Cascade and 4 ounces of liquid household bleach such as Clorox. Run the whirlpool for 10 to 15 minutes, and then drain the bath. To rinse it, fill the bath with cold water to three inches above the highest jet, and run the whirlpool for another 5 to 10 minutes. Drain the bath and wipe dry with a soft cloth.

Speed tips: Wipe the whirlpool after each use to prevent the buildup of soap scum. Better yet, enjoy a soap-free soak, and all you will need is a quick wipe of a towel to clean your whirlpool.

In a pinch: If the surface becomes dull, use an automotive-type rubbing compound followed by an application of paste wax.

Caution: Do not use abrasive cleaners on fiberglass or acrylic whirlpools. They will scratch and dull the surface. Always read product label for proper use and safety precautions.

Wicker

Wicker is a catchall term for furniture woven out of a variety of plant fibers. Most wicker is made from rattan, but canes, reeds, sea grasses, willow branches, fiber rush (twisted paper), and synthetic materials are also used.

"Everybody has a different opinion on how to clean wicker," says Joyce Brown-Tickle, owner of Wicker Works in Wilmington, North Carolina. Some advocate blasting the dirt off with a garden hose, while others say don't even get it wet. Both are right, Brown-Tickle says. It just depends on what type of wicker needs to be cleaned—synthetic or natural fibers. Synthetic, which is excellent for outdoor use, can be hosed down without being harmed. Natural fibers, however, are more likely to crack, swell, rot, or discolor from prolonged exposure to water and direct sunlight.

If you don't know whether a wicker piece is synthetic or natural fibers, look for an indication of where it was made, says Brown-Tickle. If the label says "Made in the U.S.A.," it is most likely manufactured from synthetic materials since nearly all the natural wicker is imported from China and the Philippines.

Technique: When cleaning wicker, use the smallest amount of water possible to get the item clean. Interior wicker made from natural or synthetic materials should be vacuumed first to remove loose dust and dirt. If further cleaning is necessary, mix up a sudsy solution of a capful of Murphy Oil Soap and a quart of water. Using a damp sponge, skim off the suds and apply the suds to the furniture. Use a small brush if needed to reach between the reeds. Wipe off the suds with a clean damp sponge. Be careful not to wet any wooden parts if you are cleaning a piece that is constructed around a wood frame.

Wicker used outside often requires a more vigorous cleaning technique. Scrub synthetic and raw natural wicker with warm water and a brush, and then rinse with a hose. Dry it as fast as possible so that the woven fibers will not swell or rot. Place it in the hot sun or next to a fan.

Extreme wetness will cause painted wicker to swell and the paint will flake off. Clean it with a damp sponge and wire brush to remove the loose paint. Allow it to dry thoroughly, and then repaint.

When the wicker is thoroughly dry, check the surfaces for sharp strands or fuzzy places. Sand them smooth with fine sandpaper. Then give it a coat of spray on automobile wax.

Speed tips: Vacuum wicker regularly with the brush attachment to avoid dust buildup. Cover tabletops and dresser bureaus with a sheet of glass to prevent dust from getting trapped in the weave. Then all you need is a few sprays of glass cleaner to keep the top—the part of the furniture most likely to collect dust, dirt, and stains—looking as good as the day you bought it.

To speed up drying, wash your wicker on a windy day.

In a pinch: If you don't have a vacuum, a dry paintbrush will clean dust and dirt particles from the weave.

If your wicker chair crackles and creaks when you sit down, it might need some moisture. Dry indoor heat and arid climates dry wicker out. Wipe it down occasionally with a damp sponge to restore moisture to the fibers.

Caution: Wicker needs a certain amount of humidity to prevent it from cracking, but too much will damage the fibers and cause them to rot. Keep natural wicker out of direct sunlight, dew, and rain for extended periods of time.

Windows

The trick to gleaming windows is in the drying, not in the washing. That's why professional window washers may have differing opinions on which cleaning formula works best, but the universal tool of choice for wiping it off is a squeegee. The truth is that unless they are heavily soiled, most windows can be cleaned with sudsy water. Besides costing next to nothing, water doesn't streak—even on a warm day.

THE DOUBLE-HUNG
DILEMMA SOLVED

Step 1: Cleaning the outside of a double-hung window can seem like a "can't get there from here" proposition. To start, pull the top of the double-hung window down as far as it will go. Reach out and mop the outside of the window with the scrubber. Working from above, draw the squeegee across and down the window as far as you can go. **Step 2**: Raise both the inside and outside window as far as each will go and finish the bottom of the outside window in overlapping passes.

Step 3: Lower the inside window enough so that you can reach above it and push the outside window to its lowest point. Reach out the window from above, apply cleaner to the top half of the inside window with the scrubber. **Step 4**: Raise the outside window and lower the inside window enough to repeat the scrubbing process on the lower half of the inside window by reaching out and up. Return windows to position in Step 3 to squeegee the top half of the inside window. Repeat movement in Step 4 to squeegee the outside of the lower half of the inside window.

Windows dried with a squeegee stay clean longer than windows cleaned with paper towels. Scrubbing with a paper towel builds a static charge on the window that attracts dust. It pays to purchase a good-quality squeegee. The rubber will be pliable and adhere to the window surface better for more effective drying. Ettore makes a professional-quality tool that is sold at janitorial supply houses. Your window cleaning should also include some old bath towels to catch drips, cloths to dry-wipe your squeegee between passes, a window scrubber to apply cleaning solution, and a large plastic bucket.

Technique: If you plan to clean windowsills and window frames, do it before you wash the glass. Vacuum window frames and windowsills to remove excess dirt. Clean wood or aluminum window frames with a solution of mild liquid dishwashing detergent and warm water. An old toothbrush is useful for reaching into the corners of the mullions. Rinse and dry with a cloth. If your aluminum frames are looking

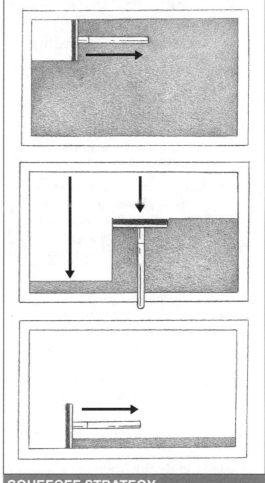

SQUEEGEE STRATEGY

Here's the ultimate no-streak, no-mess plan for using a squeegee on windows. Draw the squeegee across the top of the window to stop the flow of drips. Starting either side, draw the squeegee down to nearly the bottom of the window. Continue the vertical pattern in overlapping strokes to prevent streaks. Finish by drawing the squeegee across the bottom. *Note:* Wipe the squeegee with a cloth between passes.

gray and weathered, shine them with a cream silver polish. Window frames with natural wood finishes can be cleaned with a wax instead of soap and water.

Once the window frames and windowsills are clean, you can

MONEY-SAVERS

Three Window-Cleaning Formulas

Make your own window cleaner like the professionals. Commercial "blue" cleaners are costly and tend to leave streaks. Here are alternatives recommended by cleaning experts.

- Plain lukewarm water works just fine if your windows aren't too dirty. And it has two big advantages. No streaks if you're washing on a warm day. And it's practically free.
- Add ½ cup white vinegar to 1 quart cool water.
- Mix ½ cup sudsy ammonia, 1 pint rubbing alcohol, and 1 teaspoon liquid dishwashing detergent (don't use more, or streaking could result), and add enough water to make 1 gallon.

move on to the glass. Mix up a glass-cleaning solution that suits your preferences—alkaline solutions will remove dirt, vinegar will remove hard-water deposits, sudsy water will prevent streaking on a warm day, and adding several ounces of rubbing alcohol will cut through greasy film. Don't mix alkalis and acids, such as vinegar and ammonia, in the hope of solving two cleaning problems. One will partially neutralize the other so that neither will be fully effective.

Dampen the window scrubber and apply the solution to the window. You want to make the window wet enough to dissolve dirt, but not so wet that it's a dripping mess. Lightly draw the squeegee across the top of the window (this will help stop drips). Then draw it down the window, stopping a few inches from the bottom. In an overlapping stroke, make another vertical pass on the glass. Continue this pattern across the width of the window, wiping the blade of the squeegee with a cloth between each pass. Finish off by drawing the squeegee across the bottom. Wipe any drips around the frame with an absorbent cloth.

When cleaning window exteriors, do the windows on the top floor first. Dirty water may drip from the windowsill onto freshly cleaned glass below.

Speed tips: Always wash windows from top to bottom so that you won't get drips on the ones that you've already done. Use vertical strokes outside and horizontal strokes inside so that you'll know which side the streaks are on.

In a pinch: For small windowpanes where a squeegee just won't fit, use a chamois to dry windows. Rub a clean blackboard eraser over the just-washed window for a quick shine.

If you're thrifty, substitute a fluffy paint roller to apply your glass cleaning solution.

Caution: Ammoniated cleaners are hard on your hands and on the blade of the squeegee. Watch the temperature outside if you plan to clean aluminum window frames. Don't clean if it's below 50°F or if the aluminum is too hot to touch. And avoid the use of abrasive cleaners, which will permanently scratch the finish.

Be careful not to drip alkaline or alcohol solutions on painted or varnished woodwork. It will damage the finish.

Wine Stains

 EMERGENCY ACTION
Sprinkle a red-wine spill immediately with a liberal amount of salt. Allow the salt to absorb the wine, and then rinse in cool water. For white wine, blot up as much of the spill as you can and sponge with cool water, according to cleaning experts.

To prevent wine stains altogether, take these precautions suggested by wine experts. Learn to pour like a wine steward, slowly twisting the bottle neck to the side as you finish pouring so that drips will stay inside the bottle. Instead of laying the cork on your tablecloth, use a dish or ashtray.

Technique: If you can launder a white-wine spill before it has dried, then it is not likely to stain. Rinse the spill immediately. Apply an undiluted neutral detergent such as Liquid Tide and a few drops of white vinegar. Rinse. Launder washables in warm water. Dry cleanables should be taken to a professional if any stain remains.

Depending on the fabric and the age of the spot, red-wine stains can be impossible to remove. If you use the salt and cool water treatment for fresh spills outlined above, apply liquid laundry detergent and rinse in cool water. If the stain remains, apply a paste made from bleach-enzyme laundry soap such as Biz (mix according to package directions), soak for 30 minutes in an all-fabric bleach, and then launder.

For dried stains on durable fabrics, such as a tablecloth, hold the stained area over a bowl and cover with salt. Pour boiling water over the salt until the stain disappears. On other fabrics, soak with a few drops of white vinegar and blot, or try soaking with a solu-

HOW IT WORKS

What Puts the Red in Red Wine?

The color of wine is not determined by the color of the grape but rather by the length of time that the skins of the fruit remain with the juice. A white wine can be made with red, black, or white grapes, with the skins being removed early in the wine-making process. For rosés—or pink wines—red or black grapes are used, and the skins are removed after one to three days. In red wine making the skins remain for longer periods.

tion of hydrogen peroxide (a mild bleach) and a few drops of ammonia. Test your fabric for colorfastness first.

On rugs and carpets, immediately cover the spill with a generous amount of salt. Allow it to dry, and then vacuum.

In a pinch: For dried stains on washable fabric, pour club soda through the spot and launder as outlined earlier.

Caution: Avoid vinegar on cotton, linen, rayon, and acetate.

Woodwork

Woodwork should be cleaned according to the type of finish that is on it—such as paint, varnish, polyurethane, stain—not according to the type of wood it is.

Technique: Dust baseboards weekly in heavily used rooms and monthly in seldom-used areas of the house. Vacuum baseboards with the dust brush attachment while you're doing the floors, or use a lamb's wool duster. Most woodwork has a sealed finish and can be cleaned with water when needed. Wipe it clean with a damp sponge dipped in an cleaning solution recommended by the finish's manufacturer (follow the product directions for proper usage). Then polish dry with a clean towel. Remove black heel marks with a little mineral spirits on a cotton swab, says Colleen Dodson, vice president of Lehigh Valley Hardwood Flooring in Allentown, Pennsylvania.

Speed tips: Before you start washing down the woodwork in a room, take a damp paper towel and wipe it along the baseboard to pick up lint, dirt, and bugs so that they don't get embedded in your sponge and end up in the cleaning solution.

In a pinch: To remove grease and smoke stains from painted woodwork without damaging the finish, use trisodium phosphate (available at hardware stores) according to the manufacturer's directions and be sure to do a thorough clean-water rinse, says Jim Capehart, president of Buss Paint and Wallpaper in Emmaus, Pennsylvania.

Caution: Don't try to clean woodwork when you're washing the walls. Baseboards are usually covered with lint, hair, and dead bugs, which can stick to the sponge and then transfer onto the wall.

When using trisodium phosphate, wear protective eyewear, rubber gloves, and a long-sleeve shirt. Always read the product label for proper usage and safety precautions.

Wool

Wool stays clean longer than other fabrics. Its coiled fibers and their shinglelike structure keep dirt from penetrating the surface, says Jennifer Morgan, Ph.D., product technologist for the Wool Bureau in New York City. Stains and spills naturally bead up on the surface, while dirt caught in the springy surface hairs can usually be brushed off easily. Ironically, the same characteristics that enable

Five Basics for Keeping Your Wool in Sheep-Shape

1. Dry-clean sparingly. Once a season is usually sufficient. Wool, like hair, can be burned by overexposure to chemicals. Excessive dry-cleaning will give it a shiny appearance, according to the Wool Bureau in New York City.

2. Give it a breath of fresh air to release odors and wrinkles from the fibers.

3. Empty the pockets to prevent bulgy bumps and sags. Wool has a memory and will take on a new shape.

4. Let it rest 24 hours before the next wearing. This allows the fabric to spring back into shape.

5. Store your wool garments with cedar blocks or in a cedar-lined closet or chest to avoid moths. Clean garments prior to storing; it's the body oils that the moths are attracted to.

wool to repel dirt so effectively also cause its main laundering problem—shrinkage.

Technique: Wool garments should be hand-washed since agitation can cause the fibers to interlock and shrink. Dissolve a small amount of mild laundry detergent, such as Woolite, in lukewarm water. Immerse the garment and gently squeeze the suds through. Allow the garment to soak for three to four minutes. Using several changes of cool water, rinse thoroughly until no more suds are visible in the water. Gently squeeze the wool to remove excess moisture. Never wring or twist it. Reshape it and lay it on a flat towel to dry.

Speed tips: Brush your wool garment after every wear with a clothes brush to remove surface soil and prevent it from becoming a stain later on. Wool responds well to spot-cleaning. If you find a small spill or stain on a garment, rinse it with cold water or seltzer and blot it dry with a clean white cloth to remove it. Never use paper towels.

In a pinch: To remove wrinkles, hang the garment in a steamy bathroom.

How to Wash a Wool Blanket

Measure the blanket before washing so that you can block it or stretch it to the original shape and size after laundering. Fill the empty washer with warm or cold water—the dirtier the blanket, the warmer the water should be. Add laundry detergent or soap and agitate briefly to dissolve. Stop the washer and add the blanket, distributing it loosely and evenly around the agitator. Soak for 10 to 15 minutes. Restart the washer and advance the control until the agitation stops and the washer begins pumping the water out of the tub. After a 1-minute spin cycle, advance the washer to the rinse cycle and allow the washer to finish automatically.

Set the dryer on the high-temperature setting and preheat three or four dry bath towels, which will be used to absorb moisture from the blanket so that it will not pill in the dryer. Place the blanket in the dryer with the warm towels for about 10 minutes at the same high-temperature setting. Remove while slightly damp to avoid shrinkage. Stretch the blanket back to its original shape and finish drying it on a flat surface or over two clotheslines, says the Michigan State University Extension in East Lansing, a community education program.

Remedy for a Shrunken Sweater

The following soaking method may soften and relax the wool fibers of a shrunken sweater enough to allow reshaping, according to Jennifer Morgan, Ph.D., product technologist for the Wool Bureau in New York City. But before trying this method, test your sweater for felting. Hold it up to your ear and stretch it. If you hear a cracking sound, that means that the shrinkage is irreversible and this method won't help.

If your garment passes the test, here's how to proceed: Add ½ cup hair conditioner to 1 gallon lukewarm water. Dip the sweater until wet. Squeeze conditioning solution from the fibers; do not rinse. Reshape on a flat surface, and let it dry

Caution: Do not hang wool to dry it. With the exception of woolen blankets, do not dry wool in or near a source of heat. It will shrink. While wool knits, sweaters, and blankets can be laundered at home, dry-cleaning is recommended for tailored garments, such as suits. If a garment label states "Dry-Clean Only," take it to a professional dry cleaner.

Yard and Patio Furniture

Yard and patio furniture are made for the outdoors, which means that they can handle a good hose-and-scrub cleaning. If you do it regularly, you'll keep dirt, tree sap, and other grime from taking over. You'll save yourself a major cleaning job, and you'll have more time for your magazines and umbrella drinks.

Technique: Clean yard and patio furniture at least twice a year. Spray it with a garden hose and then wash it with a nylon brush and a bucket of warm water with a few squirts of liquid dishwashing detergent.

Avoid using steel wool and other abrasives on the furniture since most surfaces scratch easily. Some plastics and vinyls are even coated with special finishes that protect the furniture from ultraviolet rays. You don't want to remove these. Scrub joints and crevices with an old toothbrush. Rinse suds by spraying with the garden hose. Dry the furniture with clean towels or by leaving it in the sun.

Apply automotive wax or polish to most nonwood surfaces—painted metal, anodized aluminum, plastic, and vinyl. This helps protect the surface from the elements and gives it a nice long-lasting shine. "It's just like your automobile," says Mary Lou Heltemes, customer service supervisor at Homecrest Industries, an outdoor furniture manufacturer in Wadena, Missouri. "If you don't wax it, the frame finish will oxidize and dull." Always read product labels to make sure that they are recommended for your particular material. Here are general tips for materials found in most types of yard and patio furniture.

Aluminum

Although aluminum does not rust, it can discolor and corrode slightly when exposed to pollutants in the air and rain. This condition, known as oxidation, can cause pitting, which looks like fine grit stuck to the surface and does not come off easily.

Never use alkaline cleaners like ammonia, trisodium phosphate, or even baking soda on aluminum. They discolor it. If the aluminum surface is discolored, wash it with a one-to-one solution of vinegar and water. The acid in vinegar will help restore the aluminum's shine. Be sure to pretest it first on an inconspicuous area.

Do not use abrasive cleaners, such as scouring powders or steel wool. They might scratch or dull the surface.

Coat your aluminum furniture with automotive wax or a silicon spray to protect it from corrosion and pitting.

Cushions

Most outdoor furniture cushions these days are covered with water-resistant and sun-proof materials. Generally speaking, you should clean these the same way you would the furniture and dry them by standing them up in the sun. However, always follow the manufacturer's recommended cleaning instructions.

In the case of mildew, you'll want to deep clean the cushions. Fill a clean garbage can or some other large container with a solution of 1 cup liquid chlorine bleach and 1 cup powdered laundry detergent dissolved in 3 gallons warm water. (Double the solution, if necessary.) Soak the cushions for at least 2 hours, and then scrub them with a nylon brush. Do not use bleach on cushions covered in colorful fabrics. It will cause the colors to fade and bleed.

It is essential to rinse the cushions thoroughly with cold water. Otherwise, the mildew can return. "One way to do it is to take them to a self-service car wash," Heltemes says. "They have good water pressure and a drainage system, too." Dry the cushions completely by allowing them to sit in the sun for several days.

Note: Do this deep cleaning only if recommended by the cushion manufacturer.

To keep mildew off cushions, especially those with bright prints that cannot be bleached, clean them more often than normal. Mildew grows on organic materials, like cotton, leather, and paper. "Because most of the cushion materials are synthetic, the mildew feeds off foreign substances, like pollen, dust particles, or spilled juice," Heltemes says.

Speed tip: Use a leaf blower to help dry wet cushions.

Yellowing

Everything from your clothes to your tablecloths to your floors can yellow if they're not cared for appropriately. Here are some suggestions for keeping things bright.

Linens

Never wash linens with chlorine beach. It can cause the fabric to yellow. To wash common linens, such as napkins and tablecloths, use a mild laundry detergent and an oxygen-type bleach like Clorox 2. To clean fine linens, such as drapery linens, upholstery linens, decorative linens, and fine linen apparel, take them to a dry cleaner.

Caution: Do not store linens on bare wood shelves; this also can cause yellowing.

Upholstery

It's ironic, but one of the major reasons upholstery yellows is exposure to foam cleansers that are designed to brighten the fabric. Some commercial cleaners contain fluorescent brightening solutions. These make the upholstery look brighter at first, but over time, the fluorescent residue that remains on the fabric may cause yellowing. Your best bet: Don't use foam cleansers on your furniture. If you already have and yellowing has occurred, consult a professional upholstery cleaner about the best solution.

Vinyl Flooring

Vinyl flooring and vinyl tiles commonly will yellow for two reasons: exposure to intense sunlight or contact with asphalt and tar. And once vinyl has become discolored, it's hard to restore it. So, your best option is to protect your flooring before the damage occurs.

To prevent sunlight from harming your floors, keep your windows covered with shades or curtains during the brightest parts of the day. To keep tar and asphalt off your floors, place doormats inside and outside doors leading to your driveway and road.

Wood Furniture

The varnish finish on old wood furniture may yellow over time. This is normal, and the only way to change the look is to strip and refinish the piece. You should consider refinishing only if the piece is not an antique. Stripping an antique will diminish its value significantly.

Wood furniture with a white finish also may yellow, but here the culprit is likely to be sunlight or tobacco smoke. To remove the yellowing, wipe the furniture with smoker's toothpaste, then coat the wood with furniture polish.

Note: Don't rub the smoker's toothpaste into the wood. The toothpaste contains mild abrasives that could scratch or dull the finish.

Yellow Mustard

EMERGENCY ACTION
Rinse or blot away mustard with cold water.

Don't let mustard's light yellow color fool you. It's one of the toughest stains around. "It has disperse dyes, the kind used for dying polyester," explains Rajiv Jain, laboratory manager for the Association of Specialists in Cleaning and Restoration in Millersville, Maryland. "These dyes impart color by dispersing into the fiber structure."

Technique: Scrape away any excess mustard. For washables, first soak the item in cold water to remove as much of the stain as possible. Then pretreat it by mixing ¼ teaspoon clear liquid dishwashing detergent and ½ cup warm water. Apply it directly to the fabric, then lay the garment on a hard surface and pat the stain lightly with the back of a spoon. This allows the solution to get into and in between the fibers, where stains hide. Don't rub the material together; that will abrade the fibers. Next, wash as directed, either by machine or by hand, in the hottest water safe for the fabric. If the stain does not come out completely, follow the same pretreatment procedure, but this time with a solution of one part vinegar and two parts water. Never use ammonia or any other alkaline substance, which can darken a mustard stain. "It might not all come out," Jain says. "It depends on how much was spilled and when." The bigger and older the stain, the harder it will be to remove.

For fabrics that cannot be washed, either have them professionally dry-cleaned or blot the stain with a clean white towel and a spot remover, like Carbona Stain Devils or K2r, available at supermarkets, hardware stores, or discount department stores. Blot from the inside of the garment to push the stain out. Wear protective rubber or latex gloves, and use these products in a well-ventilated area.

For carpets and rugs, first blot the stain with the detergent solution using a clean white towel. Then rinse by blotting with a clean towel and water. Do not blot with laundry detergent because it often contains optical brighteners that can bleach carpet and rug dyes. Instead, if the first solution does not work, try blotting with a solution of one part white vinegar and two parts water. Rinse by blotting with a towel and water, then dry with a fresh towel.

Note: Before using cleaning solutions, always test them on an inconspicuous section of the stained item.

Caution: Always rinse out one cleaning solution before trying another. Mixing chemicals, especially ammonia and chlorine bleach, can create noxious fumes. Always read the product label for proper use and safety precautions.

Zippers

Zippers may jam or stick if they become clogged. The best way to clean them and undo the damage depends on the source of the stickiness.

Technique: If dirt, food, or a sticky drink has gummed up the zipper, brush the zipper's teeth with an old toothbrush and warm water.

If gum causes the clog, heat the zipper with a blow-dryer set on "high" for 30 to 90 seconds. Take care to keep the dryer at least 6 inches from the zipper and the surrounding fabric to prevent accidental melting. Remove as much of the gum as possible by brushing it out with an old toothbrush or picking it with a toothpick. If necessary, reheat and continue to work out the gum until it is gone. Alternatively, you may be able to remove the gum by freezing it. Hold an ice cube to the gum until it is hard, then crack it off. Remove any residue with a toothpick.

If tree sap is the culprit, treat it with rubbing alcohol. Lay the zipper on a clean absorbent cloth, then soak a cotton ball in alcohol and blot the zipper with the ball. The alcohol will dissolve the sap so it runs through the zipper and ends up on the absorbent cloth.

Note: To make sure the color of the zipper and the surrounding fabric don't run when exposed to the alcohol, test first by applying alcohol to an inconspicuous area.

If the zipper sticks after cleaning, it may need lubrication. Rub it up and down with candle wax or soap to get it operating smoothly again.

Zithers and Other Stringed Instruments

Keeping zithers and other stringed musical instruments clean is essential for maintaining their sound and integrity. Still, most professionals agree that you should never overclean your instrument.

Technique: Clean zithers, guitars, cellos, violins, and such with a soft dry cloth, preferably one made from chamois. Wipe off perspiration and buff away fingerprints. It doesn't take much more than that. (In fact, cleaning solvents, especially alcohol-based products, can ruin the thin coating of varnish covering most stringed instruments.) After playing bowed instruments, dust off the rosin that accumulates beneath the strings near the bridge and wipe away any perspiration. At least once a year, have fine instruments professionally cleaned. Call your local symphony orchestra or school bandleader for a professional referral.

Index

Underscored page references indicate boxed text. **Boldface** references indicate illustrations.

Books, 29–31, <u>30</u>
Boots, 31–32
  leather, 168–69
Borax, uses for
  cleaning agent, 263
  deodorizer, <u>185</u>, 298
Bottles, 291–93
  Thermos, 274–75
Bowling balls, 33
Box springs, 178
Brass, 33–34
  furniture hardware, 119
  pots and pans, 208, <u>209</u>
Bread, uses for
  scrubbing material, 2, 72
  stain removal, <u>300</u>
Brick, 34–35
  fireplace, 102–3
  floors, 109
Briefcases, 35–37, <u>36</u>
Brightening agents, in foam
      cleaners, <u>289</u>
Brocade, 37
Bronze, 37–39
Brushes
  decks, 81
  hair, 39–40
  leather, 127
  paint, 194–95
  sable, 11, 45, 46
  toilet, 281, **281**
  truck, 15
Buffers, rotary and orbital, 55
Burns
  cigarette, 40
  on counters, 74
Butcher block, **41**, 41–43

C

Cabinets, kitchen, 43–44
Camcorders, 44
Cameos, 44–45
Cameras, 45–47
  outdoor use, protection during, <u>46</u>

Can openers, 47–48
Canvas shoes, 229
Car(s)
  body, 53–55
  carpet, 55
  engine, 55–56
  tires, 57
  washes, selecting professional, 56
  waxes for, 54–55
  windows, 57
Carpet(s), 48–50
  allergens in, 49
  car, 55
  cigarette burns, 40
    deep, 49–51
    steam, 52
  depression marks in, 52
  gum removal from, 136–37
  new, <u>49</u>
  smoke in, 244
  spills on, <u>250</u>, 251
  stains, <u>50–51</u>
    alcoholic beverages, <u>50</u>
    banana, <u>50</u>
    cola, <u>50</u>
    egg, <u>50</u>, 98
    fruit, <u>50</u>
    gravy, 134
    grease, 135
    ice cream, <u>50–51</u>
    iodine, <u>51</u>
    jam, <u>50</u>
    jelly, <u>50</u>
    juice, <u>50</u>, 150–51
    ketchup, <u>51</u>, 152
    lipstick and lipgloss, <u>51</u>
    milk, <u>50–51</u>
    mustard, 323
    oil, 188
    peanut butter, <u>51</u>
    perfume, 197–98
    vomit, 297
    water, 305–6
    wine, 316
  volatile organic compounds in, <u>49</u>

concrete, 109
cork, 71–72
hardwood, 110
stone, 260–62
terrazzo, 110–11
tile, 276–78
vinyl, 111–12, 277–78
  yellowing, 321–22
wax buildup on, 308–9
Flour, for stain removal, 261
Flowers
artificial, 112
cleaning for shows, 112
cut, tips for keeping, 292
dried, 112
silk, 112
Foam rubber, 113
Foam upholstery cleaners, 289
Food
odors, 217
stains (see specific types)
washing, 114
Food graters, 114–15
Food grinders, 115
Food processors, 116
Formaldehyde, indoor air pollution
  from, 4–5
Formica, 205
Fountains, 116–17
Frames, picture, 201–2
Freezers, 216–18
Fruit stains, on
carpet, 50
stone, 261
Fuel spills on concrete, 68
Fungi. See also Mildew; Mold
in humidifiers, 143
indoor air pollution from, 4
Fur, 117–18
Furnace, soot from, 247–48
Furniture. See also specific types
aluminum, 118–19
antique, 11

chrome, 119
cleaning code on, 288
glass, 119
hardware, 119
lacquer, 120
marble, 120
rattan, 120–21
scratches, 122–23
upholstery, 121
water stain removal from,
  305
wicker, 120–21, 310–11
wood, 121–23
yard and patio, 320–21

G

Garden sprayers, 124
Germs. See Bacteria
Glass, 125–26, 126
doors, fireplace, 102
furniture, 119
hurricane lamps, 157
picture frames, 201–2
Pyrex cookware, 210
skylights, 239–40
Thermos bottles, 274–75
windows, 311–15
Glassware, 126–27
Gloves
drying, 128
fabric, 128
leather, 128–29
  baseball, 127
  preservation, 129
rubber, 128
Glue, wood, 295
Gold, 130
Golf bags, 174
Gore-Tex, 130–31
Graffiti, 131–33, 132
Grass stains, 133
Grater, food, 114–15
Gravy stains, 133–34

M

N